The Urbana Free Library

To renew materials call
217-367-4057

ALSO BY ANNE MENDELSON

Stand Facing the Stove: The Story of the Women Who Gave America The Joy of Cooking

MILK

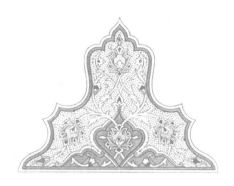

MILK

THE SURPRISING STORY OF MILK THROUGH THE AGES

ANNE MENDELSON

WITH 120 ADVENTUROUS RECIPES
THAT EXPLORE THE RICHES OF OUR FIRST FOOD

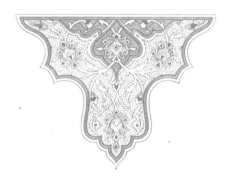

ALFRED A. KNOPF NEW YORK 2008

IN MEMORIAM

M.I.

E.S.M.

This Is a Borzoi Book Published by Alfred A. Knopf

Copyright © 2008 by Anne Mendelson

All rights reserved. Published in the United States by Alfred A. Knopf, a division of Random House, Inc., New York, and in Canada by Random House of Canada Limited, Toronto.

www.aaknopf.com

Knopf, Borzoi Books, and the colophon are registered trademarks of Random House, Inc.

Library of Congress Cataloging-in-Publication Data

Mendelson, Anne.

Milk : the surprising story of milk through the ages / by Anne Mendelson.—1st ed.

p. cm.

Includes index.

ISBN 978-1-4000-4410-8

1. Milk—History. 2. Cookery (Milk) I. Title.

SF251.M46 2008

641.3'7109—dc22   2008019620

Manufactured in the United States

First Edition

ILLUSTRATIONS CREDITS

AMERICAN MUSEUM OF NATURAL HISTORY LIBRARY, SPECIAL COLLECTIONS 9 (*top:* Richard Lydekker, *Royal Natural History* [vol. 2], 1894; *bottom:* Richard Lydekker, *Wild Oxen, Sheep, and Goats,* 1898), 12 and 13 *top* (John G. Wood, *Our Living World* [American edition], 1885), 37 (William Youatt, *Cattle,* 1834), 89 and 135 (John Lockwood Kipling, *Beast and Man in India,* 1891)

COLLECTIONS OF THE NEW YORK PUBLIC LIBRARY, ASTOR, LENOX AND TILDEN FOUNDATIONS: 11 (Jean Francois Champollion, *Monuments de l'Egypte et de la Nubie,* p. 1844–99), 13 *bottom* (*Illustrated London News,* 1864), 15 (Edward Moor, *The Hindu Pantheon,* 1810), 22 and 39 (Charles Louis Flint, *Milch Cows and Dairy Farming,* 1858), 32 (George W. Thornbury, *Old and New London* [vol. 4], 1872), 33 *bottom* (*Frank Leslie's Illustrated,* May 15, 1858), 155 (*Magasin pittoresque,* 1837)

THE NEW-YORK HISTORICAL SOCIETY 27 (*The Cries of New York,* 1845 edition, NYHS negative #54406), 33 *top* (*Harper's Weekly,* August 17, 1878, NYHS negative #80839d)

THE STATE LIBRARY OF VICTORIA 65 (*Australian Illustrated Weekly,* November 11, 1893)

RALPH SELITZER, *The Dairy Industry in America,* 1976 80, 130, 131

HEDWIG DORN, *Zur Stütze der Hausfrau,* 1918 95, 127, 136, 177, 178, 273

CONTENTS

PREFACE

This book has grown out of a lifelong love of milk and fresh dairy products. It is the culinary guidebook, dairy-chemistry-for-cooks primer, and eclectic recipe collection that I always vainly wished somebody had written. And it developed into something else that I'd always wanted to find: a geographical-historical exploration of the world's milky ways, including those that have shaped the modern American milk supply for better or worse.

Milk itself would have been a fascinating subject at any time in history. It is really and truly the First Food, at least for all members of the mammal class. The practice of milking was an anchor of many prehistoric civilizations, one of humanity's oldest and deepest bonds with domestic animals. The animals raised for the purpose are remarkable creatures, though they remain nearly invisible to most of the people who put milk on shopping lists. What they produce is a biochemical marvel that modern science has not yet finished analyzing. Its still-unplumbed complexities are exactly what make it irreplaceable in a huge number of the world's cuisines. In the ancient world it often had religious significance as a ritual offering; in India it still has sacred associations. On a more earthbound level, it has figured tremendously in the farm economies of most industrialized nations.

But I'm not sure that any previous historical juncture would have been an equally fruitful—or fraught—moment for stepping back to survey the many dimensions of milk, especially in the United States. It gets lots of headlines these days, some of them pleasanter reading than others. Among the most striking features of the early twenty-first-century dairy scene are:

- Milk in many ways exemplifies an American love-hate relationship with food, an endless tug-of-war between exalting and demonizing things on the basis of medical claims and counterclaims.
- It is also an alarming example of farming and processing technology somehow run amok, careening down ever more extreme paths with less and less connection to anything recognizable as real milk.
- On a more encouraging note, a resurgence of small-scale dairying and dairy farming is proceeding under our noses just as many people become aware of a hunger for something not satisfied by featureless, taken-for-granted, mass-produced milk and fresh dairy products. Today we have unprecedented

opportunities to taste milk, cream, butter, fresh cheeses, and other simple milk-derived foods made by, and for, people who know what flavor is.

- Most powerfully of all, milk today represents a time of change in American culinary perspective, stemming from massive change in this nation's ethnic makeup. Part of the impetus behind this book was my eagerness to share the voyages of culinary discovery that began for me in immigrant neighborhoods of northern New Jersey and ended by completely reshaping my understanding of milk's place in world history, not to say the world's kitchens. What I learned, in a nutshell, is that the usual American ways with milk and dairy products are only a narrow, anomalous sidetrack from something immensely larger, richer, and more ancient. It's my hope that other people will be as bowled over as I have been on seeing how much new Americans from diverse cooking traditions have to teach us about this humble substance.

My entry point to enlightenment was yogurt—not what I'd known from American pop versions but the plain creamy yogurt that kept turning up as sauce, drink, condiment, and just all-around player in small Greek, Bosnian, Turkish, Israeli, Persian, Afghan, and Indian restaurants. Slowly it dawned on me that in simple fermented yogurt I was tasting something that might have been eaten or drunk by Old Testament patriarchs, Sumerian lawgivers, Homeric heroes, Hindu gods, or the flower of Persian chivalry. The uses I saw it being put to in modest little eateries made me realize how little I'd really known about cooking with milk and dairy products.

As the larger picture opened up to me and I began trying to delve into chapters of the culinary past that no one else seemed to have written, I gradually arrived at a thoroughly rearranged world view of milk and things made from it.

In the first place, for most people in most parts of the world, milk has always been not a blandly innocuous food but one with decided flavors of its own. Historically it has come from not only cows—which give the mildest-tasting milk of any dairy animal—but many other creatures, suited to different climates and geographies, whose milk has distinctive flavors peculiar to their species. (Goats' milk is probably the most familiar example in the United States.) Furthermore, sweet milk—"sweet" in the sense of "unsoured"—is not really as old a part of systematic foodways as milk fermented by friendly bacteria. Since prehistory, most of the milk consumed in all dairying regions of the world has been soured into yogurt or forms resembling today's cultured buttermilk. After all, fermentation is what happens to milk within a short time of milking unless you artificially forestall the event through refrigeration. And if you keep up with the story of lactose intolerance, you will realize that more human beings can more easily digest soured than sweet milk. To use an often-abused word, soured milk is in a very real sense a more "natural" food for people past the age of weaning. Just as crucial from a cook's point of view, soured milk plays off against other flavors with a many-dimensioned verve that's missing in the sweet counterpart.

Similarly, fresh cheeses made by a few simple forms of curd-setting are not just primitive precursors of "real" cheeses that have been ripened or aged. They are both older and more globally important than any other kinds of cheese. In their own right they are anything but blah and monotonous. Since ancient times they have been marked by infinite nuances of flavor and texture, depending on local environments, the animals that provide the milk, and the manner in which the curd is set. Fresh cheeses preserved through brining, like the Greek variety we call feta, are also more ancient than European-style ripened ones and figure prominently throughout a wider geographical range—in fact, most of the same geographical range as yogurt.

In the long territorial stretch of the Old World that I came to think of as "Yogurtistan," people have until recently been much closer than we are to the primal origins of both dairying and cooking with dairy foods. The Indian subcontinent also preserves more links with an ancient past. So do the Russian reaches of western Asia along with adjacent Eastern Europe; the dominant form of sour milk there isn't yogurt, but continuity still exists with a tradition in which milk was almost invariably fermented before people thought of consuming it or cooking with it. The big global exceptions to the pattern today are northwestern Europe, Great Britain, and several parts of the world—including North America—that became British or French colonies. In the mother countries something happened, only a few centuries ago, to start a huge commercial concentration on two forms of milk that had been little known, or even unknown, among other dairying peoples. They were fresh unsoured milk and its linear opposite: ripened or aged cheese.

Before this switch of direction, there hadn't been anything remarkably odd about these regions except that they had a high proportion of people with the globally rare ability to digest the lactose in sweet milk throughout their adult lives—a genetic fluke that didn't stop sour milk and fresh cheeses from being cornerstones of household dairying for centuries or, more likely, millennia. But after cheeses proliferated as specialties destined for particular markets and sweet milk for drinking began to be produced in large volumes for urban clienteles, northwestern Europe and Britain never looked back. (The first change happened about four or five hundred years ago, the second toward the start of the nineteenth century.) It's this heritage that has chiefly shaped American perceptions of dairy foods.

Few readers of this book will need to be convinced that whether or not aged and ripened cheeses belong to the very oldest and most widespread milky ways, they are a glorious contribution to the joy of mankind. I have not tried to discuss them for the simple reason that there are already many other works treating the subject with the love and intelligence that it deserves—though sometimes also leaving the mistaken impression that fresh dairy products are really cheese manqué.

The situation is very different with fresh milk and such offshoots as fresh cream or sweet butter. They can indeed taste wonderful—I hope to convey an idea of just how wonderful—when carefully and skillfully brought to us in a state of true freshness. They can be invaluable in a savvy cook's arsenal of resources. But you will note that I've written "can be," not "are." The triumph of drinkable fresh (or pseudo-fresh) milk as the dominant popular Western form of milk started us off down the garden path to the unfortunate consequences that I mentioned before. It has left millions of us without access to genuinely fresh, excellent milk—or any sense of what we're missing.

This long deprivation is why the revival of small dairy farms and the reawakening of interest in artisanal fresh dairy products is such cause for rejoicing. It would have been a splendid turn of events at any stage in the last fifty years. Great things are happening when more and more of us have access to butter that tastes like cream, *cream* that tastes like cream, and—still more important—flavorful unhomogenized milk pasteurized by methods less "efficient" than those now standard in the industry. But by happy coincidence, or maybe not mere coincidence, these developments have arrived at the same moment as have waves of immigrants from parts of the globe where older, non-Western traditions of consuming and cooking with milk still prevail. Some of today's small farmers are developing an interest in ancient (and excellent) sources of milk that once would have seemed ludicrously far-fetched— goats galore, dairy sheep, and even water buffaloes. Anyone can see that very new Americans from very ancient milking regions will shortly be looking around for what they consider good milk, together with good yogurt or other soured milk, fresh cheeses, and perhaps even their own preferred versions of butter. I believe that with these on hand, America's culinary horizons will be rapidly and spectacularly enlarged.

As you will see, the book straddles several categories. From a pretty early stage I knew that it would have to be part narrative history, reaching back into the prehistoric past to make clear what extraordinary creatures the milch animals are and including an unflinching look at the course of modern factory-scale dairy farming and processing. People today, after all, are starting to believe that they should know where their food comes from. I was convinced that even a brief account of our Goliath milk industry would make people stand up and cheer for the hundreds of little Davids who are now appearing on the American dairying scene. I saw also that the book would have to make at least a quick foray into the chemical intricacies that are the reason milk isn't reproducible by phony substitutes. And I knew both that I wanted to present an eclectic array of recipes from dramatically differing world traditions and that what I wanted to show about the incredible versatility of milk in cooking was not going to fit any usual organization of recipes by menu category.

When all the pieces came together, they formed two pictures, both taken from many angles. One is a broad overall look at where milk comes from and what it is, the other a worldwide exploration of milk in cookbook form.

The first section opens with a historical survey of milch animals and milking traditions in the four great geographical zones where milk became a defining culinary element. It goes on to trace the strange fortunes of fresh (well, not very fresh) drinkable milk in modern Western societies, leading up to an age of intensively bred-and-fed supercows, increasingly bizarre forms of processing, and nutrition wars. And before turning to actual recipes, I sketch the biological and chemical underpinnings without which we would have neither milk nor any of the things made from it.

The cookbook portion begins with the uses of fresh unfermented milk and cream (as well as modern canned milk) and goes on to explore yogurt in many guises, other forms of cultured milk and cream, butter (with the true buttermilk that is part of the buttermaking process), and fresh cheeses. The recipes have been chosen to suggest what a wealth of experiences awaits any adventurous dairy-minded cook with the enterprise to plumb both Western European traditions based on fresh milk, cream, and butter and the still more exciting ones now reaching us from entirely different cuisines.

At bottom, *Milk* springs from both a long-standing concern about our troubled milk supply and a growing belief that we're on the road to an era of more delicious milk and simple dairy foods, including whole complexes of cooking possibilities that many of us never dreamed of a generation ago. I hope that I have done justice to the beauties of fresh milk and cream, the less familiar miracles of their freshly fermented counterparts (with yogurt occupying a position of special honor), and the pleasures of fresh as well as brined cheeses. My love affair with the subject has been a voyage of many discoveries. I will be happy if I can bring other people along on it.

PART 1

MILK, MILCH ANIMALS, AND COOKING
Beginnings and Traditions

Many thousands of years ago, somebody saw an animal nursing her young and had the eccentric, not to say dangerous, idea of getting in on the act.

This "somebody" was most likely many Neolithic somebodies, independently impelled to the same experiment. Students of prehistory have never pinpointed an exact time or place for one definitively successful attempt at milking. But they have educated guesses about when and where people got the art down pat: probably some time between 8000 and 6000 B.C., somewhere between the Anatolian plateau and the Zagros Mountains of southwestern Iran. They also know one thing about the animal in question: It wasn't a cow.

A strange custom, this, using another creature's milk for food. Even today it is anything but universal among the world's peoples. But where it took hold, other animals' milk became a staff of life and—odd though it may seem to those reared on cows' milk from cartons—a source of varied, rich, exuberant, and even exciting flavors in many cooking traditions from prehistory to the present.

The oldest places where humans mastered the skills of milking tend to overlap with the region, where the world's oldest documented cuisines originated and where some ancestral preferences still survive. Today, when mechanized or even computerized milking is a gigantic commercial enterprise in advanced societies from Australia to Argentina, food lovers everywhere can still learn much from the relationships among humans, animals, and foodways that sprang up in those primal areas, as well as patterns that followed over a few thousand years in several other parts of the premodern world (the premodern *Old* World, since milking was unknown in North and South America until after Columbus).

Virtually all the most ingenious, flexible uses of milk as a food and cooking ingredient can be traced to four seminal culinary zones of ancient Asia and Europe, each marked by characteristic preferences for certain milch animals as well as particular dairy foods. Starting with the oldest, they can be conveniently thought of as the Diverse Sources Belt, the Bovine and Buffalo Belt, the Northeastern Cow Belt, and the Northwestern Cow Belt. The four primary zones correspond respectively with the great east-west sweep from the Balkans to western Mongolia, the Indian subcontinent, northeastern Europe from the Baltic into Russia, and northwestern Europe.

You will notice one great omission fitting into none of these categories: the milking regions and traditions of Africa. My reason for leaving them out is that many crucial practices simply are not reproducible in American kitchens. Even today the uses of milk in the chief dairying areas (the east, southward from parts of Ethiopia and the Sudan to Mozambique) are stamped by ancient pastoral, semi-nomadic ways of life and particular techniques—for example, impregnating the interior surface of milk-collecting gourds with smoke from fragrant grasses or wood chips—that probably are impossible to translate into meaningful terms for cooks in industrialized societies. At least, I've found no sources of culinary information, though in the United States we're starting to get some picture of Ethiopian foodways, including a few milk-based specialties.

THE DIVERSE SOURCES BELT

At the outset, today's cooks should know that much of what's worth discovering about milk as a culinary treasure first emerged throughout a certain broad swath of Eurasia centuries (at least) before milking spread to regions north and south, and millennia before more specialized approaches carried the day in industrialized Europe. The beginnings were almost surely in the prehistoric Near East, several hundred miles from the coastal Mediterranean sites where grain crops were first domesticated: present-day Israel, Jordan, Syria, and Lebanon, starting at some point before about 8000 B.C. Somewhat eastward and many centuries later, other nameless pioneers applied the idea of domestication to the animal kingdom. They began with a few local creatures—possibly objects of sacrificial cults—that hunters had already found to be promising sources of meat and hides. In time they, and neighbors in gradually widening areas over a general eastward-westward course, extended the new practice to more species, until people throughout a several-thousand-mile range from the Balkans, Mediterranean North Africa, and the northwestern fringes of Arabia far into central Asia were herding and tending more than half a dozen kinds of four-footed livestock. Unlike people in the other principal zones, they have continued to use several if not most of these creatures as milk sources to this day.

The practice of milking didn't develop as early as other uses of domestic animals. It must be seen in contexts quite unrelated to modern milking—for example, climate and geography, which nowadays hardly impinge at all on the lives of the largest dairy-cow herds.

The cradle of animal domestication, from Asia Minor eastward into present-day Iraq and Iran, was not gentle. Most of the region was arid and had brutally hot summers, a fact that would intensely stamp the oldest chapters of dairying history. The geographic range of livestock herding gradually expanded eastward and westward in ancient times to embrace a greater range of terrains both more and less hospitable, but largely sharing some harsh features of the eastern Mediterranean and Anatolia.

Throughout the great east-west belt where milking first took root, the chief livestock animals were goats, sheep, pigs, cattle, horses, asses, and camels. Pigs were the odd ones out here. All the rest had at least dual careers as sources of meat and milk, with some also doing duty as beasts of burden.

What made them suitable for the milking part of the arrangement? Or to put the question differently, why were pigs *not* used for milking? One obvious reason is that pigs—as equal-opportunity scavengers of vegetable and animal matter—are the only nonherbivores in the lineup. No society has ever habitually consumed milk from any animal that doesn't live on grass and leaves. The preferred species have always been ruminants (sheep, goats, cattle, the reindeer of far northern Europe, the water buffaloes of India), other cud-chewing animals (dromedaries, Bactrian camels), and a few non-cud-chewers fairly good at converting vegetation into milk and meat (horses, asses).

It may be—I've never talked to anyone in a position to know—that flesh eaters and omnivores communicate some flavor to their milk that made prehistoric peoples reject it. But regardless of this point, anatomy alone would have put them at a disadvantage for being milked. The club of domestic milch animals consists of fairly, though not unmanageably, large hoofed beasts standing high enough off the ground for human hands to reach under them without great difficulty. Carnivores like dogs and omnivores like pigs give birth to large litters, which means that the mammary system is spread out along the whole length of the mother's belly. She nurses lying on her side, while with long-legged hoofed mammals both mother and offspring stand during nursing. The large grass eaters all bear single young, or at most twins or triplets. This makes it possible for the mammary gland to assume the compact (and from the human viewpoint, convenient) form of an udder beneath the animal's hindquarters. As a final advantage, all have nipples elongated into teats that hands can easily grasp.

All the major Eurasian milch animals also live and move in herds, ranging over sizable territories in search of food. They are well adapted to open grasslands of different kinds, from dry steppes to steep hillside pasturage to well-watered plains. (Pigs would starve on any such ground.) The sparser the vegetation, the more widely they need to wander. Thus they have always been a more natural fit with some form of pastoral nomadism than with settled farming on limited tracts of land. (The latter won out in most of the world, but without large-scale technology and transportation it is a difficult balancing act.) The tremendous east-west sweep of the globe running from Hungary and the Balkans across the Hellespont through Asia Minor, south of the Black and Caspian Seas and north of the Himalayas, on into Mongolia and western China is remarkably rich in grasslands that must have been the original habitats for the wild ancestors of today's milch animals. Even today, a few groups of pastoral nomads still tend roving herds of goats, sheep, cattle, camels, and to an extent horses in parts of central and western Asia. Milk has always been a prominent part of the bargain because lactating females can in essence carry part of a tribe's daily food supply on the hoof, relieving people of the need to haul it around.

THE FLAVOR COROLLARIES

From a culinary point of view, there are striking implications. The part of the world with the oldest and most deeply ingrained milking traditions is also the one where milk came from the most varied sources—animals whose milk generally had pronounced and diverse tastes. Cows' milk is blander than any of its competitors, though undoubtedly this was less true of prehistoric cows that grazed in nomadic conditions and gave scantier amounts of more concentrated milk than their modern counterparts.

The prevalence of arid climates with fierce summer heat was also significant. It meant that cows were seldom the dominant milk source, because of all dairy animals they are the least able to tolerate heat. (There are exceptions, of which more later, but not in the Diverse Sources latitudes.) Then there were the seasonal reproductive cycles of the major herd animals. Most give birth close to the time of new grass in spring, so that the mother has the advantage of the year's most plentiful grazing just as she comes into milk. Lactation continues for some months until the young are weaned, the supply dries up, and the mothers are again ready to breed. People would therefore have done most of their milking during the months when milk sours most quickly once it is taken from the ewe, mare, goat, or other source.

Clearly the earliest milk-eating experiments must have been done with milk fresh from the udder. But until very recently this did not become a favorite form in the Diverse Sources Belt, except sometimes as a food for young children. Set aside any assumptions based on the availability of refrigerators, and you will see that the natural fate of milk left to sit around in extreme summer heat is swift colonization by neighborhood bacteria. Some kinds are harmful (in fact, occasionally lethal) and some benign, but at ambient hot-weather temperatures one group of nonharmful bacteria has a certain competitive advantage. They feed on lactose, the special sugar of milk, converting it to lactic acid and incidentally rendering the milk more digestible for grown-ups who have lost the usual childhood tolerance for lactose. In the process, they lower the pH of the milk enough to make it inhospitable to many disease-carrying organisms. This isn't to say that letting milk sour is an infallible measure for keeping pathogens at bay, but it affords some protection.

The particular kinds of lactic-acid bacteria that would have got there first in the blistering summers of the Middle East and Central Asia produce something resembling yogurt, though until fairly recent times no one used that name or sought to inquire whether one group's milk-souring bugs were identical to another's. The crucial thing to realize is that in nearly all of the Diverse Sources Belt—which, as I've suggested, is nearly tantamount to "Yogurtistan"—the simplest way for most people to consume milk was soured, in the form of yogurt or its close cousins.

Two other forms became universal enough over most of Yogurtistan to suggest that they also go back to very ancient times. The first probably was hit upon after a very young kid or lamb had been butchered and eviscerated. Somehow milk came in contact with the lining of the animal's stomach and later was found to have curdled to a cheeselike substance through the action of an enzyme peculiar to the digestive systems of nurslings. Eventually people learned to use the mysterious curdling agent (the modern name is "rennet") in tandem with natural souring to produce agreeable-tasting—though short-lived—fresh cheeses in which the flavors of the original milk were both transmuted and intensified.

The second step forward followed the discovery that a strong brine solution would stop spoilage in such cheeses and enable them to be held for weeks or months. Ripening or aging in the fashion of modern European cheeses was impossible because the process requires cooler surroundings at some crucial stages. In hot, arid climates, lightly salted fresh cheeses can undergo some primitive flavor-altering and spoilage-preventing changes simply through drying out. (French *crottins* are an example.) But the requisite conditions for more sustained, complex fermentations did not exist in prehistoric times. Brining, on the other hand, was a convenient preservation technique for anyone with access to salt. Most parts of the Diverse Sources Belt thus have had some long-standing tradition of brined cheeses—that is, versions of what Americans usually call "feta."

Several features of this ancient milking landscape are bound to surprise people used to modern commercial dairy products. Maybe the most striking is the absence of blandness, not only in the milk itself but in what's done to it. For millennia, people in the oldest dairying regions consumed milk that started out with distinctive flavors mirroring individual animal sources and then acquired lively lactic-acid notes when it became something we would recognize as yogurt or the related versions of fermented milk now known as kefir or *kumys* (see pages 198–99). (Cooks should also note that eventually the habit of heating or boiling milk to be used for yogurt became almost universal, because it produces a richer and silkier-textured result.) The oldest and most universally eaten cheeses also tasted firmly of the original milk, with a briny tang superimposed in the case of the feta relatives.

Many cuisines of the Diverse Sources Belt (though not all) also used some form of butter. Where it existed, it was generally stronger-tasting than ours both because of the animals the milk came from and because it often underwent an extended period of storage, sometimes after a flavor-intensifying treatment such as long simmering with or without herbs and spices. Different versions of clotted cream—some with emphatically ripened flavors—also seem to have been widespread for many centuries. When we come to cheese, however, the range of possibilities was seriously restricted until fairly recent times. Even today only a few kinds of cheese other than fresh white cheese and feta are produced in the old Diverse Sources Belt. For the most part their descent can be traced to Western influence and modern European originals (e.g., Greek *graviera*, which takes its name from Gruyère) rather than to ancient local tradition.

As you will see from many of the recipes in this book, cooks of the Diverse Sources Belt love to set off dairy foods with pungent flavors of many kinds. Certain combinations or effects crop up again and again. Pairing chunks of brined white cheese with green herbs and crunchy raw vegetables is as natural in Bulgaria as two thousand miles away in Uzbekistan. Romanians are as fond of cucumbers with yogurt as are Iranians and Afghans, and yogurt-garlic sauces are loved from one end of the zone to the other. Perhaps the most fascinating discovery for me was the array of cereal products for soups and porridges that are made—like Greek *trahana* and Turkish *tarhana*—by drying and crumbling a fresh or fermented mixture of grain (or flour) and yogurt, often with the enrichment of vegetables and herbs.

THE DRAMATIS PERSONAE: THE ORIGINAL BIG THREE

Only three of the major Diverse Sources Belt milch animals ever achieved enough importance as milkers anywhere else to have crossed the path of most American food lovers. Camels chiefly remained in the drier areas of the primal milking zone. Horses (and their close equid relatives, asses) spread nearly everywhere in the Old World, but the intensely horse-centered way of life anciently pursued by some nomadic tribes of Central Asia didn't. In no other societies did mares' milk enjoy great popularity as a food. The Big Three that

ANCESTRAL WILD SHEEP
(MOUFLON)

eventually adapted to lands far north and south of the first milking belt were sheep, goats, and cows. For the sake of practicality my recipes generally call for dairy products based on cows' milk, but I urge you to seek out the other two wherever possible. Sheep's and goats' milk will give you at least a little idea of how much wider some people's dairying horizons used to be.

Sheep and goats (to zoologists, *Ovis aries* and *Capra hircus*) go together like firs and spruces, and were the core milch animals in more areas of the Diverse Sources Belt than any other contenders. Apparently descended from a common ancestor that lived before the last ice age, they resemble each other in so many skeletal features that zooarchaeologists often can't tell whether a few stray bones belonged to a goat or a sheep. The catchall term "caprines," or more ponderously "ovicaprids," is often applied to both.

Caprines almost certainly were the subjects of the earliest Near Eastern human milking experiments, after some centuries of being kept for meat and skins. By classical times goats and sheep were being raised side by side throughout the Diverse Sources Belt and had made their way beyond it. There was great logic to their original tandem success in and around mountainous reaches of the Near East, the region where they had evolved. Both were born to thrive in this arid land of fierce summers and bitter winters. They also had the advantage of being small enough for people to tangle with and live to tell the tale, but large enough to give amounts of milk that would repay the effort of collecting it. When raised together, they complemented each other's ways of getting the most out of local resources. Goats are light and nimble enough to climb forbidding rocky slopes—even shrubby trees—in search of food, while the heavier, shorter-legged sheep efficiently work flat, grassy pastures. Goats eat nearly anything with leaves and shoots; sheep (which seldom eat leaves) can crop grass closer than any other herd animal. Sheep, being sheepish in temperament, are also easy to keep track of and herd into folds, while the more contrarian goats range adventurously in search of anything edible.

The world's first pastoralists found that both sheep and goats obligingly came into season in the fall and gave birth after roughly five-

ANCESTRAL WILD GOAT
(PERSIAN WILD GOAT)

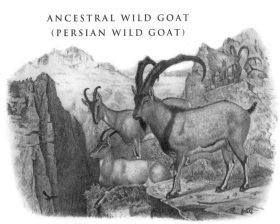

month pregnancies, in time to reach peak milk production in late spring and early summer. The milk of the two tasted as similar as you might expect of such close evolutionary cousins. But the goats, even though slightly smaller, managed to yield several times more milk than the sheep. The latter contributed a meager amount of naturally rich, concentrated milk that intensified the whole (goat-and-sheep dairyists regularly pooled the two creatures' milk, as is still common from the Balkans into western Asia) beyond all proportion to its volume.

Cattle did not become realistic candidates for domestication and milking until many centuries later. The most obvious obstacle was size, coupled with a murderous disposition.

Modern cows and bulls are descended from a great creature called the aurochs (plural, "aurochsen"), or urus, that evolved somewhere in northwestern Asia in the last ice age. By the time the glaciers retreated, the aurochs species, *Bos primigenius*, ranged widely throughout much of the Old World. Wherever they went, the fierce and kingly beasts aroused wonder, often to the point of religious awe. Full-grown bulls could stand some six feet high at the shoulder; the largest must have weighed well over a ton and a half. The huge, sweeping horns that still give pause to people looking at the painted Lascaux specimens were accompanied by an extremely short fuse.

As compared with the wild ancestors of goats and sheep, aurochsen would have been difficult to bring into the domestic human orbit even if they had not been innately menacing. They were large enough to have trouble maintaining a stable body temperature in the hot summers of the Diverse Sources Belt. (As mentioned earlier, the problem persists even with their smaller descendants.) They were also poorly adapted to arid conditions, could neither forage in the free spirit of goats nor crop short grass as well as sheep, and needed several times more food per head than the caprines. On the other hand, cows gave much more milk than either ewes or "does" (the usual dairyman's term for nanny goats).

Over many centuries or millennia, people succeeded in breeding aurochsen to produce a domesticated species, *Bos taurus*, that was smaller and gentler than its ancestor. All bovines also have the advantage of pronounced sexual dimorphism: The females are much smaller than the males and not nearly so hardwired for aggression. Bulls still were, and are, much the most dangerous of all domestic animals. But early on someone discovered that castrating them before they were full-grown would produce oxen, which nearly matched the docility of cows and are the world's strongest draft animals other than water buffaloes and elephants. Their muscle power would lead to a revolution in the human food supply.

Cattle domestication had been established in the Near East by about 7000

AN EGYPTIAN COW GIVING BIRTH

to 6000 B.C. As with sheep and goats, milking apparently did not follow for many centuries. By then, however, local societies had taken to plowing with oxen or cows, a breakthrough comparable to the later invention of tractors. Before that, would-be farmers had had to dig with handheld sticks, and settled agriculture had been restricted to tiny plots with very light soil. Neither goats, sheep, nor humans were able to drag a larger, heavier version of a stick with enough force to penetrate dense clayey soil or well-rooted sod. Domesticated cattle were the plowers that literally broke the ground for the diffusion of grain farming beyond its Near Eastern cradle.

The spread of the animals didn't necessarily go with a taste for their milk. To this day, cows' milk is less dominant in the old Diverse Sources Belt countries than in other parts of the world. Though they have been milked there since antiquity—cows are depicted in scenes of milking activity on a third-millennium B.C. frieze from Tell el-Obeid in southern Iraq—they had to be carried into far southerly and northerly regions to become *the* milch animal par excellence. No reader of Homer, the Old Testament, or Virgil automatically thought of cows on hearing the word "milk"; the main association was with goats and sheep. Locales where cows came to be prime milk sources from early times were, and are, marked by very different ways of life and culinary preferences. The first of these places was India.

THE BOVINE AND BUFFALO BELT

As Jared Diamond has pointed out in *Guns, Germs, and Steel,* Old World food crops and other resources had to overcome more obstacles in order to move north and south than east and west. The reason is that the all-important factor of temperature varies directly with latitude, not longitude.

Some plants and animals brought to new environments managed to cope with heat, cold, and other variables better than others. Goats, horses, and sheep proved to be hardy under many conditions, but tended to be challenged by tropical humidity. Cattle were another story. As descendants of creatures that had flourished in glacial chill, they would have been thoroughly defeated by Torrid Zone heat and humidity had it not been for a timely genetic freak.

ZEBU COW AND CALF

People had been husbanding cattle for meat, draft purposes, and, to an extent, milk in ancient Mesopotamia for centuries when a strange new type appeared, probably between 3000 and 2500 B.C., somewhere between southern Persia and the western Pakistan-Afghanistan fringes. The same aberration may (no one is sure) have occurred independently in another spot or two between the Middle East and Nilotic Africa. In any case, the new creature—later christened *Bos indicus* by zoologists to distinguish it from *Bos taurus*—was the reason that milking and milk-based cuisine were able to penetrate throughout the Indian subcontinent and much of Africa.

The most visible difference between ordinary cattle and the *indicus* variant was the latter's pronounced neck or shoulder hump. Eventually naturalists started calling the humped cattle of India "zebus" and a similar race in Africa "sangas." To sidestep learned debates about zebu-sanga classifications and whether *indicus* designates a subspecies or separate species, I have lumped together both humped kinds as "zebu-type."

The hump, which was larger on bulls than cows, went along with a pendulous dewlap, a narrow bony frame, thin skin, and many environmental advantages. Zebu-type animals can tolerate sweltering tropical heat, resist certain diseases and parasites, and subsist on more meager pasturage than other cows. Today the zebu-type milch cows of Nilotic Africa at least as far south as Tanzania support the world's most intensely cow-centered pastoral cultures, and those of India symbolize an entire nation—at least, as seen by militant patriots.

JUNGLE, MOUNTAIN, RIVER

The Indian milch-animal scene is riddled with strange complexities, puzzles, and paradoxes, one being that though the subcontinent is framed by regions representing the most diverse bovine gene pool on earth, most of India's Asian neighbors scorn the creatures' milk. From Assam eastward into several Southeast Asian countries, wild bovine jungle species, including gaur, kouprey, and banteng, still survive along with some domesticated offshoots. But there is little local use of either the tame animals' milk or that of zebu cattle.

YAK

To the north, the picture is different. From the western Himalayas through and beyond Mongolia, people have been herding a towering, fur-draped bovine cousin, *Bos grunniens*, for about twenty-five hundred years. Americans usually call it "yak," though Tibetan speakers protest that the correct word for the female is *dri*. In any case, not only is yak, or *dri*, milk famously cherished wherever the creature is raised, but it is traditional to exploit the phenomenon of "hybrid vigor" by crossbreeding yaks with both zebu and taurine cattle for, among other benefits, increased milk yields in female offspring. Western observers who have tasted *dri* milk report that it is a lovely golden color with an extraordinarily deep, rich flavor; some experiments with Western-style cheeses have been made in Nepal and elsewhere, and it isn't out of the question that the few small yak-husbandry ventures that have recently started in North America may generate a bit of local interest in the milk.

None of these bovine cousins encroaches on the milk-giving role of the sacred zebu cow in India proper. But an entirely different creature does. Strange as it may seem to anyone else, Indians rely less on the milk of the sacred cow than on that of this nonbovine competitor, the fourth of the world's leading dairy animals. More than half the nation's milk supply actually comes from the "river" strain of the water buffalo, *Bubalus bubalis.*

WATER BUFFALO

This formidable-looking ruminant is a long, massive, low-slung, splay-footed beast with a hide like a hippopotamus and a pair of fearsome ridged horns. Water buffaloes should not be confused with bison, which strictly speaking aren't buffaloes at all. The true buffalo's closest ancestors probably were staking out habitats in the wetlands of southern Asia at about the same time that aurochsen began roaming their own northern haunts.

Like oxen elsewhere, domesticated buffaloes were the great facilitators of a certain staple crop—in this case rice, since they can pull plows through muddy or semi-flooded paddies that other animals could never negotiate. Their meat is considered at least equal to beef wherever both are eaten. But for some reason, only India showed any interest in their milk or developed a particular strain suitable for that purpose. All other Far Eastern regions bred large, thick-set draft buffaloes of the "swamp" strain. The Indian "river" buffalo is a rangier, bonier type that diverts a great deal of food energy into lactation. In fact, it may be the most remarkable of all milch animals.

What sets river buffaloes apart from the rest of the crew is that they produce not only richer milk but *more* milk than nearly all the rest—and this with far less intensive breeding-and-feeding efforts than have gone into increasing the yields of Western dairy cows, the only higher-volume producers among the four major milch animals. Only sheep give milk that is equally or more concentrated—but, as noted, there's very little of it. A good milking ewe can, under favorable conditions, yield two or three quarts (four to six pounds) of milk a day, while two to three *gallons* (sixteen to twenty-four pounds) is by no means exceptional for a buffalo.

Buffaloes' milk has an odd glaucous appearance, suggesting that it shouldn't be nearly as creamy as cows' milk. In fact, it is much creamier. People who have tasted it fresh (I have not) say that it seems almost like a concentrated milk reduction. Judging from the buffalo yogurt and mozzarella that I have eaten, it seems to have some special earthy dimension of its own quite unlike the goaty-sheepy flavors of caprines' milk. What's more, the animals thrive and produce copiously on cheaper and coarser tropical forages than cows.

Though reliable statistics are hard to come by, there are known to be many more zebu cows than buffaloes milked in India. But the latter account for more than 50 percent of the nation's commercial milk supply. Why the animal itself never came to be revered is a mystery. Zebu cows in India became important as domestic livestock and sources of milk earlier than water buffaloes, and perhaps the quasi-divine status that they eventually acquired did not admit of diminishment by being shared with another beast.

Paradoxically, the very fact that water buffaloes are *not* considered holy may have made Indian commercial milk producers willing to undertake more aggressive, systematic management measures; though millions of cows are left to wander the countryside without anyone trying to improve their milk yield, dairying interests apparently feel freer to intervene in buffalo destiny.

Western dairyists' lack of interest in buffaloes' milk is equally puzzling. When taken from the tropics, buffaloes are surprisingly good at adapting to other surroundings. They probably ranged as far north as southern Mesopotamia from ancient times, and since then have been successfully introduced into Egypt, the Levant, and parts of Italy and the Balkans. But only today are a handful of experimenters trying to see how well water buffaloes can tolerate more northerly temperate climates. Some British and American farmers have managed to generate a little publicity for swamp buffaloes' meat as an alternative to beef, and a very few are trying to do the same for river buffaloes'–milk yogurt and mozzarella cheese.

Possessing two milk sources of equal culinary importance makes India unique among the world's

GODS AND DEMONS PULL ALTERNATELY ON OPPOSITE ENDS OF A GIANT SERPENT TO ROTATE THE MIRACULOUS COSMIC "CHURN" OF HINDU MYTH.

dairying countries. (There is some use of goats' milk in hilly northern regions, but nationally it ranks a very distant third.) Cows' milk and buffaloes' milk are used all but interchangeably for every kind of dairy product. But because buffaloes' milk is more concentrated and gives higher yields of milkfat, protein, and virtually any other milk-derived product per original pound of milk, it is more commercially profitable. Cows' milk enjoys higher prestige, undoubtedly because of its association with the sacred animal.

Brahmins have long cherished an image of the cow as a crown jewel in a complex, prohibition-fenced scheme of beliefs about the ritual purity or pollution of food. In this worldview she is the wellspring of life in palpable form, inexhaustibly pouring forth the miracle of milk, a holy substance considered to have been purified by inner fires in the grass-transforming alembic that is the cow's body. (In fact, a Hindu creation myth describes a primordial sea of milk as the stuff from which many great gifts of the world were "churned" under the direction of Vishnu.) The cow-mother also gradually became a symbol of

Mother India—originally, a benevolent symbol; now something more aggressive. Cow worship never used to have anything like the frankly militant Hinduist associations that it enjoys in today's political-religious tinderbox. (Not only is there a national prohibition against beef slaughter, but people remarking too loudly that even Brahmins used to eat beef in Vedic times are likely to incur harassment if not death threats.) Not surprisingly, modern industrialized cow dairying has proceeded somewhat cautiously in India despite a good deal of entrepreneurial interest and expertise, and despite the fact that milk is more central to cooking there than in any other nation. It is no exaggeration to say that, without milk, the doctrine of ahimsa (the inviolability of animal as well as human life) could not have achieved its primacy and the flowering of vegetarianism throughout India would have been impossible.

THE SOUL OF A GREAT CUISINE

From prehistoric times, the sweltering Indian climate ensured that, as in the Diverse Sources Belt, milk would be more often used soured than fresh. But there are several critical differences. Not only Western-style aged cheeses but the fresh and brined cheeses of the earlier milking region are conspicuous by their absence from Indian tables. In fact, so are most dairy foods made from raw rather than cooked milk.

Boiling milk after milking and before using it for most other purposes seems to be a very ancient Indian culinary tradition. It changes the milk's receptiveness to different culturing organisms, discouraging those that would produce fresh cheese. (A second anticheese factor is that killing young animals for rennet would violate the principle of ahimsa.) But boiling makes milk all the more suitable for yogurt, which depends on having "thermophilic," or heat-preferring, bacteria introduced at a temperature close to 110°F. Most of the favorite Indian dairy products start off with milk being boiled and allowed to cool until it reaches the right stage to be inoculated with a little of yesterday's yogurt.

You might not guess how thoroughly yogurt from both cows' and buffaloes' milk pervades the cuisine from the many Anglo-Indian books about food that insist on saying "curd" or "curds" for indigenous words such as the Hindi *dahi* and Tamil *thayir*. Yogurt is a dish in its own right and the foundation of various beverages and cold relishes, as well as an element in innumerable sauces, dressings, soups, and desserts. It is also the starting point of churned butter (Hindi *makkan*, Tamil *vennai*). Because of its basis in yogurt, the buttermilk (Hindi *chhas*, Tamil *moru*) resulting from butter churning has nuances that would be hard to duplicate here in America.

In fact, anything based on yogurt—highly nonstandardized throughout the subcontinent—is likely to taste different even from one Indian region to another. In addition, there will be differences between the cows'-milk and buffaloes'-milk versions. Buffalo yogurt starts out creamier and denser, and yields more butter in churning. The butter itself is almost pure white because it contains more finished vitamin A than the yellowish precursor beta-carotene that predominates in most cows' milk.

Freshly churned butter of either kind can be eaten as is, but is more often slowly simmered to produce the ambrosial cooking fat called ghee (Tamil *neyyu*), which is also yellow or white depending on the animal it came from. The long, gentle cooking evaporates any remaining water and makes it easier to "clarify" the milkfat, or separate it from any residual milk solids; without such treatment it would be extremely perishable.

Plain fresh milk does play a part in Indian cuisine, but there are distinct regional preferences that perhaps reflect different degrees of lactose tolerance. Though it is hard to sort out the many statistical claims that have been published with very hazy scientific documentation, people in the northern states appear much more likely to maintain lactose-digesting ability into adulthood. In those regions, people occasionally drink milk as a beverage—but usually when it has been heated and partly cooled, and usually with some kind of sweetening.

The north has also produced a milk-based specialty that arouses curious reactions in other regions of India. It is a kind of curd made by heating milk (sometimes buttermilk) and adding an acidulant like lemon juice that causes casein (the major milk protein) to precipitate out of the whey in a semisolid white mass. Called *chhenna* in that form, *panir* when cut into cubes, this very bland and slightly rubbery substance often turns up on English-language restaurant menus as "cheese" or something like "cottage cheese," "soft cheese," or "pot cheese." In fact it is none of the above, never having been exposed to either rennet curdling or bacterial fermentation. But it is a wonderfully versatile foil to rich-flavored sauces and purées, and in the form of chhenna makes lovely patties and dumplings.

The idea for this not-exactly-cheese may have come from either the conquering Moghuls, who swept through India from north to south starting in about 1525, or the Portuguese, who were already carving out spheres of influence before the Moghuls arrived. There was a block to its acceptance: the widespread Hindu belief that "breaking," or "cutting," milk into "parts" (curd and whey) violated the holy substance's integral nature. For some reason, the taboo was soon overcome by northern Hindus but frequently persists elsewhere. This is why chhenna and panir never became everyday foods in regions where Moghul or Portuguese influence was slight. Generally speaking, they are less important the farther you get from the first Moghul strongholds in the north.

A more widely accepted northern contribution is unsoured milk cooked down to different concentrations, usually with added sugar. Among the passionately loved specialties based on reduced milk are several forms of clotted cream (*malai*); various sweet, rich milk puddings thickened with rice; and a fudgelike concentrate known as *khoa*, which is the basis of an entire sweetmeat industry (especially in West Bengal State and neighboring Bangladesh). For non-Indians, the huge repertoire of reduced-milk confections and sweets tends to be at best an acquired taste. On their home territory, however, they are as defining a preference as whiskey in Scotland.

As in the Diverse Sources Belt, the practice of drinking milk fresh and unflavored has historically been infrequent, even in zones of widespread lactose tolerance. But today India has an aggressively progress-minded dairy industry (though it is somewhat constrained by attitudes toward cows), powerfully influenced by modern Western notions about milk drinking and eager to be a model for Western-style dairying enterprises in the less-developed Asian and African tropics. It is impossible not to wonder how the older milk-based traditions will be affected by the imposing of views originally shaped by radically different cultures and geographies.

THE NORTHEASTERN COW BELT

It took many undocumented centuries for livestock husbandry, including milking, to spread from the Diverse Sources Belt not only southward into India but northward beyond the Black Sea and the Caucasus into another east-west zone stretching from the western Russian steppes through Ukraine and north of the Carpathian Mountains into Poland, parts of the future Austro-Hungarian Empire, the Baltic lands, and the fringes of Scandinavia (where there is also an admixture of other influences from the west). With this third great dairying zone we move a little closer to the preferences that most Americans understand and that are now being exported all around the world.

Cattle held an advantage over the other domestic animals introduced to northeastern Europe: They'd been there before. That is, they were returning to parts of the chilly latitudes where their aurochs forebears had been roaming when the last ice sheet decamped for the North Pole. (Aurochsen were still at large in Neolithic times; they became more elusive as human populations took over, but they didn't absolutely disappear until one last female died in Poland in 1627.) Long, cold winters and brief, relatively cool summers with good amounts of rainfall to keep pastures green were exactly what cattle needed to thrive and produce milk. Wherever they were brought in these parts, they became the dominant milch animals.

The number-one status of cows rested not only on their environmental suitability but on a preference for their milk, clearly evident by modern times. Goats had their niche as "the poor man's cow" where grass was too meager for a real one. Sheep were mostly relegated to wool or (more sporadically) meat production, with milking a very minor priority. The comparative blandness of cows'-milk products emerged as the way many people thought dairy foods *ought* to taste. This preference was largely shared by Slavs, Balts, and the Ashkenazic Jews who diffused into many parts of the region. The contribution of Jews to local dairying from the Middle Ages on must have been vast. No one else had any particular religious motivation for exploiting varied uses of milk. Observant Jews, however, were required to prepare either "meat" or "milk" meals with no mixing of the two. Not only were "milk" meals cheaper, but it was easier to turn milk into a range of delicious forms.

As in the two previously discussed zones, people very rarely made a habit of drinking fresh milk as it came from the source—and this despite the fact that at least some northeastern Europeans have a certain degree of lactose tolerance (Ashkenazim less so). Even in northerly climes, milking seasons used to coincide naturally with the warmest weather of the year, when milk sours fairly fast without refrigeration. (Manipulation of milking cycles for year-round production is a modern commercial development.) Here and there, unsoured milk was used as a thrifty base for soups in lieu of meat, or went into the cereal porridges that were the crucial peasant mainstay everywhere. But for the most part milk was consumed in cultured form, either drunk plain or made into fresh curd cheeses. Renneted fresh cheeses from uncultured milk also had some currency, but most kinds used a combination of souring and renneting. The whey was yet another porridge vehicle. (Grain-based porridges were the basic survival dishes of the Northeastern Cow Belt, and even small amounts of milk or whey greatly increased their nutritional value.)

Brined cheeses like those of the Diverse Sources Belt never became popular except in a few Central European areas of overlap with the Balkans (for instance, Hungary and Romania). And generally speaking, neither the local kinds of sour milk nor the local fresh cheeses closely duplicated those of the more southerly milking zone. The reason is that under slightly cooler conditions, different types of bacteria with slightly different flavor effects are likely to work their will on milk either spontaneously or through inoculation. To produce what traditional yogurt eaters will recognize as yogurt, you need emphatically warm temperatures (and preferably a preliminary heating of the milk). Milk left to sit out at less sultry temperatures will attract "mesophilic" bacteria like those responsible for souring today's cultured buttermilk. Add rennet at a strategic moment and you will get something not unlike the pot cheese or farmer cheese familiar to many Americans, with a softer or firmer curd depending on very small gradations of temperature. But with patience you can arrive at a very similar, slightly tarter cheese made without rennet—the practice of observant Jews, since milk could not come in contact with an animal substance like rennet.

Cream in cultured form enjoyed greater importance in the Northeastern Cow Belt than in the lands to the south. Because cows' milk separates more quickly and fully on standing than goats' milk (though not as readily as water buffaloes' milk), it is easier to skim off the cream for use by itself, fresh or sour. Cooler temperatures also aid the process. Clotted cream, which is really cooked, did not become as important here as in other regions. Sour cream, ranging from slightly runny to nearly as thick as cream cheese, became a versatile cold sauce base, spread, and enrichment for soups and other dishes.

Northern ideas about butter diverged sharply from those in the two older milking zones. In both India and the Diverse Sources lands, butter was commonly churned from whole-milk yogurt. (It was seldom made from anything but cows' or buffaloes' milk, because producing butter from goats' milk with its very small fat globules was extremely difficult before modern centrifuges. Sheep's milk worked better, but was less cost-effective given the small amounts of milk per animal.) Most often it also underwent a slow simmering process, as for ghee. The northerners took another tack by using cream (usually soured) rather than whole milk for churning and omitting the prolonged cooking. This process produced an entirely different substance, smooth and unctuous at ambient temperatures where ghee and other forms of clarified butter would be grainy, and also containing subtle flavor notes lost in clarifying. The downside of using cream was that you got a smaller amount of less flavorful buttermilk.

The northerners' butter was also a cooking fat as excellent in its own way as ghee—a fact of crucial importance, because the region lacked any source of edible oil comparable to the Mediterranean olive or Middle Eastern sesame seed. People could, of course, render lard, beef suet, or poultry fat to be used in cooking. But the process required amounts of time and fuel that butter churning didn't. Once you had butter, you had a marvelously versatile food that could be incorporated into some kinds of rich bread and pastry doughs or spread on already-baked bread, melted over cooked foods as a sauce, worked into fresh skim-milk cheeses as an enrichment, or used as a sautéing medium that imparted a lovely flavor to anything cooked in it. Its biggest drawback was that it went rancid easily if stored long without refrigeration. As for the buttermilk, it could be either a beverage in its own right or a cooking liquid (especially for porridges).

The Northeastern Cow Belt also happens to be an unparalleled center for all kinds of brine-pickled vegetables and fruits, from sorrel and cabbage to apples and beets. Like sour milk, these depend on fermentation of carbohydrates to lactic acid (though the starting point is not milk sugar). The two kinds of lactic-acid products—bracingly sour pickles (or their brine) and smooth, more gently tart cultured milk or cream—make a wonderful marriage, especially when the pickles are garlicky. This magical combination has produced a large family of cold soups that are among the glories of Russian, Ukrainian, Polish, and other cuisines. Like many yogurt dishes of the Middle East and India, they are a lesson in milk's affinities with partners that few American cooks would have thought of a generation ago.

Until modern times the Northeastern Cow Belt shared the two older milking regions' general indifference to any kind of ripened cheese. For centuries almost no cheese was produced there other than the small fresh kinds that could be easily made at home. Of course, Jews faced the obstacle that putting rennet in milk is almost automatically a violation of kashruth. ("Almost" because under certain convoluted interpretations not accepted by all, animal rennet can be judged to have lost its "meat" status.) And for everybody including Jews, a broader limiting factor was the absence of proven markets able to repay the sustained efforts involved in producing and selling aged cheeses— which brings us to what is in many ways the strangest of the world's dairying zones.

THE NORTHWESTERN COW BELT

Geographically, this used to be the smallest of the major Old World regions where strong traditions of fresh dairy foods developed. But after some five millennia it suddenly ended up as the largest. Consequently it is enmeshed in snarls of contradiction-laced history.

The core areas are northern Germany, the Low Countries, northern France, and especially the British Isles. In southern Scandinavia, eastern Germany and the western Baltic lands, France and Germany as far south as the northern Alps, and some of the old Austro-Hungarian domains, the zone shades into traditions more akin to the Northeastern Cow Belt or the Diverse Sources Belt. And before modern times the links with such eastern neighbors were stronger everywhere. The premodern history, however, hasn't been much explored. In fact, a general failure of historical perspective set in at the dawn of the Industrial Revolution after Great Britain exported its own milk-centered customs and attitudes to all the Anglophone colonies including the future United States, Canada, Australia, and New Zealand. For all practical purposes these are now extensions of the original Northwestern Cow Belt.

From early times one huge factor has set apart the population of this zone from most of the human race: a capacity for digesting lactose, discussed from a biological standpoint in "The Story of Modern Milk." A second, almost equally important difference rooted in the northwestern European transition

from the medieval to the modern economy came into play later (and as we shall see, decisively shaped the mentality of modern dairying). But at least at the outset, the uses of milk in the future Great Britain and its near European neighbors don't seem to have been decisively different from other people's.

Livestock husbandry and dairying probably spread out from the Near East into northwestern Europe at around 3000 B.C. As in the Northeastern Cow Belt, cattle constitutionally liked the local weather and soon became more dominant milch animals than sheep and goats. By medieval times sheep's milk was highly valued by many but discouragingly labor-intensive to produce; where sheep were raised for wool, people sometimes came to ignore any other purpose. Goats tended to be preferred for milking in areas too steep or bleakly exposed for cattle grazing (for example, parts of Norway and Scotland). But this is to get ahead of the story.

How did prehistoric farmers of the northwest use cows' or other animals' milk in the unrecorded millennia before the Romans arrived? Set aside modern assumptions based on an industry that brings fresh drinkable milk to millions, and the truth is that there's very little to go on. One crucial fact is that since Neolithic times the region has contained one of the planet's most remarkable pockets of "lactase persistence," or "lactose tolerance," the ability to digest the lactose in unsoured milk long beyond infancy. Archaeologists hypothesize that the genes governing the condition occurred widely in a prehistoric culture that occupied parts of southern Scandinavia, the Low Countries, north coastal Germany, and the Baltic lands. (Other lactose-tolerant peoples are scattered in Africa and northern India, and there may be still more elsewhere.) But the *ability* to do something isn't the same thing as a preconditioned *choice* to do it all or even 50 percent of the time. There is little evidence to prove that the early peoples of northwestern Europe had as highly developed a preference for drinking milk fresh as their modern descendants. Milk sours there as regularly as in the Near East (though more slowly) and has the same advantages in that form.

WHAT THE ROMANS SAW

The first observers who might have cast some light on the prevalence or non-prevalance of milk drinking were the Romans, who described what they saw in breathtakingly unhelpful language. The problem in trying to decipher their accounts of Gaulish foodways is that they brought a distinctly southern perspective to every northern region they explored.

From a dairying viewpoint, things had taken very different turns north and south of the Alps when agriculture diffused westward into Europe. The Mediterranean coast from Italy to Iberia—the Romans' "Cisalpine Gaul"—developed a version of Diverse Sources Belt preferences without quite as wide a range of milch animals; sheep and goats became the primary sources, with cow dairying becoming competitive only in pockets. It appears that, except for fresh cheeses, the fresh dairy products that are the focus of this book either didn't acquire as much importance in the south as in the four major milking zones or were relegated to a lesser role in early modern times, when consciously market-oriented dairying choices began outstripping home-centered ones. In any case, cheeses of all kinds eventually predominated over other ways of consuming milk.

The Romans themselves were great pioneers in cheesemaking, because parts of northern Italy were lucky enough to possess both rich grazing lands and a climate cool enough for the prolonged fermentation processes that aged cheeses require. Besides, the city of Rome at its height was a magnet for specialized luxuries from the countryside that would not be equaled in Europe until the end of the Middle Ages. But the Romans had a hard time making sense of the non-Roman ways with milk—perhaps cheese—peculiar to northerners.

Because cattle were more important to both Romans and Greeks as beasts of burden than as sources of milk, neither civilization had deeply explored all the culinary qualities of cows' milk liked by other peoples. Greek observers returning from Scythia on the southern fringes of the Northeastern Cow Belt reported that people there consumed an alien stuff for which they could find no better designation than "cow cheese," or *boutyron*—a word that makes a certain amount of sense, and that became the Latin *butyrum* (and our "butter"). But when the Romans got to "Transalpine Gaul," or the Gaulish lands beyond the Alps, it is difficult to sort out just what they meant to say about the uncouth peoples' dairy foods. Their accounts present major roadblocks for anyone trying to establish in what form the peoples of the new Roman possessions liked to consume milk.

Tacitus and Pliny the Elder, both of whom had been stationed in Gaul after

Julius Caesar's conquests, unmistakably say that the barbarians ate some form of curdled milk. The term Tacitus uses is not *caseus* ("cheese") but *lac concretum* ("solidified milk"), while Pliny marvels at the very fact that cheese was *not* known among the Gaulish tribes; he vaguely describes the usual form of milk as something that they "thicken to a pleasant sour substance," but doesn't seem to distinguish this very clearly from butter. Caesar laconically says that the Gauls ate "milk, cheese, and meat," which leaves us wondering about the contradiction with Pliny (who presumably had more knowledge of the colony's peacetime domestic arts) and whether "milk" specifically meant fresh milk.

All of which goes to show that despite the odd genetic makeup of the peoples who were living in the Northwestern Cow Belt a couple of thousand years ago, conclusions about how often they actually used their unusual ability to drink unsoured milk are impossible. Certainly they did turn milk into various curdled forms (meaning ones with most of the lactose removed). But we also know that their better-documented descendants during the Middle Ages sometimes drank cows' and other animals' milk fresh, sometimes turned it into various soured products, fresh cheeses, butter, and aged cheeses. It doesn't seem unreasonable to guess that the pre-Roman Gauls also enjoyed both fresh milk for drinking and milk variously transformed by lactic-acid bacteria.

THE MEDIEVAL PICTURE

As in the other major dairying zones, no fresh milk industry existed in medieval Europe, or could have. Milk didn't change hands for money as often as it was consumed by small householders with their own cow or goat. Most farming was comparatively small-scale and unspecialized except for a few great commodities like wool. Dairy husbandry was usually a home enterprise, with peasants or smallholders milking an animal or two (rarely many more) and sometimes drinking part of the milk fresh or soured before making it into other simple products for their own use. Where larger operations existed, they were usually part of monastery or manor farms.

In most of northwestern Europe, butter was the cheapest and most plentiful of fats rather than anything epicurean. Cream was not particularly prized in cooking; when it was skimmed, it went into butter. The ever-useful by-product of that process was true buttermilk. Not too dissimilar from some of today's cultured buttermilk was whole milk fermented just long enough to become refreshingly tart but still liquid enough to drink, perhaps close to Pliny's "pleasant sour substance" and analogous to the yogurt of southern regions. People do not seem to have cooked with fresh milk nearly as much as we do; at any rate, it crops up less often in surviving medieval cookbooks than almond milk.

The fresh cheeses that were ordinarily the most practical kinds for house-holders to produce were based sometimes on the skim milk saved from butter-making, sometimes on whole milk. (In the latter case any butterfat that drained off along with the whey was separately saved for whey butter. The whey itself furnished a common drink; if people didn't consume it, it often ended up in pig swill.) Fresh cheeses ranged from simple curds, eaten either along with the whey or after being drained of it, to "green cheese," or curds allowed to take on a cheesier nature but eaten before aging. The curdling could be done by bacterial souring, rennet, or a combination of the two, with the flavor and tex-ture varying according to how strong the action of the acid or enzyme was and how far coagulation was allowed to proceed.

A NEW AGE DAWNS

So far, the region's dairying preferences had much in common with those of northeastern Europe—and even the older milking lands of the Near East, when it came to the importance of soured milk and fresh cheeses. But a few centuries or generations before Columbus, something started happening that would propel western Europe and later North America toward radically changed ideas of food, or rather of how to buy and sell it.

One way to describe the change is that the economic center of gravity began to revolve around cities, which (like imperial Rome in its day) looked increas-ingly to the countryside to supply them with food. Another way to look at it is that most kinds of specialized farming for profit got to northwestern Europe sooner than anywhere else in the world, foreshadowing the modern commer-cial production and transport of many foods. One of the first results was an expanding interest in ripened cheeses, already better known here than in any other stronghold of dairying. The larger kinds were not economically feasible to produce except through sizable cooperative ventures that pooled the milk and labor of many farmers (or a whole village or district) and rested on the knowledge that a market for the end result justified the expense of production as well as transportation to towns and cities.

During the many European economic shakeups following the Age of Dis-covery, more and more milk was diverted to large-scale manufacture of aged and other specialized cheeses, usually from cows' milk. Fresh cheeses contin-ued to be eaten in the northwest, but with snowballing urbanization and the displacement of peasants from the countryside in many areas, they were less often made and consumed in the households of people who actually owned a cow or goat. The farmers who remained either participated in large-scale cheesemaking based on milk pooled from a group of farms or carried out inde-pendent small-scale dairying for profit. Farmstead dairying was chiefly managed by women, who produced butter and fresh or aged cheeses (often bearing regional names) for nearby markets.

It began to be not only possible but highly desirable to target market segments, to put forth products that might claim distinction by virtue of novelty, unusual appearance, or manufacturing nuances reflected in some fillip of flavor or texture. In other words, western European dairyists were ready for a systematic commercial exploitation of diversity more intensive than anything in older regions. The contents of today's more ambitious cheese shops reflect the aggressive, long-continued pursuit of this aim—which incidentally diminished the importance of simple fresh dairy products that before the age of refrigeration could not be brought to market without spoiling.

Part of the reason that diversification triumphed was that the strikingly varied, broken-up geography of western Europe itself created an infinite number of environments. The seventeenth-century Dutch, still engaged in the giant engineering projects that would give them fine tracts of grazing land reclaimed from the sea, led the way in commercial dairy specialization. From the Low Countries into southern Scandinavia or southward to the Alps, westward to the Atlantic coast of France, or beyond the North Sea in the diverse topographies of Great Britain, the production of countless characteristic—even unique—local cheeses or other dairy specialties consciously tailored to particular domestic or foreign markets became an ever more lucrative enterprise. As systematization advanced, the many northwestern European microclimates enabled farmers to develop a large range of cattle, goat, and sheep breeds for milking and also encouraged dairyists to work with a great spectrum of naturally occurring microflora—bacterial strains that might present some marvelously flavorful departure from the kinds in the next district or the next valley. (This is why things that may look alike on paper—for instance crème fraîche in Normandy and sour cream in southern Germany—often seem to have come from unrelated planets when you taste them.)

THE GROUND SHIFTS

With shrinking rural populations and the growing professionalization of cheesemaking after the late Middle Ages, fresh milk for drinking became a less prominent feature of everyday country diets. The focus of milk consumption gradually began to center on towns and cities, where it was increasingly sold for cash. As will be explained in "The Story of Modern Milk," the perishability of milk would limit the shift until the nineteenth century. But meanwhile, other kinds of change were afoot in the kitchen as medieval culinary models yielded to new ideas.

Both sweet cream and (in some regions) cream cultured to local preferences became valued as tokens of luxury in Northwestern Cow Belt cooking after the sixteenth century. Discerning consumers began to recognize schools of elegant buttermaking. New families of butter-based sauces gained prominence, especially in France, while sweet cream began to find its way into ice creams and different kinds of sauces. In the west of England it was made into the renowned local specialty called clotted "Devonshire" or "Cornish" cream. Cream in whipped form was a great discovery of this period, though whipping techniques were at first limited by the comparatively primitive state of whisks (see page 87).

THE MILKMAN.

"Milluk! Milluk! Milluk ho!
Quick for I can't wait,—here I go!"

" A quart of Milk, good man, I'll take,
'Tis for my little dark-eyed daughter,—
But tell me, sir, for her sweet sake,
Ah! tell me 'tis not *Milk and Water* !"

In the sixteenth and seventeenth centuries unsoured milk had not yet acquired the commanding position it was to achieve, but it became more popular both drunk by itself and in sweetened beverages, roux-based sauces, and sweet or savory custards. The soured counterpart seems to have undergone a corresponding decline by the nineteenth century. Rural Scandinavian cooks retained the most, English and American cooks the least interest in different forms of soured milk with a real lactic-acid tang. Even in the British Isles and the new United States, a taste for true buttermilk (often though not always ripened) survived for centuries, while other locales remained loyal to particular cultured milk specialties.

Fresh cheeses had varied fortunes. Most ceased to be made at home except in country districts. Regional preferences in fresh cheeses sold at market went in highly varied directions; as a result, something like German *Quark* is only crudely interchangeable with English or North American opposite numbers. In France an impressive variety of forms appeared as objects of great culinary interest in their own right. This richness makes sense, because it was early French commercial dairyists who worked most intensively to exploit subtly differentiated strains of local bacteria—without microscopes, and long before the advent of the large industrial laboratories that today maintain colonies of microorganisms engineered to manufacturers' preferences.

The range of English (and early American) fresh cheeses appears to have been much smaller, though there was a demand for what was called "cream cheese"—a term hard to interpret but certainly not much like today's factory product. Long after the general decline of home-produced fresh cheeses, an occasional English observer would wistfully comment on curd cheeses or "bonnyclabber," still recalling the rural British past in remote Scottish or Irish districts. In the American Deep South, "clabber," or "curds and cream," was a beloved regional dish for generations. After the mid-twentieth century, universal pasteurization and homogenization of milk would wipe out many of these local favorites.

The tangled paradoxes of the northwestern European legacy wouldn't be as glaring if not for the fact that people from the region eventually became the voice of progressive diet-and-nutrition officialdom issuing recommendations to the whole human race, with little understanding of their own pre-industrial dairying past. Since at least the late nineteenth century, Western manufacturers and nutritional experts have been exporting versions of the modern Northwestern Cow Belt mentality to Latin America, developing tropical countries, and even the far older dairying zones of the Near East and India. This mindset stacks up pretty woefully against the deeper, broader heritage of northwestern European dairy foods and milk-based cooking. Luckily for us, other possibilities are gaining ground by the minute.

WHERE GLOBAL MILKY WAYS MEET: DAIRY FOODS IN TODAY'S AMERICA

At the dawn of the twenty-first century, the far-flung areas constituting the old Northwestern Cow Belt suddenly find themselves absorbing all manner of contributions from the other three primary milking zones—the gift of peoples who have immigrated from those regions. And considering the predicament to which industrial dairying "progress" has brought us here in the United States, they're arriving not a moment too soon.

In the late 1960s, just before immigration from every corner of the globe had begun to skyrocket, the American food scene represented either the collision course or the prolonged romance of two goals reflecting opposite sides of the northwestern European market ideal. One was to get as many differentiated products as possible before the buying public, the other to weed out all possible alternatives that interfere with profits. Both aims still merrily coexist, with lunatic results exemplified by, let's say, yogurt.

You can now walk into thousands of supermarkets and take your pick of "amaretto cheesecake" or "lemon cream pie" nonfat yogurt; low-fat yogurt with a choice of chocolate chips, granola, or Reese's Pieces as topping; or milk-free vanilla or chocolate soy yogurt—without necessarily being able to find any item that people brought up on the real thing would recognize as plain yogurt worth putting a spoon into.

The tide of immigration from the world's older dairying strongholds has redrawn the picture. Depending on where you live, you may have access to grocery stores or even supermarkets with fresh, creamy, and soul-satisfying plain yogurt made by small companies for particular immigrant communities. What's more, a taste for plain whole-milk yogurt from sheep's or combined sheep's and goats' milk has begun crossing over from Turkish- or Greek-born consumers to growing numbers of other Americans. Rich, intense Greek-made yogurt partly drained of whey in true Yogurtistan tradition has developed a following here among many food lovers.

Densely toothsome yogurt made from buffaloes' milk now regularly reaches some specialty food stores. Start frequenting small restaurants specializing in south Indian *dosas* (fermented rice-batter crepes), and you may soon find yourself adoring the southern-style yogurt- or buttermilk-based cold beverages that they serve, laced with whole spices, garlic, herb sprigs, and hot peppers. Where Russian immigrants have settled, wonderful sour cream and farmer cheese, *prostokvasha* (a pourable yogurt), and butter with the taste of clotted cream usually follow. The list can only grow as foreign-born cooks and food lovers put down roots here and find themselves able to introduce people raised in a narrow modern version of the Northwestern Cow Belt mentality to some of the "new" (though really old) fresh dairy products that have come to America.

And this isn't to mention a growing revolt against milk processed to a fare-thee-well before any of us can get our hands on it. For all the continued prominence of horrible examples to the contrary, today it is more possible than it's been in at least half a century for many of us to find honest, unhomogenized whole milk from small herds and dairies run by businesspeople who care about well-tended milch animals and fresh milk flavor.

In short, I think it is realistic rather than naive to hope that the United States will consummate the story of the great dairying zones by giving the best elements of all four a chance to flourish on American soil. That prospect makes a detailed historical look at the worst side of our own dairying traditions less discouraging than it might be.

THE STORY OF MODERN MILK
Or, Is This What We Really Want?

You can love fresh dairy products as some of life's best pleasures and still be saddened by the spectacle of modern dairying. Milk deserves many superlatives. But unfortunately, among them is the title of this country's most misunderstood food. Nothing more cruelly illustrates the unholy wars between desire and fear, gratification and denial, cravings and paranoias that now beset millions of American consumers.

As I have pointed out, signs of improvement are now dawning. In fact, the unhappy story I'm about to sketch may be headed for a not-so-unhappy outcome. American consumers may be ready to develop an enlarged perspective on why milk matters, a question now sunk in great historical amnesia. Even if we grew up on dull, featureless milk, we now have the advantage of living alongside many people raised in livelier traditions of milk-based cookery. And part of what they have to teach us is that something very curious happened in the Western world's use of milk starting about two centuries ago.

The story gets—to borrow from Lewis Carroll—curiouser and curiouser as it goes along. Its convolutions often reflect visions of dollar signs dancing in various heads. It zigzags through human digestive vagaries and cultural biases, science and pseudo-science, milk-processing technology, animal breeding and feeding, obscure consequences of refrigeration, the dawn of cyberfarming, and more. But little of all this could have been foretold at the outset, when popular eighteenth-century nutritional theory leapt to wrong conclusions that suggested new entrepreneurial opportunities. Late in the century, residents of the area that I've called the Northwestern Cow Belt—especially England and its North American colonies—began placing great emphasis on one particular way of consuming milk: in fresh drinkable form.

At that time, commercial trade in fresh milk was only slightly more possible than trade in the morning dew. Up to a century or two earlier, people who drank fresh milk had generally gotten it by milking their own cow or goat. City dwellers willing to gamble could buy it from someone who drove a cow or goat about the streets and milked a few cups' worth into a customer's bowl or pot, or hawked it from pails. (The gamble was on not being killed by any plagues carried by the animal, milker, or pail.) But everyone was at least as used to soured as fresh milk until an urban market specifically for fresh milk began to take shape, fostered by ideas about health that in a few generations would make fresh milk a nearly mandatory part of everyone's diet, especially children's.

Now, many very real medical considerations are involved with milk and linked with its modern commercial fortunes. But fear of catastrophe through *lack of fresh unsoured milk*—that form specifically—is the least rational of the lot. In fact, it is purely imaginary. It couldn't have originated if people in nineteenth-century England and North America had known anything about another medically loaded issue that I've only incidentally touched on until now: lactose tolerance or intolerance.

THE DIGESTIVE MAJORITY AND MINORITY

To summarize briefly: The *lactose* dissolved in whey is the principal sugar of milk, an energy supplier otherwise unknown or almost unknown in the animal or vegetable kingdom. Unlike milkfat and milk proteins, it is the same in composition from one animal's milk to another. It belongs to the family of *disaccharides* (double-barreled sugar molecules) and consists of a unit of simple *glucose* linked with a unit of another simple sugar, *galactose*.

In healthy baby mammals drinking mother's milk, an enzyme called *lactase* severs the link between the two halves of the molecule in the small intestine and frees the galactose to be converted (by yet another enzyme) into glucose, eventually releasing into the bloodstream two glucose molecules' worth of energy from each original lactose molecule. This feat of transformation becomes unnecessary when the child advances to a milkless adult diet. At that point lactase production stops—though in most cases not completely. Almost all human beings retain at least a vestige of lactase activity throughout their lives. And a few belong to odd mutant populations that never lose lactase activity in the same way as do most people or animals, a condition known as *lactase persistence* that is as anomalous as a fawn's keeping its spots once they have served their purpose. For most of the human race, when more than small amounts of unsoured milk get into the digestive system, the lactose in the whey passes almost intact into the small intestine. It draws diarrhea-producing water in its wake, while resident bacteria eventually reduce it to tatters and by-products including painful amounts of gas. (Note that this reaction, though unpleasant, is not an actual allergy. True milk allergy, potentially life-threatening but luckily rare, is an immune response in which the body reacts to milk proteins as foreign substances to be fought off with antibodies and a surge of histamines.)

As any glance at the world's dairying regions and cuisines shows, lactose intolerance doesn't stop adults from consuming milk. It usually deters them from drinking the fresh unsoured milk that suddenly acquired vast prominence in Western diets during the nineteenth century. The milk drinkers of the Northwestern Cow Belt didn't know that they were mutants able to do something very unusual. And until the vogue for fresh—that is, full-lactose—milk appeared in early modern times, even northwestern Europe treated it as only one possible form of milk among many others with little or no lactose.

PURITY AND PRESTIGE

A shift in priorities occurred in eighteenth- and nineteenth-century England. The new focus on milk for drinking reflects a "perfect storm" convergence of circumstances. First of all, cash-crop farming began to attract ambitious specialists who saw opportunities in feeding cities. City provisioning had become more complex and troubled as the rural poor, progressively dispossessed by new patterns of land ownership, migrated to urban centers. Townsfolk became both more isolated from once widespread skills like dairying and more dependent on retail sellers who came to the ever-expanding city markets or trolled the streets for customers. A smaller but notable factor was the advent of hot tea and coffee with fresh milk added. All this coincided with an emerging popular-science vogue that claimed to incorporate the discoveries of the first real modern chemists and public-sanitation pioneers.

The new idea that many substances were acids, bases, or neutralized prod-

CHILDREN OF THE AFFLUENT BEING FED MILK IN
ST. JAMES'S PARK, LONDON.

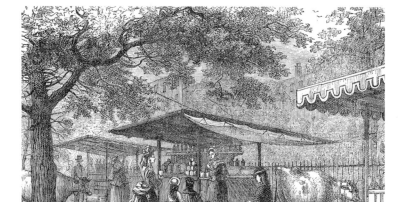

ucts of reactions between the two seems to have captured many imaginations by the end of the eighteenth century. So did the concept of "putrefaction" as a process of chemical decomposition. Putting two and two together and coming up with five because as yet nobody knew anything about bacteria, some influential would-be experts decided that acids were damaging substances and alkalis benign, while acid fermentation of foods was often a sort of dangerous putrefaction likely to lead to dyspepsia if not pestilence.

Meanwhile, more and more consumers were city people who had never acquired the home skills of fermenting bread doughs or milk, or any familiarity with the resulting sour flavors. It was not difficult for many leaders of medical and culinary opinion to convince a sizable audience that bread and milk were best when "sweet" and "pure"—the bread chemically leavened instead of leavened by yeast or sourdough fermenta-

CHILDREN OF THE POOR BEING FED "SWILL" MILK IN NEW YORK, 1878.

tion; the milk free of any sour "taint." Of course the mysteries of the lactose in sweet milk had not yet been plumbed.

By 1851 the London–street life chronicler Henry Mayhew was describing supposedly healthful "new milk" straight from the cow being sold in St. James's Park to children and "others, of a delicate constitution," who in the surly opinion of one seller would benefit more "if they was set to some good hard work." A crucial breakthrough was at hand: the ability to sell fresh (i.e., full-lactose) milk for drinking *at a higher profit than in any other form.*

SWILL DAIRYMEN MILKING A COW TOO FEEBLE TO STAND, 1858.

Yankee enterprise now showed the way to milk that would be cheap and convenient for buyers, lucrative for producers. By 1830 the demand for fresh milk had increased exponentially in the major northeastern cities of the United States. So had the supply—but much of it came from dozens or hundreds of cows herded into crowded, filthy milking sheds next to breweries or distilleries, where dairyists thriftily bought up the wastes for fodder. This opportunistic dovetailing of interests sickened or killed huge numbers of cows and provoked horrified outcries from public-health advocates who saw the watery, bluish, ill-tasting "swill milk" doing the same to people.

Farmers and middlemen shortly began working to get much better country milk to the cities. Their great ally was rail or steamboat transport of milk in sealed cans, which started in the 1840s and had decisively driven out swill milk in a few decades. Dozens of local railway lines were built to connect rural regions with cities, enabling dairy farming to become the livelihood of sundry bailiwicks such as Orange County, New York. Small though they look today, the East Coast operations begun during this era were on a scale that allowed tens of thousands of city dwellers to take up milk drinking as a relatively safe and affordable daily habit—perceived, however, as necessity, not habit.

Medical opinion now unanimously held that drinkable unsoured milk was indispensable for children and healthful for everyone else. Doctors did notice that milk seemed to disagree with more people than any other food of equal importance. But there was no way that they could have identified lactose as a culprit. In fact, more and more evidence seemed to mount that fresh milk was a godsend if not a miracle food. There were "milk cures" that had patients in sanatoria gulping six quarts a day for six weeks before returning to society in (according to adherents) a state of restoration. Less bizarrely, after about 1910 calcium and phosphorus were conclusively proved to promote healthy skeletal growth. Dairy products clearly were the richest known source of both. From World War I on, public nutrition-education programs would urgently implore mothers to feed milk to children by the quart.

Two major worries continued to dog "Nature's Perfect Food" as a continuous country-to-city pipeline materialized. The lesser was adulteration, which was very widespread but seldom involved anything more dangerous than a little adroitly administered water and whiting or plaster of Paris testifying to the premiums that fresh or theoretically fresh milk commanded. Milk-borne epidemics remained a more serious concern.

Public understanding of contagions had improved greatly with the work of the microbiologists Louis Pasteur and Robert Koch. During the last third of the nineteenth century the milk industry used such discoveries to advance factory-scale production of relatively—though far from completely—safe milk. Sterile bottling techniques on plant production lines became feasible at the same time as tuberculin testing on dairy cows (now known to be a vector for tuberculosis) and bacterial counts of milk samples under a microscope. These factors would have been tremendously important in any era. But modern technology was about to usher in others—refrigeration and pasteurization—destined to make milk in the industrialized West even more firmly identified with the sweet, full-lactose milk that non-Westerners had trouble digesting.

The earlier successes in getting milk from country to city had not solved the problem of temperature. Many bacteria, including the lactic-acid kinds that make milk go sour, can be kept in check if the milk is thoroughly chilled. Railway cars refrigerated with blocks of ice helped push back the geographical limits of milk collection and distribution after the Civil War, and by the early twentieth century mechanically refrigerated tank cars were starting to take over. Milk was already being chilled at bottling plants, and the consumers who bought it often kept it in home iceboxes until use.

The weak link here was the farm, where the milk emerged from cows (normal body temperature about 100°F) into the ambient temperature of the barn. When dairying was more of a home enterprise, many households had had springhouses for keeping things cold, but now farmers had little choice but to put the results of morning and evening milking into cans and head for the milk train. Depending on the season and the length of the journey from farm to plant, any resident bacteria might or might not have had opportunity to multiply. Thus despite many gains in understanding, milk-borne diseases were still enough of a reality at the end of the nineteenth century to spur a long, ultimately successful milk-pasteurization campaign whose most famous exponent was the New York department-store magnate Nathan Straus.

The pasteurization process that became most common after about 1900 involved running the milk into a vat, heating it beyond the tolerance of nearly any microorganism, and maintaining a certain temperature for some period of time to kill bacteria as uniformly as possible. There were competing ideas about the ideal conditions, but eventually most dairy plants opted for a temperature of about 145°F and a heating period of thirty minutes, followed by prompt chilling. Between 1900 and 1920 pasteurization, usually by this formula, became mandatory in most parts of the country.

But that wasn't the end of the pasteurization story. In the 1930s many plants began switching to another method involving not separate batches but a continuous pipe feed of milk—"high-temperature/short-time," or HTST, pasteurization. This requires a pasteurizing temperature of 161°F maintained for fifteen *seconds* (not minutes) and nearly instantaneous cooling to 40°F. Since about 1970, the even more drastic continuous-feed "ultrahigh-temperature" pasteurization—UHT or "ultrapasteurization" for short—at or above 280°F for about two seconds has been gaining ground.

Early pasteurization initiatives went along with calls for much stricter governmental supervision of sanitary conditions at dairy farms. Whatever the public-health benefits, these pushes toward modernization drove small and marginal farmers out of business if they could not afford the necessary capital investments. Meanwhile, a certain medical faction continued to oppose pasteurization as an unwarranted interference with the natural qualities of milk. For several decades the "certified milk" adherents not only kept commercial raw milk before the public (at premium prices) but energetically publicized the quite valid view that superstrict hygienic supervision and testing at critical points could reliably prevent milk-borne infections without recourse to pasteurization. Certified milk production was, if anything, a harder option for farmers, since the certifying "medical milk commissions" held them to stricter standards (especially regarding bacterial counts) than the local authorities enforcing requirements for pasteurized milk.

The one factor that both sides insisted on was a low-enough temperature to keep the milk fresh—i.e., unsoured, with the original lactose intact. By the turn of the twentieth century, the scientific means existed to distinguish "putrefaction" from benign bacterial fermentations, but advanced Western food preferences now had little room for plain sour milk. In the early days of 145°F pasteurization, Southerners, many Ashkenazic Jews, and ex-rural types nostalgic for the sour milk of their youth still could still "clabber" pasteurized milk at home by leaving it out at room temperature. More up-to-date people clapped it straight into the icebox or refrigerator. This latter practice tipped the population of invading bacteria toward the kinds called psychrophilic, or psychrotrophic, meaning "cold-preferring." Such organisms feed not on lactose but on milkfat and milk proteins. When they go to work the result is inedibly bitter, truly putrid milk. The HTST and UHT pasteurization methods that eventually carried the day posed further bars to natural souring, because the very rapid, thorough heating and cooling of the milk virtually eliminated lactic-acid bacteria along with other microbes.

Though the pasteurization and certification campaigns were a tremendous public-health success in many ways, they played a distorting role in others. In their single-minded focus on one goal, they helped to relegate naturally fermented fresh dairy products to some lesser realm and wipe out home cooks' already fading knowledge of how to work with milk for multiple purposes. They capped and legitimized both the equation of pure, first-class milk with nonsoured milk for drinking and the idea that such milk is not just one food among many but a fundamental necessity for human survival. By the time Western medical opinion belatedly noticed the phenomenon of lactose intolerance in the late 1960s, American consumers and most of their nutritional advisors were too automatically conditioned to a milk-in-every-fridge mentality to grasp two clear implications: first, that anyone can happily live without using milk in any form; and second, that drinking large amounts of unsoured milk is foreign to the habits of most dairying peoples throughout the world.

Neither of these thoughts seems to have seriously affected public-health education. By and large, unsoured milk for drinking continues to be treated as a core food or defining element of the American diet in a way that soured milk is not—and this despite the fact that it has been losing any resemblance to real fresh milk for the better part of a century. The ins and outs of the story are tortuous, but the basic reason for the debasement of quality couldn't be simpler. From early milk-train days on, milk for drinking commanded higher prices than milk meant to be changed into other forms, an irresistible stimulus toward expansion at whatever cost to quality.

As the volume of milk produced by the nation's farms grew in the twentieth century, the entire system became riddled with struggles for competitive advantage. Investment in advanced devices that reduce labor costs per unit of milk has become ever more essential to farmers' survival. Obvious instances are electric milking machines and refrigerated bulk tanks, widely adopted after the rural electrification initiatives of the 1930s and mandatory almost everywhere by about 1950. Another expensive machine that people are likely to know less about is the cow herself, as reinvented for our time.

COW AND SUPERCOW

There came up on the drive immediately before the front door, under the custody of a boy, a cow. It was an Alderney cow, and any man or woman at all understanding cows would at once have perceived that this cow was perfect in her kind. Her eyes were mild, and soft, and bright. Her legs were like the legs of a deer; and in her whole gait and demeanour she almost gave the lie to her own name, asserting herself to have sprung from some more noble origin among the woods, than may be supposed to be the origin of the ordinary domestic cow,—a useful animal, but heavy in its appearance, and seen with more pleasure at some little distance than at close quarters. But this cow was graceful in its movements, and almost tempted one to regard her as the far-off descendant of the elk or the antelope.

ANTHONY TROLLOPE
The Belton Estate (1866)

ALDERNEY COW, 1834

Bessy, Will Belton's gift to Clara Amedroz early in the star-crossed courtship at the heart of Trollope's novel, is the nonpareil of what used to be meant by a "dairy cow." Few of her counterparts today evoke thoughts of deer and antelopes. For many dairy farmers, the ideal modern cow is more like a ruminant SUV. You could call her an expanded and consolidated version of a cow, just as today's dairy farms are expanded and consolidated versions of farms. A case in point: While the number of dairy cows in this country shrank from about 18 million to 9 million between 1960 and 2005, the total amount of milk they produce increased from 120 billion to 177 billion pounds during the same period.

In 1856 the English writer George Dodd's magnificent survey *The Food of London* reported that one especially fine cow had given 28 quarts (7 gallons, or about 56 pounds) of milk a day for six weeks. In 1975 an Indiana cow named Beecher Arlinda Ellen set the dairy world on fire by pumping out a record-eclipsing average of 152.5 pounds (more than 76 quarts, or 19 gallons) a day during a year's lactation, for a total yield of 55,661 pounds, compared to a national 1975 dairy-cow average of about 10,000 pounds. Ellen's feat has since been surpassed several times, and the current 365-day lactation record is the 67,914 pounds yielded by a Wisconsin contender, Muranda Oscar Lucinda-ET, in 1997. By 2005 the national average was almost 20,000 pounds a year per cow.

The road to such "improvements"—if that's the right word—has paralleled the growth of the fluid-milk industry since about the early nineteenth century. Scientific breeders then began distinguishing the best milkers by body type and working with local breeds to accentuate their advantages.

Trollope's Bessy represents one extreme of the "dairy type." From his description it's plain that she was of what we would now call Jersey stock. Doe-eyed and curiously reminiscent of shy, tawny woodland creatures, Jersey cows are the smallest and most enchantingly pretty of the major modern dairy breeds. At the time of Will Belton's wooing, they and the slightly bigger, less deerlike Guernseys were usually lumped together as "Alderneys." Bessy probably weighed only between six hundred and seven hundred pounds; in this country the Jersey was gradually developed into a somewhat larger and coarser animal, so that a latter-day American relative might be between nine hundred and one thousand pounds.

Beecher Arlinda Ellen, a black and white behemoth who at maturity weighed 1,750 pounds, cannot ever have reminded anyone of an antelope. She and Bessy were poles apart on any scale of dairy-cow values. But both exemplify a talent that breeders have been exploiting and amplifying for the last two centuries: the gift of converting more of what they eat and drink into milk than other cows. At one glance cows of advanced dairy type, whether tiny or enormous, are easy to tell from beefy counterparts who put more food energy into gaining weight than lactating. They are not exactly gaunt, but their pelvic bones jut starkly from hollow, angular flanks and their ribs are either plainly or almost visible under a very thin layer of flesh. Their entire system is concentrated on making milk, not infrequently to the point of endangering life and limb.

But what are we calling milk? The Bessies of the dairy world direct a phenomenal amount of caloric energy from their food into manufacturing a rich, concentrated source of nutrients, chiefly milk proteins and milkfat but also important amounts of lactose and minerals. The Ellens also channel just about everything they ingest into milk—extraordinary volumes of milk so diluted that it can almost be said to have been watered inside the cow. (The average milkfat percentage from Ellen's famous 1975 lactation—2.9—was far below the mingy federal minimum standard of 3.25 per-

cent for whole milk.) Genetic propensities to give richer milk and *more* milk tend not to go together. It's possible to manage both, but not easy. The first is economically advantageous if the milk is intended for purposes like butter- or cheesemaking. The second became the be-all and end-all for many or most dairy farmers when golden opportunities opened up in the fluid-milk market.

Early nineteenth-century English breeders tackling the quantity-quality equation produced the progenitors of four major breeds that later were adopted and revamped by American dairymen: the Channel Islands cattle (Jerseys and Guernseys), the somewhat larger, lyre-horned red and white Ayrshires, and a branch of the beefy Durham, or Shorthorn, race specially engineered for milk. Later in the century American breeders began experiment-

A "COW OF THE FIRST CLASS,"
CIRCA 1860

ing with a strapping, strong-framed Alpine cow that would become the American Brown Swiss. They also became interested in a large black and white (sometimes red and white) kind from the northern Netherlands that was first called "Dutch" or "Friesian." In most countries its descendants still have the name "Friesian," but American breeders unaccountably preferred "Holstein-Friesian" or just "Holstein."

Literally dozens of other breeds have their adherents on the American dairy scene, but the ones we hear about most in popular reporting are Jerseys and Holstein-Friesians. Cows like Ellen—you probably don't need to be told that she was a Holstein-Friesian—are what food writers generally associate with the latter. It's a wrong stereotype, for there are many Holstein-Friesian dairy herds managed at least as much for quality as quantity of milk. To farmers who grew up understanding flavor, quality means rich percentages of both milkfat and "SNF," or "solids nonfat," which includes everything else except water. Nonetheless, the real reason that Holstein-Friesians now make up more than 90 percent of today's U.S. dairy-cow population has to be volume, both in its own right and in relation to milk-production costs per cow. The average yield per year of Jersey cows is now about 16,000 pounds of milk, compared to 21,500 pounds for Holstein-Friesians.

The picture really isn't all that simple. Because many breeds can have particular virtues, dairy herds with "grade" stock (purebred or close to it, but not officially registered), mixed stock, or deliberate crosses of several breeds are more common than ones made up of single-breed registered stock. Many a "grade" Holstein-Friesian herd owes its fine milkfat and SNF records to a strategic admixture of Jersey genes. But higher and higher volume per cow certainly is a universal (though not exclusive) goal.

Merely breeding dairy cows generation after generation for skinny contours and brimming milk pails would not have brought daily record yields from the neighborhood of 56 pounds (28 quarts) to 152.5 pounds (76 quarts, for Ellen) or roughly 186 pounds (93 quarts, for Lucinda) between the mid-nineteenth and late twentieth century. The early "scientific" breeders worked before it was possible to apply Mendelian genetics to the cows or chemical analysis to the milk. Not until these tools were mastered and coupled with artificial insemination (starting in 1938) and advanced record-keeping techniques did breeding for actual genotype heat up. There seemed almost no limit to yields once farmers could identify heritable milking qualities in the daughters of a particular sire who could then impregnate hundreds or thousands of other cows. But breeding by itself was only half the story behind today's super-high-producing cows. The other half was feeding, which has been revolutionized as drastically as applied cattle genetics by modern information technology.

BREED, FEED, AND EXCEED

The unimproved cows of yesteryear suckled their calves while eating what cows were made to digest: grass. Like human mothers, some produced more milk and some less. The higher producers might eat more to compensate for the greater amounts of energy and nutrients being channeled into their milk, but the energy-balance system was largely stable and self-regulating. Genetic selection for abnormally high yields complicated the picture. It meant that the "best" cows were always in a sort of metabolic race to outrun "negative energy balance," with capacity for intake being pitted against capacity for output.

Calves left to their own devices start experimentally nibbling grass within days of birth and are at least partly weaned in a few months. Suckling a calf places lesser demands on the mother's body than being completely milked out in a milking parlor twice (or even three times) a day for a year or more at a time. A little arithmetic shows that the 1,750-pound Ellen was directing close to 8.75 percent of her own weight a day into that 152.5-pound milk output. Few cows can eat and drink fast enough to keep up with such losses.

Now, a ruminant's stomach does not resemble a human stomach. It is a series of chambers that postpone the business of digesting food by gastric juices in the fourth stomach, or *abomasum*, until the cellulose of grasses has first been partly broken down by trillions of microbes in the gigantic fermenting-tank system formed by the *rumen* and *reticulum* (the first two stomachs) and ground fine by the many-leaved walls of the *omasum* (third stomach). Even the role of the mouth is different, for what the animal eats gets two chewings, one perfunctory, the other a more thorough "rumination" of a bolus of cud regurgitated from the rumen. Ruminants live in delicate symbiosis with their bacterial and protozoal guests, a multispecies population swimming in a reticulo-ruminal soup replenished by gallons of saliva per hour. As well as breaking down fiber, the microbes begin the work of elaborating the particular proteins and fatty acids that the host animal needs.

For millennia after cattle were domesticated, different sorts of grass (or hay) continued to be virtually their whole diet. The resident ruminal bacteria need it to maintain a stable balance of different microbial organisms. Altering the diet kills off some species while encouraging others, until the entire chemistry of the rumen may be thrown out of whack. This does the cow no good but, depending on what you're feeding her, may make her give more milk. For generations it has been known that you can stimulate dairy cows to higher yields by keeping them on low-fiber, "high-energy" rations with large amounts of "concentrate" (mostly meaning grains, especially corn). Concentrate translates into more net caloric energy per pound than fiber, which siphons off more energy into the work of digestion. But at high levels it also changes the only slightly acid environment of a normal rumen to a lower pH. The unhappy animal often loses her appetite. She is constantly thirsty and tries to right matters by drinking more water, which means more (if thinner) milk and explains why one can speak of milk watered inside the cow. She may develop full-blown ruminal acidosis.

Here we arrive at one of several déjà-vu-all-over-again moments in recent dairying history: Cows may no longer be munching distillery wastes in hideous city sheds, but it still is in at least some people's interest to feed them substances injurious to their health. In acute and even subacute acidosis, the walls of the rumen become ulcerated, releasing infectious bacteria that often travel to the liver, where they cause abscesses, or generating by-products that migrate to the interior of the hooves, where they cause a painful foot inflammation called laminitis. (This condition probably was the reason that the "downer cows" surreptitiously filmed by the Humane Society at a California slaughtering plant early in 2008 had to be goaded onto their feet by electric shock.) In addition, lowered ruminal pH is ideal for encouraging the growth of *Escherichia coli* bacteria that can survive through the entire digestive tract (ending up in manure and fertilizer made from it) and often include the virulent 0157:H7 strain.

The elite, high-producing stars of dairy herds are the cows who suffer most drastically on large amounts of concentrate. Already pushed by genetic makeup to the threshold of negative energy balance, they are easily nudged over the edge by any loss of appetite. But the breeding-and-feeding stresses on high-producing cows don't end there. Since the mid-1990s farmers have made them even higher-producing through injections of the hormone bovine somatotropin (BST), also called "bovine growth hormone" (BGH). Or more precisely, the Monsanto Corporation's laboratory-engineered "recombinant" version of the cow original, known as rBST or rBGH. Much controversy rages around rBST—and we now reach another *plus-ça-change* moment. Adulteration scandals, it seems, didn't end with the practice of dyeing the milk. An angry faction has denounced rBST as a harmful foreign substance. Monsanto reasonably enough points out that it is indistinguishable from the BST made by cows and naturally found in milk. Its detractors, also reasonably, want to know whether consuming it can increase human blood levels of a potential carcinogen that occurs at higher concentrations in treated cows' milk, "insulin-like growth factor-1" (IGF-1).

No clear medical consensus has emerged on these issues. On the other hand, it's obvious that whatever increases milk production in already high-yielding cows also increases the physical stress on organisms that are stressed to begin with. Not only is rBST a serious additional risk factor for mastitis (infection of the udder), to which today's stressed-out cows are highly prone, but it tends to shorten the animals' life expectancy—which in any case has been on a downward slope over the last half century. In 1950, farmers might have kept many or most cows milking for a dozen years after their first lactation at (usually) about age two. In 2007 a production span of three years before "culling" to be sold for cheap beef wasn't uncommon. Forget the fact that in the Dark Ages of dairying a well-treated cow might often have lived out something close to the twenty-year potential of the species; enlightened modern management ensures that during their short term on this planet many of today's cows will have to be repeatedly dosed with antibiotics to pull them through their latest bout of mastitis or laminitis. Antibiotics are banned from milk sold for any food purpose whatever, and the milk from cows under antibiotic treatment is supposed to be dumped. Nonetheless, contamination is regularly caught in inspections of farm-to-plant milk shipments, and whether it is sometimes *not* caught is anybody's guess.

The pressures on cows mirror those on farmers—a word I use for want of a better one, though their job is really more like applied industrial engineering under the most unforgiving conditions. Farming to supply the fluid-milk market is an incredibly competitive business with painfully slender profit margins that make shaving a few cents from production costs for a thousand pounds of milk a matter of survival or collapse for large operations. And all operations are inexorably becoming larger. In the late 1940s sixty-cow farms looked as modestly middle-sized as three-hundred-cow farms do today. Only at the level of two thousand cows do dairyists start to talk about *big.* There are operations with eight or nine times more. The San Joaquin Valley in California has dairy farms so huge that the methane gas given off by ruminal bacteria and belched by the animals as they chew the cud is now regarded by air-quality experts as a major local pollutant.

Many small dairy farms stand, or stood before they disappeared, in the path of real-estate juggernauts in the ever-expanding orbit of cities. Those that survive often do so by leaving the fluid-milk market for arrangements with local makers of other dairy products; ripened or aged cheeses are an increasingly lucrative destination for milk with good fat and protein content.

Meanwhile more and more of the fluid-milk supply comes from huge farm operations completely dependent on high-producing cows bred, fed, and injected to be still higher-producing. On many farms, the animals never see a blade of grass—not because farmers are unnatural villains but because pasture management for hundreds of ground-trampling twelve-hundred- to eighteen-hundred-pound Holstein-Friesians is a time-consuming luxury. Besides, grazing in an actual pasture distractingly complicates the job of evaluating any one cow's performance in a several-thousand-cow herd.

The crucial task of tracking performance is now done by computer on most dairy farms. A cow may have a name, but she also has a number recorded on an ear tag, possibly one with a computer chip. She enters the herd along with crucial milking statistics from her dam's and sire's lineages. Everything she eats and drinks is measured against her milk-output data (weight as well as fat, SNF, and water content), which go into the computer from the milking machine. Her food ration is a customized recipe based on readouts of her milking record. It typically includes chopped hay, cornstalk or other silage, corn or cornmeal, ground soybeans or cottonseed, and beet pulp or molasses, not to mention chemical buffers like sodium bicarbonate, dicalcium phosphate, or powdered lime to lessen the risk of acidosis. The milking data dictate adjustments in the exact proportions of different nutrients.

This isn't at all a matter of robotic programming replacing thoughtful human care, because every dairy farmer has his or her own priorities. Computer-monitored rations can be a tool for wringing the last drop of watery milk out of creatures on the edge of metabolic collapse, or a way of balancing quantity and quality while maintaining the animals in good health. But it's fair to say that any cow who performs poorly enough to bring down the herd average for desired characteristics will rapidly be culled.

If a cow proves really remarkable in an outstanding herd, she may well be chosen for supermotherhood via ET, meaning "embryo transfer" or "transplant" (hence the initials at the end of Muranda Oscar Lucinda's name). She must first be induced to "superovulate"—release multiple ova instead of the normal single ovum—through a series of hormone injections, then inseminated with semen from a bull of proven excellence as a dairy sire. After some days her uterus is washed out with a saline solution that is microscopically scanned for fertilized eggs (too small to see with the naked eye). Meanwhile, several destined surrogate mothers have been brought synchronously into heat through rBST injections and are ready to be impregnated with the new embryos. The donor cow can thus become the mother of perhaps six or more calves almost simultaneously—all daughters, if the bull's semen has been sexed to choose only sperm with X chromosomes. And the process can be repeated at intervals.

The steam that drives current breeding-and-feeding technology along with the rest of the production engine is, of course, the bizarre exaltation of milk drinking over other forms of milk consumption since the nineteenth century. It can't be too often repeated that pushing fluid milk into this extraordinary role has not made it more worth drinking (by those who can digest it) for the sake of flavor.

Dairy farmers are not to blame for the punishing realities of modern commercial milk production. Not only do they supply a food that everybody else takes for granted without understanding the first thing about it, but they were hit hard in the late twentieth century as the Nature's Perfect Food myth began to be challenged by authorities on coronary artery disease and heart attacks. When the diet-and-health battle heated up, the nation's milk processors had some useful strings to their bow. Unfortunately these would provide no magic answers for farmers.

BRAVE NEW MILK

The cholesterol wars arrived several generations after three strategic developments that didn't do much for the cause of good plain milk but would enable the industry to reinvent itself under fire. In the end, these bits of technical progress would give dairy processors the tools for taking Nature's Perfect Food apart and—the really decisive factor—putting it back together with selling points that nature hadn't thought of.

The first breakthrough, in the 1880s, was the mechanical separation of cream by centrifuge, far more thorough than any hand skimming. The next came in 1890, when a University of Wisconsin dairy chemist invented the eponymous Babcock test for measuring the precise fat content of milk—at the time, the chief indicator of quality. These two advances led to intense growth in the butter industry, which became the most lucrative destination for milk. Old-style farmstead buttermaking declined, while dairying regions became dotted with small factories called creameries that bought up shipments of high-Babcock-score milk and produced butter from cream so efficiently centrifuged that, like the cream my parents remembered buying in tiny Creamery, Pennsylvania, it had to be spooned rather than poured.

The third crucial achievement was homogenization, or the technique of crushing milkfat globules into droplets too small to rise to the surface in a cream layer. Homogenization had to overcome several obstacles before it could be coupled with the first two advances. It disrupted the chemical structure of the milkfat so drastically as to release a torrent of enzymes that promptly turned raw milk rancid. Even when dairy chemists learned to sidestep rancidity by combining the steps of pasteurizing (which inactivated the enzymes) and homogenizing, there remained the age-old consumer habit of judging milk by its richness—i.e., the thickness of the cream layer on top. When packaging in glass bottles came in toward the start of the twentieth century, one of its advantages from a buyer's point of view was the plainly visible "creamline." The fact that homogenized milk in glass tended to acquire an unpleasant oxidized flavor on exposure to light more rapidly than creamline milk was another strike against it.

As a result, until shortly after World War II few people saw any reason to want homogenized milk. Milk for drinking was almost without exception available in only two degrees of richness: with or without all the original fat. Skim milk, or what was left when the cream was separated for other purposes, was the ugly sister. Health experts warned mothers that it was paltry stuff, deficient in crucial nutrients. (Most states required that it be fortified with vitamin A to replace the fat-soluble beta-carotene that disappeared along with the cream; this step is still mandatory for fat-free and most reduced-fat milk.) At the nation's creameries skim milk was an unvalued by-product, often dumped for lack of any profitable use.

As early as the late 1930s a few dairy processors had been trying to win people over to homogenized milk. The turning point came with a postwar shift to opaque paper or cardboard containers in place of returnable milk bottles. This in turn accompanied another shift away from home delivery and toward supermarket purchases of milk. Consumers and supermarket managers adored the convenience of throwaway packaging, Milk processors and distributors loved the fact that cardboard couldn't be seen through, which incidentally solved the oxidation problem. It was the perfect moment for abolishing creamline milk and substituting a product whose appearance had previously weighed against it.

From an industry perspective, homogenization meant not simply homogenizing milk as it came from Bessy, Ellen, or Lucinda but being able to play with it. A commercial dairy could now calculate the amount of fat in incoming milk, completely remove it, and homogenize it back into the milk *in any desired proportion*, while putting any surplus to other purposes such as butter or ice cream. In effect, "whole milk" could now be whatever the industry said it was.

Publicity campaigns successfully persuaded housewives that homogenized milk was both handier and—a particularly Orwellian stroke—creamier-tasting than messy old-fashioned milk with the cream on top. The fact that few milk drinkers now had ever met a cow was a great help. Very soon even the few diehards who preferred milk in glass had forgotten about creamlines, and today curiosity seekers tasting unhomogenized milk for the first time often find the appearance and "mouthfeel" vaguely unnatural. The dairy-processing industry was free to set the standard milkfat content for supposedly "whole" milk at 3.25 percent by weight—the minimum specified by the Food and Drug Administration in the Code of Federal Regulations, though some states mandate a slightly higher percentage.

In 1929 a survey of the composition of milk produced by major dairy-cow breeds showed milkfat ranges from 2.9 to 8.4 percent; though a similar listing today would show some ironing-out of extremes, a real average for American dairy herds probably would be around 4 percent, with the best herds easily achieving 5 or 5.5 percent. Yet after more than half a century of almost universal homogenization, it would be fiscal insanity for most processors to sell anything mirroring the composition of real whole milk. Indeed, consumers have trouble grasping that the usual homogenized product is *not* whole, in the sense of being entire or intact.

FROM MILK GLUTS TO NICHE MARKETING

This tale of pseudo-progress must be seen against a backdrop of permanent crises in milk allocation. As dairy farming became more capital-intensive and productivity per cow increased, chronic supply-and-demand mismatches arose that led to price regulation during the New Deal era. I will not attempt to describe the labyrinthine USDA milk price–support system, which baffles my comprehension and probably hasn't been understood by the last five secretaries of agriculture. Suffice it to say that for about seventy years the prices paid to dairy farmers have been calculated by formulas based on both geographical location and intended use, meant to ensure a steady supply of drinkable fresh milk from rural dairying regions to population centers. "Class I" fluid milk for drinking occupies a privileged rank and ordinarily commands the highest prices, while most of the milk destined for other uses (for instance, in butter, cheese, powdered milk, and various manufactured foods) is placed in a confusing array of generally less lucrative pigeonholes. It probably will surprise no one to learn that, regulatory machinery or no, the country is periodically flooded with regional or nationwide surpluses of fresh fluid milk, while many (perhaps most) dairy farmers barely break even.

Special-interest gimmickry promised an out. Dairy processors had investigated it to an extent after World War I, the success story of chocolate milk being one 1920s example. But their efforts were mere dabbling until the miracle of "standardization" by homogenizing came along. And even that might not have had the spectacular results it did if not for a swift reversal of nutritional orthodoxy about the benefits of whole versus skim milk during the late-twentieth-century cardiac donnybrooks summarized further on (page 50). Suddenly milkfat was not proof of quality, but one of nature's blunders in designing an otherwise virtuous food. From the '60s or '70s on, hasty public-health re-education campaigns sought to convert consumers to "the less, the better" attitudes regarding fat percentages in milk, with zero being the new ideal.

Zero was easily attainable through centrifuging, but centrifuged skim milk lacked the flavor-saving smidgin of cream that remained in the milk after hand skimming. Some people uncomplainingly adopted zero-fat milk; many more balked. The milk-processing industry eventually arrived at a spectrum of products starting with 0 percent milkfat milk and progressing through various homogenized gradations of fat content: 0.5 percent (officially "low-fat"), 1 percent, 1.5 percent, and 2 percent (these last three "reduced-fat"). Not all are equally available everywhere, but in most states you will find at least three or four of them. All quickly acquired fan clubs that are now an entrenched part of American culture. For a long time the hardest sell remained skim milk, and for good reason: The usual commercial versions are a singularly thin, vapid travesty of decent hand-skimmed milk. But eventually processors hit on the stratagem of using dried skim milk solids to add body and selling the result under names like "Skim Milk Plus." (Despite any promotional malarkey on the label, the real difference between this and plain skim milk is not extra "creaminess" or "richness" but more lactose and casein.)

Other possibilities opened up with news of the lactose-tolerance issue, which began reaching consumers in the 1970s and seriously sank in about a decade later. Instead of acknowledging that people do not in the least need to drink fresh milk, dairy chemists eagerly began working to produce something that would approximate fresh milk without the usual lactose content. In all fairness, this head-in-the-sand approach must be attributed less to industry guile than to cultural biases so deep that even intelligent public-health advocates don't recognize them as biases.

Making lactose-free milk turned out to be far more difficult than making fat-free milk. Lactic-acid bacteria do it all the time—but no one wanted the souring and thickening that are part of their wizardry. Instead, the human wizards had to directly expose milk to the lactase enzyme. Unfortunately for flavor, the result was a release of very sweet free glucose into the milk when the original lactose—one of the *least* sweet sugars in nature—was enzymatically chopped into galactose and glucose. More recently, advanced techniques have been developed to physically extract the lactose from the milk instead of splitting it into component sugars. No technique so far makes lactose-free or lactose-reduced milk taste particularly like plain unmodified milk. Taste, however, doesn't seem to be the point.

Regardless of the new products' deficiencies, they have brought us still more value-added categories of fluid milk. Along with the aforementioned kinds of fat-free or reduced-fat milk, supermarket dairy cases now display lactose-free or reduced-lactose "whole" (i.e., homogenized 3.25 percent), skim, 1 percent, and 2 percent milk. If your head isn't already spinning from this surfeit of choices, some retail sources also tout calcium-fortified milk— either "whole" or reduced-fat, full-lactose or reduced-lactose. Why add calcium to a food that already happens to be a rich source of calcium? Well, call it the Nothing Succeeds like Excess theory of nutrition. Despite the fact that neither osteoporosis nor childhood skeletal maldevelopment is more prevalent among well-nourished people in societies where no one consumes milk than in the United States, it would take a lot to displace the "no milk, no strong bones" syllogism from popular nutrition education. You can even buy milk fortified with fiber, undoubtedly in response to some perception of a market.

Among the final absurdities in this sequence of nutritional bad jokes is the rehabilitation of "filled" and imitation milks, once synonymous with cheap impostures. In the era when creameries were awash in unwanted skim milk, various quick-buck artists conceived the idea of buying it up for a song and emulsifying ("filling") it with some kind of vegetable oil, perhaps partially hydrogenated to mimic the "mouthfeel" of the milkfat in whole milk. Dairymen's associations and health experts—who in those days usually furthered each other's agendas—denounced the budget-price results as unwholesome shams. They were still louder in condemning the nutritional deficiencies of "imitation milks" compounded from vegetable oil, sugar, corn-syrup solids, some protein source, and emulsifiers.

Who could have foreseen that one day we would see these old ringers peddled in new guises as more healthful than what now passes for plain milk? The American Heart Association serenely certifies a product called SunMilk, made by emulsifing skim milk with sunflower oil. Soy-based imitation milks are rapidly encroaching on real fluid-milk sales. Quite unrelated to the plain fresh soy milk sold in small Chinatown groceries, they are created from improbable farragoes of ingredients with heavy doses of sugar and added flavorings to counteract an underlying "beany" pong. Today's dairy aisles are crammed with filled milk and soy milk in such flavors as strawberry, chocolate, green tea, and mango, proudly billed as "lactose-free," "casein-free," "cholesterol-free," and "heart-healthy." Dairy farmers may regard the trend with dismay—but not the world's largest conglomerate of milk processors, Dean Foods, which has hedged its bets by acquiring the Silk and Sun Soy brands of soy milk.

Can this spectacle get any crazier? It can and will. Dairying experts everywhere are trying to see whether adding substances like fish oil to dairy cows' rations will result in milk with more unsaturated fatty acids. It has been difficult to administer feed supplements that won't either impart off flavors to the milk or end up being turned into saturated fatty acids after all by the ruminal bacteria. But at least one success story is now on retail shelves in Ontario: Dairy Oh!, developed by members of the University of Guelph's renowned dairy science department. Similar products will eventually jostle for U.S. shoppers' attention with the already dizzying roster of value-added twists on milk that we now take for granted.

THE FAT FACTOR AND THE FEAR FACTOR

We all know the reason behind the bastardized products flooding the market: the reputation as a killer that milk acquired during successive debates on heart disease in the last half of the twentieth century. Today a great deal of the diet-and-cardiac-mortality gospel as originally promulgated has had to be profoundly revised or, in some cases, thrown out. But for some reason the milk parts of the creed have never come in for serious re-examination.

Many facts of the case are undisputed. In the first place milkfat as found in all full-fat dairy products is very rich in saturated fatty acids. (For the nuts and bolts of the saturation concept, see the description of butter, page 234.) Beginning as unsaturated precursors in the fresh grasses or hay eaten by the cow, these acquire their saturated form in the great chemist's workshop of the rumen with its population of fermenting bacteria. The same is true of other ruminants like goats, sheep, and water buffaloes. All produce milkfat with more saturated fatty acids than any vegetable-derived fats except coconut oil, palm oil, and palm-kernel oil.

The picture is clear from a few simple comparisons. A 100-gram portion of most commercially available vegetable oils contains about 10 to 18 grams of saturated fatty acids and 82 to 90 grams total unsaturated fatty acids, with widely varying proportions of monounsaturated to polyunsaturated fatty acids. The figures for olive oil are about 14 grams saturated fatty acids, 77 grams monounsaturated fatty acids, and 9 grams polyunsaturated fatty acids. But 100 grams of cows'-milk butter that has had the water mechanically removed would—allowing for large variations in composition among different animals—probably average out at roughly 62 grams saturated fatty acids, 29 grams monounsaturated fatty acids, and 4 grams polyunsaturated fatty acids together with a few grams of other milk-derived substances.

Undisputed though all these figures are, the interpretations different people have placed on them are anything but. We can start with the campaign to point out saturated fatty acids—and foods like milk that contain a great deal of them—as artery-clogging menaces. This movement was led during the '50s and '60s by the energetic, influential Ancel Keys, whose country-by-country comparative studies of diet data and mortality statistics provided the initial evidence for a sustained public-health war on saturated fats and cholesterol.

Several aspects of this battle, however, remained strangely underreported for many decades. One is that Keys's attempts to link national dietary habits and coronary heart disease ignored many populations in which high consumption of saturated fats wasn't accompanied by high rates of atherosclerosis. (The most obvious examples are parts of Asia, Africa, and the Near East with heavily milk-dependent diets, and various tropical regions where palm or coconut oil historically was the cooking fat of choice.) Another is that his contentions about the genesis of arterial plaque have proved surprisingly hard to verify in detail as he first proposed them. And from the start, many equally qualified frontline researchers came to conclusions different from those of Keys.

As time went on, both interpretive disagreements and official course corrections began to strain the public patience, until a certain popular backlash erupted late in the 1990s. The first hints of trouble to come appeared when Ancel Keys and his allies in the public-health sector realized that they had oversimplified the saturated/unsaturated–fat dichotomy by telling people that "more unsaturated" automatically equaled "more life-saving." To their surprise, monounsaturates turned out to afford more cardiac benefits than the polyunsaturates in which they had initially placed their trust. Links between dietary cholesterol and the levels that show up in the bloodstream as builders of arterial plaque also failed to meet early expectations. Some years later researchers realized that blood-serum cholesterol was not one uniform substance but an amalgamation of different fractions with different effects; moreover, its path from dinner table to artery wall didn't match the beautiful simplicity of the first formulations. A yet more jarring discovery was that the labels "saturated," "monounsaturated," and "polyunsaturated" were inadequate to indicate different fatty acids' roles in triggering or protecting against atherosclerosis. Certain saturated fatty acids in milk and meat didn't seem to raise blood cholesterol levels. Certain monounsaturates appeared to be desirable, others quite the opposite. As for polyunsaturates, they turned out to come in several molecular configurations that now are thought to play dramatically different roles in cell chemistry and plaque formation.

Epidemiologists surveying twentieth-century mortality figures further weakened the Keysian argument by failing to agree on whether there had ever been an "epidemic" of fatal heart disease, as opposed to statistical shifts during a period of increasing longevity and decreasing likelihood of dying from diseases of childhood or youth before cardiac conditions had had time to manifest themselves. Another embarrassment surfaced in the early 1990s, when the authorities had to do a highly public about-face on blanket recommendations of shortenings and margarines. Far from being beneficial, it developed, the partially hydrogenated vegetable oils responsible for these test-tube wonders contained possibly atherogenic trans fatty acids in hugely greater amounts than plain butter. The turn of the twenty-first century saw a far worse setback: The general lean-and-trim diet blueprint to which the antisaturated fat agenda belonged was thrown into disarray when a vocal wing of dietary specialists denounced low-calorie, low-fat alternatives to such traditional full-fat foods as milk, butter, and cream as factors in a rising national tide of obesity and diabetes.

By the mid-1990s some rebellious types were heretically celebrating a return to steak. A few years later red meat and eggs—early victims of nutritional McCarthyism—were getting a small, grudging rehabilitation from the self-constituted food police. Not so butter and full-fat milk, though they happen to have a striking piece of negative evidence on their side. As shown by USDA and census statistics, consumption of both whole milk and butter was steadily *declining* during the 1950s and '60s while the number of fatal heart attacks rose—along with decreasing use of animal fats overall and increasing use of vegetable oils. Yet to this day the American Heart Assciation—which readily accepts money from manufacturers in return for putting AHA approval stickers on products like Cocoa Puffs breakfast cereal and Smart Balance De Luxe Microwave Popcorn—still inveighs against milk with the milkfat that is simply part of the nature of milk. And the shakiest tenets of the Keysian party line continue to inspire tinhorn politicos like the school-district administrators who have succeeded in getting whole milk banned from public schools in both Los Angeles and New York City. Probably most people who think of themselves as nutrition-savvy would be astonished to learn that evidence of whole milk's being a ticket to an early grave is conspicuous by its absence.

How did a good and useful food come to be buried in such misunderstanding? For one answer we can look to well-meaning authorities on nutrition and disease who have spent fifty-plus years repeatedly issuing blanket dietary recommendations for the whole population without waiting to think through many ifs, ands, or buts that have had to be inserted piecemeal at erratic intervals. Their pronouncements, as rehashed by a corps of food and health journalists, have reached most of us as a series of disjointed bulletins compared to which the blind men's reports on the elephant were marvels of coherence.

Add an endless chorus of commercial persuasions to buy more and more (for obvious reasons, never less) of this or that value-added niche product targeted to real, imaginary, or highly misrepresented needs and deficiencies, and you have what I can only call a schizoid mentality. Consider the millions of people taught to fear and distrust a common food to the point of banishing it from their diet. Do they look elsewhere for ideas about eating that don't involve its use? On the contrary, they rush forth to spend extra bucks on crude artificial mimicries of the dreaded offender.

NOT ALL THINGS TO ALL PEOPLE

This sad ending might have looked like the only ending a decade or two back, but I see increasing evidence that it doesn't have to be.

Seventeen years ago I went to a "milk tasting" organized by the New York branch of a national gastronomic organization, meant to illuminate some of the factors affecting milk flavor, like what animals it comes from and what sort of processing it undergoes. The next week a *New Yorker* "Talk of the Town" reporter—unable to taste any particular difference among the six samples on display "except for the chocolate milk, which tasted like chocolate"—had a quiet snicker at the general foofaraw (especially the lunatic aspirations of any anti-pasturizers trying to turn a public health hazard into "*chic milk*," in scornful italics). Moral of story, as of 1991: Modern dairying had been working to treat an innately variable, highly perishable biological secretion like a bulk commodity long enough for wags to chortle over even a modest attempt to call this absurdity into question.

I doubt that an exercise designed to stimulate curiosity about milk from various animals, handled in different ways, would draw the same sort of putdown today. The idea that milk doesn't have to be a gastronomic neuter wished on the public under misguided dietary assumptions, but actually is capable of *tasting* like something, is not quite as foreign to people who eat and think about what they eat. What now seems to be happening, for at least some of us, is a more liberating perception of food in general as a source of both sustenance and pleasure.

Notwithstanding the Babel of sales pitches and ideologies charging us to view everything we put in our mouths as either a miracle cure or a death warrant, a gathering conflux of the independent-minded is recognizing the really great thing about today's food scene: It gives us the stuff of *several different kinds of enjoyable and nutritious diets* based on time-honored foodways of peoples everywhere in the world. It feeds and nourishes a mentality that seeks varied, flexible answers to the question of what to eat rather than competing Doctrines of the Faith about what *not* to eat. There are, for instance, different ways to be a vegetarian, inspired by eating patterns from parts of the Far East, Near East, Mediterranean basin, and India—routes paved with choices of pleasure, not deprivation, and blessedly free of products arm-wrestled into simulations of what they are not.

If this dietary liberation theology has any prime doctrine of its own, it's that starting with a "what to eat" firmly centered on a very wide spectrum of minimally processed fresh fruits, vegetables, and vegetable protein sources ought to free us from agonized struggles to ration out other foods—for example, milk—by miserly formulas from this or that ministry of fear. No food has to pretend to be all things to all people. Nothing has to suffer exaggerated reactions against false labels like "Nature's Perfect Food."

Or to put it another way: If we can shed the notion that chugging down so much milk a day is a duty, perhaps we will be free to discover different forms of it as a joy. People whose ancestors never consumed milk products may be able to make up their own minds about it without well-meant ethnocentric mistakes distorting the picture. Those with the right genes may taste the really, truly fresh milk and cream just starting to reach certain retail sources and for the first time realize what exquisite works of nature these are. And those whose understanding of milk products and milk-based cooking has revolved around a few narrow Western models may rejoice in the glorious culinary plenty and diversity now opening up to all of us.

In short: Everyone who honestly loves fresh dairy foods should tune out the noise of hucksterism and fearmongering, and recognize what milk can contribute to the pleasure of not all but very many sound and satisfying diets.

RAW VS. PASTEURIZED,
ORGANIC VS. CONVENTIONAL
A Minority Opinion

People who learn that I'm writing a book about dairy products often ask whether I think raw or pasteurized milk is better for children and adults, or how organic milk stacks up against conventionally produced versions. Unfortunately, I don't have any clear-cut answers.

Certainly the questions spring from sincere concerns about the potential of a basic foodstuff to nourish us or bring down disasters on our heads. But I find the usual course of public debate troubling. It is waged with great eagerness to discuss issues of food and health by slinging around as many claims and counterclaims as possible in the service of preformed agendas, and all too often without elementary caution, fair-mindedness, or patience to entertain any answer that falls between two stools. And in the case of milk, the loudest opinions often come from people who know very little. I can only offer my own opinions in the hope that they'll be of help to someone.

RAWNESS AND RATIONALITY

To be blunt: Every time I hear or read any discussion of raw milk in any public forum, I know I can look forward to endless repetitions of a few misleading, simpleminded claims on both sides, with either no attention to or no technical understanding of taste factors (which are *my* preformed agenda).

Most of those who want consumers to have unfettered access to raw milk insist that pasteurization destroys nutritional value. Sometimes they also assert that raw milk tastes better, period. Neither claim is unconditionally true. On the other side, adherents of pasteurization are bent on warning the public that without it we can expect the unhindered spread of milk-borne pathogens that used to kill people en masse but are eliminated in the pasteurizing process. This, too, is only partly true.

To start with flavor, though it's the last thing many of the polemicists think of: Certainly a glass of raw milk sampled at the farm is going to taste different from the supermarket milk in somebody's refrigerator. But pasteurization is only one of the industrial processing steps responsible for the difference. As explained earlier (see page 45), virtually all the pasteurized milk that reaches us has been centrifugally separated, recombined to standardized milkfat percentages, and homogenized. These steps do more to denature milk than anything else that happens to it in manufacturing. The creamier "mouthfeel" and fresher flavor of whole raw milk at a well-run Jersey cow dairy farm (and, by the way, plenty of Holstein-Friesian farms) reflect not just actual freshness but the fact that the basic milk structure is intact. You can get nearly all of the same effect from unhomogenized pasteurized milk—at least, if it comes to you very fresh and was pasteurized by the right method.

This brings us to the second great factor usually left out of the debate: There is pasteurization and pasteurization. As we've seen, at one time it was routinely done at a comparatively low temperature for a long time by pumping batches into and out of a vat. This method eliminated harmful bacteria with minimal impairment of flavor. The more cost-effective approaches that are almost universal today involve higher temperatures with near-instantaneous heating and cooling by continuous flow. They tend to impart a slightly more cooked flavor while denaturing some of the water-soluble milk proteins—but it's hard to attribute particular flavor effects to these techniques alone, because they are almost always carried out together with homogenization.

Then there is the intrinsic quality of the milk itself. Rawness and pasteurization have nothing to do with the plain fact that milk produced by farmers with sane breeding-and-feeding priorities tastes better than milk cranked out with an eye only to volume. Some of the best milk I've tasted has been raw, and so has some of the worst. I have awful memories of one watery, dismal brand that I naively tried several decades ago when New York State permitted retail sales of raw milk in health-food stores.

When we come to the question of health and safety, people on both sides usually seem to have their minds closed before they open their mouths. The most frequent argument I hear about the health-giving properties of raw milk is that the heat of pasteurization destroys the vitamin C and most enzymes present in raw milk. Quite true—but not of great importance to anyone's health. Compared with other plentiful sources of vitamin C (most fruits, some vegetables), milk contains very little in the first place; the loss through pasteurization isn't going to drastically affect our access to an adequate natural supply of this nutrient.

As for the large array of enzymes that disappear in heating, they are a highly species-specific aid to the digestive systems of newborn calves and don't need to greatly concern nonbovines—except cheesemakers, who are sorely handicapped when intricate sequences of enzymatic changes are interfered with through pasteurization. With due respect to people who swear that raw milk cleared up their children's ear infections or other problems, I have yet to see convincing proof that it automatically improves our general nutritional welfare.

But I am only marginally more sympathetic to the claims of the other side. The health authorities who have brought about blanket prohibitions on the sale of raw milk in most states seem to me to represent muddled governmental thinking at its officious worst. They are perfectly correct in pointing out that raw milk is a known vector for spreading such deadly diseases as tuberculosis and brucellosis. They are just as wrong in trying to impose the presumption that all raw milk is guilty of such evils until proven innocent. In fact, the means have existed for more than a century to ensure that it *is* innocent: very frequent, very scrupulous inspection of cows, milking facilities, and milk.

What spreads disease is not raw milk but raw milk contaminated by harmful bacteria—or in some cases, *pasteurized* milk contaminated by bacteria. Pasteurization is a great blessing that does indeed keep most fresh dairy products from spreading lethal infections. As practiced today, it also saves a lot of money for all parties. But it is a crude and imperfect solution to a problem that ought to admit of more than one solution.

Treat milk by continuous-feed pasteurization methods at high temperatures, and you will not (usually) cause mass outbreaks of disease by pooling the output of many thousands of cows on many dozens of farms at colossal processing facilities hundreds of miles from the point of production, then shipping it over equal or greater distances to many hundreds of retail stores where it may reach consumers close to a week after milking. Clearly, there are precautions that have to have the force of law if that's the only way anyone is to get milk—but why *should* it be? What's wrong with devising other precautions for milk to be sold without pasteurization?

The real answer is cost-effectiveness. Anyone can see that producing and distributing raw milk in the same way as HTST (high-temperature/short-time) or ultrapasteurized milk (see page 35) would be an invitation to disaster. Economies of scale are impossible here. The milk must be handled and stored in much smaller volumes, transported (if at all) over much shorter distances, and sold within a much shorter time than milk for mass distribution. And any given unit of HTST or ultrapasteurized milk is not only cheaper to produce for retail sale than the same amount of raw milk, but cheaper to *regulate*. It would be insane to allow the sale of raw milk without frequent official inspections of herds and facilities, ultravigilant testing of all cows, and a strict schedule of bacterial counts done on the milk—all of which adds up to longer man-hours and higher personnel budgets than the far laxer supervision of HTST and ultrapasteurized milk. No wonder that most state regulatory agencies faced with any suggestion about licensing raw-milk operations automatically switch to the "How Not to Do It" mode of Dickens's Circumlocution Office. If they had concrete motives for figuring out how to *do* the job, clean raw milk could be gotten (at a price) to the small number of consumers who want it.

Even under the strictest supervision, raw milk can't be guaranteed to be uniformly and absolutely free from pathogens. But neither can pasteurized milk. Any fair-minded person will recognize that pasteurization is a generally effective public-health measure that hugely reduces bacterial populations in milk. But occasional cases of recontamination after pasteurizing not only occur but seem to be on the increase, especially in certain kinds of cheeses made (for Latin American clienteles) by direct acidification instead of lactic-acid fermentation. The pathogen *Listeria monocytogenes* crops up oftener than any of the other usual suspects. The question of whether it can actually survive the pasteurization process has not yet been conclusively settled. Most authorities now think that it can't, and that episodes such as the 1983 outbreak of listeriosis in Massachusetts—traced to pasteurized milk from several different dairy herds, after forty-nine people had been sickened—represent recontamination that escaped monitoring.

I don't mean to soft-pedal the danger of pathogens in "natural" or "alternative" foods beloved of some counterculturalists—indeed, I'd seriously caution anyone against galloping off to the nearest dairy farm and trying to buy raw milk with no questions asked. But it's only just to point out that every year more and more cases also come to light of pathogens spread through mass-distribution channels—let's say, in hamburger—and undetected at the time by the usual public-health regulatory machinery. The difference is that nobody as far as I know is proposing to bring raw milk to the public through mass-distribution channels.

As a food writer, I believe it is irresponsible to recommend certain raw animal products—oysters or clams on the half-shell, fish in sashimi or Andean *tiraditos*, beef in steak tartare or carpaccio, unpasteurized milk—without pointing out that they are better disease vectors than most other fresh raw foods. You don't have to regard all raw milk as a deadly poison in order to think that people looking to buy, sell, or regulate it should pay superfanatical attention to the cleanliness of cows, milking equipment, and storage conditions. But if produced and handled under eagle-eyed supervision it should be no riskier than other raw foods that command happy followings among food lovers—indeed, probably less risky than raw clams and oysters, which sicken dozens or hundreds of people every year.

The monkey wrench in the analogy is that these other foods never inherited the bizarre nutritional mythology of fresh fluid milk. Consumers feel free to enjoy any one of them or not, without imagining that they must shovel it into their children or themselves as a scientific duty. If the "Milk Is Indispensable" notion were not so entrenched, the subject wouldn't rouse such passions. In fact, if we all had access to sources of good, fresh, locally produced unhomogenized milk batch-pasteurized by slow methods, less nonsense might be spouted about rawness and pasteurization. Meanwhile, it certainly isn't irrational to point out that the risk of spreading disease through raw milk lies not in its rawness but in the absence of carefully designed, well-enforced regulations requiring that it be handled under very much stricter supervision than the HTST or ultrapasteurized milk in ordinary retail stores.

"ORGANIC": IMAGE AND REALITY

The second major controversy that has pitted mainstream interests against people looking for better alternatives concerns organic versus conventional farming practices. Here again, I usually wish the debate could be conducted with more reason and less yelling. But there are two other thorny factors: a hazy public understanding of what is meant by the word "organic" and a rapidly shrinking distance between mainstream and organic agriculture.

"Organic" is a term tricky enough to pin down when applied to plant crops, and becomes ridiculously arbitrary where livestock are concerned. The organic criteria submitted by the National Organic Standards Board in 2002 exclude any crop raised with pesticides and synthetic fertilizers, though there is a certain amount of hair-splitting about just what falls under those categories. Organic milk is supposed to come from animals that have been fed nothing prohibited under organic-crop guidelines. Treatment with recombinant bovine somatotropin (see page 42) is also forbidden. But what consumers think they're getting when they see the words "organic" and "milk" together on a package label goes considerably beyond these yardsticks.

This is not the place to review the entire meaning of organic agriculture or evaluate its promise for better soil management and better food. But pious-sounding rhetoric and pictures of contented cows on milk cartons are no guarantee of either humanely tended animals or more "natural" milk. For better or worse, organic agriculture is big business. The bigger it gets, the more eager many producers are to interpret organic requirements in ways that serve the bottom line instead of reforming conventional agriculture's faults—for example, haggling over how long an interval should pass before cows originally raised by nonorganic regimens can be deemed free enough of banned substances to be milked as part of an organic herd. And they bank on the assumption that consumers don't know enough about milk to look beyond the "organic" label and compare concrete markers of production values. Here are some jarring facts to take into account before ascribing any ethical or other advantages to organic milk:

- The organic dairying business is tremendously concentrated, with the great preponderance of milk coming from three or four very large producers owned by vast agribusiness conglomerates. The biggest facilities are in the Rocky Mountain and West Coast states, and milk regularly travels thousands of miles from there to reach retail shelves throughout the country. As with conventional milk, gigantic farm operations with several thousand cows now dominate the business.
- The largest farms depend on the same breeding-and-feeding methods as their conventional counterparts, including high-energy rations to increase volume (see page 41); thrice-daily milking; and as much confinement with as much restriction of access to grazing as the managers can get away with. (The NOSB regulations mention "access to pasture" and to the outdoors generally, without spelling out how much or little.)
- Milk entering the pool at large organic dairies is separated and homogenized by the same arbitrary numbers games as conventional milk.
- The milk is also usually ultrapasteurized, the better to transport it across vast distances and permit weeks rather than days between time of milking and time of use.

So far, the major organic-dairy producers have managed to cash in on the widespread popular view of pure, simple, pastoral, animal-friendly organic food without acknowledging how little their wares justify the image. In fact, milk is one of the fastest-growing segments of the organic market. Sales of organic dairy products reached about $2 billion in 2005 and are increasing by about 20 to 25 percent annually; Horizon brand is now familiar in mainstream supermarkets from coast to coast. But this is one gift horse that really should be looked in the mouth. Why should we support new-style versions of factory farming clad in airs of moral superiority to factory farming?

Other people may come to other conclusions. But I ignore every organic brand of dairy products on the shelves unless it has some solider selling point than simply being "organic"—for example, also being unhomogenized, or coming from small dairy operations in my own part of the Northeast. I try to support these whether or not they have organic certification. I urge other consumers to exercise some judgment about the "organic" label, and to seek alternatives to mass-produced conventional milk in places such as farmers' markets or a few specialty retail sources that encourage locally based agriculture.

WHITE MAGIC 101

I'm sure that no institute of higher learning offers a course called "Milk Science for Dummies," but in my opinion it would be a blessing for cooks and consumers. To learn even a few basics about the biology and chemistry of this supposedly familiar substance is to see a bottle or carton of it with new eyes. And without new eyes few Americans can look past the externals to see milk's connection to living animals (the biology part) or fathom the reasons it tastes and behaves as it does (the chemistry part).

MILK AND MOTHERHOOD,
OR LACTATION IN A NUTSHELL

Every carton of milk in every supermarket started out inside an animal, in most cases a cow, who was giving milk because she had given birth. This will make perfect sense to any human mother who has done the same.

Cows and women both have nine-month gestations, compared with about five months for goats and sheep. Milk wouldn't exist if mothers' bodies didn't undergo intricate hormonal changes during the process. These cause the specifically female apparatus that lends its name to the class Mammalia (*mamma* is Latin for "breast") to crank up from neutral into high gear. Between conception and delivery a semi-undeveloped system of ducts and lobes that has been biding its time in the mother's breast, udder, or mammary gland by any other name expands tremendously, putting forth subdivided lobules and the minute capillary-embroidered sacs called alveoli that do most of the milk synthesis. (A nursing cow's or goat's udder, by the way, is not a hollow space that gets filled with liquid like a water balloon, any more than is a nursing woman's breast. It has a lot of room for internal expansion depending on how much milk has been secreted, but most of what's inside is living tissue in a somewhat spongelike, elastic arrangement.)

Until the actual onset of labor, pregnancy-sustaining hormones inhibit this future life-support system from producing true milk. In the last few days or hours, however, a kind of pre-milk equipped with various immunological weapons begins to be secreted. The start of labor triggers a cascade of drastic hormonal readjustments that produce more of this substance—a thick, serous yellowish fluid with a slightly laxative effect, known as colostrum. It is exactly what the newborn needs to get through the transition from placental to oral nourishment.

Colostrum functions solely as an interim support, and doesn't look or taste at all like any animal's normal milk. Within a week or two in most species, the real milk supply appears in response to a sequence of hormonal commands. Mother and infant establish an intricate but (usually) efficient feedback in which a mouth clamping around a nipple causes the "letting down" of the milk that has collected in the alveoli and ducts since the last nursing.

No animal except man has ever thought of decanting milk into receptacles other than baby animals, or of consuming the milk of any species other than its own. In fact, most interspecies substitutions would be disastrous for newborns because of the crucial matches between milk composition and the physiological needs of different animals. The milk of two kinds is no more interchangeable than the placental blood that supports life within the womb before milk takes over the job.

Cast your mind over the many destined environments that infant mammals must confront during the period of adjustment made possible by nursing. Arctic waters, for instance, or grassy savannas. If your first duty in life is to grow an insulating layer of blubber, you would die on milk meant for creatures whose immediate task is to build the muscle power to run with the herd. The situation is less critical for humans past the age of weaning who choose to consume another creature's milk, since it will ordinarily share attention with a number of other foods instead of being anyone's only sustenance.

If you know anything about the dairy industry, you know that the milk in one supermarket carton really started out inside not one cow but hundreds, whose milk has been pooled and sent to gigantic processing facilities where it is brought as close as possible to uniformity. Commercial milk is expected not to show any detectable variation throughout the 365 days of a year. A lactating mother's milk, however, is anything but uniform, and isn't meant to be produced over a whole calendar year. A natural breeding cycle would dictate that at a certain point the baby starts sampling other food. As it gradually loses interest in nursing and graduates to an adult diet, the mother's milk supply synchronously changes composition and dries up, and the mammary system reverts to pre-pregnancy mode.

In the smaller herd animals such as goats and sheep, mothers are ready to conceive again just when the young are fully functioning on their own. In fact, the spring lambs and kids will themselves be able to breed in autumn. The breeding interval is a year longer with cows, but a calf left to its own devices will be grazing and independent of the mother by eight or nine months. In all three cases nature has programmed the mothers to stop lactating before the time of poor grass or no grass and again come into milk when spring vegetation is at hand.

If you could see and taste the milk of one cow's, doe's, ewe's, or woman's milking cycle, from the time she stops producing colostrum to the time when the young animal says farewell to nursing, it would be shot through with huge variations. Milk shifts in makeup not only throughout one lactation but from the beginning to the end of one *day*. Indeed, the first and last mouthfuls that an infant swallows at a single nursing ordinarily differ in composition (the final dribs and drabs being the highest in fat). And this is to ignore the question of how one individual cow's, doe's, ewe's, or woman's milk differs from that of others in her species, herd, or bridge club.

We can imagine how visible such differences must have been to cottagers who milked only one animal. Composition could be averaged out to an extent when the milk of a whole herd was pooled. Still, the limits of interference with the biology of milk production were stringent in early times. The first way that prehistoric dairyists discovered to prolong lactation far beyond the needs of infants was to get lambs, kids, or calves weaned to some transitional ration as soon as possible and milk the dam twice (or more) a day as aggressively as the hungriest offspring. Usually she accepted this more willingly if the little one was kept close enough in sight to trigger the let-down reflex.

A well-known illustrated encyclopedia of the world's cheeses has an extraordinary photograph illuminating the point better than a thousand words. It was taken among the semi-nomadic Qashqa'i people of southern Iran, who still herd sheep and goats as people might have five or six thousand years ago. On an expanse of stony hardscrabble, a woman wearing the richly patterned Qashqa'i skirt and tunic sits hunkered down at the hindquarters of a shaggy, longhorned black goat that she is milking into a large pail. The animal looks trustingly up at the second member of this classic pre-industrial milking team: another woman who bends down to grasp the goat gently under the chin with one hand while using the other to restrain a tiny black kid, half hidden in the folds of her skirt.

After some days or weeks the mother may be coaxed to let down her milk without the baby in sight. And if someone keeps milking her with might and main long after her real offspring would have gone on to other food, her body can be fooled into thinking that a young one still needs the peak milk supply that she was pumping out a month or two after giving birth.

Of the Big Four milch animals, cows are the easiest to manipulate into prolonged lactation. And because they accept alterations of their natural breeding schedule more readily than the other three, they are the easiest to maintain on a year-round lactation (or as long as two or three years) if you can solve the formerly intractable problem of how to feed them through the winter with no pasturage. Today's dairy-cow rations can be—and often are—bought and administered with no relation to local climate or vegetation, meaning that for many of the animals, twelve- or eighteen-month lactations are routine. Modern dairyists often actually inseminate cows a few months into lactation, allowing a drying-off period of only about six weeks before they "freshen," or give birth and again come into milk. (Probably this strenuous regimen has much to do with the short life spans of modern cows. Ganmaa Davaasambuu, a researcher on hormones in food, has also discovered that routinely milking pregnant cows channels possibly harmful amounts of pregnancy-triggered estrogens into the American milk supply.) By staggering the breeding schedules of different cows in a herd, a farmer can achieve something like a uniform general output throughout every season. (Goats, sheep, and buffaloes obstinately prefer a more seasonal reproductive schedule.)

The impersonally standardized form in which most of us now encounter milk tends to blind us to the realities of nursing for each and every mammal. At the onset of lactation any animal mother's body starts channeling everything she eats into what is not just "nature's perfect food" but nature's *only* food for a newborn navigating the complex early stages of growth and development. Of course, nature never meant this precious substance to enter the outside world. It's worth re-emphasizing that milk as it emerges from the nipple is as much a living fluid as blood, designed to go straight from the mother's mammary system into the infant's digestive system with no detours. Once it is sidelined into a pail or tank, its major components begin undergoing multiple interactions with the forces of irreversible chemical change. What we call cooking is one way of capturing and using these forces.

A LITTLE HANDS-ON DAIRY CHEMISTRY

In the age of "molecular gastronomy," few food lovers will need to be told that every tastable quality in food rests squarely on chemistry. But in the case of milk, even the crudest chemical analysis is too long to fit between the covers of a cookbook. Rather than try to list the many thousands of substances present in any single arbitrarily chosen form of milk (for example, the homogenized and pasteurized cows' milk usually, if incorrectly, labeled "whole"), I would like to send you into the kitchen to conduct some simple experiments that show milk's major components at work.

You will get more out of these exercises if you first understand that, to food chemists, all animals' milk is a structured system with three principal "phases." Each phase, by the way, contains complexities that the utmost powers of science today can barely describe, much less duplicate. Put the three together, and you have something still more mind-boggling.

All milk starts out with water, and the simplest of the three phases to visualize is an *aqueous* (water-based) *solution* with molecules of different substances dissolved in it. But milk is also a *suspension,* meaning that it contains minuscule undissolved solid particles floating in the aqueous medium. In the third place, it is an *emulsion* shot through with small dispersed globules of something that can't be either dissolved or suspended: fat.

The dissolved substances include minerals such as calcium and potassium, several proteins known as lactalbumins and lactoglobulins, and the special sugar of milk, lactose. The suspended particles, which are larger than even the large globulin and albumin molecules, are called micelles and are intricately cobbled together out of more calcium as well as casein, a unique form of protein that furnishes the main protein reservoir for the newborn. The still larger emulsified fat globules are made up of countless different lipids (fat-related substances) linked up in still more innumerable configurations, each globule being surrounded by a delicate but sturdy membrane that keeps the contents from spilling into the milk.

The three fundamental phases can be clearly seen in any sample of milk under a microscope. But people actually knew of them long before microscopes. The kitchen-lab experiments that I suggest re-enact some major pre-industrial discoveries of dairying peoples. (A note to people who have trouble digesting lactose: Unless you suffer from extraordinarily severe lactose intolerance, you should be able to taste small samples of full-lactose milk without ill effect. In this sequence of exercises, the two things most likely to cause symptoms are the *unsoured* milk and whey. Little of the original lactose will remain in the soured versions, and the cream in several experiments has much less lactose than milk. Skim milk has proportionally more than whole milk.)

EXERCISE 1 Begin by getting enough pasteurized, *unhomogenized* whole cows' milk to work with, preferably a gallon but at least half a gallon. (I'm all in favor of rescuing raw milk from the public-health doghouse, but will leave that battle to others.)

What if you hunt frantically through a dozen stores and can't find unhomogenized milk? Or are appalled at how much it costs compared with "regular" homogenized milk? Well, look on the bright side—you've already learned something! Without spending a cent on anything except gas and shoe leather, you have just discovered one of the true idiocies of the American milk industry. Illogical as it may seem, milk that retains its three basic phases in unmonkeyed-with form is—when you can find it—usually at least three times as expensive as milk that has been put through a complicated, energy-intensive alteration of the original structure. Go figure. But if you completely strike out, buy a gallon or half a gallon of skim milk (preferably without added milk solids, another distorting bit of interference) and half a pint of heavy cream (preferably unhomogenized—simply look for a label that doesn't say "homogenized"—and non-ultrapasteurized). If you have to use these expedients, skip the first two exercises and go on to the third (page 66).

Pour the cold milk into a glass or stainless-steel bowl that is deep enough not to spread out the contents in a big lake but wide enough to admit a scooping/skimming tool such as a shallow ladle or large spoon. You may find the mouth of the bottle or carton partly stopped up with what used to be called a "cream plug," a thickened blob testifying to the fact that your milk probably took several days to get to the store. (When unhomogenized milk was more common, it moved much faster and was likelier to reach the family doorstep with a liquid cream layer than a definite plug on top.) Break it up, if necessary, by gently whisking until it is smoothly recombined with the milk.

Before going any further, taste the milk. Concentrate your attention on what's in your mouth: something ethereally subtle but concretely *there*. This milk has a kind of roundness or depth that the homogenized equivalent doesn't. The reason is that the contrast between its leaner and richer components hasn't been ironed out but remains just delicately palpable. Its flavor is not so much flavor as a sensation of freshness on the palate that scarcely translates into words. "Sweetness" is as close as anything, but it's an elusive note on the thin edge of perception rather than sugar-in-your-coffee sweetness.

What you have just sampled is, for humans past the age of weaning, one of the world's oldest beverages after water. It was never drunk everywhere in the fresh liquid form you are encountering; the reasons,

PITCHER TO MEASURE THE DEPTH OF CREAM, WHICH USED TO BE THE MEASURE OF QUALITY IN UN-HOMOGENIZED MILK

as we have seen, vary, from human digestive quirks to the ubiquity of milk-souring bacteria. You should also recall that goats' and sheep's milk, with their more distinctive flavors, are still older in human experience, and that your sample has undergone a few significant changes through pasteurization. Even so, you are getting close to something primeval.

EXERCISE 2 Let the milk sit in the refrigerator, covered, until a well-defined layer collects at the top. Layering will start within hours, but it may take from twelve hours to two days before the "top milk," as people used to call it, is really well separated.

Why such wide variation? Take this as the first concrete illustration of what you just read about the non-uniformity of milk in a state of nature—something you should get used to if you plan to work much with milk in your own kitchen. If your sample came from Jersey cows, it will separate faster and more distinctly than Holstein-Friesian milk. Goats' milk would take several days for a somewhat incomplete separation, while water buffaloes' milk would separate quite clearly in much less time than cows' milk.

Use your skimmer to remove the top layer to a smaller nonreactive container such as a small glass bowl or measuring cup. You won't be able to get all of it without a little remixing of top and bottom. Another lesson: The two layers can't be fully separated by hand (it takes a mechanical centrifuge). But you have now performed your first feat of applied dairy chemistry. You have used gravity to isolate (though incompletely) the emulsified phase from the other two milk phases.

Of course you know that the thicker liquid in the smaller container is cream. It rose, or "creamed," because it is lighter than the rest of the milk. ("Heavy cream" is a misnomer as regards specific gravity.) It contains nearly all the milkfat, still emulsified in a small amount of the original water-based solution; traces of the suspended micelles also remain. The reason for differences in creaming time is variation in the size of milkfat globules; larger ones, like those in buffaloes' milk, rise faster than the much smaller ones in goats' milk. With cows' milk there are well-known differences among breeds.

When cream separates more promptly there's also more of it. A gallon of good rich Jersey milk may give you as much as two or three cups of cream. But don't be surprised if your sample yields less than half that amount—again pointing to the unpredictability of mothers in comparison with machines. Taste it. Maybe if it were shocking pink or moss-green, one wouldn't have the same reaction, but its ivory sheen and caressing smoothness suggest some stunning union of virginal and carnal. Put it back in the refrigerator for the nonce.

EXERCISE 3 Your original container of milk is now a container of "skim milk," which means the solution and suspension parts of the three-phase system that you started out with. Stir any vestiges of cream back into the whole, pour out a small amount, and taste it. It will be very slightly sweeter than the milk you sampled before. (The cream will be sweet, too, but the two kinds of sweetness are indefinably different.) Notice how much richer and finer this feels on the palate than any commercial skim milk, even or especially the kind enriched with intrusive-tasting milk solids. In hand-skimmed milk the residual trace of cream creates an effect you wouldn't guess from its minuscule volume.

If you weren't able to obtain unhomogenized milk, proceed with a gallon or half a gallon of skim milk. In any case, pour half of the milk into a saucepan, half into a nonreactive bowl or wide-mouthed jar. Stir a little cultured "buttermilk" into the second half—we'll come later to the reason for the quotation marks. Plain yogurt is not as suitable because yogurt cultures really require special cosseting. But it will work as a second choice. Whichever you use, the label should unmistakably say that it contains active cultures.

Relative amounts aren't terribly important, since different samples will vary with the strength of the culture. Half a cup of "buttermilk" or plain yogurt should be more than enough for two quarts of skim milk. What you are doing is "inoculating" the milk with microorganisms that will convert some of the lactose into lactic acid. Cover the container and let it sit undisturbed at room temperature until it is slightly soured. This happens faster in a warm room, but timing will be unpredictable no matter what—eight hours, twelve, sixteen. You will get a thriving colony sooner or later and shouldn't worry if it's later. (The only reason for complete failure would be antibiotic contamination of the milk—illegal and rare, but not absolutely unheard of.)

Keep tasting the milk at intervals until it has a perceptible sourness and a bit of body. Now pour yourself a little and drink it. You are tasting something that most of the world's milk users are far more familiar with than fresh sweet milk. Plain soured milk brings history to life, or more accurately, prehistory. It harks back to the earliest chapters of human culinary discovery—the knowledge of how to change one flavor into another.

EXERCISE 4 While the inoculated batch is souring, turn your attention to the remaining skim milk. For each quart of milk you will need about 2 tablespoons of freshly squeezed lemon juice or 1 to 1½ tablespoons of distilled white vinegar (please, no fancy vinegars here!).

Quickly bring the milk to a boil. Turn off the heat, stir in the lemon juice or vinegar, and take the pan off the stove. The milk will quickly separate into a soft fluffy-looking (the technical term is "flocculent") substance and a thin greenish-white liquid. If the separation is not fairly distinct, add more lemon juice or vinegar (about 1 tablespoon per quart of milk).

Dampen a piece of tight-woven cheesecloth (*not* the gauzy stuff) or a large cotton handkerchief, wring it out, and use it to line a colander set over a deep bowl. Pour and scrape the contents of the pan into the colander, then gather up the corners of the cloth and tie them together securely to make a bag. After a few minutes' draining, lift up the bag and put it somewhere to drain more completely. I usually suspend it on a long wooden spoon placed across the top of a pail or deep stockpot. Leave it until the liquid stops dripping, which may be anywhere from four to more than eight hours.

Meanwhile, taste some of the greenish liquid that drained into the bowl. You probably know that this is "whey" and the solider white stuff is "curd," or "curds." The flavor of whey depends on the method used for separating it from the curd. This batch may be almost imperceptibly sour from the lemon juice or vinegar, but there will still be something definitely milky about it—though without the body of whole or skim milk. Set it aside, at room temperature or in the refrigerator. When the curd is drained, transfer it to any convenient container and taste a spoonful. It will be quite bland and delicate, a little like a closer-grained ricotta cheese (which is based on a similar idea).

You have now removed the *suspended* phase of the milk from the aqueous *solution* that it was suspended in. The solution is no longer white and opaque because it has lost the components—milkfat globules and still more importantly casein—that make milk milky-looking by refracting light off their surfaces. Line up the whey, curd, and previously separated cream, and you will see the three phases of milk side by side, as well isolated from one another as they can be by low-tech home methods developed thousands of years ago.

There are really several possible means of separating curd and whey. The one given here happens to be the simplest for American home cooks. It is a classic method in northern India, where Western-style cheese is unknown. Like all other ways of producing curd, it persuades the tiny casein micelles to come together in large enough clusters to literally fall—chemists say "precipitate"—out of the whey by the force of gravity. What you did was to combine the action of heat and an acidulant, which join forces to precipitate curd faster than any other method.

You can eat the curd as is, or perhaps turn it into a spread with a dash of salt and some minced scallion and/or green chile. It is the chhena described more fully on page 106 and used in several of my Indian recipes (see Vegetarian Malai Kofta, page 108, and Saag Panir, page 111).

EXERCISE 5 You can easily see that your efforts have produced more whey than anything else. In earlier and thriftier dairying eras, all the whey drained from curd got used. Today millions of pounds are literally thrown down the drain—except where prohibited by local environmental regulations—because the amount that can be put to any halfway profitable purpose is only a fraction of the volumes produced in commercial cheesemaking. But if you seriously love making the dairy foods that yield whey as a by-product, you will eventually want to try finding a good use for it.

Whey comes in two basic forms. You have just tasted one of them, "sweet" (i.e., unfermented) whey. This is very bland, because the acidulant that you used to curdle the milk was too mild to impart much of an acid taste. The alternative is "sour" whey. To make it, inoculate the bowl of whey with live-culture "buttermilk" or plain yogurt by stirring in anything from ¼ to ½ cup per quart just as you did with the first batch of skim milk; leave it to culture in exactly the same way, tasting it occasionally to follow the souring process.

You may already be familiar with another excellent version of sour whey, the liquid that separates from drained yogurt. For more about forms of whey and their uses, see "Fresh Cheeses." But for a first experiment I suggest either mixing sweet whey with enough sugar and lemon juice to jazz it up a bit or seasoning sour whey with a vigorous pinch each of salt and dried mint. Both versions are extremely refreshing poured over ice cubes.

EXERCISE 6 The cream obtained in Exercise 2 has one more trick to play, if you haven't already put it on strawberries. For those who couldn't get unhomogenized milk and are working with "boughten" cream, the general idea is the same. In both cases you are going to get two results—very small in quantity, but thought-provoking for any real cook—from one batch of cream.

I suggest doing or at least trying to do this by hand. It's laborious, but enables you to track critical stages of change more closely than any other method. People who have had to settle for ultrapasteurized cream may need to use a handheld immersion blender, but I recommend first seeing how far you can get without it.

Have the previously skimmed cream or half a pint of commercial heavy cream in a small glass bowl or measuring cup. Both cream and container should be very cold when you begin, because the amount is small enough to easily become overwarmed through simple friction. Start rapidly agitating it with a small wire whisk. Large bubbles will appear, then stop appearing. The whole consistency will gradually become heavier. (This will take longer with ultrapasteurized cream.) Keep plying the whisk until you recognize the beginnings of whipped cream.

In technical terms, you have incorporated air into the mass while partly knocking apart the remarkably constructed membrane that surrounds each milkfat globule. Some dislodged components of the membrane now form walls around the air bubbles. Whipped cream is not your present goal, so go on beating the cream stiffer and stiffer until the whisk will scarcely move through it. Keep watching the pace of change. After a longer or shorter interval (once more depending on variables beyond your control) you will see a bit of liquid seeping from the stiff, heavy foam. Keep on whisking, and the whipped cream will resolve itself into a grainy yellow-white substance and a thin, cloudy whitish liquid.

Scrape the wires of the whisk as clean as you can, and beat the half-separated components with a small wooden spoon to separate them further. Drain the liquid into a small cup; work the yellow stuff with the spoon to force out any more residue, and drain that off, too.

You have now produced butter and true buttermilk by wrestling your way through a phenomenon known as *phase inversion*. The cream at the start of the proceedings still consisted of milkfat globules emulsified in the underlying solution, which held the fat globules as a fabric may hold tiny beads or sequins. The solution—not too far removed from the whey you saw in the curd experiment—at that time formed what is known as a *continuous phase*, with the milkfat globules sprinkled throughout as a *dispersed phase*. (The suspended casein micelles that later came together as curd were a whole different dispersed phase; you may now be starting to see why food chemists never tire of pointing out that milk is an incredibly complex substance.) Agitating the system forcefully enough eventually causes the separate globules of fat to unite in a coherent mass, squeezing out most of the original wheylike solution. Most of this liquid will drain from the mass as you work it, but not quite all.

In a switch of roles, the previously dispersed milkfat has become the continuous phase: butter. The tiny amount of the original solution/suspension that hasn't drained off now remains scattered through the mass in minuscule droplets of true buttermilk as the dispersed phase of a suddenly inverted emulsion.

Examine the buttermilk. Its main difference from the whey that you obtained before is that it retains whatever casein was in the original cream. (This is why it looks whiter.) Taste it. In spite of starting with a gallon of milk, you unfortunately don't have enough to do anything more with, but at least you can recognize it as a pleasant cousin of both sweet whey and milk. If you had cultured the cream before churning it, the buttermilk—the liquid residue of the phase-inversion process—would be more like soured milk. (What is sold in today's America as "buttermilk" is really a kind of soured milk similar to the version you tasted in Exercise 3.) In dairying parlance, the culturing of cream for butter often is called "ripening."

If you ever make ripened butter by the directions in "Butter and True Buttermilk" and sample the resulting buttermilk, probably you will scratch your head in puzzlement at the complete unavailability of real ripened buttermilk in any part of this country.

The small amount of cream used here yields only a little butter—but oh, what celestial stuff! Put it in the refrigerator to chill briefly. (Butter most emphatically is *not* among the foods that reveal their ultimate perfections when left to bask in the warmth of an American kitchen.) Dig out a bit on a spoon and eat it, trying to concentrate on every microsecond of its delicate passage from solid to melted. Spread some on a plain cracker or piece of sturdy bread and eat it. If there is enough left, scrape it out onto a helping of piping hot cooked vegetables or noodles. It is like the Platonic essence of the cream you tasted earlier, containing tiny, elusive vestiges of the original fresh skim milk together with the suave, luscious, ineffable newly churned butter. It is not as wonderful in consistency as butter made by very good professionals who know the ideal temperature for different batches of cream. But the flavor ought to make any butter lover wonder how manufacturers have the nerve to call some of their wares "butter."

WHAT HAVE WE BEEN MISSING?

Now, what exactly have you proved by all these exertions? After all, anyone can buy the results of the foregoing experiments (or nearly all of them) as separate products. Most of them won't taste as good, but doesn't the convenience of being able to get ready-made butter, skim milk, and so forth compensate for some small loss of quality?

Well, yes and no. If you've eaten good fresh dairy products, you'll know that the loss of quality is not small. But there's something else at issue here. You started out with *one single batch of milk* that was as close as practicable to the state in which it emerged from the cow. (True, it was pasteurized, but that didn't greatly impair its fitness for our purposes.) The amount was not huge. But through an alchemy not hopelessly beyond everyday American kitchens, it supplied you with not only delicious whole milk but wonderful fresh cream, skim milk fit to drink with pleasure rather than resignation, refreshing soured skim milk, nutrient-rich curd and whey (whose versatility I've barely hinted at), a bit of truly lovely butter, and a tantalizing soupçon of real buttermilk. It could have yielded still other transformations—for instance, yogurt, yogurt "cheese," junket, pot cheese and several other fresh cheeses, or clotted cream. Some of these can also be made from the so-called whole milk that we're all familiar with—it bears repeating that by no stretch of the imagination is commercial U.S. whole milk really whole—or from other standard offerings in the supermarket dairy case. But they are better when they are, so to speak, mined from the original ore that is true whole milk.

Why should all the white magic be left to the big dairy processors and not the home cook? It's as if the only way people could buy wheat were as cake flour, prepackaged cake mix, biscuit mix, white sauce mix, frozen bread dough, flavored instant bulgur, and so forth. How could any cook ever learn to understand what wheat itself is all about? How could any consumer ever fathom the sheer wastefulness of a corporate machinery geared up to make one of the world's most ancient foods available only in the form of superspecialized prod-

ucts meant to fill arbitrary little retail-sales slots, while excluding the incredibly versatile basic material that could furnish better homemade versions of
them all?

Since none of us lives in some ideal realm of pristine ingredients, most of
my recipes are based on easily obtainable versions of cows' milk, butter, and so
forth. But I would like users of this book to keep thinking of the tangible,
tastable culinary magic that is ancient applied dairy chemistry. Not so long
ago, millions of ordinary people could readily perform this magic in their own
homes. We still should be able to recapture it. If more cooks understand that
they, too, can manipulate the miraculous complexities of milk to splendid culinary purpose, their voices may move the American dairy industry to bring us
the basic substance in less technologically manhandled and denatured form.

PART II
RECIPES

FRESH MILK AND CREAM

Chinese "Fried Milk"

Rice Pudding

Chocolate Pudding

Panna Cotta and Relatives

Cremets d'Angers

Lemon Sponge Pudding

About Vanilla Ice Cream

Vanilla Ice Cream I: Custard-Based

Vanilla Ice Cream II: Philadelphia-Style

Crème Anglaise (Stirred Custard)

Cajeta Mexicana (Mexican Dulce de Leche)

Dulce de Leche with Canned Condensed Milk

Batidos (Latin American Milkshakes)

Thai-Style Iced Coffee

Hot Chocolate

Chocolate Malted

Hoppelpoppel: Eggnog with a Difference

Milk Punch

To most American cooks, the idea of ordinary milk or cream as a vehicle of vivid or concentrated flavors comes as a surprise. We're more used to encountering them in gentle contexts where no one expects them to be anything but bland, and where that quality can be seen as a virtue. Indeed, sometimes it *is* a virtue. But there's a lot more to milk-based cookery than mild-mannered innocuousness.

A simple first step for starting to think outside the box: Take about two cups of milk—any kind from skim to whole will do—and a few ounces of strong-flavored smoked fish like chub, whitefish, Finnan haddie, or kippered herring. If none of these is easy to find, substitute a chopped raw onion. Put the fish or onion in a small dish, pour the milk over it, and let sit for four to twelve hours, well covered, in the refrigerator or at room temperature.

Strain the milk through a fine mesh sieve and taste it. It will have picked up either a distinct fishy-smoky edge or an equally definite pungency from the onion. Even plain water will leach out salt from foods, but water doesn't have the property of becoming subtly and complexly infused with other essences. One of milk's signature qualities is the tenacity with which its more volatile or reactive components latch on to reactive counterparts in more strongly fla-vored foods. This really should be considered a useful talent. Your fishy or oniony milk would make a wonderful cooking liquid—say, as part of a roux-based milk sauce or the foundation of a chowder.

As this mini-exercise suggests, American cooks usually have very limited experience in exploiting some fascinating aptitudes of plain milk and cream. Models of suavity and creaminess we have aplenty, and I'm certainly not turn-ing up my nose at those qualities or planning to forgo demurely luscious incar-nations of milk such as whipped cream. But it must be said that the familiar English- or French-derived uses of unsoured milk or cream seldom are notable for piquancy, intensity, or multidimensional verve. Probably our most notable milk-based dishes are sweetened puddings, which can be excellent but represent only a tiny fraction of what we could be doing.

Opportunities for enlarged horizons have become more obvious as America has become progressively enriched by the cooking traditions of new immi-grants, and will be still more so in years to come. Recent arrivals from north-ern India have introduced millions of us to the firm cheeselike delicacy—not a true cheese—that is called panir or chhenna and eaten in marvelously spiced sauces. Clotted cream, which depends on very slow heating to thicken the top cream layer of unhomogenized milk into a dense, nutty-tasting crust, has long been known to people who travel in the West Country of England, and is now taking up permanent residence in this country thanks to Turkish immigrants devoted to their own riper-flavored counterpart, *kaymak*. People from the Asian and Latin American tropics are bringing preferences of their own that usually include a love of sweetened, concentrated dairy products such as canned condensed milk or the still intenser *dulce de leche*—also condensed, but by heating in an open kettle rather than under a vacuum. Latin Americans are also crazy about their own versions of milkshakes (*batidos*) based on many different kinds of tropical fruits.

In short, today's uses of fresh milk and cream in starring roles add up to more of an expanding galaxy than anyone could have predicted a few years ago. There also seems to be more hope of persuading a few independent-minded farmers and dairyists to improve the quality of what we have to work with.

LABEL BABEL: BUYING MILK AND CREAM

The usual commercial choices in this department unfortunately have more to do with arbitrary niche marketing than simple, unvarnished milk or cream. Nonetheless, some of the questions I'm most frequently asked are about the meanings of different designations on labels of fresh milk and cream. Clearly there is a hunger for more information. Here, in ascending order of richness, are the kinds usually available in retail markets. A preliminary caveat: Very few fresh dairy products have been assigned any formal FDA "standard of identity" in the Code of Federal Regulations; it may be frustrating to learn that things bearing the same name often vary in composition from one state (or indeed one manufacturer) to another, but such is unfortunately the case.

- Fat-free or nonfat milk: Still informally called "skim milk" by some, though the term has disappeared from most labels. It contains the whey and casein of milk with none of the butterfat, and is fortified with vitamins A and D. Proportionally it contains more lactose than any other form of fresh milk. (The proportion of lactose decreases with every increase in milkfat content, so that heavy cream contains only minute amounts.) It also curdles more easily with the heat of cooking. When it comes from well-managed herds of cows producing a lot of protein in the milk, it can be quite satisfying. The fat-free milk from large commercial dairies, however, is at best indifferent-tasting. There are versions with added nonfat dry milk solids, which in my opinion just plaster an extraneous cheesiness over dull-tasting milk. Note that they have more lactose than plain skim milk.

  All other gradations manufactured by large commercial processors are based on fat-free milk homogenized with certain standardized percentages of milkfat.

- Low-fat milk: Made by homogenizing fat-free milk and cream to 0.5 percent milkfat content. Fortified with vitamins A and D.
- Reduced-fat milk: Usually made by homogenizing fat-free milk and cream to 1 percent, 1.5 percent, or 2 percent milkfat content. Fortified with vitamins A and D.
- Whole milk: The designation "whole," though legally sanctioned, is misleading inasmuch as the milk has been separated by centrifuge and recombined to an arbitrary standard. In most states, it means a mixture of nonfat milk and cream homogenized to 3.25 percent milkfat content. Fortified with vitamin D.

Cream, as processed for mass distribution, is also usually homogenized, but not as universally as milk. The unhomogenized kind, in all gradations, is much creamier-tasting. On standing for a while, it will develop a layer of skim milk at the bottom, clearly visible when the cream is sold in glass. This is not a defect but a sign that the cream retains milkfat globules large enough to separate from the thinner milk, not having been crushed to a fraction of their original size through homogenization.

For more about cream, see the essay on whipped cream (page 83). Today's usual retail-store choices—nearly always ultrapasteurized—are:

- Half-and-half: A term with no uniform meaning. Long ago it hazily designated a mixture of half milk, half cream by volume. Modern manufacturing percentages (by weight) range from 10.5 to 18 percent milkfat in different states, or even in the same state as processed by different manufacturers. Note that percentages are only sometimes stated on labels. Nearly all half-and-half is homogenized. I hope it isn't necessary to say that the product brazenly labeled "nonfat half-and-half" in supermarkets is utterly unrelated to the real stuff and should not be used in any of my recipes.
- Light cream: The least precise of all designations; ranges from 18 to 30 percent milkfat. Thus the terms "half-and-half" and "light cream" can overlap in meaning. If milkfat percentages don't appear on labels, trial and error is the only way to tell how rich or light local brands of half-and-half or light cream are. Often homogenized.
- Heavy cream: Must contain at least 36 percent milkfat; anything richer is very rare. Often homogenized.

In most places today it is uncommon to find the intermediate gradation "light whipping cream" for cream with a milkfat percentage between 30 and 36. Where it exists, it is often homogenized.

As explained on page 46, milk in many gradations is also sold with value-added features such as lactose reduction. In consequence, dairy-section shelves are filled with a huge number of products that, if you believe the marketing moguls, represent a wonderful diversity of choice inviting cooks to exploit innumerable subtle differences in the kitchen. In my opinion, they add up to the kind of niche-marketing-gone-hogwild spectacle that you see in the toothpaste aisle. I don't suggest buying any kinds from supermarkets except whole milk and heavy cream (sometimes light cream or half-and-half). When unhomogenized, truly whole milk, good skim milk, and nonultrapasteurized cream are available to cooks everywhere without search missions to expensive specialty food shops, then we can start congratulating ourselves on *choice*. Meanwhile, cooking with milk and cream is best done with the plainest, least-fiddled-with versions you can find.

There is one notable category of exceptions to this rule: canned milk, a food intended for emergency situations that in some parts of the world ended by taking on gastronomic dimensions of its own. Gail Borden, who introduced a vacuum-evaporation method of condensing and canning heavily sweetened milk shortly before the Civil War, reaped a considerable wartime reward by supplying it on a large scale to the Union Army. A different process perfected in the late 1880s yielded unsweetened evaporated milk. The two new products had a lively success over the next century throughout the industrialized West, where they still command a following. But it was in the Latin American and Asian tropics—regions with brief dairying histories or none—that they would make their biggest mark.

Canned milk accompanied the colonial powers to much of southern Asia, where no society except India had any taste for milk as it came from cows or other milch animals. That it *didn't* taste like other forms of milk was all to its advantage. The condensed kind, which Borden had intended to be diluted

AN EARLY CANNED MILK ADVERTISEMENT

with up to five or, in a pinch, seven times its volume in water before being drunk like usual milk, had (when undiluted) a densely syrupy quality that people greatly enjoyed. Evaporated milk was less sweet and heavy, but also had a sufficiently strong caramelized note to drown out the disliked flavor of unprocessed milk.

In Central and South America, European-style dairy farming has been extensive enough to make fresh milk known wherever milch animals can be raised. But the love of canned milk seems to run deeper. Both there and in Asia, condensed and evaporated milk are primarily used not as major elements of the diet but as enrichers of sweetened beverages—for instance, Thai-style iced coffee and tea, or the Latin American equivalents of eggnog. In Latin America, they are also preferred for flans and used in desserts such as the celebrated "three milks," or *tres leches*, a cake made with condensed milk, evaporated milk, and cream. It is important to realize that in these cases canned milk is not a poor relation of "real" milk but an ingredient prized for its own qualities.

Finally, there are two other forms in which unsoured milk reaches a large clientele: the long-keeping fluid version and the powdered kind.

LONG-KEEPING MILK IN ASEPTIC PACKAGING has been advertised as a great convenience because it needs no refrigeration until opened, though afterward it is as perishable as any other kind. One brand, Parmalat, now seems to have become a permanent fixture in U.S. supermarkets. When I've tried it, the flavor has seemed at least as fresh as that of conventionally packaged milk at the end of the usual journeys to supermarket and home refrigerator. I don't buy it myself, but this is one case where aseptic technology seems to produce something no worse than the prevailing conventional technology—though that isn't saying much. Every dish in this chapter (except for those using canned milk) will taste better if made with very fresh unhomogenized milk or cream. But many of them can be reasonably managed with mass-produced whole milk, including the long-keeping versions. (I don't recommend any of the reduced-fat gradations.)

DRIED OR POWDERED MILK has been around longer than the aseptic-packaged fluid version, and strikes me as the least desirable way you can buy unsoured milk. But it is important enough to many people to deserve some attention. Its history is bound up with the chronic surpluses confronting milk producers. Surpluses of something notoriously perishable are harder to deal with than surpluses of, let's say, salt.

From the late nineteenth century on, manufacturers were looking into the possibility of converting unsoured milk into a form still more durable than canned milk, and cheaper to handle and package in large volumes. Early versions had a sweetish, cooked flavor, slightly mitigated as the technology improved. The Great Depression and World War II brought about large-scale diversion of milk surpluses, in dried form, to domestic food-assistance programs and international relief agencies. These still are financial mainstays of the industry. Huge amounts also find their way into commercial confectionery, baked goods, canned soups, frozen foods, and many more uses. As pointed out earlier, nowadays dried milk solids are often used to "enrich" commercial skim milk, though I find no real richness in the result. But for decades, a stubborn drawback discouraged retail sales of dried milk: the difficulty of dissolving the powder quickly and smoothly in cold water. The problem was solved in the mid-1950s by a new technique of getting the powdered grains to aggregate in minute crystals. Millions of consumers took to instant dried milk as a thrifty alternative to fresh milk. For a while it was the darling of nutrition-minded recipe developers, who encouraged home cooks to put supposedly vitalizing doses of dried milk into sauces, puddings, and breads.

Another technical problem was more intractable: the tendency of milkfat to develop spoiled or harsh flavors in the drying process. Dairy processors did find solutions, but they were expensive enough to make mass-produced whole dried milk economically infeasible. This is why virtually all commercial brands are nonfat, though there is some distribution of whole dried milk in health-food stores.

As the shelf life of fluid milk in cartons has been extended, dried milk reconstituted at home has lost some of its appeal for consumers. Its great selling points are cheapness, durability, and—for people in remote locales with little access to other dairy products—convenience. In my view dried milk is the least appetizing form of either skim or whole milk. I don't cook with it myself, and would not recommend using it in any of my recipes. The only form of dried milk I ever use is malted-milk powder, which isn't meant to produce an imitation of fresh milk, and whose caramelized flavors are part of its appeal. (See Chocolate Malted, page 141.)

Dairy Maid

CREAM, WHIPPED AND UNWHIPPED:
SOME THOUGHTS

It isn't exactly news that most people today cannot find plain pasteurized (much less raw) cream. In fact, some users of this book probably have never encountered any that wasn't ultra-pasteurized. To them, anything else may not taste quite normal. But if you can possibly get hold of some basic pasteurized heavy cream (preferably unhomogenized) to compare with the more usual kind, you'll be better able to understand why it's the ultrapasteurized version that's really not normal.

The main difference is that the heat of ultrapasteurization (carried out in a rapid, high-pressure continuous feed at 280°F) affects particular kinds of whey proteins called agglutinins that otherwise would bond with the membranes of milkfat globules in well-chilled milk or cream and encourage separate droplets of fat to cluster closely together. Through this clustering action the milkfat "creams," or rises to the top as a visible cream layer.

When skimmed or removed by centrifuge, this risen, or agglutinated, cream has a satisfyingly slow-flowing quality that we think of as "heavy," though as regards specific gravity it's really *less* heavy than the rest of the milk. Heat tends to damage the agglutinins; the effect is negligible with old-fashioned, low-temperature batch-pasteurization methods but quite destructive at the higher temperature required for ultrapasteurization. As a result, ultrapasteurized cream is thinner than cream pasteurized by slower methods.

If you've been able to line up a pasteurized and an ultrapasteurized sample of heavy cream and taste both, you may think I've got it dead wrong, because the ultrapasteurized cream will seem quite viscous and heavy. You will find the reason in the ingredients list printed on both cartons. Plain pasteurized cream will list nothing but "cream" (or perhaps "milk"). The ultrapasteurized label is more romantic reading, with enticements like "carrageenan" or "guar gum," "polysorbate 80," and "mono- and diglycerides." It is purely because of such fixes to the thinness problem that the contents seem heavier than nonultrapasteurized cream. If you put both on berries or other acid fruit, the ultrapasteurized sample will react by turning quite a bit thicker—also thanks to the same extraneous agents. And the finish of the plain pasteurized cream will be cleaner and fresher, without the cooked or overcooked note of the other.

The proof of the pudding is in the whipping. Since ultrapasteurized cream has been in existence, old-school cooks have been loudly complaining about how difficult that process has become. You will see why if you put two equal-sized samples (anything from ½ to 1 cup) of both kinds into separate bowls, chill them well in the refrigerator, and read on a bit.

Raw or plain pasteurized cream not only creams faster than its ultrapasteurized lookalike but also moves more easily to another useful step, a kind of bubble formation that depends on intact agglutinins helping clusters of milkfat globules come together. For best results the cream (preferably unhomogenized, for reasons to be explained) should contain at least 35 percent milkfat. If it is agitated through whipping with a set of wires or blades, air is introduced into the cream mass. (You have already seen the principle at work if you tried the brief "White Magic" Exercise 6 on page 69.) The friction and commotion of whipping causes the complex, delicate milkfat-globule membranes to shed slippery bits of their own inner and outer walls. The agglutinins that they previously took up from the whey now help dislodged membrane-wall remnants to cooperatively join and to create new, differently constituted walls of film around the air pockets. At the same time, part of the fat starts to be released from some formerly unbreached globules.

With more agitation, eventually the still-chilled cream enters a delicate intermediate state: lightened and expanded to about twice its original volume from the incorporation of air in a film-supported network of bubbles, with the remaining milkfat starting to be jammed closer between bubbles but not yet cohering in a buttery mass. This is what we call "whipped cream."

Check the time on the clock. Take the bowl of nonultrapasteurized cream and start whipping with any preferred beating tool. An immersion blender, wire whisk, rotary eggbeater, or hand mixer will do. So will a food processor, but it will be harder to follow the different stages by eye. Cream, container, and beating device should be very cold for the quickest and most thorough results—meaning the most efficient action of agglutinins on milkfat-globule membranes. The agglutinins bond most easily with membrane surfaces, thus encouraging the clustering of globules, at temperatures around 40°F. Their work is progressively impeded as the cream warms to anything like usual room temperatures.

As you beat and the cream moves from the globule-clustering stage to the partial rupture of globule membranes, you will see it looking loose and gloppy, a little heavier, noticeably expanded and thicker, and finally transformed into a light blossomy cloud. *Do not let it turn to butter.* People have preferences for more softly or stiffly whipped cream; I like it about as stiff as it can get but usually find myself in the minority on that question.

When it's whipped to your satisfaction, look at the clock to see how long the whole process took. This will be highly variable, depending on several factors beyond your control. Put the lovely stuff back into the refrigerator and try to reproduce the experiment as exactly as possible with the ultrapasteurized heavy cream.

The cream will go through the same stages on the road to becoming whipped cream, but somewhat more slowly and (if you're using a whisk or rotary eggbeater) more effortfully. The reason is that you have less in the way of membrane walls and agglutinins to start the clustering process and the buildup of film. The difference in time will be most marked if your non-ultrapasteurized sample was also unhomogenized; shattering milkfat globules to smithereens by forcing them through the minute nozzle openings of a homogenizer leaves crushed remnants too small to cluster easily and cream that takes longer to whip.

The more easily cream whips, the better-tasting the result. (The best comes from Jersey cows, whose milkfat occurs in large globules that give the cream a leg up on the clustering process.) Still, even ultrapasteurized and homogenized cream make infinitely better whipped cream than any of the pressurized prewhipped commercial substitutes. Even when they contain real cream, they have a vapid wishy-washy consistency quite unlike the full-bodied quality of freshly whipped cream.

It is true that home-whipped cream on standing displays a tendency to start leaking a bit of liquid, but this is not a serious drawback and can be partly offset if you beat in a small amount of sugar (a teaspoon to a cup of cream) partway through whipping and plan to very lightly rewhip it just before serving.

One cup of heavy cream will yield about 2 cups of whipped cream. There is no more agreeable dessert topping or pastry filling, whether the cream is plain or flavored with more sugar (2 to 3 tablespoons to each starting cup of cream), a jolt of any preferred spirit or liqueur, or a dash of vanilla or almond extract.

HISTORICAL UPS AND DOWNS

Given everything that I've said about the inferiority of ultra-pasteurized cream, how did it come to crowd out old-fashioned pasteurized cream so decisively in the last thirty or forty years? The short answer is lack of public demand for cream, period. Cream has had its heydays and lean times in the history of Western cooking, and we seem to be well into one of the latter.

There are plenty of reasons that fresh cream hasn't always been a prominent feature of every dairying region. It can exist, in theory, in any location with milch animals whose milk has large-enough fat globules to form a cream layer on standing. The best are cows and water buffaloes. But in hot climates the creaming phenomenon is somewhat diminished and the cream sours quickly. Thus the northerly milking regions of Europe were about the only areas where unsoured cream could have figured in cooking. Northeastern peoples, however, firmly gravitated toward sour cream. This was never a preference of the far northwestern reaches—but neither was fresh cream, for a long time. We have no evidence that most English or northern French cooks held any form of cream in high regard until close to the dawn of specialized modern dairying. It was after the late seventeenth century that cream-based dishes became common in English and French cookbooks, and that particular districts became known for the excellence of their cream as well as butter.

The culinary prestige of cream increased swiftly with advances in cooling milk. Creaming, or the formation of a well-defined cream layer, was found to take place faster and more thoroughly in a dairy with a running cold spring than in a warm room. With the developing nineteenth-century ice trade, followed late in the century by mechanical refrigeration, people discovered that very deeply chilled milk creamed still better. Not long after this, centrifugal separators took over the job, and cream so rich that it had to be thinned with milk before whipping in order not to turn to butter reached urban consumers' iceboxes as a matter of course.

This development coincided with the advent of improved beating devices. Before the nineteenth century nothing better than bundles of straw or twigs existed for beating cream or egg whites. You had to whip cream a little at a time, skimming off the whipped froth from the top and placing it in a sieve to drain off any still-retained liquid while you went on with the rest of the batch. Whisks of thin wooden or metal rods seem to have been available by midcentury, but were not much more efficient. Over the next fifty years these were superseded by sturdy balloon whisks and rotary eggbeaters, just as ice cooling, centrifuging, and the rise of dairy-cattle breeds such as Jerseys and Guernseys (noted for the quality of their cream) put other pieces of the puzzle in place. By the turn of the twentieth century any cook could produce beautifully and completely whipped cream in a matter of minutes, whereas Isabella Beeton in her renowned 1861 manual had estimated that a pint of cream ought to take an hour.

A golden age of cream-enriched cooking was now at hand in countries with modern dairy technology. In the United States, whipped cream became the embellishment or filling of choice for any really dazzling dessert. In France and all places touched by French culinary influence, rich fresh cream (whipped or unwhipped) became the magic ingredient in mousses, quenelles, custards, Bavarian creams, and sauces that would symbolize grand cuisine for many from the belle époque to the 1970s.

Influential cooks and writers of the period leading up to the so-called gourmet revolution habitually placed cream in a starring role. As an aspiring young cook, I thought it was impossible for anything to be too creamy. And I was far from alone in that opinion, which now looks as quaint as yesteryear's fashionable kitchen color schemes.

One reason for cream's fall from grace was, of course, the general move away from full-fat dairy products that began several generations ago. Recently, the rationale of this trend has been called into question. But cream has been one of its economic casualties. For dairy processors, most of the cream obtained when milk is centrifuged at the plant has become a chronic embarrassment. Some profit can be salvaged from the bulky, inconveniently perishable substance by putting it to such manufacturing purposes as butter and ice cream—or giving it a longer shelf life through ultrapasteurization. For the industry as a whole, ultrapasteurized cream is the only form that makes economic sense.

It's a sad development, because when real creaminess is what you want, there is nothing like fresh cream. Still, even cream-loving cooks nowadays understand that creaminess can all too easily become a kind of blanket spread over individual textures, softening other flavors to the point of mawkishness. (Especially ultrapasteurized cream, with its faint sludginess and lack of clean finish.) There are occasions when too much cream is just enough, but also many when less is more.

Enough of a market for decent-tasting cream remains to keep a few small dairies supplying specialty stores here and there, especially in large cities. I'd hazard a guess that demand will increase rather than decrease, given the resurgence in small-scale farm dairies and the many doubts now being cast on the superior healthfulness of low-fat dairy products.

RECIPES

CLOTTED CREAM

Many people fall in love with the Devonshire or Cornish versions of this celestial substance without realizing that a similar idea has occurred to people elsewhere, from Serbia (*kajmak*) and Turkey (*kaymak*) to India (*malai*). The necessary raw material is a kind of milk that on standing acquires a thick, well-defined top layer of cream. Water buffaloes' and cows' milk are the best for this. Goats' milk, with its very small fat globules, will not develop the requisite degree of separation. Sheep's milk also has fairly small fat globules, but is sufficiently more concentrated than goats' milk to make good clotted cream anyhow. In parts of the Diverse Sources Belt, milk from two or more species is sometimes combined.

What's crucial in all cases is an unhomogenized distribution, with cream on top and the thinner milk on the bottom. For English clotted cream the unhomogenized milk is put in a wide, shallow pan and subjected to a very slow, gentle heating that causes the cream to form a thick, semisolid blanket. Heating cream by itself without a bottom layer of milk doesn't work the same way. Though most of the milk will eventually be removed at the skimming stage, it somehow communicates better flavor to the cream. Besides, the thinner milk on the bottom acts as a heat insulator and modulator, letting the top gradually reach temperatures that will half-coagulate it without directly exposing it to the stronger heat coming from the floor of the pan.

Heat alone won't produce the desired result. There also has to be some evaporation of water from the surface, promoted by the width of the pan and the further step of letting the milk stand at least overnight before starting to warm it. The incomparable flavor doesn't depend on bacterial action, though probably a small amount of ripening takes place during the initial standing phase. (Ignore recipes that tell you to put sour cream in with the milk.) The main factor is *cooking without boiling,* which transforms the taste of simple fresh cream into something wonderfully warm and nutty.

English-style clotted cream is quite simple to make at home if you can get hold of unhomogenized milk and cream. It is not true (though often asserted) that the real thing depends on unpasteurized milk. *Unhomogenized* milk is the key, since its comparatively large milkfat globules easily come together in a good substantial body. The few people who can get milk from Jersey or Guernsey cows are the luckiest, because the milkfat globules are larger than in the milk of other breeds and the cream almost begs to form a rich clot. (Devotees of the stuff can be spotted by the fact that they find the word "clot" poetic.)

In the English West Country, milk alone was traditionally used to make clotted cream, but you must remember that it was milk from very backward cows that knew no better than to give small amounts of very rich milk. The best plan today (for those lacking their own Jersey cow) is a combination of unhomogenized milk and cream, in the ratio of 1 cup cream to 1 quart milk. You can make a stab at clotted cream with homogenized whole milk and heavy cream, but the separation will be less complete and the yield more meager.

I don't recommend making clotted cream with less than about 1 to 1½ quarts of milk (that is, milk-cream mixture), because under the best of circumstances you won't get much more than a cup of clotted cream per quart. (I find a two-quart batch best.) You will need a wide, shallow nonreactive skillet or sauté pan that will hold the milk without spilling when moved from one spot to another. If you have two suitable pans you can distribute the milk between them. But note that you'll have to clear space in the refrigerator for the postcooking phase, which may complicate the planning with two pans. An instant-reading thermometer is a help.

YIELD: About 1 cup clotted cream, 4 cups leftover milk for each starting quart of milk and cup of cream (Results will vary depending on the quality of the milk and how long it heats.)

1 or 2 quarts unhomogenized milk
1 or 2 cups nonultrapasteurized heavy cream, preferably
   unhomogenized

Combine the milk and cream in a shallow nonreactive pan (see above), preferably one with a heavy bottom. Let it stand at least 12 hours, loosely covered, in
a cool room. Lacking a fairly cool room, you can use the refrigerator, but the
milk won't clot as firmly; increase the standing time to 16 to 24 hours or until
the cream layer is well defined.

Set a Flame Tamer or other heat-diffusing device on a stove burner, and
very carefully set the pan of milk on it over the lowest possible heat. (If put
directly on a burner the milk may boil, which ruins the gradual coagulation
process.)

Watch the pan closely through the various heating stages. The slower the
process the better. First you will see tiny beads of fat appearing around the rim
of the pan. Then small blistery stipplings will form just under the surface,
which will begin to look filmy. Eventually the surface will acquire a yellow cast
and begin to wrinkle, then coalesce into a more deeply and completely wrin-
kled crust. The milk will take on a faintly cheesy smell. The temperature,
meanwhile, must reach something between 140° and 180°F, and has to remain
in that range long enough to encourage the maximum amount of clotting. If
you snatch the pan from the stove as soon as you see wrinkles, you will end up
with less cream. Try to keep it within the right zone for about 4 hours. (I'm
skeptical of people who say they can make clotted cream in half an hour.)

Very, very carefully remove the pan from the heat, and let cool to room temperature before sliding it into the refrigerator and leaving it for at least
8 hours, preferably overnight; the clot will not firm up until it is deeply chilled.
With a slotted spoon, spatula, or anything else that will work, gently lift the
thick yellow crust into a small bowl, letting the residual milk drain back into
the pan.

Part of the clotted cream will be firm, part slightly fluid. You can gently stir
it together to even out the contrast, but I like it as is. It will keep in the refrigerator, tightly covered, for 5 to 7 days. Proudly serve it on biscuits, scones,
toast, bread, or anything else that takes your fancy. It is a glorious partner to
fresh fruit, and perhaps even better with compotes or stewed dried fruit.

Going through a two- or three-day process for far less cream than milk may
sound like a spendthrift idea, but the leftover milk is actually lovely for such
purposes as scalloped potatoes and chowders. It also makes absolutely wonderful rice pudding.

MASCARPONE

Mascarpone originated close to the Lombard city of Lodi. Technically it is one of the noncheese cheeses, like Indian panir, made by simple acidification instead of lactic-acid fermentation or enzymatic action. The cheap and handy original acidulant was tartaric acid from the tartar that crystallizes out of wine onto barrel walls during the aging process. Cream of tartar, a potassium salt of tartaric acid that is available today in most supermarkets, ought to be just as good, but I have never had success using it. I get good results with the other common acidulant for mascarpone—citric acid, the "sour salt" that once flavored some versions of borshch. Look for it in health-food stores or markets catering to a Jewish clientele, and also in some Indian and Turkish groceries. Its advantage over such agents as vinegar or lemon juice is that a very small amount will both curdle the cream and add a suggestion of pleasant, neutral tartness free of other distracting notes. The flavor you want is lightly cooked (not boiled) cream with a delicate hint of acid.

This beautiful quasi-cheese would be a cinch to make if one could find the right sort of cream—which *isn't* a cinch. Plain heavy cream when chilled yields a result I don't care for, clayey rather than silky. Most half-and-half won't set up. The best choice would be cream with about 20 to 25 percent milkfat, nonultrapasteurized and if possible unhomogenized. Some old-fashioned "light cream" fits the bill. Otherwise, use a combination of heavy cream and half-and-half matching the consistency of light cream. I use 2 cups each of half-and-half and heavy cream. (But note that the name "half-and-half" covers products of varied milkfat percentages in different areas; depending on where you live, you may have to experiment with other proportions.)

The uses of mascarpone, beyond the familiar tiramisù, are legion. I love it with dried or fresh fruit, but even more in savory contexts. Try eating it on bread with salt. Or put a dab each of mascarpone and Gorgonzola on bread or crackers for an improvement on the commercial version called *torta*. In *The World of Cheese*, the late Evan Jones described mascarpone in the Trieste region being given something like the Liptauer cheese treatment (page 303). This sounds like a wonderful avenue to explore.

YIELD: About 2½ to 3 cups mascarpone, 1 to ½ cups whey
(Proportions will vary with the milkfat content of the cream.)

1 quart nonultrapasteurized cream, either all light cream or equal
   amounts of half-and-half and heavy cream
½ teaspoon citric acid (see above)

You will need a double boiler or an equivalent arrangement such as a stainless-steel bowl fitted over a saucepan of water. Start the water warming over medium-low heat. Pour the cream into the top part or bowl and let it slowly heat to about 185°F, checking the temperature at intervals on an instant-read thermometer.

When the temperature reaches 185°F, turn off the heat. Stir in the citric acid and let stand until you see the cream turning decidedly thicker. If this doesn't happen, very gently stir in another pinch of citric acid.

Have ready a colander lined with tight-woven cheesecloth or a large cotton handkerchief, set over a large bowl. Carefully pour the contents of the top vessel into the colander, and let drain until the whey is barely dripping. Refrigerate the colander arrangement for 8 to 12 hours—having, I hope, first removed anything smelly from the refrigerator.

Turn the mascarpone out into a mixing bowl and beat it smooth with a wooden spoon before packing it into a clean container. It will keep, tightly covered, for 4 to 5 days in the refrigerator.

NEW ENGLANDISH CLAM CHOWDER

Any claim to present an "authentic" New England clam chow-der is a sure way to start a fight about a dish that has had some serious career changes over the years. Today we all associate it with a soul-satisfying hot milk–based soup enriched with salt pork and full of clams and potatoes. But American chowder in general—the word "chowder" probably comes from a Norman-Breton fish soup called *chaudrée* and the idea seems to go back to eighteenth-century English, French, and North American coast dwellers—seems not to have started off as either a milk-based soup or a soup at all.

Early versions suggest a one-pot meal made by arranging layers of sliced salt pork, cut-up fish, and ship's biscuits (for thickening) in a pot with some seasoning like onion, adding enough water to cover the ingredients, and simmering the whole thing for an hour until the elements melded into a hearty dish. In the course of the nineteenth century two innovations appeared: the addition of potatoes to the layered ingredients and, starting around the middle of the century, the use of milk to replace all or part of the water— eventually, enough milk to convert the dish into a soup.

I would guess that milk came into the picture in this dish—as it did in much of our cooking—along with the nineteenth-century rise of a specialized dairy industry in the northeastern United States. In any event, the layering idea gradually disappeared along with the ship's biscuit; New Englanders came to understand "chowder" as a soup made of milk; and the hand-cranked meat grinders that appeared in many households after about 1880 were called into play to grind up the salt pork, onions, and clams before they went into the pot. Awful things happened a few generations after that, eventually leading to the sort of restaurant incarnation that may be almost any hot soup with a clam or two, enough milk to make it white, and enough flour and potatoes to make it nearly solid enough to walk on.

My favorite clam chowder is simply the kind that was considered old-fashioned in my youth. It should have a certain rockbound plainness; I like it more milky than creamy, and innocent of any seasonings fancier than maybe a bay leaf or some thyme. I thicken it with nothing but the potatoes. If you feel strongly about having it thicker, make up 2 to 3 teaspoons of beurre manié (see page 254), whisk it into the hot milk, and cook for a couple of minutes until it thickens.

YIELD: About 6 servings

30 large hardshell clams (quahogs or chowder clams)
2 ounces salt pork, cut into matchstick-sized pieces
1 large onion, cut into medium-sized dice
2 large potatoes (I prefer a mealy type), peeled and cut into medium-large dice
1 cup whole milk
1 cup cream, either all half-and-half or part half-and-half and part heavy cream
Freshly ground pepper to taste
Minced parsley for garnish

Shuck the clams or have them shucked by the fishmonger; save the liquor. Rinse away any grit, coarsely chop the clams, and strain the liquor through a cheesecloth-lined strainer.

Put the salt pork in a small soup kettle or large, deep saucepan over medium heat to render out the fat. Cook for 8 to 10 minutes, stirring occasionally, until browned and crisp but not burnt. Scoop the fried bits out of the hot fat and drain on paper towels.

Add the onion to the fat and sauté it over medium heat, stirring occasionally, until translucent. Add the diced potatoes and the strained liquor from the clams. Bring to a boil and cook over medium heat until the potatoes are almost soft enough to disintegrate, about 15 minutes. Mash the potatoes slightly with a wooden spoon (most should still be intact; some will half-dissolve into the cooking liquid).

Heat the milk and cream to a boil and simmer a couple of minutes over very low heat. Add the chopped clams, let the milk return to a boil, and pour it over the potatoes in the soup pot. Taste the chowder for seasoning and add a few grindings of pepper (it probably won't need salt). Serve at once, garnished with minced parsley and the reserved salt-pork bits.

CREAM OF TOMATO SOUP

Real cream of tomato soup isn't worth making with anything but dead-ripe, sweet, juicy local tomatoes in season. Even good canned tomatoes will lack the right summery sprightliness. If a batch of tomatoes is a little wan-flavored, I sometimes resort to a small dollop or two of homemade tomato paste or a combination of regular and sun-dried tomato paste.

Cream may curdle, though not as badly as milk, when heated with an acid solution such as tomato broth unless the mixture is stabilized with some kind of starch. A small amount of beurre manié does the trick here.

YIELD: About 7 cups

3 tablespoons unsalted butter
6 to 7 shallots, coarsely chopped
7 to 8 very ripe, juicy medium-sized tomatoes (about $3\frac{2}{3}$ pounds), well rinsed
1 cup heavy cream
1 cup (or to taste) well-flavored chicken, beef, veal, or vegetable stock
2 to 3 teaspoons beurre manié (page 254)
1 teaspoon salt, or to taste
1 to $1\frac{1}{2}$ tablespoons tomato paste (optional, see above)
A pinch of sugar (optional)
Minced scallions, chives, or parsley for garnish

Melt the butter in a medium-sized saucepan over medium heat; when it foams and sizzles, add the shallots and sauté until translucent and tender. Cut the tomatoes into wedges, add to the pan, and simmer, covered, until they are swimming in their own juice, 20 to 25 minutes.

While the tomatoes are cooking, bring the cream to a boil in a small saucepan and let it reduce over low heat to about ½ cup. Heat the stock in another saucepan.

Pour the cooked tomatoes, with their juice, into a heatproof bowl, then work them through a food mill into the pot they cooked in. Discard the skins and seeds. Heat the purée just to a boil and add the hot stock. Whisk the beurre manié into the reduced cream, then whisk into the soup along with the salt; cook just until slightly thickened. Taste for seasoning. If you think it needs a little enrichment or some softening of the acid, add a dollop of tomato paste or, as a last resort, a pinch of sugar. Serve hot, garnishing each serving with a little minced scallion, chives, or parsley.

APPLE-ONION CREAM SOUP

Cream soups are best when they have something more than creaminess going for them. A good cold-weather example is this robust sweet-tart combination of apples—use a good local fall variety in season—and onions with some crisp bacon for counterpoint. It's best when made with a strong, full-flavored beef broth.

YIELD: 8 to 9 cups

4 to 6 thick slices of bacon, coarsely diced
3 to 4 tart, juicy apples, pared, quartered, cored, and coarsely diced
4 tablespoons butter
4 large onions, coarsely diced
3 cups good beef broth, or as needed
6 to 8 whole allspice berries, lightly bruised
1 cup heavy cream
1 teaspoon salt, or to taste
Freshly ground black pepper
A dash of lemon juice (optional)
1 teaspoon caraway seeds, lightly bruised (optional)

Cook the bacon slowly in a heavy skillet to render out all the fat. When it is crisp, scoop it out of the fat and drain on paper towels. Sauté the diced apples over medium heat in the same skillet, stirring occasionally, until cooked through. Scoop out a few spoonfuls of the apples for garnish and set aside.

Melt the butter in a large heavy saucepan. When it foams and sizzles, add the chopped onions and sauté very patiently over low heat, stirring frequently, for 15 to 20 minutes, until the onions are well softened and starting to brown. Scoop out a few spoonfuls for garnish and set aside with the reserved apples. Add the rest of the apples to the onions, pour in the broth, add the allspice, and simmer until everything is nearly dissolved, 10 to 15 minutes.

Fish out and discard the allspice. Purée the soup in batches in a blender or food processor, making sure to leave the texture slightly coarse. Return the soup to the pot, heat to a boil, and stir in the cream. Let it come to a boil again, add the salt and a grinding of pepper, and taste for seasoning; if it seems too bland, squeeze in a little lemon juice. If it is too thick for your taste, thin it with some hot water. Serve garnished with the reserved bacon, apple, and onion. I like a scattering of caraway seed as well.

VICHYSSOISE

Chilled cream soups do not go back very far in the annals of either French or American gastronomy. Before modern refrigeration, the whole business of chilling food at any season but winter was expensive, difficult, and almost wholly reserved for fancy aspics and ice creams. *Crème vichyssoise glacée*, the best-known chilled cream soup of the twentieth century, saw the light of day in or around 1917 as a summer cooler, the international hybrid offspring of a simple French leek-and-potato soup and a developing American enthusiasm for new dishes based on refrigeration technology. The soup's inventor was Louis Diat, chef at the Ritz-Carlton Hotel in New York, who designed his brainchild for the summer menu of the hotel's rooftop-garden restaurant and named it for the city of Vichy, close to his Bourbonnais home.

The idea struck a chord with American cooks and diners. Recipes for Diat-inspired vichyssoise had been published even before he officially set down his version in the 1941 *Cooking à la Ritz*. The new soup became the prototype of innumerable chilled puréed concoctions that people kept "discovering" over at least the next thirty years; *Gourmet* magazine's mailbox was regularly filled with readers' offers to share family improvisations on the theme (puréed cooked something, mixed with a lot of cream and served ice cold) using any vegetable from asparagus to zucchini. Electric blenders made it possible to invent more elaborate mixtures—there is no telling how many people independently stumbled on "Fishyssoise"—at the push of a button.

But strange to say, or perhaps not so strange, the taste for these voluptuous imaginings never spread far beyond the United States. Vichyssoise and the rest remained far outside mainstream French preferences. The cautious embrace of vichyssoise in Elizabeth David's *French Provincial Cooking* seems to depend on toning down the general milk-and-cream content of the original—and no one could possibly question David's credentials as a cream lover. It strikes me as significant that chilled soups freighted with heavy cream became synonymous with American gourmet cooking at just the time that honest-tasting unhomogenized whole milk with its intrinsically creamy quality was disappearing from the American table. Part of what filled the vacuum was cream, with sometimes good but often regrettable results.

By my lights, the fall from grace that cold cream soups underwent a few decades back was not wholly unmerited. But vichyssoise as made by Diat was certainly the best of them, a genuinely pleasant soup that doesn't deserve the "updates" or "makeovers" or "tweakings" commonly visited on it in recent years. A few points have to be kept in mind if it is to taste like anything:

1. Being thick and heavy by nature, it doesn't need to be drowned in superrich cream. Diat calls for much more stock or water, milk (meaning unhomogenized whole milk), and "medium cream" (I use light cream or rich half-and-half) than heavy cream.
2. The potatoes should have plenty of mealiness and flavor.
3. Because it is served very cold, it needs a lot of salt.

I don't see how Diat's straightforward cold soup can be improved on, unless by a dash of acid such as lemon juice or good wine vinegar. My puréeing device of choice is a hand-turned food mill, though the original uses just a strainer. This amount, which according to Diat ought to serve eight, seems more suitable for ten or twelve, since it makes about 3 quarts. The recipe can easily be halved.

4 leeks, white part only, sliced thin
1 medium onion, sliced thin
2 ounces unsalted butter
5 medium potatoes, peeled and sliced thin
1 quart water or chicken broth
1 tablespoon salt
2 cups milk
2 cups light cream or half-and-half
1 cup heavy cream

Melt the butter in a medium saucepan, add the leeks and onion, and sauté gently until scarcely browned. Add the potatoes, water or stock, and salt, and cook over medium-low heat until the potatoes are tender, about 35 to 40 minutes. Put the mixture through a food mill set over a bowl. Return to the pan and stir in the milk and light cream. Season to taste and bring to a boil before letting cool to room temperature. Stir in the heavy cream and chill thoroughly. Serve very cold, garnished if you like with minced chives.

MILK TOAST

This dish is one of our last remaining links with "soup" in its oldest sense. The word originally meant bread, often toasted stale pieces or the hard crust of a loaf, put to frugal use by being soaked ("sopped") in something wet—water, broth, ale, wine, or milk. The last of these was certainly the most nutritious alternative in many parts of Europe where during bad times some people were lucky to see meat a few times a year. Somehow the "soup" idea was first transferred to the soaking liquid and then reattached to a whole class of liquid dishes minus the sopped bread. Today there are only a few soups that we routinely associate with bread crusts or croutons. And few people would be likely to think of the spoonable breakfast or supper dish called "milk toast"—once routinely fed to nursery-age children and invalids—as having the slightest connection with soup.

Even divorced from its old associations with thrifty medieval foodways, milk toast has its charms. It can be a lesson in the happy affinity of bread and milk; read the milk-toast entry (in which two people revel in a no-pains-spared version at a supremely elegant restaurant) in M. F. K. Fisher's *An Alphabet for Gourmets*. Of course, it can also be dreary beyond belief. The difference is all in the caliber of the two star players. The bread must be firm and nicely toasted, the milk fresh and creamy. Detail-minded cooks used to specify "rich milk." I can't see making it without unhomogenized whole milk from a good small dairy; if that's out of the question, mix homogenized whole milk with a dash of cream or a few dashes of half-and-half. (You can indeed splurge by using nothing but cream, for what used to be called "cream toast.")

Here is the general idea: You will first need some fresh hot toast, from slightly stale bread. (Give coarse, hearty bread a day or two to acquire the right texture; let fine-textured, dainty bread stand overnight.) Allow about as much toast per serving as one greedy person might eat for breakfast. I prefer it sliced rather thick and toasted to a good rich brown on both sides. Butter the hot toast on both sides—this keeps it from getting too soggy too fast—and put it in individual serving bowls, preferably rather deep ones. Some people tear or cut the toast into bite-sized pieces.

Meanwhile, have some "rich milk" slowly warming in a small saucepan, preferably with a large pinch of salt and a grinding of pepper to each cup. There is a slurpy-is-better school that uses a generous cupful to two substantial slices of toast, and another wing that likes about half that amount, or just enough to be almost absorbed by the toast. When the milk is too hot to stick a finger into, pour it over the toast in the bowls. Serve at once, while the toast has a little bite to it.

VARIATION: Serious milk-toast lovers should investigate a splendidly bold-tasting Balkan counterpart usually called *popara*, enriched with feta cheese. My version is slightly modified from the directions in Maria Kaneva-Johnson's *The Melting Pot: Balkan Food and Cookery*. Crumble an ounce or two of feta cheese into a bowl, cover it with creamy whole milk, and let soak for 30 minutes to an hour. Drain off the milk into a saucepan. Meanwhile, take some robust, slightly stale country-style bread, broken into bite-sized pieces, and divide it among four ovenproof serving bowls. Dot the surface with bits of butter and heat the bread in a preheated moderate (300°F) oven for about 20 minutes. Briefly scald the milk, with or without a little sugar. (The proportions, by the way, should be such that the milk will be almost completely absorbed by the bread.) Scatter the drained cheese over the bread in each bowl and pour the hot milk over it. If desired, sprinkle a dash of Hungarian or Turkish paprika over each serving.

"WHITE SAUCE" OR SAUCE BÉCHAMEL MAIGRE

Milk sauces thickened with flour did not become common in European cooking until the eighteenth century. After that, however, they took a sharp upturn paralleling the rise of modern dairying and modern flour milling. By the turn of the twentieth century, milk sauces overshadowed other kinds in most middle-class American and English kitchens. When up-to-date cooks of Fannie Farmer's era thought of "sauce," milk-based white sauce was what they most often had in mind.

Standard white sauces of a century ago usually involved either a briefly cooked mix of flour and butter with milk added, or a slurry of flour (or starch) and cold milk that thickened in cooking. With small variations like the addition of tomato or egg yolk, they could be rechristened by many other names. Similar mixtures were the base of cream soups. When made very thick, they were the starting point for croquettes.

After the 1970s, white sauces as a class were largely relegated to the culinary Hall of Shame, an understandable fate in view of what most of them had come to taste like by midcentury. But we should not forget that butter was generally more buttery and milk creamier during the first heyday of white sauces in American kitchens. In other words, they weren't necessarily as insipid as they would become. And the founding white sauce that gave birth to them wasn't insipid at all. It was the French béchamel, a sauce that demanded scrupulous, thoughtful attention and judgment. A true béchamel must be cooked a long time with extreme delicacy so that it stays white instead of browning; at the same time, it develops real flavor of its own.

The béchamel version that became classic, after being championed by Carême in the early nineteenth century, used a rich mixture of cream and an elaborate, painstakingly reduced meat stock as the liquid. A little later, milk came in as a substitute in the version called *sauce béchamel maigre. Maigre,* meaning "lean," designates dishes that are meatless or otherwise suitable for Fridays, fast days, and Lent, when nothing on the table is supposed to be *grasse*—non-"lean," or meat-based. (The word means literally "fat," or "fatty.") The family of modern American white sauces originated as short-cut versions of béchamel maigre.

Béchamel grasse has nearly vanished today, even in France, but I would recommend the following version of béchamel maigre to anyone willing to put a little more time and effort than usual into white sauce. Admirers of Madame E. Saint-Ange's noble twentieth-century cooking manual will recognize that my version is adapted from hers.

(A parenthetical note: To reconstruct a decent if not super-ambitious béchamel grasse, replace the milk with any preferred combination of stock and cream—nonultrapasteurized, it should go without saying. To get closest to the spirit of the original, use a rich veal stock.)

YIELD: About 2 cups

The few simple enrichments and aromatics given here make all the difference between a subtly flavored sauce and what critics not unjustly call "library paste."

1 small onion or half onion
1 small carrot or half carrot
A bit of celery stalk
A few parsley stems

A few mushroom trimmings
¼ cup unsalted butter
A few scraps of dry-cured country ham or prosciutto (optional)
3 generous cups whole milk (preferably unhomogenized)
¼ cup flour
1 bay leaf
1 to 2 sprigs of fresh thyme, or a large pinch of dried thyme
Salt and freshly ground white or black pepper to taste
Freshly grated nutmeg

Chop the onion, carrot, and celery into medium-fine dice. Coarsely cut up the parsley stems and mushroom trimmings.

Melt half the butter in a small heavy saucepan over low heat. Add the onion, carrot, celery, parsley, and mushroom and optional ham scraps. Cook, stirring, for 8 to 10 minutes, being careful not to let the vegetables brown. Scrape out the sautéed aromatics into a bowl and melt the rest of the butter in the same pan over very gentle heat. Meanwhile, heat the milk just to boiling in another small, heavy saucepan.

Add the flour to the butter and cook over low heat, stirring gently, until the mixture is smooth. It must not brown. Whisk in the hot milk. Return the sautéed aromatics to the pan and add the bay leaf, thyme, salt, pepper, and a discreet grating of nutmeg. Bring the sauce to a boil. Simmer, uncovered, over low heat for 30 to 40 minutes, stirring occasionally. The sauce should become somewhat thicker than heavy cream, without sticking or browning on the bottom.

Pour the sauce through a mesh sieve into another pot or heatproof container, gently pressing with a spoon to extract as much liquid as possible from the cooked vegetables without getting any of the pulp. It is now ready for use. If it has to stand for a while, melt a little more butter over the surface to keep it from forming a skin; reheat very gently, stirring, over a heat-deflector such as a Flame Tamer. (Alternatively, put it in the top of a double boiler and reheat over hot water.)

AJÍ DE LECHE
(VENEZUELAN MILK-CHILE INFUSION)

A*jí* is Caribbean and South American Spanish for "chile peppers," as well as the name for various sauces or infusions based
on them—for instance, this Venezuelan table sauce made with
milk, to which I was introduced by the endlessly knowledgeable
Maricel Presilla. Maricel loves it with fish. I could eat it with nearly
anything. Like the little experiment with smoked fish or onion on
page 77, it is an object lesson in how milk absorbs and transforms
strong, penetrating flavors. (Do not expect the consistency to
resemble a chunky salsa; it will be as thin as milk.)

By all means save the puréed chile-herb mixture after straining
off the infused milk. It will keep for a few days in the refrigerator,
tightly covered, and makes a wonderful addition to anything from
cream cheese to cornbread batter. See Spicy-Milky Peanut Sauce
(page 105) for another excellent use.

YIELD: About 3 cups

4 small green or red hot chiles (habaneros, Scotch bonnets, jalapeños,
   or any preferred combination of different kinds)
2 to 3 scallions, cleaned and trimmed
2 garlic cloves
About ¼ cup cilantro leaves stripped from stems
3 cups whole milk
1 to 2 teaspoons salt

Stem and seed the chiles; coarsely chop them with the scallions and garlic. Put
them in a blender or food processor with the cilantro and about half a cup of
the milk; process to a purée, turn off the motor, and add the salt with the rest
of the milk. Pour the mixture through a medium-mesh strainer into a bowl,
pressing hard to extract every last bit of milk from the puréed aromatics. Store
the infused milk in the refrigerator, tightly covered, for up to 4 to 5 days, and
serve as a table sauce with any kind of simply cooked meats, fish, or vegetables.

SPICY-MILKY PEANUT SAUCE

Here is a bit of lagniappe for anyone with a batch of the above Ají de Leche and the leftover seasonings used to make the heady milk infusion. You can use it as anything from a dip to a noodle sauce. It also makes a great dressing for cold chicken or potatoes, and can profitably be substituted for tahini in pita sandwiches.

The exact proportions don't matter. It can be thickish or thinnish, tame or blazing hot. You will find that peanuts vary in their ability to absorb water and oil.

YIELD: About 2½ cups

8 ounces peanuts, dry-roasted or oil-roasted
¼ to ½ cup Ají de Leche (See preceding recipe.)
¼ to ½ cup any preferred vegetable oil
½ to 1 teaspoon salt
1 to 3 tablespoons puréed seasoning mixture from Ají de Leche

Put the peanuts in a food processor and grind briefly, stopping before they start to form peanut butter. Add ¼ cup each of Ají de Leche and oil. Process the mixture to a coarse paste; if it's too heavy for the blades, add more milk sauce and oil a little at a time until the texture is slightly thinner than peanut butter. Add ½ teaspoon salt and 1 tablespoon of the puréed aromatic mixture; taste for seasoning and work in as much more of each as you like.

The sauce will keep in the refrigerator, tightly covered, for about a week.

PAN GRAVY WITH CREAM

This is the sauce of sauces for any meat browned in a skillet or roasting pan. It's like a tiny flavor blossom in the mouth and is meant to be dished out by the spoonful, not the cupful.

Cream-enriched pan gravy is another of those pleasures that almost defy recipes. But here is the simplest possible outline of the process as applied to any basic pan-broiled meat. You might choose loin lamb chops for an example—or steaks or hamburgers or "lamburgers."

I will assume that you already know how to pan-cook the meat in a heavy skillet—NOT nonstick—so as to brown it well on all sides without extreme charring. Remove the finished meat to a warmed platter. If a lot of fat has rendered out of the meat, simply pour it off. Immediately splash a little water into the hot pan. Forget exact measurements. Every case is different. Anything close to half a cup for a medium-sized skillet or a little more for a large one will do. You can use wine (any kind you like) or stock (ditto) instead of water, but the principle is the same. Turn up the heat to medium-high. With a wooden spoon or spatula, start "deglazing"—that is, scraping up all the browned bits from the pan so that they can melt back into the liquid. Try to be thorough, but fast. Turn down the heat a little if it's bubbling away too fast to keep up with, but not so much as to discourage the liquid from reducing by more than half and forming a rich brown glaze.

Now add about as much heavy cream as the amount of water you started with. Stirring rapidly, let it reduce in the same way, but stop while it is still pourable. Pour the sauce over the meat and serve at once.

What you have just done is to superimpose a reduction on a reduction—slightly concentrated cream amalgamated with a concentrated solution made from everything that initially caramelized and sizzled as the meat juices met the heat of the pan. The same technique, on a larger scale, can be applied to the pan glazes or drippings of any meat or poultry—even a Thanksgiving turkey, if you share my opinion that a smidgin of this precious substance is better than a bucketful of anything else.

CHHENNA AND PANIR

As I've explained, milk coagulated through the addition of acid at a high temperature isn't really cheese. But it is the only cheeselike food that took root on the Indian subcontinent, or at least parts of it. (The taboo against "breaking" milk into curd and whey—see page 17—prevented its acceptance everywhere.) And it has been greeted with great enthusiasm in the United States. I have even found frozen supermarket versions in New Jersey.

If you tried your hand at "White Magic" Exercise 4 on page 67, you've already seen acid coagulation at work. Larger batches involve just the same principle: Bring milk to a boil and while it is still hot, add some acid ingredient that makes it at once break into a mass of fluffy curds floating in whey. Once the major part of the whey is drained, you hang up the curd in a cloth to drain or press it under a weight. Chhenna is what you get if you stop at a fairly soft, moist stage and leave the curd in a mass. Taken to a firmer, more thoroughly drained stage it is panir, which is most often added to sauces in sliced or cubed form after a light browning in ghee or oil.

In India, the curd for chhenna and panir is usually coagulated with citrus juice or commercial citric-acid crystals. There are various other possibilities, including whey saved from a previous batch, sour whey drained from yogurt, or yogurt itself. (Vinegar would also do the job, but it is scarcely used in any Indian region but Goa.) Since judging necessary amounts of whey or yogurt takes some experience, I have given directions using only lemon or lime juice. You can easily double the recipes, using the ratio of 2 tablespoons juice per quart of milk. Whole milk (homogenized or unhomogenized) gives the best results.

CHHENNA

YIELD: About 8 ounces (1 cup) chhenna, 7 cups whey

2 quarts milk
¼ cup freshly squeezed lemon or lime juice

Pour the milk into a heavy-bottomed 4-quart saucepan. Bring to a boil over high heat, stirring to keep the bottom from scorching. When it starts boiling up in earnest, remove from the heat and promptly strain the lemon or lime juice into the milk, stirring it in gently. The milk should rapidly separate into clouds of white curd in a sea of greenish-yellow whey. (If this doesn't happen, add another spritz of juice.) Let stand for 8 to 10 minutes.

Line a strainer or colander with tight-woven cheesecloth or other clean cotton cloth, set it over a deep bowl, and use a skimmer or shallow ladle to carefully lift out the larger clumps of curd into the cloth. Very gently pour in the whey with the remaining curd.

Let drain for a few minutes. Tie the corners of the cloth into a bag. Holding the bag by the tied corners, briefly rinse the curd under cold running water to remove a little of the lemon taste. Gently squeeze the bag in your hands to press out some of the water. Now you can either hang it up to drain further until it is a little softer than cream cheese (usually about 1½ to 2 hours; suspend it on the kitchen faucet or a wooden spoon set over a deep bowl) or speed the process as follows: Flatten the bag of curd into a rough disc or rectangle, put it on a plate, and cover it with another plate. Place a weight (a heavy can, a couple of large beach pebbles) on the top plate and let stand for about 30 minutes, periodically draining off any overflow. It can then be used as is, but will be easier to work with if you cream it with a large wooden spoon in a bowl or with the heel of your hand on a flat work surface. Imagining that you are creaming butter for a cake or putting a *pâte brisée* through the stage called *fraisage*, work the cheese very, very smooth a little at a time. If you are not using it at once, pack it into a container and refrigerate, tightly covered. It is extremely perishable and should be used within 3 to 4 days.

PANIR

YIELD: About 8 ounces panir, 7 cups whey

2 quarts milk
¼ cup freshly squeezed lemon or lime juice
2 tablespoons ghee (page 251) or vegetable oil

Follow the directions for chhenna to the stage of draining or pressing. The cheese should now be drained for 4 to 5 hours or pressed for 1 to 2 hours, until firm enough to be cut with a knife. Shape it into a block roughly 4 by 4 inches and cut into approximately 1-inch cubes with a heavy sharp knife. It will be both firmer and more flavorful with a quick browning: Heat the ghee in a heavy medium skillet, either nonstick or very well seasoned (panir sticks tenaciously to most pan surfaces). Add the cubes of panir and cook, stirring and turning constantly, until they are golden brown on all sides. Scoop out of the hot fat to drain on paper towels until cooled to room temperature. Store as for chhenna and plan to use within 3 to 4 days.

VEGETARIAN MALAI KOFTA

This is a name that I have never really figured out. "Kofta" refers to meatballs or meatball-shaped things like dumplings and croquettes. "Malai" ought to indicate that thick cream is involved, but many dishes labeled "malai kofta" haven't a smidgin of cream. Be that as it may, Indian restaurants in this country regularly attach the name to a vegetarian dish of meatless croquettes in a creamy sauce with Mughlai touches—that is, real or fancied borrowings from the Moghul conquerors of India, usually including nuts and sweet dried fruits. The versions I like best are based on chhenna, the slightly moister cousin of panir. Usually the cheese is bound with potatoes or chickpea flour and shaped around a dab of fruit and nut filling before being dipped in a simple batter of chickpea flour and water and deep-fried in oil or ghee.

The sauce is made separately and can take many different forms. I'm partial to one with onions, cream, yogurt, and a mixture of finely ground nuts—this last closely copied from the "Fragrant Masala with Nuts" in Neelam Batra's inexhaustibly rich *1,000 Indian Recipes*. It is complex enough to be best made in stages.

YIELD: About 4 large servings as a vegetarian main dish

FOR THE SAUCE:
12 to 15 green cardamom pods
4 to 5 black cardamom pods
½ teaspoon ground cinnamon
½ teaspoon black peppercorns
2 to 3 whole cloves
1 tablespoon raw cashews
1 tablespoon pistachios
1 tablespoon almonds
4 to 6 quarter-sized slices of peeled fresh ginger, coarsely chopped
1 to 2 long green chiles, stemmed, seeded, and coarsely chopped
3 to 4 garlic cloves, coarsely chopped
3 to 5 tablespoons ghee (page 251) or vegetable oil
½ teaspoon cumin seeds
½ teaspoon Indian brown mustard seeds
8 to 10 fresh curry leaves
3 medium onions, chopped
2 to 3 ripe plum tomatoes or 1 large globe tomato, peeled, seeded, and finely chopped
1½ teaspoons salt, or to taste
Any chopped fruits and nuts left over from stuffing the croquettes (see below)

FOR THE CROQUETTES:
12 ounces chhenna (page 107; use 3 quarts milk)
About 1 tablespoon each raw cashews, pistachios, and/or almonds
1 scant tablespoon golden raisins
1 or 2 Turkish sweet dried apricots (optional)
1 to 2 teaspoons salt
1 medium-large potato, all-purpose or waxy
¾ cup Indian chickpea flour (usually labeled "besan" or "gram flour")
A large pinch each of ground cumin and ground coriander (optional)
Vegetable oil for frying
Cilantro for garnish

To make the sauce, remove the seeds from the cardamom pods. Put the cardamom seeds, cinnamon, peppercorns, and cloves in a small heavy skillet and roast over medium-low heat, stirring, until the spices are fragrant but not scorched. Remove from the heat and let cool slightly before grinding everything to a fine powder in an electric coffee or spice grinder.

Put the nuts in the same skillet and roast over medium-low heat, stirring frequently, until they are fragrant and lightly browned. Remove from the heat and let cool to room temperature before grinding to a powder in a mini–food processor. Combine the ground spices and nuts in a small bowl and set aside. (This nut masala mix can be prepared a week or several days ahead; store in the refrigerator, tightly covered.)

Mince the ginger, chiles, and garlic together almost to a paste. Heat 3 tablespoons of the ghee or oil until fragrant and rippling in a deep heavy skillet. Add the cumin, mustard seeds, and curry leaves and cook, stirring, for a few seconds. Add the minced ginger mixture, and let it sizzle briefly before you add the onions. Cook, stirring frequently, over medium-high heat until the onions are softened, about 15 minutes.

Let everything cool slightly and process to a coarse paste in a blender or food processor. Add the tomatoes and nut masala, and process briefly.

Rinse out and dry the skillet. Add the remaining 1 to 2 tablespoons ghee or oil, and heat over medium-high heat until fragrant and rippling. Add the sauce, which should sizzle vigorously. Cook, stirring frequently, until you see the fat beginning to separate from the sauce, 20 to 25 minutes.

Remove from the heat and let cool. The sauce can be prepared to this point several hours ahead and reheated while the croquettes are being fried. If you have any leftover fruit and nut filling, add it to the sauce in reheating.

For the croquettes: Make the chhenna and work it smooth; see page 107.

Coarsely chop together the nuts, raisins, and optional dried apricots.

Boil the potato until tender in plenty of salted water; peel while still warm, and grate the flesh on the coarse side of a box grater. Add the potato and ½ to 1 teaspoon salt to the chhenna and work it with your hands into a soft dough.

Lightly oil your hands and a couple of plates. Divide the chhenna-potato dough into 8 equal-sized portions. Roll each into a ball between your palms, then pat it into a disc about 2½ inches across and set it on a plate. Place about a teaspoon of the nut-fruit mixture in the center of each disc. Gently fold up the edges, and reshape it into a ball enclosing the filling; roll smooth between your palms. Set the filled croquettes on a plate.

Sift the chickpea flour into a bowl with the remaining ½ to 1 teaspoon salt and optional cumin and coriander. Add a large dash of vegetable oil and ⅔ cup water, and whisk to make a smooth batter.

Reheat the sauce if it has cooled, dumping in any unused fruit-nut mixture.

Pour oil into a wok, Indian *kadhai*, or deep skillet to a depth of about 1½ to 2 inches, and heat to about 350°F. Immerse half the croquettes in the batter; lift out with a skimmer and quickly add them to the hot oil. Fry, turning several times, until they are golden brown on all sides, and lift out to drain on a plate lined with paper towels. Repeat with the remaining croquettes. Slide the croquettes into the hot sauce and let warm through for a minute. Arrange the croquettes and sauce in a serving dish, garnish with a little cilantro, and serve at once. Steamed basmati rice is an ideal accompaniment.

SAAG PANIR OR PALAK PANIR

When Indian restaurants began multiplying in the United States during the 1970s, one of the quickest hits with diners everywhere was a northern-style dish called *saag panir* or *palak panir* that has now become as all-American as spring rolls or shish kebab. It consists of panir cubes—eclectically minded cooks are known to substitute firm tofu or drained pressed ricotta—in a sauce of chopped or puréed leafy greens. "Palak" is Hindi for "spinach"; "saag" can be any kind of leafy greens. The faintly nutty blandness of the panir marvelously contrasts with and complements the slight bitterness of spinach or the more assertive character of Swiss chard, collard greens, or any other greens you care to experiment with.

There are no rules about the composition of the sauce. Anything goes—greens or spinach creamed or simply tossed in a little hot oil or ghee with a few quasi-Indian seasonings, or sumptuous presentations of puréed greens simmered in a "wet" (saucelike) masala and flavored with a dry masala (spice mixture). My version is neither more nor less "authentic" than a hundred others.

YIELD: About 5 to 6 servings as a vegetarian main dish

12 ounces chhenna (page 107), made with 3 quarts of milk and
⅓ cup of lemon or lime juice
6 tablepoons ghee (page 251) or vegetable oil
2 pounds fresh spinach or other preferred leafy greens, or two 10-ounce
packages frozen leaf (not chopped) spinach or greens, thawed
4 to 5 quarter-sized slices of fresh peeled ginger, coarsely chopped
1 long green chile or 2 small hot green chiles, stemmed, seeded, and
coarsely chopped
2 garlic cloves, coarsely chopped

A large pinch each of cumin seeds and Indian brown mustard seeds
(optional)

1 medium onion, chopped

1 ripe medium tomato, peeled, seeded, and chopped (optional)

1 teaspoon salt, or to taste

⅛ to 1 teaspoon (or to taste) garam masala (any preferred homemade or
commercial blend)

½ to ¾ cup well-drained creamy plain yogurt

½ to ¾ cup heavy cream

Make the chhenna as directed. Press it firm, cut into cubes, and brown in
3 tablespoons of ghee or oil, following the directions for panir on page 108.

Rinse fresh spinach or greens very zealously to remove the last trace of grit
or sand. Shake off a little of the water, put it in a large heavy-lidded saucepan,
and cook, tightly covered, over high heat just long enough to wilt the leaves,
3 to 4 minutes. Frozen spinach or greens can be used as soon as thawed. In
either case, drain off excess liquid and squeeze as dry as possible between your
hands. Pick over the spinach to remove the coarser stems. Chop it very fine
with a heavy sharp knife. (You can roughly purée it in a food processor, but first
chop through the stems in several places to keep them from wrapping around
the spindle.)

Mince together the ginger, chile, and garlic until they are almost a paste.
Heat the remaining 3 tablespoons of ghee or oil until rippling in a large deep
skillet or medium saucepan. Add the optional cumin and mustard seeds. When
the seeds start to pop, add the minced ginger paste, let it sizzle for 10 to 20 seconds, and add the onion. Cook uncovered over medium heat, stirring frequently, until the onion is well cooked, about 15 to 20 minutes. Add the
optional tomato, and cook for another few minutes before stirring in the
spinach and salt. Add the garam masala in any amount you prefer, from a large
pinch to more than a teaspoon. Cook uncovered, stirring frequently, about
20 to 25 minutes, or until the spinach and onion have formed a dense, fragrant
sauce and the fat is beginning to separate.

Add the panir to the sauce and let heat through. Gently but thoroughly stir
in ½ cup each of thick drained yogurt and heavy cream. Check the consistency
and add a little more of one or both if desired. Serve with plain steamed basmati (or other) rice.

"CORN KEES"
(GUJARATI STOVETOP CORN PUDDING)

This pretty dish originally came from a small Indian paperback, *100 Easy-to-Make Gujarati Dishes* by Veena Shroff and Vanmala Desai. Our corn and watery milk undoubtedly produce a thinner, sweeter result than the starchy, filling corn and richer milk of India, so I replace some of the milk with cream and add a little starch in the form of wheat flour. To me, corn here seems plenty sweet without the added sugar, but this is a matter of individual taste.

Asafetida, once available only in Indian grocery stores, now turns up in more venues (my local Whole Foods supermarket, for one). It deepens all the other flavors just as the turmeric deepens the color.

Dishes like this are regularly made with either cows' (or buffaloes') milk or coconut milk; in both cases the milk brings out the "corny" quality of the corn. In a pinch you can substitute three 10-ounce packages of frozen corn kernels, first giving the corn a very short spin in a blender or food processor to bring out the juice while leaving the texture coarse.

YIELD: 4 to 6 servings as main dish, 7 to 8 as side dish

6 large ears of corn, shucked and cleaned
6 small hot green chiles (any preferred kind)
A 1-inch chunk of fresh ginger, peeled
3 tablespoons ghee (page 251) or vegetable oil
¼ teaspoon Indian brown mustard seeds
1 tablespoon flour (optional)
1½ cups milk and cream, combined in any preferred ratio
   (I use 1¼ cups milk and ¼ cup heavy cream)
1 to 2 teaspoons salt, or to taste
2 teaspoons sugar
A pinch of ground asafetida
½ teaspoon ground turmeric
Juice of 1 lemon
Minced cilantro for garnish

Cut and scrape the corn kernels from the ears with a sharp knife.

Chop the chiles (deseeded if you prefer) and ginger together until they are almost a paste.

CORN KEES (CONT.)

Heat the ghee or oil in a deep wide skillet or sauté pan and add the mustard seeds. When they start to splutter and pop, add the corn and stir over pretty brisk heat for a few minutes. Add the optional flour, stirring well to eliminate lumps. Add the chile-ginger paste, milk-cream mixture, salt, sugar, asafetida, and turmeric. Cook uncovered over medium heat, stirring frequently, for about 15 minutes. The texture will thicken somewhat if you have used flour and remain a little runny otherwise. Remove from the heat, stir in the lemon juice, and serve garnished with a sprinkling of minced cilantro.

VARIATION: To convert this into Spiced Corn Chowder, omit the flour and use 5 cups of the milk-cream mixture, 8 to 10 chiles, and a 2-inch chunk of ginger. Proceed as directed above, doubling the amount of all other seasonings and making any further adjustments when you taste the soup after it has come to a boil.

IRISH CHAMP
(MASHED POTATOES WITH MILK AND GREENS)

In some parts of the Old World milk or buttermilk was very nearly the only everyday source of protein for poor people until modern times. Ireland, where millions would have starved if the family cow had starved, remained a case in point far later than most parts of England or Europe.

When "Irish potatoes" arrived from the Americas, marriages of milk with the new vegetable proved to be a nutritional blessing to the nation. Supplementing these two ingredients with some green vegetable (usually spring onions or leeks, though young green nettles were also a favorite) put more vitamins into the mix and added a bit of fresh verve. This combination was called "champ," and was a main dish—more accurately, an *only* dish, a meal in itself—on thousands of Irish tables for generations. Like many peasant standbys, it was usually served in one communal bowl that everyone dug into with his own spoon. I think it still makes a fine main dish for a simple meal, though of course no one today commands the services of a small Irish cow giving the excellent milk for which Ireland was once renowned. Anybody who can get good unhomogenized milk should use it here.

The important principle in dishes like champ is that cooking anything oniony in milk creates an entirely different effect from sautéing it in butter. For champ, what you want is not a sautéed flavor but the one that results when the milk is directly infused with an oniony character (the same principle applies if you use some other kind of greens). In this way, the butter that's added at the end will be a fresh touch of luxury not foreshadowed by anything else in the dish.

Use either leeks or scallions, or (if you can get them) the fresh white bulb onions with green stalks still attached that are often sold as "spring onions" or "jumbo scallions." Other possibilities: a large handful of chives, new peas, parsley, or—if you're a field forager—young nettles.

YIELD: About 6 servings (4 as a main dish)

5 to 6 large russet or other mealy (baking-type) potatoes
    (about 1¾ to 2 pounds), peeled and cut into large chunks
2 to 3 small leeks or medium spring onions or 6 large scallions, cleaned
    and trimmed; include an inch or two of the green part (more for
    scallions)
2 cups whole milk, preferably unhomogenized
Salt and freshly ground pepper to taste
4 to 8 tablespoons butter, cut into chunks

Boil the potatoes in salted water until tender. While they are cooking, cut the chosen onion relatives into thin slices. Put them in a small saucepan, pour in the milk, and bring to a simmer. Cook, uncovered, until tender, about 10 to 15 minutes (a little less for scallions). Strain off the milk, return it to the pan, and keep it warm, reserving the onions separately.

Drain the cooked potatoes and briefly return them to the pan over low heat to let them dry out a little, shaking the pan to prevent scorching. Put them in a large, deep bowl, and start mashing with a wooden spoon or potato masher. Mash in the drained onions while adding as much of the hot seasoned milk as the potatoes will absorb without getting soupy (the amount will vary according to the starchiness of the potatoes). Some lumps are all to the good. Season with salt and pepper to taste and serve at once, as hot as possible. Each person makes a well in his or her portion and puts in a lump of butter.

SCALLOPED POTATOES

Scalloped" is a culinary term for which no reasonable definition exists. As far as I understand, it murkily emerged late in the nineteenth century from a welter of antecedent words, including "collop" (a thin, cutletlike slice of meat), "escalope" (the French equivalent), and "scallop" (the mollusk). Many cooks came to apply it to things that were "escaloped" in the sense of being cut into slices, presented in a nice layered or overlapped serving arrangement. By the turn of the twentieth century, "scalloped potatoes" usually meant a sturdy standby made by building up layer on layer of sliced raw potatoes in a dish and baking them, covered with milk, until very tender.

The dish takes well to a little jazzing up with onion and a salty accent like diced ham (a Swedish cousin, "Jansson's Temptation," is liberally seasoned with anchovies). But it really is only as good as the potatoes and the milk; you must remember that it originated in an age when many people dug their own potatoes and attached real meaning to such terms as "rich milk" and "new milk." If you're stuck with supermarket homogenized milk, you might want to replace a little of it with half-and-half or light cream. As for the potatoes, they should be mealy to the nth power. Use a heavy hand with the salt.

A slight soupiness and curdled appearance are perfectly normal for this dish.

YIELD: 6 to 8 servings

4 large mealy-type potatoes (russets—no substitutes)
1 medium or 2 small onions
3 tablespoons flour
4 ounces smoked ham, coarsely diced (optional)
1 tablespoon salt, or to taste
Freshly ground black or white pepper
Minced parsley (optional)
3 to 4 tablespoons butter
1½ cups (or as needed) milk, preferably unhomogenized (you can
    replace about ¼ cup of the milk with half-and-half or light cream)

Preheat the oven to 350°F.
Peel the potatoes and onion and cut into very thin slices. Butter a 2-quart

baking dish, preferably wider than deep, and arrange a layer of potato slices over the bottom. Dust with a little of the flour. Scatter a little of the onion and optional ham over the potatoes; season plentifully with salt, pepper, and the optional parsley and dot with bits of butter. Add another layer of potatoes and continue in the same way, finishing with a layer of potatoes and any remaining butter. Pour enough milk over the potatoes to nearly but not quite cover them; the amount needed will vary with the shape of the baking dish.

Bake, tightly covered with a lid or several layers of aluminum foil, for 40 to 45 minutes. Remove the cover and bake another 35 to 40 minutes, until the milk is nearly absorbed. Let stand for 5 to 10 minutes before serving.

CREAMED SPINACH, MADAME SAINT-ANGE
(ÉPINARDS À LA CRÈME)

Fans of creamed spinach are legion, but they all seem to understand something different by the term, from a little spinach in a lot of white sauce to a lot of spinach with a little reduced cream. Neither of these exactly takes my fancy. I think that for many spinach lovers the following recipe by the great twentieth-century French cookbook-writer E. Saint-Ange will come as a revelation. The main thing that sets it apart from other versions good, bad, or indifferent is adding plenty of butter to the hot spinach *at the last minute* so that it has no time to lose its just-melted suavity.

This is my general take on the sturdy classic with measurements given in standard American units. Experienced cooks will understand that before cooking, the spinach should be rinsed and lightly shaken to remove excess moisture, and that today's equivalent of pushing a pan to the corner of an old-fashioned range is putting it on a burner over very low heat. The ever-methodical Madame Saint-Ange notes, "The cream used here can be replaced by the same amount of milk, reduced by half," and gives estimated total preparation time as "one and a quarter hours, including all prior preparations."

(For anyone interested in further pursuing the acquaintance of *La Bonne Cuisine de Madame Saint-Ange* I recommend Paul Aratow's complete translation.)

YIELD: 7 to 8 servings

3 to 3½ pounds spinach (gross weight, before trimming)
3 ounces (6 tablespoons) butter
scant 2 tablespoons flour
⅞ cup cream (or 1¾ cups milk, reduced to ⅞ cup)
Salt
Pepper
Nutmeg
Large pinch of granulated sugar

Put about 1 tablespoon of the butter in a medium-size "sauteuse" pan; add the spinach and wilt on high heat, stirring it, for 4 or 5 minutes.

Remove from the heat. Season with: a good pinch of salt; the pinch of granulated sugar; a small pinch of pepper and grated nutmeg. Dust with the flour, mix well, and stir again on the heat for just 2 minutes.

Now add the cream, little by little, and *off the heat*. Next let it come to the boil, stirring continually. Then remove the pan to the corner of the stove. Cover and let it gently simmer for *20 to 30 minutes*. This part of the cooking can also be done in the oven: in that case, place a round of buttered [parchment] paper over the spinach under the lid. Just a few seconds before serving, add to the spinach what you have left of the butter, by small bits. From that moment do not let boil. If the spinach has to wait a little while, it would be best to put off adding the butter, and not to do this until the very [last] moment: otherwise it loses its creamy effect.

[Once the spinach is arranged in a serving dish, Madame Saint-Ange suggests garnishing it with small triangular butter-fried croutons or sprinkling it with 5 to 6 tablespoons of hot cream, seasoned with a small pinch of fine salt.]

Butter Boat

CHINESE "FRIED MILK"

The popular idea that the Chinese have always shunned milk products is quite inaccurate. So is the notion that lactose intolerance accounts for the very widespread modern Chinese dislike of milk, butter, and any dairy product that doesn't come out of a can. The French historian Françoise Sabban exposed these mistakes more than twenty years ago. As she shows, descriptions of milking practices, dairy products, and the use of milk in cooking are routinely found in many sources, including agricultural and culinary treatises from the sixth to the eighteenth century.

Why the dominant Han Chinese ethnic population eventually developed an aversion to the mere idea of tasting milk or butter, and why the use of these foods became almost entirely limited to a few ethnic minorities in the Mongol or Uighur outposts of the empire, are among the great puzzles of history. Certainly the use of cows' milk today is a piece of Westernization that has penetrated very unevenly into Chinese society. But in recent times an intriguing dish called "fried milk" has achieved currency in some of the areas most deeply affected by European contact, chiefly in Kwangtung (Canton) province and Hong Kong. It should not be confused with another local dish of the same name, a dessert made out of a superthick, starchy milk-based custard cut into squares or diamonds and then deep-fried in a batter coating in the same way as its probable inspiration, the Portuguese *leite frito*.

The second or savory kind of "fried milk" slightly resembles *fu yung*, at least the very delicate versions that use only egg whites. It, too, could be described as a custard, but a lightly set savory one made with a combination of milk, egg whites, and a little cornstarch, all stir-fried to the texture of scrambled eggs. When I've had it in Chinatown restaurants, it usually contains crab or shrimp and sometimes is served on a bed of fried cellophane noodles or rice sticks. Browned pine nuts are the usual garnish.

This version of fried milk is great as part of a simple Chinese dinner menu. I've also found that people who won't touch egg yolks with a ten-foot pole like it as a breakfast or brunch dish—especially with the vegetarian substitutions suggested below. It's a useful recipe to know about when you're wondering what to do with a bunch of egg whites after making something like lemon curd or Hollandaise sauce.

I first came across the dish in Ken Hom's fascinating book *Fra-*

grant Harbor Taste, a tribute to the food of Hong Kong, and have followed his recipe for many years with only minor deviations. Hom suggests a combination of fresh and canned evaporated milk. I've also had good results with all fresh milk. Experiment with the recipe to your liking; it seems to work equally well with larger or smaller proportions of milk, egg white, starch, and seafood or meat.

YIELD: 5 to 6 servings

2 tablespoons cornstarch
1 teaspoon salt
1½ to 1¾ cups whole milk (all fresh, or about two parts fresh to one part evaporated)
8 egg whites
4 ounces lump crabmeat or peeled shrimp (whole if small, otherwise diced)
2 to 3 ounces unsmoked Smithfield-style ham, coarsely chopped
A handful of pine nuts
2 to 3 tablespoons peanut oil
Cilantro for garnish

Mix the cornstarch and salt to a smooth paste with a few tablespoons of the milk. Add the remaining milk and egg whites and use a whisk to stir—*not* whip—the mixture until well combined but not quite perfectly blended. Stir in the crabmeat (or shrimp) and ham.

Toast the pine nuts in a small dry skillet, stirring occasionally, until lightly browned. Scoop them out into a bowl before they can scorch.

Heat the oil in a wok over medium-high heat. When it is not quite smoking, pour in the milk–egg white mixture and begin to stir-fry, scooping and scrambling with a spatula (preferably a wok spatula). At first it will be thin and soupy; after a couple of minutes you will notice some thickening on the bottom. Reduce the heat to low and continue to stir-fry for a few minutes longer, until the milk custard has the consistency of scrambled eggs. (Total cooking time is usually about 5 to 6 minutes.) Toward the end it will take on a cheesy consistency and "break," giving up a lot of liquid. Now pour the contents of the wok into a mesh strainer set over a bowl to let the watery part drain off before turning the "fried milk" out into a serving dish. Serve at once, garnished with the toasted pine nuts and a handful of cilantro leaves.

VARIATIONS: You can replace the shellfish and ham with a few ounces of cooked chicken breast, diced or shredded. For a vegetarian version, eliminate the shellfish and ham and substitute a dozen or so dried shiitake mushrooms (soaked in hot water, drained, and coarsely chopped) along with a large handful of scallions or Chinese chives (trimmed and coarsely chopped), slender asparagus tips (blanched or briefly stir-fried), or seeded chopped tomatoes.

RICE PUDDING

Rice puddings exist around the globe in boiled, baked, steamed, and other forms that range from nursery to banquet fare (say, from German *Milchreis* to French *riz à l'impératrice*). We in the West are most familiar with puddings based on whole rice, such as Spanish or Latin American *arroz con leche*, Norwegian *riskrem*, and the eggy kind at American delicatessen counters. But where rice puddings reach even greater glory, from Turkey to India, they are often made with rice flour. This is entirely understandable, since the essence of rice pudding is the alchemy that takes place between the sweetened milk and the starchy or floury part of the rice grain. (The same is true in parts of Southeast Asia where the "milk" in question is coconut milk.)

Of the European- and American-style rice puddings, I always unhesitatingly opt for members of the stovetop branch made without eggs. (Or for that matter, without raisins—I like to put raisins plumped in hot water and a little Scotch *on* the finished pudding, not *in* it.) Nothing is wrong with baked egg-enriched rice puddings, but to me they lack the clean elegance of the ones simmered in a saucepan.

The long-grain rice of American supermarkets can be used in a pinch but really is not starchy enough to suit the purpose. The kinds I recommend are called "short-grain" by some people, "medium-grain" by others, and—just to complete the confusion— "round-grain" by many British pudding lovers. They are starchy, but not as starchy as the varieties used for risotto (arborio, *vialone nano*, etc.). My favorite is *baldo* rice, which is grown in Italy largely for the Turkish market and shows up in Turkish and Greek groceries. I've also had good results with a kind widely sold in Hispanic markets under names like "Valencia" (which it is not) or "Valencia-type."

The reason for fussing over the choice of rice is that you want it to gradually release a certain amount of starch in cooking—just enough to bind the mass of softened grains in a velvety matrix that conveys a sense of creaminess even when you use skim milk. The other important thing to realize is that as regards the amount of rice you're using in proportion to liquid, less is more. It's astonishing how little rice you need for the most beautiful effect. When you use too much, somehow the lovely puddingy consistency never develops to the full and the milk can't really blossom in your mouth. Some old-fashioned recipes used to specify a few tablespoons of rice to a quart of milk. Other versions, like mine, use both water (for precooking the rice) and milk (for completing the cooking).

The best rice pudding I ever made was a happy accident using the leftover milk from a batch of clotted cream (page 89).

YIELD: About 5 to 6 servings

⅔ cup (generous) baldo or other medium-grain rice
1½ cups water
4 cups milk (whole, skim, or any desired percentage)
½ cup sugar
1 teaspoon salt
A 4- to 5-inch piece of vanilla bean
Zest of half a lemon, peeled in long strips
Either a 3-inch piece of cinnamon stick or a generous grating of nutmeg

Put the rice and water in a heavy-bottomed 1½- or 2-quart saucepan, bring to a boil, and cook tightly covered over very low heat for 15 minutes. Don't worry if not all the water is absorbed in that time.

Add the milk and remaining ingredients, stirring to dissolve the sugar. Bring it to a boil, and simmer over medium heat for 45 to 50 minutes, stirring frequently. After about 15 minutes fish out the vanilla bean, slit it lengthwise with a small sharp knife, and scrape out the contents. Return the vanilla bean and seeds to the milk, which will still be very thin. It should begin to thicken slightly in another 15 to 20 minutes. Keep stirring vigilantly as more of the starch dissolves out. The pudding is done when it has a creamy, full-bodied texture.

Remove the vanilla bean, lemon peel, and cinnamon stick (if using). Rice pudding can be served warm, but I prefer to let it cool to room temperature before transferring it to a bowl and chilling thoroughly. Some people dislike having any skin form on top and try to prevent this by pressing plastic wrap directly over the surface. I simply stir it back in a few times and don't worry if a little more re-forms.

CHOCOLATE PUDDING

This recipe is taken with little alteration from the first chocolate pudding recipe I ever used, in my mother's copy of Fannie Farmer. It's a good representative of the cornstarch-based milk pudding tribe, which for a time nearly disappeared from up-to-date cookbooks. Some of us, however, remember that such puddings used to be one of the most popular uses for milk in American cuisine.

Don't judge this kind of pudding by chocolate mousse standards. The texture, though less airy and creamy than that of a mousse made with beaten egg white and whipped cream, is smooth and satisfying in another way. What happens in cooking is that as the starch molecules link with the water molecules of the hot milk, new compounds form from the softened, reconfigured ("gelatinized") starch and the no-longer-free water. The butterfat of the milk keeps the mixture from turning into a pasty stodge as it cools to near-solid consistency—at least, as long as the proportion of starch to liquid isn't high.

Being very lowbrow in my approach to chocolate, I use any brand of plain unsweetened chocolate. If the new high-cacao-solids premium chocolate brands now reaching this country are your passion, by all means experiment with them (reducing the amount of sugar slightly if the chocolate is already sweetened).

YIELD: 4 servings

2 cups whole milk, or part milk, part half-and-half
2 ounces unsweetened chocolate, broken into pieces
3 tablespoons cornstarch
⅓ cup sugar
½ teaspoon salt
1 teaspoon pure vanilla extract
Whipped cream for garnish

Reserve ¼ cup of the milk. Pour the rest into a small heavy saucepan with the chocolate and heat over medium-low heat, stirring occasionally with a wooden spoon or heatproof rubber spatula, until the chocolate is melted. (You may prefer to use a double boiler, which will give some insurance against scorching when the pudding starts to thicken.)

While the milk heats, put all the dry ingredients in a small bowl and mix in the reserved ¼ cup milk to make a smooth paste. Stir this into the milk-chocolate mixture, increase the heat slightly, and cook, stirring frequently, until it starts to thicken, 5 to 8 minutes. Stir in the vanilla, reduce the heat slightly, and cook for another 5 minutes, stirring slowly but regularly. (Overly vigorous stirring may break down the starch links.) Remove from the heat, and continue to stir (very gently) as the pudding cools almost to room temperature. Gently pour into 4 small serving dishes, such as glass custard cups; press a piece of plastic wrap over the surface of each to keep a skin from forming. Refrigerate for at least 2 hours, until thoroughly chilled, and serve with a bowl of unsweetened whipped cream.

PANNA COTTA AND RELATIVES

When *panna cotta* rode into town in the 1990s, people of a certain age did a double take. This maiden-white concoction of gelatin-set sweetened cream (with or without milk) took some of us back to the early '60s, when the women's magazines and newspaper food columns periodically urged everybody to try something that went by the name of "Russian" or sometimes "Swedish" cream. These attributions of nationality now sound to me like food editors' games of pin-the-tail-on-the-donkey. But the idea behind "Russian" cream was gorgeously simple. It consisted of heavy cream and sour cream in any preferred proportion, with sugar and enough gelatin to make a sort of cream-on-cream aspic. I adored it. The sour cream just redeemed it from insipidity without detracting from the stunning super-hyper-creaminess of the thing. I've never cared equally for the blander panna cotta, except when given a little kick with citrus zest or something else by way of contrast.

Where did the whole idea originate? I suspect that panna cotta ("cooked cream") doesn't have particularly old Italian roots. Probably it and its cousins elsewhere started as latter-day simplifications of the medieval blancmange, which originally was made like the chicken-breast pudding (*tavuk göğsü kazandibi*) that is still a beloved dessert in Turkey. After the Middle Ages, blancmange was successively transformed into an almond-milk custard and a starch-bound milk pudding. When commercial isinglass—predecessor to today's gelatin—appeared in the eighteenth and nineteenth centuries, it gave rise to still other changes on the milk-pudding theme. There was an English version called "stone cream," which involved a layer of fruit preserves covered with a layer of isinglass-set sweetened cream. (In her 1961 *The Continental Flavor,* Nika Standen Hazelton passed along an old recipe with the comment "Said to be one of Queen Victoria's favorites.") Early in the gelatin era something similar turns up in American cookbooks as "Velvet Cream." My guess is that modern gelatin manufacturers helped revive the general idea from time to time in the twentieth century.

The proportion of cream to milk is entirely up to the individual cook. In *Marcella Cucina,* Marcella Hazan points out that when a panna cotta mixture made with American gum-stabilized ultrapasteurized cream is allowed to boil, it leaves a strange residue on the pan bottom. Take the pan off the stove just before the cream boils (or look for nonultrapasteurized cream).

YIELD: 6 servings

1 envelope (2¼ teaspoons) unflavored granulated gelatin
1 cup milk
2 cups heavy cream (or half heavy, half light cream), preferably
    nonultrapasteurized
½ cup sugar (¾ cup if you like it sweet)
A pinch of salt
About ½ teaspoon finely grated lemon zest (optional)
1 to 2 teaspoons freshly squeezed lemon juice (optional)

Put the gelatin in a small saucepan with the milk and cream. Add the sugar, salt, and optional lemon zest and juice; heat gently, stirring to dissolve the gelatin and sugar thoroughly. If using ultrapasteurized cream, do not quite let it boil. Otherwise, bring just to a boil and remove from the heat. (Make sure the gelatin is dissolved; if necessary, reheat briefly.) If you wish, pour through a fine-mesh strainer to remove the shreds of lemon zest. Let the mixture cool just slightly.

Have ready six lightly oiled 6-ounce or 4-ounce heatproof glass custard cups. Pour in the mixture and refrigerate until set, 3 to 4 hours. (If keeping longer, cover with plastic wrap; it's best eaten within a day.) Unmold by briefly dipping the bottom of each cup in hot water, then inverting onto a serving plate. Serve with lightly sweetened fresh fruit or a pureed fruit sauce like raspberry coulis.

VARIATION: For "Russian Cream"—I have grave qualms about the authenticity of the name—omit the milk. Using 1 envelope gelatin, 2 cups heavy cream, and ¾ to 1 cup sugar, heat to (or just under) a boil in the same way.

Remove from the heat, and add 2 cups sour cream, stirring it in very thoroughly. Pour or spoon into 8 custard cups or a 5-cup serving bowl and chill for 4 hours. Don't try to unmold this; it's too creamy. The perfect foil is an instant sauce made by gently melting about a cup of thin-cut Seville orange marmalade in a small saucepan and adding a shot of Scotch.

CREMETS D'ANGERS

This specialty of the Loire Valley is cream lovers' heaven, pure and simple: whipped cream napped with plain heavy cream. The whipped cream is brought to an ethereal airiness by being lightened with stiffly beaten egg whites and drained in a mold or wicker basket (often heart-shaped) lined with muslin. You then serve it with summer berries and sugar, "sauced" with unwhipped cream.

There are Angevin versions of *cremets* based on a very soft, fresh *fromage blanc* beaten smooth with cream and/or egg whites. Something like this, with a cream-cheese mixture replacing the fromage blanc, is the usual model for the *coeur à la crème* recipes in American cookbooks, which I find stolid by comparison with the whipped-cream kind described by Curnonsky (in *Recettes des Provinces de France*) and Elizabeth David (in no less than *three* of her books—she must have been crazy about it).

This is a dish best reserved for your local summer fruit season, no matter how brief. Since there is no last-minute preparation, it's an ideal dinner-party dessert. (But the recipe can easily be halved for a smaller number of people.)

Because there is nothing to disguise the essence of cream, I'd try to hunt down glorious heavy cream from a small dairy (preferably one that does batch-pasteurizing without homogenizing) before undertaking this exercise in unvarnished simplicity.

Ultrapasteurized cream just won't yield the same effect. But if you can find good crème fraîche, a few spoonfuls will add a little pizzazz to ultrapasteurized cream.

Please note the use of uncooked egg whites. The risk of salmonella infections from raw eggs has been greatly reduced in the last twenty years (and is smaller with eggs from free-range hens than birds raised in factory-farm conditions), but it has not been eliminated.

YIELD: About 10 servings

About 3½ cups heavy cream, preferably nonultrapasteurized and
    unhomogenized
4 egg whites
Superfine sugar
Fresh seasonal fruit (raspberries, very sweet and ripe strawberries,
    or sliced peaches or apricots)

Using a chilled bowl and chilled beaters, whip 2¼ cups of the cream very stiff (almost to butter stage).

Beat the egg whites to stiff peaks in a separate bowl. Thoroughly fold the egg whites into the cream.

Line a perforated mold (a coeur à la crème mold, if you have one) or colander with *tight-woven* cheesecloth or a large cotton handkerchief, letting the edges hang over the rim. Spoon the whipped mixture into the mold and loosely cover with the overhang. Set it over a bowl to drain and place the whole arrangement overnight in the refrigerator (which should be free of anything smelly). At serving time, turn out the cremets into a dish. Pass around the cremets, sugar, fruit, and remaining unwhipped cream for everyone to help himself. Or you can pour the cream directly over the serving bowl of cremets.

VARIATION: Recently I was introduced to a very similar dish called "Fontainebleau," or "Fromage de Fontainebleau," in a surprising but delicious Americanized version using both sugar and yogurt. Begin by stirring together 2 cups plain yogurt (preferably a rich, creamy kind) and 1 cup superfine sugar until the sugar is well dissolved. Whip 2 cups heavy cream; separately beat 3 egg whites. Fold together cream, egg whites, and sweetened yogurt; drain as described above and serve with fresh fruit and (if desired) fresh cream.

LEMON SPONGE PUDDING

It's a cake, it's a custard, it's what lemon curd (page 269) would be if it took a fancy to hobnob with milk and flour in a baking dish. Some nineteenth-century versions of this two-layered milk pudding were made in a pastry crust at a time when the terms "pie" and "pudding" were somewhat interchangeable in American kitchens.

The *Joy of Cooking* "Lemon Sponge Custard" was one of the first dishes I ever attempted from that contribution to human happiness, and I still make it by more or less the same formula. The amounts given below will fill an 8-inch square Pyrex baking dish. Note that you will also need a larger pan for a water bath.

YIELD: About 8 to 10 servings

1½ cups sugar
4 tablespoons butter
A pinch of salt
Grated lemon zest to taste (anything from ½ to 2 teaspoons)
6 eggs, separated
⅓ cup flour
⅓ to ½ cup freshly squeezed lemon juice
2 cups milk

Preheat the oven to 350°F. Cream together the sugar, butter, salt, and grated zest. Work in the egg yolks one at a time. Combine the lemon juice and milk. Add the flour and the milk mixture alternately in three or four increments each, being sure each one is thoroughly incorporated before adding the next. Beat the egg whites to stiff peaks, and stir into the batter, which will have an odd half-curdled look (don't worry). Butter a shallow 2-quart baking dish and gently pour in the mixture.

Have ready a kettle of boiling water. Set the baking dish in a slightly larger pan, slide the whole thing almost all the way into the oven, then carefully pour enough hot water into the larger pan to come about an inch up the sides of the dish. Bake for 1 hour; the top will be something like a sponge cake and the bottom will be a creamy custard. It can be served hot, but I prefer it well chilled. The Rombauers' recommended accompaniments of "thick cream or raspberry sauce" cannot be improved on.

ABOUT VANILLA ICE CREAM

The effect I love most in ice cream is delicacy, not over-the-top richness or flavors revved up to something like bombing-raid intensity. Give me "plain vanilla," which to my mind is anything but plain when made with that rarest of treasures, very fresh unhomogenized cream.

There are two general American approaches to ice cream making. Custard-based ice cream (sometimes called "French") uses a cooked mixture similar to crème anglaise (see page 132), and acquires a voluptuous finish and rounded flavor from eggs or egg yolks. "Philadelphia" ice cream is chancier but, I think, more beautiful in its simplicity. Its basic texture rests on nothing but a combination of cream and sugar, its flavor (in the vanilla version) only on sweetened cream and vanilla. There is nothing to disguise the quality of the cream and vanilla; if they're indifferent, the ice cream will be nothing special. And freshness is everything in Philadelphia ice cream. Serve a particularly good batch within hours of freezing, and you will taste ice cream as the great nineteenth-century Philadelphia cookbook author Eliza Leslie meant it to taste.

VANILLA ICE CREAM I: CUSTARD-BASED

This is what Eliza Leslie, in the 1851 *Miss Leslie's Directions for Cookery*, labeled "Frozen Custard"—as opposed to "ice-cream, for which it frequently passes." Today, however, it is probably the most familiar American style of ice cream. The main reason is that first-class cream from small local dairies no longer exists as an option for most manufacturers; custard-based or French ice cream doesn't expose the indifferent quality of the basic ingredient as glaringly as the Philadelphia counterpart.

Because of the richness lent by the eggs, I prefer to use a combination of heavy and light cream with milk. See page 83 for more on the crucial gradations of cream.

YIELD: About 6 cups (exact volume may vary markedly with different ice cream–maker models)

1 large vanilla bean, preferably Mexican
1 cup whole milk, preferably nonultrapasteurized and unhomogenized
2 cups light cream or rich half-and-half, preferably nonultrapasteurized and unhomogenized
1 cup heavy cream, preferably nonultrapasteurized and unhomogenized
2 large eggs, or 4 egg yolks
⅔ to ¾ cup sugar (I prefer the smaller amount)
A pinch of salt
½ to ¾ teaspoon pure vanilla extract, preferably Mexican (optional)

If necessary, put the bowl of your ice cream maker in the freezer to chill in advance.

Slit the vanilla bean lengthwise with a small, sharp knife and scrape the seeds into a small, heavy-bottomed saucepan. Pour in the milk and cream, add the halved bean, and slowly heat to just under a boil.

Whisk together the eggs or egg yolks, sugar, and salt. Slowly pour the hot cream and vanilla bean into the whisked eggs, stirring with a wooden spoon. Pour the mixture back into the saucepan and cook over medium-low heat, stirring gently. As the mixture starts to thicken, stir more rapidly, being sure to scrape the custard from the entire pan bottom. When the pan bottom starts being exposed and the custard coats the spoon, quickly remove the pan from the heat before the eggs can curdle. Pour the custard through a medium- or fine-mesh strainer into a heatproof bowl and let cool completely, stirring several times. Taste for seasoning and if desired, stir in a little vanilla extract to reinforce the flavor. (All flavors will be muted in freezing.) Let the custard chill thoroughly in the refrigerator before freezing according to manufacturer's directions.

OLD-FASHIONED GEAR-DRIVEN ICE CREAM FREEZER

VANILLA ICE CREAM II: PHILADELPHIA-STYLE

The quality of the cream you use is all-important here. Ultrapasteurized cream will often impart a faint sludginess to the texture, the result of the gums and thickeners used to offset a loss of viscosity that occurs in the manufacturing process. If you can find unhomogenized cream, the larger size of the fat globules will make the ice cream feel heavier and creamier on the palate—not, however, that you want the absolutely heaviest and creamiest effect possible. It will be more delicate made with a combination of heavy and light cream than with all heavy cream. For the crucial gradations, see page 83.

YIELD: About 6 cups (exact volume may vary markedly with different makers' models)

1 large vanilla bean, preferably Mexican
2 cups nonultrapasteurized light cream or rich half-and-half, preferably unhomogenized
2 cups nonultrapasteurized heavy cream, preferably unhomogenized
¾ to ⅞ cup sugar (I prefer the smaller amount)
A pinch of salt
¼ to ½ teaspoon pure vanilla extract, preferably Mexican (optional)

Slit the vanilla bean lengthwise with a small, sharp knife and scrape out the seeds into a small saucepan. Add 1 cup of the light cream and the halved bean. Heat slowly to just under a boil. Let the cream cool to room temperature before proceeding.

Combine the remaining light and heavy cream with the sugar and salt. Stir until the sugar is thoroughly dissolved. Discard the vanilla bean and add the infused cream to the rest. Taste for seasoning and if desired, stir in a little vanilla extract to reinforce the flavor. (All flavors will be muted in freezing.) Let the ice cream base chill thoroughly in the refrigerator before freezing according to manufacturer's directions.

CRÈME ANGLAISE
(STIRRED CUSTARD)

Crème anglaise, so baptized by the eighteenth-century French writer François Massialot, is about as English as Scotch tape is Scotch. Never mind. This simple stovetop custard is one of the most delicious dessert sauces ever invented—a beautiful accompaniment to fruit and an indispensable element in cake-based assemblages such as trifles.

Among egg-based custards, crème anglaise (also called "stirred custard") is neither so fragile as hollandaise sauce nor so sturdy as baked custards. The addition of a little sugar and a lot of milk or cream enables the eggs to cook—with constant stirring—to around 180°F without curdling, though 175°F is more prudent. The consistency can be manipulated to your preference by three factors, starting with the creaminess of the liquid used. This is not an occasion for using skim milk, but either whole milk, various milk-cream combinations, or all cream will make a fine custard. The larger the proportion of cream, the faster the custard will thicken and the less likely it is to curdle. In my opinion the best results come from light cream, half-and-half, or equal parts of milk and any preferred grade of cream (nonultrapasteurized, please).

Then there is the ratio of eggs to milk. Not surprisingly, a higher proportion of eggs means a heavier, thicker sauce. But the third variable—whole eggs versus egg yolks—doesn't work exactly as you might expect. Using both yolks and whites makes the custard set up firmer, but paradoxically with less roundness and body. Yolks alone produce not only a softer, more pourable consistency but also a more velvety richness.

In its simplicity, the sauce is like a blank slate waiting to be written on. Vanilla (preferably a whole bean, not the cruder-tasting extract) is the favorite flavoring, but various spices, herb infusions, and accents like citrus zest have their adherents. Probably the liveliest variations involve small amounts of brandy, whiskey, eau-de-vie (any preferred kind), or liqueur beaten into the partly cooled custard. I like the juice from finely grated ginger (squeeze a few drops through a garlic press).

Because crème anglaise stands up to a little more heat than other custard cousins like lemon curd or hollandaise sauce, I usually make it over direct heat. Some people prefer a double boiler for extra insurance against curdling.

YIELD: About 2 cups

1 vanilla bean
2 cups whole milk, nonultrapasteurized half-and-half, or equal parts
    milk and nonultrapasteurized cream
5 egg yolks, or 2 whole eggs and 1 yolk
⅓ cup sugar
A pinch of salt

Have ready a large bowl of ice, a heatproof storage bowl, and a fine-mesh strainer.

Slit the vanilla bean lengthwise and scrape out the seeds. Put the seeds, empty bean, and milk in a heavy-bottomed saucepan and heat to just under a boil.

Gently whisk together the egg yolks, sugar, and salt. If using whole eggs, beat more vigorously, but try to froth them as little as possible. Slowly pour the hot milk into the whisked yolks or eggs, stirring with a wooden spoon. Pour the mixture back into the pan and cook over medium-low heat, stirring gently. As it starts to thicken, stir more rapidly, being sure to scrape the custard from the entire pan bottom. When it coats the spoon and every stroke exposes a clean trail on the pan bottom, remove the pan from the heat.

At once pour the sauce through the strainer into the storage bowl, set it on ice, and whisk to partly cool it down. You can use it now if it is to be served warm. Otherwise, whisk again every few minutes until it is quite cold and refrigerate, uncovered, for an hour before covering tightly. It will set up more as it chills, but will remain loose rather than firm. Plan to use it within a day or two.

NOTE: A custard that threatens to turn grainy and "break" during cooking can usually be salvaged in acceptable condition if you instantly snatch it off the stove, pour it through a strainer as directed above, and whisk strenuously until it cools.

CAJETA MEXICANA
(MEXICAN DULCE DE LECHE)

If you take milk and sugar, cook them down thicker than heavy cream in an industrial vacuum pan, and put the result in a can, you get commercial condensed milk with an ivory-tan color and the double sweetness of two caramelized sugars (lactose and sucrose). Do the condensing yourself by boiling down a milk-sugar mixture a few steps further to a nearly taffylike consistency, and you have the world's best caramel sauce-cum-candy, known as *dulce de leche* throughout Latin America and *cajeta* (literally, "little box") in Mexico. Nearly all Latin countries have their own commercial brands, some of which are sold here. I'm not crazy about any of them except for the Coronado brand cajeta from San Luis Potosí in Mexico. The rest are generally thickened with starch, which is cheaper than using more milk and boiling it down longer, but introduces something faintly stodgy into the texture.

You have to be careful about saying "cajeta." In Mexico it historically referred to various kinds of sweet preserves cooked down to dense pastes and formerly sold in small wooden boxes. Unfortunately, the same word in some parts of Latin America is vulgar slang for the vagina, so it is a poor idea to ask for dulce de leche as cajeta in the local pan-Latin grocery. Just as unfortunately, commercial Mexican milk cajeta—also sometimes called *leche quemada*, or "burnt milk"—is much less widely available in the United States than brands of dulce de leche from other countries.

Mexican cajeta is often (not always) made from goats' milk or a combination of cows' and goats' milk. I find that using part goats' milk adds a lot of flavor and character to the homemade version; cows' milk alone gives an almost cloyingly sweet blandness. In this case it doesn't matter if the only goat's milk you can find is ultra-pasteurized. Cajeta or dulce de leche is much used for fillings and icings in Latin America, but I have to say that I never do anything with it other than either scarfing it up by the spoonful or warming it enough to pour over vanilla ice cream for the best butterscotch sundae I remember since Schrafft's.

To make cajeta at home, prepare to stand attentively over the pot for about an hour. (It helps to have another person to switch off with.) If like me you adore all things butterscotchy, it's worth it. But for a streamlined version, see Dulce de Leche with Canned Condensed Milk (page 136).

YIELD: About 2½ cups

1 quart whole cows' milk
1 quart goats' milk
2 cups sugar
¼ teaspoon baking soda

Choose a large (at least 6-quart) deep saucepan, thick enough not to start scorching on the bottom before the milk is half cooked. An enameled cast-iron pan is good; any other pan should be nonreactive and heavy-gauge. Pour the milk into the pan; dip out about ½ cup and reserve.

Add the sugar to the pan of milk, stirring to dissolve it with a wooden spoon. Bring just to a low boil. Remove the pan from the heat while you stir the baking soda into the reserved milk, then add that to the hot milk, which will froth up at once. Set it over medium heat and continue to cook, stirring frequently, for about 30 minutes. The mixture will start to look more like a syrup as the water evaporates and the temperature rises. Now you must stir constantly, gradually reducing the heat as the syrup darkens and thickens, for about another 30 minutes (less if it seems about to burn). When a stroke of the mixing spoon exposes the bottom of the pan and the syrup is slow to close in again over the track, remove the pan from the heat and let sit until the molten stuff is partly cooled but still liquid enough to pour into small containers. Let cool to room temperature before covering. It will keep for weeks at room temperature, for months in the refrigerator. It may, however, crystallize like long-stored honey. If this happens, set the container in hot water until the crystals melt.

DULCE DE LECHE WITH CANNED CONDENSED MILK

Everyone in Latin America is familiar with the convenient version of cajeta, or dulce de leche, made by immersing an unopened 14-ounce can of condensed milk in enough boiling water to cover it thoroughly, simmering it for several hours, and opening it when the contents have slowly cooled. (Not just in Latin America, either; the prison-camp inmates in Solzhenitsyn's *The First Circle* knew the same trick.) The method works fairly well, and some people even prefer the result to dulce de leche from scratch. But it has been known to end in serious injury when a sealed can exploded, either because it was defective to begin with or because the forgetful cook let the water boil away so that the contents of the can became superheated. Some commercial manufacturers now provide directions for cooking the milk out of the can, which is safer. This version is based on a method suggested by the Borden Company.

YIELD: About 1½ cups

A 14-ounce can of condensed milk

Preheat the oven to 425°F. Scrape the milk into a shallow heatproof glass baking dish such as a 9-inch pie plate. Cover it snugly with several layers of aluminum foil. Place the dish in a slightly larger ovenproof vessel, put the arrangement in the oven, and carefully pour enough boiling water into the larger container to come partway up the sides of the glass dish. Bake for 1 hour, lift out, and let cool as for Cajeta Mexicana (page 134).

BATIDOS
(LATIN AMERICAN MILKSHAKES)

The mom-and-pop restaurants in mixed Hispanic neighborhoods seldom do much in the line of wine and beer. The
choice of beverages usually boils down to good coffee, a few freshly
squeezed juices, some bottled or canned fruit and cola drinks, and a
multitude of blender specialties. In my town—which is in effect a
New Jersey outpost of Miami—the blender drinks come in milk-
based and milkless varieties. Cubans call the milkshake kind *batidos*.
(I have given up trying to remember all the names used by people
from different parts of the Latin tropics; *licuados*, *refrescos*, and
vitaminas barely scratch the surface.)

The Miami-on-the-Hudson batidos can be made from some
pretty unexpected materials, the most unexpected perhaps being
puffed wheat. But most use fruit, anything from strawberries or
peaches to remote Amazonian exotica. The tropical-fruit batidos
are almost universally based on frozen fruit. Our local stores carry
a huge array of imported fruit pulps or chunks in 14-ounce packages. These are not mediocre "convenience" ingredients; they
usually have much fresher flavor than the whole fresh fruits would
after being shipped from Central or South America, and they are
the first thing people reach for when they want to make most
batidos. Passion fruit, tamarillo, pineapple, cashew fruit, mango,
guava, *guanábana* (soursop), cherimoya, tamarind, papaya . . . the
list of possibilities seems to expand every year.

It is impossible to give one fixed formula, since every kind of
fruit will vary in sweetness (always start with a small amount of
sugar and cautiously add more to taste) and intensity. A very rough
rule of thumb is about 3 or 4 cups of milk to a 14-ounce package of
frozen pulp; you may want to halve this for a maiden attempt. Here
is a model recipe of sorts using my favorite among the frozen tropical fruits that reach these parts, mamey sapote, which everyone
except botanists calls simply "mamey." Now and then fresh mamey
sapotes in good condition briefly show up in our stores from
Florida, especially at the end of summer. Seize the moment if you
see this wonderful fruit. An exterior like a furry tan football con-
ceals salmon-colored flesh with a custardy avocadolike consistency
and a perfumed sweetness, so good for simply eating with a spoon
that you may never get around to making a batido.

YIELD: About 3 cups

Half a 14-ounce package of frozen mamey pulp, partly thawed (or the
    flesh of one large fresh mamey, peeled, pitted, and roughly cubed)
2 cups whole milk, very cold
¼ cup sugar, or to taste
½ cup shaved or finely crushed ice

Combine the mamey pulp and milk in a blender with half of the sugar. Process
for a few seconds and taste for sweetness. Add the ice and more sugar to taste;
process to combine thoroughly. Add a little more mamey pulp to thicken it
slightly, more milk to thin it. It tastes best served at once, straight up or over
ice cubes.

VARIATION: Batidos are often enriched with ice cream. Omit the crushed
ice and add half a scoop (or more to taste) of slightly softened vanilla ice cream
to the fruit pulp and milk, reducing the amount of sugar to compensate.
Process just until combined.

THAI-STYLE ICED COFFEE

Southeast Asia is among those parts of the world where "milk" as
generally understood means only the canned kind, either evaporated or condensed. Introduced by French and Dutch colonists
who also hoped to strike it rich with coffee plantations, canned
milk became a favorite addition to coffee as drunk hot or iced in
Thailand, Vietnam, Indonesia, and other ex-colonies of the region.
Eventually American restaurant-goers fell in love with the iced
version.

There is no single standard recipe. In most places, you simply
brew the coffee ultrastrong, cool or chill it, and drink it with the
canned milk—though cream has some recent adherents—and ice.
With condensed milk, further sweetening is optional (though it's
supposed to be ferociously sweet); with evaporated milk, you
sweeten the coffee with sugar or sugar syrup before putting in the
milk. Some people combine the sugar and coffee from the start, in
the brewing.

A somewhat different approach arose in Thailand, where coffee
drinkers invented a unique preground combination of roasted
coffee beans with other ingredients, usually roasted corn kernels,

sesame seeds, and soybeans. This mixture, called *oliang*, or *oleng*, is commonly brewed in a "coffee sock," a sock-shaped cotton filter on a metal rim that also happens to be much used in parts of Central America and can often be found in pan-Latin stores.

There is no substitute for oliang. But if you can't find it, lavishly sweetened strong coffee brewed by any preferred method, combined with canned milk, and served over ice makes a refreshing drink in the right spirit.

YIELD: About 6 servings

½ cup oliang (Thai ground coffee mixture)
Sugar to taste
4 cups boiling water
Plenty of ice
Canned evaporated or condensed milk (or heavy cream—
    inauthentic but good) to taste

Measure the oliang into a coffee sock set over a carafe or heatproof pitcher. If you are using evaporated milk, add about 2 tablespoons sugar for a slightly sweet or 4 tablespoons for a very sweet brew. Pour the boiling water over the oliang and sugar and leave it to steep in the carafe for 8 to 10 minutes before removing the sock. If you don't have a coffee sock, simply put the oliang and sugar in a small saucepan, pour the boiling water over them, let sit 8 to 10 minutes, and strain through a coffee filter into a carafe or pitcher. If you are using condensed milk, either omit the sugar or add only about 1 tablespoon.

Let the brewed coffee cool to room temperature. In hot weather, you may want to chill it. Taste for sweetness. If using evaporated milk, fill tall serving glasses up to the brim with ice cubes or crushed ice and pour in the coffee, leaving a good inch or two at the top. Add evaporated milk to taste, gently pouring it over a spoon so that it will gradually eddy down into the coffee in pretty swirls.

Condensed milk needs a lot of mixing, which is best done by adding about ⅓ to ½ cup of the thick, heavy stuff to the carafe of cooled coffee and stirring vigorously. Taste for sweetness, fill serving glasses with ice cubes or crushed ice, and top up with the coffee-milk mixture.

HOT CHOCOLATE

It's high time for the food-minded to discover that despite much confusion in labeling, hot chocolate is not the same as hot cocoa. The latter is made from a mixture using ground cacao partly denatured by removal of the cacao butter that is an intrinsic part of real chocolate. I can see the point of cocoa in a few uses—but not in chocolate for drinking, which has been one of the finest fruits of Old World–New World cross-fertilization since Spanish conquerors returning from Mexico with cacao beans and reports of native chocolate-drinking traditions inspired the nations of Europe to develop their own counterparts. To have the right body it has to be made with full-fat chocolate. Unfortunately, there is no formal labeling requirement.

Cows' milk, which was unknown in pre-Columbian Mexico, probably didn't enter the picture during the first few generations of European chocolate drinking. (Until the late nineteenth century, chocolate was scarcely used for any purpose *but* drinking.) To this day there are fine versions of hot chocolate made without a drop of milk. But where the tradition of milk-based hot chocolate took hold, what people loved about it was the effect of marrying two remarkably similar forms of fat. Cacao butter happens to be a closer match for the saturated/unsaturated lipid "profile" of milkfat (see page 232) than any other culinary fat, which is why the "mouthfeel" of chocolate somewhat resembles that of butter. Put them together as a hot drink, and you have something utterly luscious.

This kind of hot chocolate is better approached as an idea than a recipe: Melt some chocolate and mix it with some previously heated rich, creamy milk. (Since rich, creamy milk has all but ceased to exist, I recommend the best whole milk you can find combined with a little light or heavy cream.) The chocolate can be as recherché or ordinary as you like. When I first started making hot chocolate, the usual base was Baker's brand unsweetened chocolate, to which you added a little sugar. Nowadays most fans probably would opt for some version of semisweet or bittersweet eating chocolate. Follow your general taste in chocolate, whether it's for one of the superdense and superexpensive kinds (Scharffen Berger, El Rey, Valrhona) or one of the humbler European or American brands. Most people prefer dark chocolate, but there's no reason not to use milk chocolate. Here is a general scenario:

For one large serving, allow 1 ounce of semisweet, bittersweet, or unsweetened chocolate per cup of whole milk or milk-cream combination (say, 1 tablespoon heavy cream or 2 tablespoons light cream to a cup of milk). Real chocoholics probably will want to use more chocolate for greater intensity, but I recommend first trying the 1 ounce per cup ratio so that you'll have a standard of comparison for next time. If the chocolate is unsweetened or on the very bitter side of bittersweet, allow 1 to 2 tablespoons sugar per ounce of chocolate (less or more to taste). Otherwise, omit sugar.

Break the chocolate into small pieces, and put it in a small saucepan with a few tablespoons of water and the sugar (if using). Put the milk in another small saucepan. Start warming both over low heat, keeping an eye on the milk to prevent it from scalding. Whisk together the slowly melting chocolate and water; when the chocolate and optional sugar are smoothly dissolved, start gradually whisking in the warmed milk. Heat to just under a boil, whisking constantly, and pour into chocolate cups or small mugs.

People vary the basic formula in many different ways—for example, letting some whole spice like cinnamon, cardamom, allspice, or vanilla bean briefly steep in the hot milk before straining it over the chocolate, or lacing each cup with booze (whiskey, rum, or any preferred liqueur or eau-de-vie). Whipped cream (plain, sweetened, or flavored) is a favorite topping.

CHOCOLATE MALTED

I belong to the era of drugstore soda fountains, a species unknown to about the last two generations of Americans. In those days, moderately priced everyday ice cream was generally creamier, since plebeian and superpremium brands were not as firmly segregated into marketing niches as they are today.

It seems to me that soda-fountain fare then was far more satisfying and less contrived than the ice-cream extravaganzas now served up in multistar restaurants. I can't imagine anything ever tasting better than a simple butterscotch sundae—or this unpretentious combination of milk, vanilla ice cream, chocolate-flavored syrup, and malted-milk powder.

Since my youth both the syrup and the malt powder have deteriorated somewhat. It takes some doing to find chocolate-flavored syrup containing more cane sugar than corn syrup. Malted-milk powder lends crucial depth to the whole, but this also can take some searching for, and the few surviving brands tend to be additive-laden. (Plain old ground malted barley and powdered milk used to be nearly the only ingredients.) On the other hand, the advent of handheld immersion blenders has made it easier for home cooks to produce the right consistency.

In my day malteds were in high nutritional repute and thought to be made even better for growing children by the addition of a raw egg. I like the extra body that this gives, but raw eggs have to be viewed with some caution nowadays.

YIELD: One large (about 2 cups' worth) milkshake or 2 small ones

3 generous scoops vanilla ice cream, preferably a
   premium brand made with vanilla bean
⅔ cup very cold milk, or as needed
3 tablespoons plain (not chocolate) malted-milk powder
Chocolate-flavored syrup, preferably made with cane sugar
1 raw egg (optional)
1 heaping cup finely crushed or shaved ice

Put all the ingredients into a 1-quart glass measuring pitcher or other sturdy pitcher and begin blending with a handheld immersion blender. (If you don't have one, combine everything in the jar of a regular blender; it's a little harder to gauge progress, and you may need to pulse on and off to get a uniform texture.) As it starts coming together and becoming drinkable, try to judge the consistency and thin it with a little more milk if you like. Pour the shake into a deep, well-chilled glass and slurp it up with a straw.

VARIATION: Chocolate fans may want to substitute chocolate ice cream for part or all of the vanilla ice cream. Note, however, that superchocolatey kinds may drown out the malt flavor.

HOPPELPOPPEL: EGGNOG WITH A DIFFERENCE

Distilled liquor figures in a tribe of heavily sweetened drinks enriched with eggs and cream or milk. Often they are associated with the Christmas or Easter holidays. In the Hispanic Americas these rich concoctions go by such names as *rompope* (Mexico) or *crème de vie* (Cuba), and are usually based on eggs and canned condensed milk, with or without evaporated milk, coconut milk, and fresh milk and/or cream. In most English-speaking countries the equivalents are made with fresh cream or milk-cream combinations, and are generically called "eggnogs." The "nog" part has been rather shakily traced to an old dialect word for strong ale or beer; an early cousin called an "egg flip" was made by "flipping" a mulled beer-egg-sugar mixture from one container to another to raise a good head of froth.

In America, eggnog seems to have had some popularity at least since the early nineteenth century. Lettice Bryan's 1839 *The Kentucky Housewife* has a family-sized recipe that would look quite familiar now if it didn't call for "rich sweet milk." But the big nineteenth-century cooking manuals usually give only single-serving formulas as "restorative" or "fortifying" drinks for invalids. Not until the repeal of Prohibition did the major kitchen bibles regularly print recipes meant for a crowd.

By the time of my introduction to eggnog, creamy milk was a thing of the past and recipes usually called for cream or a cream-milk mixture. Most versions that I've encountered are cold, and involve separately beaten egg yolks and whites as well as whipped cream. You beat the yolks with sugar and booze (usually bourbon, Scotch, brandy, or rum) before adding the whipped egg whites and cream, which create a thick frothy topping. Some lily gilders also add more sweetening via a block (or individual dabs per serving) of vanilla ice cream, which gradually melts into the rest of the drink.

I confess that I have lost the taste for cold, very sweet, frothy eggnog. I like it warm or hot, straightforwardly creamy, and offset by something astringent. To those who share my opinion I offer this version of the north German *Hoppelpoppel,* closely taken from Horst Scharfenberg's lovely book *Die deutsche Küche.* (To the bewilderment of non-Germans, "Hoppelpoppel" can also refer to a dish of fried eggs and potatoes.) Its starting point is strong brewed tea sweetened with *Kandiszucker,* or lump sugar. Use the French A la Perruche lump sugar if you can get it.

YIELD: 4 to 5 cups

2 cups hot tea, brewed rather strong (use a plain unscented kind)
About 3 ounces French white lump sugar (see above; about ½ cup) or
　　5 to 6 tablespoons granulated sugar
4 egg yolks
2 cups cream (half each heavy and light, or any preferred combination)
½–1 cup dark rum or any preferred spirit

Mix the tea and sugar until the sugar is completely dissolved. Whisk the egg yolks smooth (not frothy), then whisk in the cream and the sweetened tea. Strain into the top of a double boiler set over hot water on low heat. Whisking constantly, warm the mixture until it is hot and slightly thickened. Carefully stir in the rum and serve at once in heatproof punch cups or demitasse cups.

VARIATION: Some people make Hoppelpoppel with black coffee instead of tea.

MILK PUNCH

The star chemistry between milk and liquor used to be common knowledge, and deserves to be so again. Not just milk reinforced with eggs and cream to make eggnog; not just the industrially concentrated canned milk that goes into many Latin American holiday drinks. Given a little sugar and spice, plain old *milk* is a delightful partner for brandy, rum, whiskey, sherry, and nearly anything that goes into other sorts of punch.

There is just one hitch, and by now you probably can repeat it by heart: Plain old milk isn't what it used to be. Without fresh, creamy unhomogenized milk, much of the reason for making milk punch disappears. Recipes used to call for "rich milk," "top milk," and other tokens of yesteryear. Perhaps with the reappearance of fresher and better milk from small dairies, such terms will regain their former meaning. Milk punch made with mass-produced homogenized milk will win few converts, because it won't have the dewy delicacy of fresh milk with the cream still present as a distinct element. If you can get hold of this necessary ingredient, I suggest the following general proportions per two servings:

1 cup very fresh, creamy unhomogenized whole milk
1 tablespoon very fresh unhomogenized light or heavy cream (optional; use if the milk seems on the lean side)
2 tablespoons sugar syrup
1½ jiggers bourbon, rye, or brandy
Freshly grated nutmeg

Briefly beat or whisk the cold milk in a small bar pitcher and add the optional cream. Stir in the syrup and liquor and pour into punch cups or small tumblers. Grate the nutmeg over the top and serve at once.

YOGURT

Punjabi-Style Sweet Lassi

Mango Lassi

Tarhana, Trahana, and Relatives

Homemade Greek-Style Sour Trahana

Turkish Tarhana Soup I and II

Yogurt is as amazing a piece of human intervention in the destinies of foodstuffs as wine or bread. Probably it is as old as those other two miraculous discoveries, if not older. Like them, it first came into being somewhere around the eastern Mediterranean, or perhaps not far from the Fertile Crescent. (All eulogies of the "Mediterranean diet" that ignore the role of yogurt in the first-settled parts of the Mediterranean basin are leaving out something crucial.) The somewhat later prehistoric spread of dairying from its first core areas to realms as remote as Kenya, southern India, and the western ranges of the Chinese empire went hand in hand with the spread of yogurt.

To understand yogurt in its glory, you must set aside some of the images attached to today's commercial Western versions. Yogurt as made for millennia throughout huge chunks of the Old World usually isn't called by that name; it goes by dozens (or more) of local names of which the Turkish "yogurt," pronounced something like "yaawwhhrt" with a prolonged vowel, happens to be the one that got picked up in English during the early twentieth century. In its old strongholds it does not come in a choice of flavors. It has its own intrinsic flavor, combining the taste of a particular animal's milk (sheep, goat, camel, cow, buffalo, or others) with some degree of lactic-acid sourness. Nobody expects to buy it already sweetened. Sweetness is only one possible flavor effect, achieved by adding honey or fruit preserves—or in India, unrefined palm or cane sugar—when you eat it. It may or may not have a consistency resembling anything you've bought in the supermarket yogurt section. Undoctored yogurt can be nearly as pourable as cream or as firm as a thickened pudding, again depending on the animal that gave the milk. It is beautifully creamy, because people born to yogurt-making are also born to the use of unhomogenized whole milk. It is one of the joys of life.

Yogurt was also one of the *staffs* of life, from prehistoric times on, in the regions I have called the Diverse Sources Belt and the Bovine and Buffalo Belt. Nobody knows how ancient it is. Though archaeological sites can be troves of evidence for such things as animal bones and plant seeds, less durable foods like milk products generally disintegrate and disappear fast. But yogurt must be almost as old an article of diet as unfermented milk in the first Near Eastern centers of animal husbandry—and certainly became more important as regards settled culinary practice. Under the once inescapable reality of being produced during very hot weather with no refrigeration, milk is a fickle cooking ingredient; it turns into yogurt or something yogurtlike within a matter of hours. In that state it is not only more stable than unfermented milk, but digestible by more people because of its reduced lactose content.

Here it probably is a good idea to define yogurt, or to explain that it's not strictly definable. The simplest description is: a mildly sour fermentation of milk colonized by lactic-acid bacteria of the general kind called thermophilic, or "heat-loving." These not only tolerate but prefer temperatures that would knock some kindred microorganisms out of commission—110° to 120°F, a level not at all hard to achieve on a summer's day in Yogurtistan or India.

Of course, the ambient air anywhere in the world is a soup of many miscellaneous bacteria, and the first wild fermentations of raw milk must have been a microbiological free-for-all with all kinds of edible, inedible, or positively dangerous results. Perhaps a series of lucky experiences encouraged populations of the right bugs to cluster around places where milk was being collected. Then at some unknown point, people learned to modify wild fermentation and give the desired bacteria a leg up on the competition by saving some of the last batch and using it to inoculate a new batch of milk.

It is tempting to think of yogurt-culture lineages stretching back into antiquity like royal dynasties. But as the professionals who grow bacterial cultures for industrial use know, keeping any strain pure and unchanging is impossible without the tools of modern science. From time to time natural yogurt "starters" will become easy prey for microbial enemies, or either lose their potency or develop somewhat different flavor effects through mutation. Nonetheless, it's a reasonable guess that most yogurt through the ages has involved the combined action of two particular lactic-acid bacteria, or their ancestors. As they exist today, they are usually known as *Lactobacillus bulgaricus* and *Streptococcus thermophilus*. (In the last twenty years, specialists have rebaptized both with new names, but the older ones are still the most common.) As I use the term in this chapter, "yogurt" is the product of these two principal actors' colonizing any sort of milk.

The starter method of putting certain chosen bacteria to work was a major if not completely foolproof advance in reliably turning milk into yogurt. A second leap forward—also of unknown date—came when people learned that yogurt became thicker and more flavorful if you boiled the milk and let it cool to just the right temperature range before inoculating it with the starter. (This also helped the starter bacteria more reliably get there first and multiply until they created a slightly acid environment hostile to many harmful microorganisms.) Heating the milk to a boil, or even letting it cook down quite a bit before inoculating it, became a nearly universal practice among the world's yogurt-making peoples. This is why anyone who knows yogurt will raise an eyebrow at the words "raw-milk yogurt"; I either avoid buying anything so labeled or try to question the seller about the term. If the milk really was raw, the yogurt will lack something in flavor and texture.

Certainly the first yogurt-makers didn't scientifically classify the organisms that worked their wonders on milk. There are many thermophilic lactic-acid bacteria in addition to the two I've mentioned. In different regions, yogurt and yogurtlike foods probably involved combinations of organisms whose multiple alliances and shifts—and, incidentally, flavor effects—we may never be able to fully document. Sometimes the two basic yogurt bacteria got mixed in with others that preferred temperatures between about 90° and 100°F—the so-called mesophilic organisms, which could start multiplying after the milk cooled below optimum yogurt-setting temperatures and might introduce other flavor notes of their own. In parts of the Caucasus and Central Asia, people also learned to introduce yeasts that triggered carbon-dioxide fermentation and produced some alcohol.

(For more on the resulting kefir and kumys, as well as the fresh fermented products that were developed in the cool climates of northern Europe, see "Cultured Milk and Cream.")

EAST IS EAST, AND WEST IS WEST— SOMETIMES THE TWAIN SHALL MEET

The vigorous state of yogurt sales in Europe and the United States belies the fact that many people in the Western world still don't really *get* the taste of yogurt as found east of the Adriatic. It was a very late import to the modern West—that is, a few immigrants here and there probably had managed to bring cultures from places like Greece or Syria before the twentieth century, but no one else had heard about it until 1907.

At that point grandiose reports from the Paris-based émigré Russian biologist Élie Metchnikoff began to put yogurt on the Western map. Metchnikoff had concluded that yogurt as consumed by generations of hardy Bulgarian peasants was the secret of a greatly extended life span. The culturing organisms in yogurt, he thought, were in effect microbial policemen that could be deployed to keep the human colon free of crime—i.e., toxins produced by "putrefying" bacteria. These colonic pollutants were the essential cause of aging, but luckily the bacteria that manufactured them could be knocked out by yogurt cultures. Without exposure to the "autointoxicating" products of the wrong germs, presumably everyone could live to the astonishing ages said to be commonplace in rural Bulgaria.

Today most of this scenario looks either oversimplified or positively crackbrained. But Metchnikoff's claims meant the start of a new Western career for yogurt, far from its places of origin. France was the first center of yogurt boosterism (and still is an important one). But pro-yogurt publicity circulated around the rest of western Europe from Metchnikoff's lifetime (he died in 1916 at the respectable but scarcely breathtaking age of seventy-one) throughout the 1920s and '30s. Bulgarian cultures were exported and propagated in various countries. A dogged if not delighted clientele embraced yogurt in the spirit that Evelyn Waugh ascribes to John Beaver's mother in the opening scene of *A Handful of Dust* (1934): "She held the carton close to her chin and gobbled with a spoon. 'Heavens, how nasty this stuff is. I wish you'd take to it, John.' "

There is an irony here: Metchnikoff had achieved an accurate enough knowledge of the operative culturing organisms to make possible the scientific commercial manufacture of finished yogurt—something that hadn't existed in the countries where an incubating batch of yogurt was a daily kitchen miracle, not a standardized retail product to be sold in packages. Its new Western aficionados understood nothing about it but that it was supposed to be good for you, "nasty" or not.

On yogurt's home territory, people had always eaten it not for health reasons but because it was a beloved food made and handled by well-known methods that controlled the final flavor. Without thinking, people knew how to make yogurt that was sourer, "sweeter" (i.e., less sour), creamier, milkier, thicker, thinner, or variously aligned along other scales of quality. To the early twentieth-century European sophisticates who bought yogurt as an exotic panacea, such niceties were meaningless. They disliked the lactic-acid sourness but assumed that it was a given, not an effect to be heightened or toned down by simple means like adding the starter under slightly altered circumstances (e.g., minute temperature variations) or draining whey at some optimal stage.

Gradually some European—and later, American—devotees began to like the taste of the early commercial yogurts. For those who didn't, help eventually arrived in the form of sugar.

The Greek-born Spanish entrepreneur Isaac Carasso founded one of the first yogurt-making businesses in Barcelona a few years after Metchnikoff's death, naming it "Danone" for his son Daniel. During World War II, Daniel Carasso brought a new branch of the family business—which had already expanded into France and elsewhere—to the United States, changing the name to "Dannon." By this time some European producers were experimentally adding sweetened fruit preserves to yogurt. The American Dannon company, originally a tiny Bronx-based supplier to ethnic communities, adopted this tack in 1947. By the late 1950s sweetened yogurt was making giant strides on both continents.

Different approaches, for instance, "sundae-style" with sweetened fruit on the bottom or "Swiss-style" with the sweetening mixed in, gathered enthusiastic followings. Many—probably most—manufacturers soon took to using skimmed or partly skimmed instead of whole milk, offsetting the lack of body by adding powdered skim milk. The change reduced sweetened Western yogurt's already tenuous connection with any sort of natural milk flavor but enabled promoters to call it "low-fat" or "fat-free." Some manufacturers also lengthened the product's shelf life by pasteurizing it after incubation. Of course, this killed the live cultures that have always been part of yogurt. But since live cultures weren't (and currently aren't) mentioned in the FDA's standards of identity, it didn't stop anyone from calling the result "yogurt." At about 1970 a new sales arena opened with the development of frozen yogurt, the most highly sugared avatar yet, which was inaccurately but very successfully promoted as a "lighter," more healthful alternative to ice cream.

The bigger the business grew, the less it had to do with the yogurt of Bulgaria, Turkey, or anywhere else in the eastern birthplaces of this remarkable food. In effect, yogurt had been turned into a kind of premixed sweet-and-sour pudding or pseudo–ice cream, and whatever conflicted with that image came to be viewed as a defect by makers and consumers alike.

Most real yogurt, for example, "breaks," or releases whey, if it's allowed to stand after a spoon is dipped in it. There is a simple reason for this. To dairy chemists, yogurt is technically a fragile semisolid "gel" formed during the culturing process when the lactic-acid content gets high enough to lower the pH of the milk and cause some changes in the shape of the casein micelles. Their surface becomes bumpy and irregular enough to let them link up in a spongy lattice of casein strands holding whey in the interstices of the sponge. The casein and whey remain in this delicate arrangement—somewhere between the original milk structure and the kind of decisive curd precipitation that happens with cheesemaking—as long as the yogurt is left alone. Dip into it with a spoon, and you disturb the unstable gel enough to let whey leak out of the sponge. This harmless change does not affect flavor, and can be simply though temporarily reversed by stirring the whey back in. But because the separating phenomenon (chemists call it "syneresis") bothered many consumers, manufacturers routinely started adding such fixes of the imaginary flaw as starches, gums, and/or pectin to keep the body of the yogurt intact.

Through all these vicissitudes, plain unflavored yogurt with nothing added retained a scattered following among Western consumers, mostly though not entirely in ethnic enclaves. Then a small but sturdy renaissance began to dawn for real yogurt.

Some of the impetus came from the counterculture of the 1960s, which adopted homemade yogurt as a sort of "lifestyle statement." Unlike some fashions of the time, this one has continued to gather converts ever since. Today nearly any cookbook claiming to be an all-purpose American kitchen bible will have directions for making yogurt. This certainly doesn't mean that the general cooking population has a solid acquaintance with the age-old marvels of well and truly made yogurt, but at the very least we can say that no one now sees home yogurt-making as a hippie affectation.

At the same time, several other developments contributed to a serious upturn in the American fortunes of yogurt. One was a lively outpouring of cookbooks by such writers as Paula Wolfert, Claudia Roden, and Madhur Jaffrey, celebrating cuisines to which real, fresh, rich, flavorful yogurt was crucial. This encouragement was eventually followed by a modest return of local artisanal dairying and a growing curiosity about a range of fermented foods, as well as tremendous waves of immigration from India and many parts of the old Yogurtistan.

In other words, Americans who really want to explore yogurt now have unprecedented freedom to do so. Without wanting to diminish the importance of other fermented dairy foods, I have to say that for sheer culinary richness and diversity, the basic yogurt traditions of the eastern Mediterranean, the Near East, Central Asia, and India stand apart from anything else.

It should be pointed out that these are not the world's only yogurt traditions. Yogurt or something close to it flourishes today among the pastoral peoples of East Africa and some sizable ethnic minorities of China. But I don't know of any work that's been done to document its uses in either area in terms intelligible to American consumers. On the other hand, people in this country can learn a great deal about the genius that people in India and the old Yogurtistan homelands have brought to cooking with yogurt. The recipes in this section barely scratch the surface.

YOGURT AND HEALTH: A CAUTIONARY VIEW

Health claims on behalf of yogurt have persisted, and undoubtedly helped keep it before the public eye during the transition from a strange new import to a permanent part of the American diet. But I think it's not easy to disentangle reality from myth. The only claims I'd subscribe to are that plain yogurt can be both a delicious and a nutritious food, that sufferers from moderate lactose intolerance can digest it more readily than unfermented milk, and that it may help people get over gastric upsets.

There does seem to be evidence that when certain bacteria are introduced into the colon they may help keep undesirable counterparts in check. But the basic yogurt-producing organisms (*S. thermophilus* and *L. bulgaricus*) aren't among them, because they cannot survive on their own in the human gut. Just which lactic-acid bacteria can and can't form viable populations in the colon, and what that implies about choices in fermented dairy products, are questions on which the jury is mostly out. The most plausible claims are for a lactose-digesting organism called *Lactobacillus acidophilus*, which appears able to live on its own in the colon. On the strength of this capacity, it is often added to yogurt cultures though it is not one of the heat-loving, or thermophilic, bacteria responsible for basic yogurt fermentation. In my opinion, the merits of acidophilus should be debated by people qualified to talk about lactose-digesting problems, not good food.

On the lactose-intolerance question, I'd simply point out that people's digestive capacities can vary across a wide spectrum and that the amount of lactose in yogurt also can vary a good deal. The fermentation is never carried to the point of changing a hundred percent of the original lactose to lactic acid. But as discussed later on in the basic yogurt recipe, the world's habitual yogurt eaters have almost invariably finished the culturing process by draining much or most of the whey. This eliminates nearly all the lactic acid and remaining lactose together. Unfortunately, sufferers from very severe lactose intolerance may be affected by even the small amounts found in drained or undrained yogurt; trial and error is the only way to find out. Generally speaking, lactose content is highest in yogurt made from nonfat milk, especially with added nonfat milk solids.

BUYING AND USING PLAIN YOGURT

I have been happy to see the plain-yogurt fan club grow in the last few years as good new versions come on the market. (The preflavored kinds, though hugely popular here, appeal to a different cluster of preferences and aren't appropriate for any of my recipes.) Savvier shopping has been one result. It starts with careful label reading.

The first thing to look for is the presence of live cultures. Don't buy anything that doesn't mention them. The label may say simply, "live active cultures" or list them by name, in which case the ones to look for are *Streptococcus thermophilus* and *Lactobacillus bulgaricus.* There are brands that list numerous others, but adding more kinds of bacteria doesn't confer any intrinsic flavor advantage, at least to my taste. If you find that you like yogurt prepared with a large number of different organisms, by all means follow your own preference.

The fewer other ingredients, the better. "Milk," or "milk and cream," is all that's necessary. I avoid everything containing either thickeners (starch, gum, tapioca, pectin) or additives accompanied by health claims (inulin, fructo-oligosaccharides). The additive hardest to avoid is nonfat milk solids, meant to give wan, insubstantial yogurt more body. I'd prefer to see the goal pursued by other means like using better milk in the first place, but sometimes can't find anything made without this would-be improvement.

Please be aware that real yogurt is not a low-fat or low-calorie food. (On its home territory people not only made it from whole, unhomogenized milk but often reduced the milk by long cooking to enrich the yogurt.) If you have tasted good full-fat yogurt, you will realize how inferior the reduced-fat versions are. As for commercial nonfat yogurt, it is inexcusably awful. Calorie counters and fat-watchers had best treat yogurt as a rich food to be used with discretion, not shorn of its true character. Everyone else should know that the higher the listed fat content, the creamier the yogurt. When possible, look for yogurt from unhomogenized milk, though unfortunately this information isn't always on the label.

Yogurt is best bought as fresh as possible. It becomes sourer with long sitting. Check expiration dates and try to find younger rather than elderly specimens. Once bought, it will stay fresher longer if you drain the whey as suggested on page 158. Some (usually imported) brands will say "strained," indicating that they already have been partly drained. These are usually creamier and fresher-tasting than ones with all the whey still present.

The range of available brands varies greatly in different parts of the United States. The best are almost invariably more expensive than most of the popular national brands. Small producers often sell their yogurt in local farmers' markets, and I urge you to explore these before any others. Otherwise, my hands-down favorite is Old Chatham Sheepherding Company yogurt, an advertisement incarnate for the flavor of sheep's milk. Just about as good (and expensive) is the sheep's- and goats'-milk yogurt imported from Greece under the brand name Fage Total.

Total also produces a good whole cows' milk yogurt. But I usually prefer the full-fat cows'-milk yogurts often sold by the quart in Turkish neighborhood groceries, with labels stating that they are made from "whole milk" containing at least 3.5 percent milkfat—a small but quite perceptible improvement over the usual 3.25 percent kind.

I also like the thick, dense buffaloes'-milk yogurt made by the Woodstock Water Buffalo Company of Vermont, though I wish it were unhomogenized and put up in larger containers. My favorite goats'-milk yogurt is the refreshing drinkable Yo-Goat from Coach Farm in New York State. As explained later (page 159), goats'-milk yogurt is naturally thinner than that from other animals, a quality that the Yo-Goat people happily embrace instead of trying to disguise it with thickeners as do most other makers.

A final note to cooks: Yogurt curdles on exposure to heat. This doesn't hurt the flavor, but looks rather unappetizing. Depending on the dish, you may be able to sidestep the problem by warming a sauce through without letting it boil after adding yogurt. Or for a popular Middle Eastern method, mix yogurt with a small amount of flour, cornstarch, or egg white and heat briefly before using it in hot dishes. (In India, people often use chickpea flour.) The usual proportions are about a tablespoon of flour or starch, or 1 egg white, to 4 cups of yogurt. Begin by mixing the flour or starch smooth with a little cold water or lightly beating the egg white. Put the yogurt in a saucepan and whisk or stir until it thins. Add the chosen stabilizer and bring the yogurt barely to a boil, stirring. Let it simmer for a few minutes before adding to the rest of the dish.

WALLACHIAN SHEEP
WITH SPIRAL HORNS

RECIPES

HOMEMADE YOGURT: SOME THOUGHTS

If you never have made yogurt before, it's only fair to tell you in advance that what you end up with may not in the least resemble the kinds you're used to buying—and there's no reason it should. Perhaps the most important thing to understand is that real yogurt varies widely in natural consistency, depending on factors like the source of the milk.

In the regions I think of as Yogurtistan, the comparatively thin body of unmodified cows'-milk yogurt (as compared to sheep's or water buffaloes' milk) isn't seen as a defect to be got around by adding any of the thickeners frequently put into commercial American yogurt. If people want to thicken yogurt, they do it by subtraction, not addition. Once it is set, they put it in some kind of strainer and leave it until it has lost from a third to half its volume in whey—at least, that's a usual treatment of cows'-milk yogurt. Pure sheep's-milk yogurt sets up much thicker because it's more concentrated to start with, and the pure goats'-milk kind isn't expected to set up at all; you drink rather than eat it.

The advantages of draining are several. Thin, undrained yogurt gets sour faster than drained yogurt because the retained whey continues to ferment after the yogurt sets, making it sourer without making it any firmer. Yogurt connoisseurs from places like Turkey, Greece, and Armenia always say that good yogurt is "sweet"—meaning not sugary but beautifully milky, fresh, and clean-tasting. The texture will be suave and silky without heaviness. Yogurt thickened by draining also produces better results in cooking. And the whey has its own uses as a refreshing cold drink, light soup base, or cooking liquid for pilafs.

The best analogy to explain the effect of draining is with simmering a broth or stock to reduce it. You are not merely removing liquid but deepening and focusing the original character of the yogurt in a way that can't be reversed. Sour yogurt is all very well, but compared with very fresh "sweet" yogurt it is unremarkable. Make the attempt, and I think you will be convinced.

I am often asked where to find professional-quality yogurt cultures for starting a first batch. But the fact is that after various experiments I see no great advantage in them for home yogurtmakers. My advice is to use a few spoonfuls of any plain, unflavored commercial yogurt that you find particularly good.

It's also unnecessary to buy yogurt "kits" with little individual-sized cups, or any kind of special yogurt-making equipment. I do find an accurate thermometer to be a help, but it's not essential. You can make do with a few ordinary kitchen items once you grasp the basic stages of the process that you will be putting the milk through. They are:

- Heating and partly cooling
- Inoculating with a starter
- Incubating in a warm environment protected from jostling
- Draining

None of these is difficult as long as you look through the recipe in advance and make mental notes about the equipment you'll need. The only thing that may require any special advance planning is the incubation period, when the milk has to stay warm for at least 4 to 6 hours. Some people pour the milk into a crockery bowl, cover it with a plate or plastic wrap, and leave it in a warm, draft-free place (for instance, a turned-off gas oven with a pilot light—alas, the newer gas stoves usually don't have oven pilot lights). My usual solution, which maintains a good even temperature for a long time, is one or more wide-mouthed plastic containers of the kind you can keep liquids hot or cold in, like the inexpensive half-liter Stanley Heatkeeper Food Jars from Aladdin Industries. The good news is that even if the incubating yogurt cools off below the optimum temperature of about 110°F, all is not lost—it will just take longer to set and may be a little thinner. Making yogurt really is pretty foolproof as long as the starter contains active cultures and the milk doesn't get jounced during incubation.

HOMEMADE YOGURT: BASIC RECIPE WITH COWS' MILK

I usually double the recipe, but suggest starting with these amounts for a maiden effort. Have all equipment as clean as possible before starting.

YIELD: About 2 to 2½ cups finished yogurt, 1½ to 2 cups whey (Exact amounts will vary from batch to batch.)

1 quart whole milk, as fresh as possible and preferably unhomogenized
2 tablespoons plain unflavored yogurt containing live cultures

Heating and cooling: Pour the milk into a heavy saucepan and gradually heat it to or just below boiling. Let it partly cool until not quite hot to the touch, about 110° to 115°F. (You can speed the process by immersing the pan in a sinkful of cold water.)

Inoculating: Put the yogurt into a small bowl; it's your "starter." When the milk reaches the right temperature, stir about 1 cup of it into the yogurt, then stir the mixture back into the pot of milk.

Incubating: Gently pour the milk into your chosen container (see page 157). To repeat the crucial mantra: *It must not be disturbed by any jiggling or shaking*, so set it far from any bumptious goings-on in the household. Let it stand until set to the consistency of a delicate custard, not a heavy pudding. Timings vary widely, but usually yogurt will be well set after 4 to 6 hours if the temperature can be steadily maintained at about 110°F. (Nothing can stop it from taking its own time, so be patient.)

Draining: As explained above, draining the whey once the delicate gel is set makes all the difference between unremarkable and really beautiful yogurt. Line a colander or mesh strainer with *tight-woven* cheesecloth, butter muslin, or a large cotton handkerchief. Set it over a pot or bowl deep enough to hold up to two cups of whey per original quart of milk. Pour or scrape the yogurt into the colander and drain until it has lost close to half its volume in whey, usually about 3 to 4 hours. Turn out the drained yogurt into a large bowl, and stir or beat it as smooth as possible with a stout wooden spoon. It is now ready to eat, and will never taste better.

The yogurt will keep its incomparable freshness for a day or so if refrigerated in a sealed container. After that it will start to take on the still good but less magical flavor of sour yogurt.

If you want to keep a batch going more or less permanently, save a few tablespoons from the last batch and use it as starter for the next. It will most reliably keep up its activity if you use it within a week (preferably less) of making.

VARIATION: Goats'-milk yogurt can be made by exactly the same method using a quart of goats' milk (nonultrapasteurized) to two tablespoons of starter. But the casein in goats' milk has a different composition from that in cows' milk. (Four major forms of casein play a part in the uses of milk, and each has a different configuration in the milk of different species.) As a result, yogurt from goats' milk will remain liquid. Some books suggest correctives ranging from rennet to kosher gelatin. In fact, it needs no corrective. It is just as good for drinking as other yogurt is for eating.

SERVING SUGGESTIONS: Whether you prefer sweetened or unsweetened yogurt, starting with the best plain kind you can make (or for that matter, buy) will open up a whole world of flavor possibilities. For instance, any preferred sort of honey put on creamy plain yogurt creates an exquisite contrast of tastes not to be matched by any presweetened commercial version. The same is true of fruit preserves, or flavorful unrefined sugars such as Indian *gur*, or jaggery. Real "sweet" yogurt on fresh berries or fruit is also a revelation. Or pass a bowl of it (perhaps seasoned with fresh mint, dill, or cilantro) to accompany just about any meal based on east-of-the Adriatic traditions—Serbian, Greek, Middle Eastern, or Indian. And don't forget its uses with garlic (page 162). There is no more marvelously adaptable culinary chameleon.

YOGURT "CHEESE" AND "CHEESE" BALLS

What is usually called yogurt cheese is no more cheese than cultured buttermilk is buttermilk. True, there are commercial cheeses (leaning toward the mild, rubbery, and forgettable) based at least partly on yogurt. But most often the term "yogurt cheese" refers to yogurt taken a stage or two beyond the draining suggested in the main yogurt recipe. Usually it has had enough of the whey drained from it to produce something about as firm as a medium-soft cocktail spread. This is what's often called *labneh*, or *lebne*, by Arabic-speakers. Sometimes you can buy it under that name in Middle Eastern groceries (but don't confuse it with *laban*, which is yogurt generally).

It's hard to give precise directions for turning yogurt into yogurt cheese, since different batches will take a longer or shorter time to drain to a given consistency. But for drained yogurt thick enough to use as a spread or fairly full-bodied dip, I would put either homemade or store-bought yogurt in a cheesecloth-lined colander (nonreactive, please) or the clever mesh-lined draining device called a "yogurt cheese funnel," set it over a deep bowl, and let it drain until dripping has completely or almost stopped. If it is still rather messy, gather and tie the cheesecloth corners into a bag that can be hung from a stick (I use a long-handled wooden spoon set over a pail), or put a small plastic-wrapped weight (e.g., a can of beans) on the funnel, and leave until you see no further dripping and the yogurt is the consistency of a dip or spread. The whole process may take anywhere from 6 to 24 hours—sorry, but that's the nature of the beast. It will happen faster at room temperature than in the refrigerator.

For yogurt cheese balls, you must get the mass to give up still more moisture. In the hot, dry climates where yogurt originated, this is not difficult. In many American kitchens, it will be easier said than done. I suggest that you follow the procedure for yogurt cheese, but first mix the yogurt with a little salt (about ½ teaspoon per starting pint of yogurt), to facilitate drainage. Let it sit still longer, until it resembles a very thick spread. Scrape it into a wide, shallow container (or more than one) like a Pyrex pie plate or baking dish, spreading it out no more than about ⅓ inch thick. If you are blessed with hot, dry summers and blazing sunshine, set it in a sunny place (loosely protected with thin cheesecloth) for 6 to 10 hours, or until it is as thick as cream cheese and the surface is dry. Otherwise, put it in a warm, dry room and wait for the same result, which may take two or three days. Be patient; it will be most satisfyingly cheesy if you wait until the yogurt is no longer tacky to the touch and you see a few dried-out cracks on the surface.

Now lightly rub your palms and a plate with olive oil. Scoop up the yogurt a small handful at a time and roll it into balls about 1 to 1¼ inches in diameter. Set them on the oiled plate as they are done; re-oil your hands as necessary. You should get about 5 to 6 cheese balls per original starting pint of yogurt.

If everything is terribly sticky when you are done, briefly refrigerate the plate before carefully transferring the cheese balls to a screw-top glass jar and pouring in enough olive oil to cover them. They will keep in the refrigerator for two to three weeks. The oil will congeal around them, so be sure to let the jar sit at room temperature long enough to liquefy the oil before scooping out as many cheese balls as you need. Mixed with a little of the oil, they make a lovely spread for crackers or good pita bread with a dusting of black pepper, oregano, or thyme; the sumac-thyme-sesame mixture called *za'atar*; or Turkish hot red pepper flakes (Aleppo, Maraş, or Urfa pepper).

TARATOR
(COLD YOGURT SOUP WITH CUCUMBERS AND WALNUTS)

This splendid Bulgarian soup is closely related to a Turkish nut sauce of the same name. It is perfectly designed to exploit yogurt's affinities with garlic, walnuts, and cucumbers. My recipe is loosely based on one in Maria Kaneva-Johnson's invaluable *The Melting Pot: Balkan Food and Cookery*, an extraordinary survey of the many interwoven strands that make up the Balkan cuisines.

In the Balkans, cold soups like this are often served with a little ice floating in the bowl. Dill is the usual herb for *tarator*, but some cooks use fresh mint instead. The yogurt should be fresh and sweet, not sharply acidic. Look for a nutty-flavored walnut oil; some health-food brands are so tasteless that olive oil is preferable. I like the French-made J. Leblanc.

For all yogurt-cucumber combinations I suggest using the small, thin-skinned cucumbers often sold here as "Persian-type," which are increasingly available even in supermarkets. When chopped or grated they release less water than the large, usually waxed American ones, and add better cucumber flavor. If you're stuck with the big, coarse kind, you can slightly improve results by first peeling and seeding them, then grating them, sprinkling lightly with salt, and letting some of the liquid drain off before mixing them with the other ingredients. Follow this procedure in any recipe using grated or chopped cucumbers.

YIELD: 4 to 5 servings (about 4 cups)

2 to 3 large garlic cloves
1 teaspoon salt, or to taste
1 cup (4 ounces) walnut meats
2 to 3 thick slices of sturdy-textured bread, soaked in water and
    squeezed dry
¼ to ⅓ cup well-flavored walnut oil or strong young extra-virgin
    olive oil
2 cups rich, creamy plain yogurt
3 to 4 small thin-skinned Persian-type cucumbers or 1 English
    hothouse cucumber
1 tablespoon freshly squeezed lemon juice
½ cup ice water
A large handful of fresh dill, snipped
Lemon wedges for garnish

TARATOR (CONT.)

Pound the garlic and salt to a paste with a mortar and pestle. Set aside a hand-ful of walnut meats; pound the rest smooth with the garlic. Add the bread and pound the mixture to a paste. Work in 2 to 3 tablespoons of the oil.

Whisk the yogurt in a mixing bowl with the walnut-bread paste. Whisk to combine. Coarsely grate the cucumbers or dice them very fine and add to the yogurt. (If using a hothouse cucumber, peel and seed it first.) Stir in the lemon juice.

Let the soup chill for at least an hour in the refrigerator. It will thin slightly as the cucumbers release their juice. Meanwhile, chop the remaining walnuts fine. At serving time, stir in enough ice water to make it the consistency of a thick soup. Taste for salt and add a bit more if you like. Put an ice cube or a lit-tle cracked ice in each bowl. Serve garnished with plenty of fresh dill; pass the lemon wedges, chopped walnuts, and the remaining 2 to 3 tablespoons of wal-nut oil for everyone to add to taste.

YOGURT-GARLIC SAUCE

The best sauce may be hunger, but some combination of garlic and yogurt runs a close second from Serbia to the western Himalayas. It appears on local tables as universally as simple tomato salsas in Mexico and is put on all kinds of meats and vegetables—though in many regions, not on fish or seafood; there are widespread taboos against combining fish and dairy products.

YIELD: 1 cup

2 small garlic cloves, coarsely chopped
½ teaspoon salt, or to taste
1 cup plain whole-milk yogurt, preferably thick and creamy
  (otherwise lightly drain before measuring)

Pound the garlic and salt to a paste using a mortar and pestle; stir in the yogurt. Serve at once for the mildest flavor, or let it sit in the refrigerator for several hours to bring out the garlic.

VARIATION: The recipe for "Mast-o Mooseer" in Margaret Shaida's *The Legendary Cuisine of Persia* is an interesting spin on the yogurt-garlic idea call-ing for 8 peeled and chopped shallots (reduce or halve this if the shallots are large) to 1 cup yogurt. Soak the shallots in cold water for several hours (overnight if they're strong) and let dry thoroughly before seasoning with salt and pepper and mixing into the yogurt.

CACIK AND RELATIVES

All cuisines of the Diverse Sources Belt—or original Yogurtistan—have their versions of yogurt combined with fresh vegetables and herbs. In English such preparations are variously and lamely described as salads, soups, relishes, dips, spreads, cold side dishes, or sauces, though none of these exactly fits the bill. Perhaps the best-known of them is the cucumber-yogurt mixture called *cacık* (pronounced "jajik") in Turkish and *tzatziki* in Greek; other names include *khyar bi laban* (Arabic) and *mast-o khiar* (Farsi). Any ten different people probably will give you fifteen ideas on how to concoct it—say, with thick sweet yogurt to make it mild and dense, ice water to make it soupy, lemon juice to make it sour, oil to make it satiny, chopped cucumbers presalted to draw off moisture, or grated cucumbers allowed to contribute all the moisture they want. There is invariably some kind of herb, but whether it is parsley, dill, scallion, cilantro, fennel, dried mint, fresh mint, several combined, or none of the above depends on whom you're talking to. Cucumbers, yogurt, salt, and garlic are about the only constants (and even the last can be omitted).

The following is the version I like best, but don't hesitate to try any of the embellishments I have mentioned. There is no right or wrong way to make it. I will say, however, that the quality of the cucumbers and the yogurt you start with will come through very distinctly. If you have just made a particularly excellent batch of your own yogurt, there is no finer purpose you could devote it to.

If you have to use the thick-skinned American-type cucumbers, see the suggestion on page 161.

YIELD: About 3 cups

3 small Persian-type cucumbers or 1 English hothouse cucumber
About 1 teaspoon salt
2 small garlic cloves
2 cups drained plain yogurt (a thick, creamy kind)
2 teaspoons Turkish dried mint, crushed
Freshly ground black pepper
2 tablespoons olive oil

Peel and seed the cucumbers; cut into very fine dice and put them in a small bowl with ½ teaspoon of the salt. Let stand for about 20 minutes, or until they

CACIK (CONT.)

have given up some of their juice. Drain them and squeeze as dry as you can in a few thicknesses of paper towels.

Crush the garlic and remaining salt to a paste with a mortar and pestle. Thoroughly mix the cucumbers with the garlic paste, yogurt, dried mint, and pepper. Taste for salt (probably it will have plenty). Beat in the olive oil, and let sit for at least an hour to meld the flavors; serve at room temperature as a dip, relish, or just generally useful dish.

VARIATION: This becomes a light, pleasant vegetarian cold soup for two or three people with the addition of 1 cup ice water and perhaps an extra pinch of salt. Some people put an ice cube in each soup bowl.

CUCUMBER RAITA

The yogurt-based Indian preparations called *raitas*—there is no good English word, since they might equally well be called salads or relishes—are of innumerable different kinds. There is scarcely a vegetable or fruit that can't be turned into a raita. This cucumber-based version happens to be the best known to diners in Indian-American restaurants. At a glance, it somewhat resembles the preceding Turkish cacık or Greek tzatziki. The main differences are that cucumber raitas are made without garlic and usually are laced with a dash of spices (cumin, black pepper, red pepper, sometimes others). Chopped tomato figures in some versions. Like many dishes of the subcontinent, raitas receive a different treatment in southern India as well as a different name, *pachadi*.

If you have to use the thick-skinned American-type cucumbers, see the suggestion on page 161.

YIELD: About 3 cups

3 small Persian-type cucumbers or 1 English hothouse cucumber
1 small ripe tomato (optional)
2 cups drained plain yogurt (a thick, creamy kind)
½ to 1 teaspoon cumin seeds, briefly toasted and ground with mortar and pestle
¼ to ½ teaspoon freshly ground black pepper
½ to ¾ teaspoon salt
1 small green chile pepper, seeded and minced (optional)

A handful of fresh mint or cilantro leaves, coarsely chopped
 (leave a few whole for garnish)
A dash of cayenne pepper or hot paprika

Either cut the cucumbers into very fine dice or shred them on the coarse side of a box grater. Squeeze out any excess moisture. Peel and seed the optional tomato and chop very fine.

Put the yogurt in a small bowl and whisk smooth. Mix in the cucumber, tomato, cumin, black pepper, salt, optional minced chile pepper, and chopped mint or cilantro. Serve garnished with a dusting of cayenne or paprika and a few whole mint or cilantro leaves.

Some people make this hours ahead and let it sit to marry the flavors. I like to serve it freshly mixed.

VARIATION: For Cucumber Pachadi, follow the directions for raita but use cilantro leaves and 1 or 2 small green chiles. Heat a little ghee (page 251) or vegetable oil (1 tablespoon or less) in a small skillet and toss in ⅛ teaspoon Indian brown mustard seeds and a few curry leaves. (You can also add a pinch of ground asafetida; 1 teaspoon each whole *urad dal*, also called "black gram"; and *channa dal*, Indian split chickpeas; and/or a small dried red chile.) When the mustard seeds begin to pop, pour the contents of the skillet over the yogurt-cucumber mixture and stir to combine.

OTHER SUGGESTIONS: Raitas and pachadis can be made with any vegetable that takes your fancy, crisp and raw (let's say, sliced or grated radishes) or cooked (sautéed diced eggplant, chopped spinach). There are onion raitas, mint raitas, sweet-potato raitas, mixed raw vegetable raitas. . . .

BANANA RAITA

A favorite among the many Indian fruit raitas. It is served in the same way as the preceding cucumber version, but in my opinion goes best with Indian rice-based dishes. Banana raitas can be sweet and mild, or—like this one—distinctly punchy. Tone down the chile if you like, but please do *not* use any sort of low-fat or nonfat yogurt.

YIELD: About 4 cups

3 medium-sized ripe bananas
Juice of half a lemon
2 cups well-drained plain yogurt, preferably a very creamy kind
1 teaspoon salt, or to taste
2 long green chiles, seeded and chopped (not too fine)
A large handful of cilantro, minced
½ teaspoon ground cumin, or to taste

Cut the peeled bananas lengthwise into quarters and crosswise into thin slices. Put them in a bowl, season with lemon juice, and toss to coat well.

Beat the yogurt and salt very smooth with a wooden spoon. Add the bananas and all other ingredients, reserving a little of the cilantro for garnish. Give it all a good stir and let stand for at least half an hour at room temperature to marry the flavors; serve garnished with the extra cilantro. It does not keep, so plan to serve it within an hour or two at most.

WALNUT-YOGURT CHUTNEY

Why walnuts should frequently be combined with yogurt in some of the oldest Eurasian cuisines is no mystery. Dairy animals and yogurt-making historically flourished in many of the Old World regions where walnut trees grew—Greece, the Caucasus, the Vale of Kashmir. (For another example, see Tarator, page 161.) There are many variations on the theme—coarse-textured and minimalist, bound with bread or pot cheese, enriched with stock, a little vinegary, a little sweet. This versatile Kashmiri condiment is only one possibility among many. It is traditionally made with the local medium-hot chile peppers, which can be used green but more often are dried when ripe and pulverized to make a seasoning somewhat like ground dried New Mexico chiles. Hot Hungarian paprika (or a mixture of sweet and hot) will do. Experiment with any kind of hot, mild, fresh, or dried chile you like. The proportions can be elastic; for a looser-textured sauce, increase the yogurt to 1 cup.

It is worth looking for young, sweet walnuts; the skins don't have the harsh tannic bite of older ones. Stores catering to immigrants from Turkey or the Caucasus often have excellent walnuts.

YIELD: About 1 cup

1 cup walnut meats
1 tablespoon (or to taste) ground dried New Mexico chile,
    or 1 ½ teaspoons each Hungarian sweet and hot paprika
1 teaspoon salt, or to taste
A large pinch of garam masala, or a pinch each of ground cumin and
    cinnamon
½ cup thick, creamy plain yogurt

Grind the walnuts in a food processor, stopping just when the pulverized bits start coming together in a paste. Scrape out into a small bowl; add the ground chile, salt, garam masala, and yogurt and stir to combine thoroughly. Serve at room temperature as a condiment for meats and vegetables, or a dip with crudités and any Indian bread.

LAMB KÖFTE IN YOGURT SAUCE

Among the many ways of cooking lamb meatballs in the Diverse Sources Belt, baking them in a custardlike yogurt sauce is one of the most delicious. For this Turkish version, be sure to use a good rich yogurt. I like the meatballs quite tart (from lemon juice and sumac) and a bit hot (from Turkish red pepper and paprika), with a strong jolt of cumin. Any of these can be cut back to gentler proportions.

YIELD: 8 meatballs

2 cups creamy whole-milk plain yogurt
3 to 4 thick slices of a small day-old roll or baguette, crusts trimmed
1 medium onion
2 garlic cloves
4 eggs
1 pound ground lamb
½ to 1 teaspoon Aleppo pepper or other Turkish ground red pepper
¼ teaspoon Turkish paprika
¾ teaspoon ground sumac
2 to 3 teaspoons ground cumin
1 to 3 teaspoons lemon juice
¼ cup minced parsley
1 teaspoon salt
Plenty of freshly ground black pepper
⅓ to ½ cup olive oil

Set the yogurt to drain briefly in a cheesecloth-lined colander; soak the bread in a little warm water until well softened. Preheat the oven to 350°F.

Grate the onion on the coarse side of a box grater, and mince the garlic very fine. Thoroughly beat one of the eggs. Wring the water out of the bread. Place the onion, garlic, egg, and bread in a large mixing bowl with the ground meat. Add the Aleppo pepper, paprika, sumac, cumin, lemon juice, parsley, salt, and pepper. Mix everything very thoroughly with your hands and shape into 8 oval meatballs.

Heat the oil to rippling in a heavy medium skillet. Working in two batches, brown the meatballs well on both sides. As they are done, remove them to a shallow 2-quart baking dish like an 8-inch Pyrex pan.

Beat the remaining 3 eggs and stir in the partially drained yogurt. Pour this mixture over the meatballs and bake for 40 to 45 minutes. Serve at once.

ÇILBIR
(TURKISH POACHED EGGS IN YOGURT SAUCE)

All the yogurt homelands possess some simple dish based on the unbeatable combination of yogurt and eggs. Any egg-loving cook should be able to come up with marvelous ways of pairing the two. This Turkish example, which is always glorified with paprika-reddened butter, may start your imagination going.

YIELD: 4 servings

A double recipe of Yogurt-Garlic Sauce (page 162)
1 tablespoon distilled or cider vinegar
8 eggs, the freshest possible
Salt and freshly ground black pepper to taste
¼ cup butter, preferably unsalted
1 tablespoon (or to taste) mild or hot Turkish paprika, Maraş pepper,
    or Aleppo pepper

Preheat the oven to the lowest setting. Divide the yogurt sauce among four ramekins of about 1½- to 2-cup capacity, and set in the oven to barely warm.

Fill a shallow saucepan about 1½ to 2 inches deep with water, add the vinegar, and bring to a boil. Reduce the heat to a bare simmer. Poach the eggs, two or three at a time, by breaking them into a saucer and slipping them into the simmering water; let cook about 3 minutes or just until set. Carefully lift out the eggs with a slotted spoon, letting them drain briefly, and put them into the warmed ramekins (two eggs to each). Season with salt and pepper.

Gently melt the butter in a small saucepan and add the paprika or crushed red pepper. Tilt the pan to let the solids settle to the bottom, drizzle a little of the clear red-orange butter over each portion, and serve at once.

VARIATIONS: Instead of making the garlic sauce, mix creamy plain yogurt with a little finely crumbled feta cheese and dried Turkish mint. The dish is also very good with eggs fried sunny-side up rather than poached.

"CURD RICE"

To English-speakers in India, "curd" is the local equivalent of yogurt. The popular southern dish "curd rice" is a sort of rice salad using plain cooked rice, some diced cucumber with or without other fresh seasonings, and a *tarka* (special enrichment) of dried spices briefly sizzled in hot ghee or oil, the whole thing being bound with a yogurt-milk dressing. Now that so many of us have access to Indian dals and spices, it deserves to be discovered by non-Indian cooks. I find curd rice endlessly useful as a lively room-temperature side dish that can be made hours ahead. And it wouldn't take much (some more diced or slivered vegetables, cooked chickpeas, leftover chicken or meat) to turn it into a main dish, vegetarian or otherwise.

This is one time that you aren't aiming for fluffy, dry rice with every grain beautifully distinct. Nor should you spring for basmati rice; any plain, nonconverted long-grain rice will do. You don't want it wet when cooked, but it should be just very slightly soggy.

There is nothing tricky about curd rice, but remember to let the yogurt drain well in advance. The two kinds of dal used in the aromatic tarka are not absolutely necessary, but their crunchy nuttiness is a big plus.

If you have to make do with thick-skinned American cucumbers, see the suggestion on page 161.

YIELD: About 6 servings (5 to 6 cups)

1 cup long-grain rice
2 cups drained plain yogurt, preferably a creamy whole-milk kind
About ⅓ to ½ cup whole milk
1 scant tablespoon whole (not split) urad dal (also called black gram)
1 scant tablespoon channa dal (Indian split chickpeas)
1 teaspoon Indian brown mustard seeds
1 small dried hot red pepper, seeded
6 to 8 fresh curry leaves
A pinch of asafetida
About 1 tablespoon ghee (page 251), mustard oil,
    or vegetable oil for frying the spices
3 to 4 small Persian-type cucumbers or 1 English hothouse cucumber
2 small serrano chiles or other small hot green peppers
A 1-inch chunk of peeled fresh ginger

A large handful of cilantro leaves, plus more for garnish if desired
About 2 teaspoons salt, or to taste

Put the rice in a small bowl, and cover with cold water. Rinse it in several changes of water until the water runs clear. Let soak half an hour, and pour into a sieve to drain briefly.

Meanwhile, beat the yogurt as smooth as possible with a whisk or wooden spoon. Beat in enough milk to give it the consistency of a thick but not pasty dressing.

Prepare the ingredients for the tarka: Rinse the urad dal and channa dal under cold running water to remove any grit or dust, blot dry with paper towels, and put them in a small bowl. Put the mustard seeds, dried red pepper, curry leaves, and asafetida in another bowl and have the ghee or oil ready for frying.

Cook the drained rice by any preferred method. (I spread it in a wide, shallow lidded saucepan, cover with about 1½ cups boiling water, add 1 teaspoon salt, bring to a boil, and cook tightly covered over very low heat for about 16 to 18 minutes, or until the water is barely absorbed and the rice is tender but still a little moist.)

While the rice cooks, dice the cucumber very fine. Seed the green chiles and mince them together with the ginger and cilantro.

Turn out the hot rice into a large mixing bowl and mash it for a few seconds with a potato masher, leaving the grains mostly whole.

Heat the ghee or oil very hot in a small heavy skillet. Add the urad dal and channa dal and fry, stirring, for about 15 to 20 seconds (don't let them scorch, but they should get slightly crisp). Add the mustard seeds, dried pepper, curry leaves, and asafetida, stirring briskly. When the mustard seeds start to pop, empty the entire contents of the pan over the hot rice. Add the cucumbers, minced chiles, ginger, and cilantro, and 1 teaspoon salt; toss to mix thoroughly. Lastly, add the yogurt-milk mixture and toss well. Taste for seasoning and serve warm or at room temperature, garnished with extra cilantro if you like.

CHICKEN SALAD À LA TANDOOR

À la tandoor" may be a misnomer for something that never gets anywhere near an Indian tandoor oven or any American substitute, but fans of the real thing will get the idea: cold chicken in a dressing based on yogurt and the usual elements of a tandoori chicken marinade. In lieu of the red dye that is usual in tandoori dishes, I use some Hungarian sweet paprika. Naturally this doesn't have the same intensity as the tandoor-seared original. But it's a good dish in its own way and, unlike genuine tandoori chicken, can be made ahead as the centerpiece of a cold lunch or dinner.

The proportions of spices given here are only a suggestion; improvise as you like. Use only a creamy, fresh-tasting yogurt. It's worth lavishing a newly made batch of your own on the dish, which will taste very dreary if made with thin, sour supermarket yogurt.

YIELD: About 4 servings

A 4-pound chicken, skin removed, cut into 6 to 8 pieces
2 large garlic cloves
A 2-inch chunk of peeled fresh ginger
3 tablespoons any bland vegetable oil
½ teaspoon ground cumin
½ teaspoon ground coriander
¼ teaspoon ground turmeric
A large pinch of ground cinnamon
1 teaspoon ground cayenne pepper
1 tablespoon freshly squeezed lime or lemon juice
1 to 1¼ cups very fresh, creamy plain yogurt, briefly drained before
    measuring
½ to ¾ teaspoon salt, or to taste
1 medium onion
2 to 3 teaspoons Hungarian sweet paprika
Cilantro leaves for garnish (optional)

Poach the chicken until tender (about 20 to 25 minutes for breast meat, 35 for legs, thighs, and wings) in about 4 cups water. While it is cooking, mince the garlic and ginger together until they are almost a paste. Heat the oil until almost smoking in a small heavy skillet, add the garlic-ginger mixture, and let it sizzle (but not scorch) for 30 to 60 seconds. Stir in the cumin, coriander, turmeric, cinnamon, and cayenne; let cook until the fragrance of the spices is a little deepened.

When the chicken is done, remove the pieces to a platter. (Save the cooking stock for another purpose.) As soon as it is cool enough to handle, pull the meat from the bones and cut it into neat (or not too messy) pieces. Place the meat in a bowl and toss with the lime juice. Quickly add the garlic-ginger-spice mixture, then the yogurt. Toss to combine well and add salt to taste, a little at a time. (Remember that some seasonings will be muted as it chills.) Slice the onion into paper-thin half-moons and add along with most of the paprika. Toss again, arrange in a serving dish, and sprinkle with the remaining paprika. Garnish with a little fresh cilantro if desired, and chill thoroughly before serving.

ZUCCHINI-YOGURT SALAD WITH FRESH DILL

Yogurt lends agreeable depth and verve to a vegetable that can be pretty one-dimensional. I usually prefer this without the garlic, but both versions are good. A combination of green and golden zucchini makes an especially attractive dish.

YIELD: About 6 servings

4 medium-small zucchini or similar tender summer squash (about
    1 ½ pounds)
2 teaspoons salt
10 to 12 scallions, cleaned and trimmed
¼ cup olive oil
1 cup well-drained mild, creamy plain yogurt or Yogurt-Garlic Sauce
    (page 162)
Freshly ground black or white pepper
Plenty of fresh dill, snipped

Trim the ends of the zucchini and grate them on the coarse side of a box grater. Put the grated squash in a colander set over a bowl; add the salt and mix well with your hands. Let stand for 20 minutes to drain off some of the moisture.

Meanwhile, cut off the scallion tops where the green begins. Slice the white part into rounds and set aside; chop the tenderer part of the greens and reserve separately.

Firmly wring out as much liquid as you can from the salted zucchini. Heat the oil to rippling in a large lidded skillet over pretty brisk heat, add the scallion whites, and sauté for a few minutes until translucent. Add the drained zucchini and cook, stirring and tossing to coat them well with the oil, for 3 to 5 minutes. Adjust the heat to medium-low. Add the reserved scallion greens, cover the pan, and cook for about 5 minutes or until the squash is slightly wilted. (Check occasionally for scorching.)

Remove the pan from the heat and let cool slightly, uncovered. (Too much heat will curdle the yogurt, though it won't harm the flavor.) Add the yogurt, pepper, and most of the dill. Toss to combine everything well and serve warm or at room temperature, garnished with the remaining dill.

SHRIKHAND
(SAFFRON-SCENTED YOGURT DESSERT)

Gujarati *shrikhand* is one of the world's simplest and most exqui-site desserts. There is nothing to it but well-drained yogurt—the creamier the better—sweetened to your preference and gilded with a little saffron. It can be lightly spiced and garnished, but the satiny and voluptuous character comes only from yogurt and sugar (I use confectioners' sugar). It's worth making a batch of fresh yogurt just for this purpose; otherwise, look for the creamiest possible whole-milk yogurt.

The following recipe is no more than a rough guide. Omit the cardamom or other flavorings if you want; the pistachios are a great touch, but it will be delicious without them.

YIELD: about 3 ½ to 4 cups (6 to 8 servings)

6 cups plain whole-milk yogurt, preferably an unhomogenized
    Turkish-style brand with 3.5 percent milkfat
1 to 2 tablespoons milk
A large pinch of saffron
½ to ¾ cup confectioners' sugar (or to taste), sifted
A pinch of salt (optional)
A large pinch of freshly ground cardamom (seeds from 2 to 3 green
    cardamom pods), nutmeg, or cinnamon (optional)
A dash of rosewater (optional)
A handful of chopped pistachios for garnish (optional)

Scoop the yogurt into a cheesecloth-lined colander or a couple of plastic yogurt cheese funnels (page 160), set over a bowl or bowls. Let drain at room temperature for 4 hours. It will lose about 1 ½ to 1 ¾ cups of whey, depending on the individual batch of yogurt. Save the whey for another purpose.

When the yogurt has pretty much stopped dripping, turn it out into a mixing bowl. Heat the milk in a small pan, crumble the saffron into it, and remove from the heat.

Begin beating the confectioners' sugar into the yogurt with a wooden spoon, a few tablespoons at a time. When it is sweetened to your taste, beat in the optional pinch of salt; strain the saffron-infused milk and gently work it into the mixture. If the shrikhand seems lumpy, force it through a coarse-mesh sieve into a bowl. Now beat in any preferred seasoning (or none). Refrigerate for 2 to 3 hours and serve very cold, garnished if desired with pistachios.

(*Charoli* nuts would be as usual as pistachios in Gujarat, but these small and faintly celery-accented nuts can't always be found here, even in Indian groceries.)

Shrikhand is supposed to be served in elegantly small portions, but don't count on your guests' feeling the same way.

VARIATION: Shrikhand De Luxe: One day I happened to have both some very good Turkish-style yogurt and some labneh on hand. It occurred to me that together they ought to produce something like shrikhand concentrated to the ultimate power, and I was right. Later that day I took some to a family gathering. "I don't *eat* yogurt," muttered a supremely unimpressed teenager, and stuck a spoon in it, then devoured two large helpings.

The ingredients are the same as for the previous version, except that for the 6 cups of yogurt you substitute 4 cups (1 quart) of very creamy unhomogenized plain yogurt (3.5 percent milkfat, if possible) and 2 cups (1 pint) of labneh (page 159). Beat them together in a mixing bowl, force the mixture through a mesh strainer, and drain for 4 hours as directed above. Sweeten, season, and garnish as for regular shrikhand. Sometimes I add a dash of almond extract (anomalous but good). Sweet Turkish dried apricots are a fine accompaniment. Or for a completely unorthodox variation, omit the seasonings and spoon the mixture over fresh berries or sliced peaches.

REVANI
(YOGURT-SEMOLINA CAKE WITH LEMON SYRUP)

In Greece and Turkey, *revani* is the general name for a family of cakes made (usually) with durum-wheat semolina or a semolina-flour mixture, which are soaked after baking in some kind of syrup. When taken from the oven they are heavy, coarse-textured, and a little gritty from the hard, stubborn semolina. But the syrup bath moistens and flavors the cake without making it disintegrate as a fine-textured European cake would. Yogurt is a frequent ingredient, with or without some other source of fat like butter or olive oil. The acid will slightly tenderize the crumb.

This simple lemon-flavored version comes with little change from Özcan Ozan's splendid book *The Sultan's Kitchen*, a must for any fan of Turkish food. It uses only drained yogurt (page 158) with no other fat except the egg yolks, so it's crucial to start with the richest, creamiest yogurt you can make or buy. Be sure to buy semolina fine enough for cakes, not the coarser kind for puddings. Allow at least 4 hours after baking for the cake to soak up the syrup. It is traditionally served with kaymak, the Turkish version of clotted cream, often sold in Turkish groceries. English clotted cream and plain whipped cream are reasonable substitutes. Any of them will be an excellent foil to the intense sweetness of the lemon syrup. A tiny serving goes a long way.

YIELD: One 8-inch square cake (16 small servings)

SYRUP:

1 cup water
1 ½ cups sugar
4 scant teaspoons freshly squeezed lemon juice

CAKE:

Butter for greasing baking dish
Flour for dusting baking dish
4 eggs, separated
¼ cup sugar
Zest of half a lemon (more, if preferred)
½ cup fine semolina
⅓ cup plus 1 tablespoon all-purpose flour, sifted
1 teaspoon baking powder
A pinch of salt
1 cup well-drained yogurt (an extra-creamy kind, either homemade or
    Turkish-style with 3.5 percent milkfat)
Chopped pistachios for garnish (optional)
Kaymak (see above), clotted cream (page 89), or whipped cream
    for topping

Make the syrup by heating the water and sugar in a small saucepan. When it reaches a vigorous boil, turn the heat to low and simmer for 15 to 20 minutes. Add the lemon juice and set aside to cool completely.

Have all cake ingredients at room temperature. Butter and flour an 8 x 8-inch Pyrex baking dish. Preheat the oven to 350°F.

Beat the egg yolks, sugar, and lemon zest until light and frothy. Combine the semolina, flour, and baking powder and stir them in. Add the yogurt; fold and stir to incorporate as smoothly as possible.

Beat the egg whites to stiff peaks with a pinch of salt and fold them into the yogurt batter in two or three increments. Spread the batter in the pan. It will make a flat layer just about covering the bottom. Bake for 35 to 40 minutes, or until lightly browned.

Remove the cake from the oven and instantly cut it into 16 squares—or if you are good at geometry, diamonds. Pour the cooled syrup over the hot cake, which will be swimming in syrup. Let sit at room temperature for 4 to 6 hours; the syrup will be gradually absorbed. Garnish with the optional chopped pistachios and serve with the kaymak or cream.

ABOUT YOGURT-BASED DRINKS

All peoples who make yogurt—indeed, soured milk generally—also drink it in some form or other. The oldest traditions belong to the many lands making up my imaginary "Yogurtistan" (the ex-Yugoslavia to Central Asia). The richest traditions, however, developed on the Indian subcontinent. In most places where yogurt is a drink, it is a savory one flavored with nothing but salt and perhaps some dried mint. But in India and neighboring parts, people took to mixing drinkable forms of yogurt with a fragrant spectrum of other ingredients, both "salty" (meaning savory) and sweet. Though I find cold unsweetened yogurt drinks more refreshing than the ones with sugar or fruit, I would like to see all the traditional kinds, in their delightful diversity, earn a larger place in American diets.

Americans, who are by and large little acquainted with any of the real yogurt-drinking traditions, tend to be confused by the many different names and approaches. It is easiest to begin not with the remarkable world of Indian yogurt drinks but with the simpler and more ancient kind known throughout Yogurtistan: plain yogurt thinned with a little water and flavored with a dash of salt and (often) a little mint. The name most familiar in this country is the Turkish *ayran*, or *airan*. Some parts of the Arab-speaking world also call it ayran, but more often it has no name of its own other than "yogurt" (laban). In Iran and Afghanistan, where it is commonly made with carbonated water, the usual name is *doogh*, or *abdoogh*. By whatever name, it is a lovely restorative.

AYRAN OR DOOGH
(TURKISH- OR PERSIAN-STYLE YOGURT DRINK)

Newcomers to yogurt traditions may be puzzled by the instruction to thicken yogurt by draining the whey and then thin it by adding water. But to harp again on a crucial point, the draining step really changes the character of the yogurt, especially delicate, newly made yogurt. It is fresher-tasting this way, and the salt and mint register more brightly.

From ancient times, yogurt for drinking has been made with the milk of any and all local dairy animals. If you can find sheep's- or goats'-milk yogurt, give them a try (for using goats'-milk yogurt, see Variation below). Greek yogurt from a combination of sheep's and goats' milk is excellent.

YIELD: 1 serving

1 cup very fresh plain whole-milk yogurt, lightly drained,
    preferably a creamy kind from cows' or sheep's milk
Salt (anything from a large pinch to ⅛ teaspoon)
½ teaspoon Turkish dried mint, crumbled, or 1 sprig of fresh mint,
    lightly bruised (optional)
½ cup very cold water or (for doogh) plain chilled seltzer or soda water
Ice cubes or crushed ice

Mix the yogurt, salt, and optional dried mint in a prechilled bowl and gradually whisk in the water. Serve in chilled glasses, poured over ice cubes or crushed ice. Alternatively, whip until frothy in a blender with crushed ice and serve garnished with a mint sprig.

VARIATION: For goats'-milk ayran, be sure to use goats'-milk yogurt (about 1¼ cups per serving) made without any of the thickeners added to most commercial brands. As explained on page 159, unadulterated goats'-milk yogurt (I use Yo-Goat) will be thin enough to drink as is. Skip the added water, stir or blend in the seasonings, and pour it over the ice.

ABOUT LASSI AND OTHER INDIAN
SOURED-MILK DRINKS

Where culinary terms are concerned, the United States and English-speaking India certainly are two nations divided by a common language. Take "buttermilk," sometimes given as a translation of the Hindi word *lassi* as well as counterparts in several other Indian languages that you may find on the menus of regional Indian restaurants in this country. The thing meant here is not at all identical to American commercial cultured buttermilk. For reasons explained in the discussion of cultured buttermilk and the organisms used to make it (page 247), diluted plain yogurt comes closer to the taste and texture of Indian buttermilk than our cultured version. Of course, there's no reason that people who prefer American buttermilk shouldn't use it.

Lassi is most often associated with the Punjab, where people regard it with the sort of patriotic local pride that Buffalonians bestow on chicken wings. It and its variously named Indian cousins generally are made with more emphatic and varied seasonings than ayran and company. Even the simplest "salty" and sweet versions of lassi are usually stamped with such flavor accents as cumin in the savory or rosewater in the sweetened kind. Fruit purées, most often mango or banana, often figure in sweetened lassi. So do mustard seeds, cardamom or coriander seeds, peppercorns, fresh ginger, curry leaves, cilantro, and/or chile peppers in "buttermilk" drinks of southern India. You can and should experiment with any flavors that take your fancy. There is no "wrong" way to make lassi as long as the yogurt is good.

Lovers of special cooking tools may want to try mixing lassi with the traditional churning stick (*kavvam* or *madhani*, sometimes sold in Indian grocery/housewares stores) instead of a blender or processor.

SALT LASSI

Indians swear by the combination of "curd [yogurt]," salt, and cumin as an antidote to torrid summer heat, and believe that hot spices help you cool off by making you sweat. I couldn't agree more. Nothing is more blissfully restorative at summer's worst than salt lassi in any version.

I like to drain the yogurt before adding water, but it is not necessary. Just don't try to play calorie games by substituting nonfat yogurt, which gives no idea of the right consistency. (In India the yogurt or buttermilk used for this purpose most often comes from water buffaloes' milk, which is much richer than cows' milk. Indians living here sometimes even spike the yogurt with a tiny bit of cream for more body.) Cumin, either the regular kind or Indian black cumin, will add more flavor if you briefly toast it in a small heavy skillet and grind it yourself. If you can find Indian "black salt" (a unique kind of rock salt, really pink when ground), its distinctive sulfur flavor is wonderful in lassi. Use slightly less black salt than plain salt.

The following is a very simple salt lassi. Start with the smaller amount of yogurt, and add more to taste if it seems to need it.

YIELD: 1 serving

½ to 1 cup very fresh plain whole-milk yogurt,
    preferably a creamy unhomogenized kind
Ground cumin or Indian black cumin to taste
    (anything from a large pinch to ⅛ teaspoon)
Sea salt or Indian black salt to taste (anything from
    a large pinch to ⅛ teaspoon), ground fine if coarse
Very cold water in any preferred proportion
Crushed ice from 2 to 3 ice cubes (or more to taste)

Whisk ½ cup yogurt smooth in a small pitcher and start adding seasonings and water a little at a time—more yogurt as well, if you like—until the taste and consistency are close to what you like but on the concentrated side (the ice will dilute it slightly). Most people prefer lassi somewhere between the thickness of heavy and light cream. Pour the mixture into a blender or food processor, add the ice, and process until smooth and frothy. Serve at once in a tall chilled glass.

VARIATIONS: The fun begins when you elaborate on this minimalist formula by adding other seasonings, which are usually de rigueur in the regional kinds known as *chhaach*, *neer* (meaning "water-thinned") *moru*, and *majjiga*. You can start by experimenting with some coarsely ground black pepper or toasted and ground coriander seeds, and go on to a pinch of ground asafetida; small fresh chile peppers (slivered); fresh ginger (grated or slivered); or a tarka of South Indian seasonings made by heating a little ghee or oil in a small skillet and adding a large pinch each of Indian brown mustard seeds and cumin seeds, a few lightly bruised curry leaves, and, if desired, a couple of tiny dried red chile peppers and sizzling them in the ghee until the mustard seeds pop; you then whisk the whole thing into the yogurt. Or if you have a favorite version (commercial or homemade) of garam masala or the tarter *chaat masala*, try adding a pinch.

Fresh cilantro or mint leaves, pulled from the stems and lightly bruised or chopped, are a delightful final addition to all forms of salt lassi.

PUNJABI-STYLE SWEET LASSI

Punjabis, who love lassi with proprietary zeal as the fruit of native Punjabi genius, often use milk rather than water to thin the yogurt. (You can try this in salt lassi as well.)

YIELD: 1 serving

½ to 1 cup very fresh plain whole-milk yogurt,
   preferably a creamy unhomogenized kind
1 ½ to 2 ½ tablespoons superfine sugar, or to taste
Rosewater (a dash to 2 teaspoons; different kinds vary greatly in
   intensity)
Very cold water or whole milk in any preferred proportion
Crushed ice from 2 to 3 ice cubes (or more to taste)
Mint leaves or dried edible rose petals for garnish (optional)

Proceed as for Salt Lassi, but begin by whisking the yogurt as smooth as possible with part of the sugar, then adding the rosewater and more sugar to taste a little at a time. Serve at once in a tall chilled glass, garnished with the optional mint or rose petals.

VARIATIONS: Other essences and extracts are also popular in sweet lassi. If you can find *kewra* (screwpine) or sandalwood essence at an Indian grocery, try adding it a drop at a time. Or make an infusion of a few saffron strands in a tiny bit of hot milk and strain the fragrant saffron milk into the sweetened yogurt. Orange-blossom water and genuine vanilla extract are, as far as I know, quite inauthentic, but delicious.

MANGO LASSI

The favorite version in Indian-American restaurants. In all honesty, frozen mango pulp is better than many of the fresh mangos sold here.

YIELD: About 3 cups

1 medium-small, very ripe mango or ¾ cup frozen mango pulp
2 cups very fresh plain whole-milk yogurt, preferably a creamy
    unhomogenized kind
A dash of freshly squeezed lime or lemon juice, or to taste
A dash of salt, or to taste
Crushed ice from 8 to 9 ice cubes
Superfine sugar (optional)
Mint sprigs for garnish (optional)

If you are using a fresh mango, detach the flesh from skin and pit as follows: Hold the mango upright on a work surface, narrow edge facing you and the flat and rounded sides to your right and left. With a small sharp knife, slice vertically down through both flat and rounded sides so as to just miss the flat pit. Skin side down, score each of the cut halves into ¾-inch dice. Push from the skin side to open up the scored side; slide the knife blade under the flesh to detach from the skin. Slice away as much of the remaining flesh as you can from around the pit and cut into small dice. If using frozen mango pulp, simply thaw to refrigerator temperature.

Place the yogurt, mango flesh or thawed pulp, lime juice, salt, and ice in a blender or food processor; process until the ice is slushy and the mixture is frothy and well combined. Taste for flavor and sweetness. It should need no sugar unless you have a rather insipid mango; if necessary add a teaspoon or two of superfine sugar and process to blend. If it seems a little bland, add another jolt of fresh citrus juice and/or salt. If it is too thick for your taste, dilute with a little ice water. Serve at once in tall glasses, garnished with the optional mint.

TARHANA, TRAHANA, AND RELATIVES

If I had the power to dictate the next all-the-rage ingredient, my first nominee might well be tarhana or one of its many cousins—trahana, *kishk*, *kashk*, and more. By whatever name, they belong to a large, amorphous family of staple foods that has no good general label. In *Mediterranean Grains and Greens*, Paula Wolfert—who along with Diane Kochilas has done much to publicize these treasures—suggested "rustic pasta." I lean toward "proto-pasta," because tarhana and the rest of the clan undoubtedly existed before any other sort of pasta in the regions that were the cradle of both cereal-growing and dairying. All consist of wheat (or occasionally barley) in some form—crushed, cracked, ground, or as cooked whole berries—combined with a liquid element like milk, then dried enough to be reduced to pellets, granules, or morsels. Once dried and kept dry, they last forever without refrigeration.

If you were to catalogue every variety that exists on earth, the list would stretch from egg barley and Pennsylvania Dutch *rivvels* to Sardinian *fregola* and the many forms of couscous. But probably the oldest members (and for me, the shining lights) of the family are kinds found from the Balkans far into the Middle East that are made with soured milk, buttermilk, or yogurt, particularly from goats' or sheep's milk. The interplay between tart milk and grain flavor has to be tasted to be understood.

The most varied and complex of the soured proto-pastas were developed in Turkey, where their collective name is "tarhana," and Greece, where they are called "trahana" or *xinohondros* ("sour cracked wheat," a Cretan specialty). The simplest kinds consist of nothing but flour and yogurt or soured milk, partly dried and crushed or crumbled to the texture of coarse flour or fine meal. The most elaborate ones are slowly fermented, sometimes with the aid of yeast, and use a battery of other ingredients that may include sweet and hot peppers, tomatoes, and chickpeas, with or without herbs and spices. Some kinds are made into coarse, rough-textured crumbs, some into bite-sized pieces. There are versions with sour fruit like pomegranate or quince. Every village, indeed every family, used to have its own variation. A version even came to Hungary as *tarhonya*, though today the name usually applies to a form of egg barley made without yogurt.

The long drying period produces a vividly fused concentration of all the original flavors together. Unfortunately, the drying step will be the chief logistical problem for many people seeking to duplicate this marvelous specialty in the United States. In Anatolia and Greece, the year's supply was traditionally made from combined sheep's and goats' milk in late summer, when lactation was starting to wind down (resulting in scantier but richer milk) and fiercely hot, dry sunlight prevailed everywhere. Those of us in areas of high humidity can expect the drying process to take a day or several days longer than can people in Arizona. Depending on how stubborn it's being, you may want to finish it off in a home dehydrator. Some cooks suggest an oven at lowest setting, but I don't recommend this unless you can reliably keep the temperature below 150°F.

The chief use of tarhana/trahana (which is "kishk" or "kashk" in most of the non-Turkish Middle East) is as a kind of porridge, or a soup base or thickener. It also goes into some wonderful fillings for savory pies or stuffed vegetables. Making it from scratch is undeniably the sort of extended project that people either are or aren't game for, like homemade pasta or sourdough bread. Come to think of it, sour-milk tarhana is not unlike a combination of the two, since sourdough is also a product of lactic-acid fermentation.

I have successfully made Turkish-style tarhana at home from a recipe in Özcan Ozan's excellent *The Sultan's Kitchen*. I recommend his version to anyone who wants to master this incredibly labor-intensive—but also incredibly good—staple of Turkish cuisine; otherwise, there are several good commercial brands. For most cooks, the recipe for Greek-style Sour Trahana on page 186 will be a more practical undertaking.

I suggest trying a commercial Greek brand before deciding whether to embark on the adventure yourself. Look for the pebbly-textured Vlaha or Krinos brands of trahana labeled "sour" or "xinos," meaning that it was made from milk in soured form. (If it says "sweet" or "glykos," it was made from unsoured milk—perfectly okay, but not as interesting as the other.) The best, though unfortunately scarcest, imported tra-hana I know—the coarse-textured Pittas brand—comes from Cyprus and consists of cracked wheat and sheep's-milk yogurt formed into pieces about the size and shape of Tootsie Rolls.

Tarhana imported from Turkey is often very sharp-flavored, from the complex mixture of vegetables and seasonings worked into the original ferment and left to ripen over a long period. Baktat, Coskun, and Sera are the most common com-mercial brands here. They are finer than most Greek trahana, a gritty powder with a strong pink or orange-red tinge from red peppers and tomatoes.

TO COOK TARHANA/TRAHANA: BASIC METHOD

In Turkey and Greece, people regularly eat tarhana/trahana as a breakfast porridge. This is one of the most forgiving and foolproof dishes in existence. Allowing roughly ¼ cup of dried cereal per serving, you stir it into about four to six times its volume of boiling water and cook it, stirring occasionally, over medium-low heat until the water is absorbed and you have a thick, well-softened mush or porridge. The time will usually be between 15 and 30 minutes. If the water starts boil-ing off before the grain is tender, simply add more water and cook longer. If you've inadvertently used too much water, turn up the heat to evaporate it faster. Or if you decide you'd like to try it in a soupy condition, that's fine, too. Serve it with butter, creamy yogurt, crumbled feta or grated Parmesan cheese, or any desired fresh herb. And note that the Greek kinds—especially those using bulgur—make an excellent lunch or dinner side dish for grain fanciers.

Tarhana/trahana is often briefly soaked in water before being brought to a boil, to shorten the cooking time. Another variation is to cook it pilaf-style, briefly sautéing the cereal in butter or olive oil (sometimes along with chopped onions or garlic) before adding liquid—stock instead of water, if you want a rich man's version of what is in its origins an exceed-ingly thrifty dish. By all means experiment with tarhana/trahana to thicken and enrich soups or stews; see the recipe for Turkish Tarhana Soup on page 187.

The most exciting array of recipes using trahana that I have seen—far surpassing my few suggestions—is presented by Diane Kochilas in *The Glorious Foods of Greece*.

HOMEMADE GREEK-STYLE SOUR TRAHANA

This is a several days' project, though it involves very little real work. It makes a coarse-textured trahana that will be a hit with bulgur fans. My version is modeled on a recipe in Aglaia Kremezi's *The Foods of Greece*—or was; over time it's wandered some distance from the original. As noted above, the drying process may stretch out quite a while.

YIELD: About 2 ½ pounds (7 cups)

2 cups milk, preferably goats' milk
2 cups rich, creamy plain yogurt, preferably
    Greek goats'- and sheep's-milk yogurt
About 4 cups coarse bulgur
About ⅔ cup fine semolina
1 heaping tablespoon salt
2 to 4 tablespoons olive oil (optional)
Flour or more oil for handling the dough

Bring the milk nearly to a boil, and cool to room temperature. Stir in the yogurt, and let stand overnight in a warm room, loosely covered.

Pour the soured milk into a large saucepan with the bulgur and semolina. Mix everything together and set the pan over low heat, stirring, for several minutes. The goal is only to soften the bulgur enough so that it will absorb the liquid. Different batches will vary quite a lot in absorption capacity. You want a dough about the consistency of a dense meatloaf mixture. If it is much thicker than that, thin it with a little water; if it's loose and runny, add some more bulgur or semolina. Work in the salt and oil (oil isn't absolutely necessary, but it helps the dough cohere).

Let the sticky, pebbly-textured dough cool until you can handle it. Scoop out handfuls the size of medium meatballs and flatten them into patties, occasionally moistening your hands with oil or dusting them with flour to keep from sticking. Set the patties on parchment paper spread on a tabletop or cookie sheet. Let stand, turning several times a day, for two to three days, or until bone-dry. In weather too damp for complete drying, the final stages can be accomplished in a home dehydrator on the lowest possible setting.

Break and crumble the patties to coarse crumbs until the largest lumps are no bigger than a raisin. Store at room temperature in a glass jar or jars.

TURKISH TARHANA SOUP I AND II

Tarhana in a soup acts as both flavor agent and thickener. The thickening effect, of course, comes from flour—but flour magically transformed by having been set to ferment as a dough in the company of yogurt and vegetables. A tarhana-thickened soup is not floury but somehow rustic, suave, and fortifying at the same time.

Tarhana soup is so familiar to Turkish cooks that recipes are scarcely necessary. "Dissolve some dried tarhana in some simmering water" is the gist of it. "Water or broth" is one way of enlarging the possibilities, but there are dozens more. Preferred ratios of tarhana to liquid range from about 1:4 (very thick) to 1:8 (thin).

Tarhana soup makes a great breakfast or lunch, and is a splendid main-dish soup for an otherwise light supper. The following two recipes—one minimalist, one a little more fleshed out—are only rough outlines of something that defies exact formulas.

TARHANA SOUP I

YIELD: 4 to 6 servings

6 cups water or broth (lamb, chicken, beef, or veal)
¾ to 1 cup Turkish tarhana
1 to 2 teaspoons Turkish dried mint, crushed (optional)
Freshly squeezed lemon juice to taste (optional)
Aleppo, Maraş, or Urfa red pepper flakes to taste (optional)
Salt to taste
Freshly ground black pepper

Bring the water or broth to a boil in a saucepan. Reduce the heat to low and add the tarhana in a trickle, whisking to eliminate lumps. Cook, stirring frequently, for about 15 to 20 minutes, or until thickened to the consistency of a light cream soup. In the last few minutes, stir in any of the optional seasonings along with the salt and pepper. Serve at once, piping hot.

TARHANA SOUP II

YIELD: 4 to 6 servings

3 to 4 tablespoons butter
1 medium onion, chopped
1 small Italian frying or cubanelle pepper, cored, seeded, and cut into
    thin strips
6 to 8 ounces ground lamb or beef (optional)
1 large ripe tomato, peeled, seeded, and chopped
6 cups strong broth (lamb, chicken, beef, or veal) or water
¾ to 1 cup Turkish tarhana
1 to 2 teaspoons Turkish dried mint, crushed
Freshly squeezed lemon juice to taste (optional)
1 tablespoon tomato paste (optional)
Aleppo, Maraş, or Urfa red pepper flakes to taste (optional)
Salt to taste
Freshly ground black pepper to taste
About 1 to 1 ½ cups cubed or coarsely crumbed bread from any
    preferred kind of sturdy-textured loaf, slightly stale

Melt 1 tablespoon of the butter in a saucepan, add the onion, and sauté until translucent. Add the pepper strips and sauté briefly. Crumble the optional ground meat into the pan and cook, stirring to break up lumps, until it loses its red color. Stir in the tomato, let simmer for a minute, and add the broth or water. Bring to a boil, reduce the heat to low, and add the tarhana in a trickle, whisking to eliminate any lumps. Cook, stirring frequently, for 15 to 20 minutes, or until lightly thickened. Add the mint, any of the optional seasonings, and salt and pepper.

Heat the remaining butter in a small skillet until fragrant, sizzling, and not quite browned. Add the bread cubes or crumbs and let brown lightly, tossing to coat well with butter. Serve the soup at once, piping hot, garnishing each portion with some of the croutons.

CULTURED MILK AND CREAM

Buttermilk Potatoes

Fried Bananas with Crema

Southern Buttermilk Pie

Hangop (Dutch Buttermilk Dessert)

Buttermilk as Drink

Yogurt is so hugely important in so many of the world's cuisines as to cast most other kinds of cultured milk into comparative shade. But they exist in diverse forms wherever milk exists, because milk naturally attracts lactic-acid bacteria and sometimes other organisms, including particular molds and yeasts. We know very little about their history. Still, the reason for their diversity is obvious: As dairying spread out from its first centers into most of the Old World, local climates favored wild local microorganisms.

As explained earlier, over many centuries all dairying peoples learned to culture milk by exposing it in a fairly controlled way to certain organisms that prospered in their own haunts, usually in the form of a starter taken from a previous batch. Or to put it another way, they learned to domesticate bits of the local microflora. Probably no one will ever be able to identify the multiple versions of cultured milk made throughout the world. (Modern science is not close to identifying all the microscopic species and subspecies used to produce them.) What they have in common is that, like yogurt, they are allowed to ferment just until there is enough casein precipitation to form a partly liquid gel, not the firm curd of cheese. But unlike yogurt, most involve not the thermophilic (heat-loving) bacteria endemic to Yogurtistan but mesophilic species that need cooler conditions to thrive.

The most exotic kinds, from an American consumer's viewpoint, were native to Central Asia and the western fringes of China, where horse-herding nomads used complexes of bacteria and yeasts to ferment the very lactose-rich mares' milk into a sour, slightly effervescent alcoholic drink called "kumys" (or "kumis," "koumiss"). Today it is rare and perhaps headed for extinction, at least as made from mares' milk. A milder-flavored and less-alcoholic cousin, "kefir," evolved in the mountainous reaches between Georgia and southern Russia. (Unless sugar was added, it never developed the same kick, because no milch animals except horses and asses give milk with enough lactose to support much alcoholic fermentation.)

Another family of regional cultured-milk specialties little known in this country originated in Scandinavia or the Netherlands and is known among dairy chemists by the collective name of "ropy milks"—"ropy" in the sense that a spoon dipped into the milk will come out trailing long viscous strings that non-Scandinavians find disconcerting. This unique quality comes from special mutations of several common mesophilic bacteria. Old-timers are said to consider ropy milk more flavorful and sustaining than any other kind of soured milk. The culinary historians Yvonne and William Lockwood report that diehards in the Finnish communities of Michigan's Upper Peninsula still keep alive the Finnish version, "long *viili*," while the younger generation offers unflattering comparisons to mucus or slime and sticks to "short *viili*," which is more like our cultured buttermilk.

These are all too familiar stories of former knowledge going the way of the two-bit subway fare. Such changes are usually more subtle than the loss of mares'-milk kumys or ropy milk. The plainest examples in the United States and most of western Europe are the replacement of home-soured milk and true buttermilk by cultured buttermilk as a universal stand-in, and the parallel case of home-soured cream and cultured sour cream. Today the cultured versions are all that many people know of fresh fermented milk.

It is easy to suppose that "buttermilk" as we know it connects us with a homespun culinary past. But until about a hundred years ago, recipes mentioning buttermilk—or sour cream—by name appeared less often in cookbooks than today. If you made butter, you regularly had some buttermilk on hand and knew how to use it without recipes. And if you had more fresh milk or cream on hand than you had immediate use for, you were bound to have sour milk or sour cream as soon as the lactic-acid bacteria in your home started colonizing them.

The results were anything but uniform in quality. Any batch might differ from preceding ones, though experienced cooks could partly control things by keeping track of the ambient temperature (everything soured faster in summer) and using the last of one batch to carefully inoculate the next. Different households or regions as well as different ethnic groups had their preferences about how sour or mild, thick or thin sour milk and cream should be. Clearly, local complexes of lactic-acid bacteria can't have been identical from one region (or even neighborhood) to another. The bottom line: Sour milk, buttermilk, and sour cream were simply facts of kitchen life, capable of infinite gradations that no one tried to capture in cookbooks.

Hints of change appeared around 1800, but it took more than a century to erase the diversity of American cultured milk. One factor was the introduction of alkaline leaveners for quick-raised breads and cakes, the predecessors of today's baking soda. Sour milk at once took on a particular role in a new kitchen department that claimed to be more modern and enlightened than yeast breads or cakes—chemically raised batters for quick breads, biscuits, muffins, or pancakes. Batters using potash, pearlash, or the first versions of "saleratus" depended on a reaction that instantly generated carbon-dioxide bubbles in the mixture before it went into the oven or onto the griddle. This chemical change depended on the addition of something acid. Cream of tartar was the recommendation of the scientifically minded, but sour milk was cheap and universally available. It thus began acquiring a greater prominence in written recipes.

But sour milk's days in the kitchen were numbered. The triumph of fresh, unsoured "sweet" milk was dawning. When pasteurized milk began to drive out raw milk, cooks reaching for sour milk increasingly found that they had none on hand. The usual improvised substitute was sweet milk rapidly curdled with a little lemon juice or vinegar. It was at this point, by about the late 1920s, that American dairy producers started selling the product known as "cultured buttermilk"—a slightly thickened soured milk based on commercial mixtures of mesophilic bacteria. Of course it was not real buttermilk, which was the residue left from churning butter and varied in flavor along with the character of the butter itself (page 70). But by the time of World War II, few consumers knew enough to quibble over the difference. Recipes calling for buttermilk became more numerous in cookbooks, and cooks came to assume that they represented a taste of the colonial or early American past.

The good news in this tale of shrinking horizons is that at least we still have access to a useful and sometimes quite flavorful product: plain cultured buttermilk. The less happy aspects are that neither consumers nor producers really think of cultured buttermilk as a delicacy and a privilege, and that no enterprising manufacturer has tried offering, say, half a dozen subtly varied versions of bacterially soured milk (as opposed to additive-laced travesties aimed at dieters) to knowledgeable buyers. All that is needed are excellent fresh milk (perhaps unhomogenized) and different combinations of bacteria to bring out different flavor nuances. I will wager that if even a few more differentiated kinds of honest sour milk were available, the public would respond. The story is much the same with sour cream, though I think sour milk or "buttermilk" either whole, low-fat, or nonfat has richer, more varied possibilities.

Even now, the best cultured buttermilk is a great culinary resource. Its uses are somewhat interchangeable with those of plain yogurt, but it harmonizes more discreetly with some flavors because of the different character imparted by the mesophilic bacteria. It's still a useful leavener, in tandem with baking soda, for many kinds of biscuits, muffins, griddle cakes, and quick breads. As a marinade naturally helped out by lactic acid, it's even better than sweet milk at taming fishy-flavored fish, and also is popular for tenderizing chicken. A very vocal Southern fried-chicken school insists on soaking the pieces in buttermilk for several hours or even overnight before cooking.

To me, cultured buttermilk is most irresistible as a cold drink—with or without other flavorings; see page 227 for suggestions—or soup. As "sour milk," it was the foundation of various *Kaltschalen*, a tribe of slightly sweetened

North German cold soups that were much loved a few generations ago. Farther to the east, sour milk was the chief underpinning of distinctively sour-flavored cold soups as richly varied as Spanish gazpachos. Today cultured buttermilk is our chief tool for reproducing, or at least approximating, these disappearing legacies.

Cultured sour cream is nearly as versatile an ingredient. Its American success, however, came a little later. Before pasteurization, cream left at room temperature gradually acquired a lactic-acid tang, though it stayed less sharp than sour milk because the colonizing bacteria didn't have as much lactose to work on. Before homogenization, it also set up quite thick in a couple of days. Though cooks have always used sour cream, it wasn't especially visible in American cookbooks until fairly recently. Ashkenazic Jews from the Pale of Settlement were the first group to use it extensively as a delicacy in its own right.

Bottled versions of cultured sour cream were available from some commercial dairies by about 1930. It started being called to wider attention as a "gourmet" ingredient during the 1940s. By 1951 *The Joy of Cooking* urged "the uninitiated" to suspend any prejudice roused by the name and give it a try, or even make it at home with cultured buttermilk if they couldn't buy it.

Within a generation a broad spectrum of American cooks had learned that cultured sour cream was a marvelous enricher of pastry doughs and cakes, a good alternative to fresh cream in some kinds of mousses, and (with a little draining) a lovely dessert topping. Its primary use, however, was—and still is—in cold sauces, dips, and spreads (see page 212 for suggestions).

As time went on, the commercial product increasingly diverged from its homemade precursors. A "double homogenization" process introduced in the 1960s enabled manufacturers to get a firm body that really isn't intrinsic to sour cream. Eventually they watered down the milkfat content to about 18 percent (the borderline between half-and-half and light cream) and started using rennet or vegetable enzymes to set up the cream in a state between a gel and a soft curd, usually adding gum thickeners for extra insurance.

Some of us now have a higher-priced but less technologically convoluted alternative in various boutique brands of crème fraîche—to my mind, clear proof that manufacturers of cultured dairy products have everything to gain from thinking outside the box. Most American crème fraîche versions suggest to me what sour cream could be like if someone had the initiative to use richer cream, discard some of the usual processing steps and additives, and experiment with slightly different combinations of lactic-acid bacteria in order to play on different flavor possibilities.

In fact, the time seems ripe for introducing an adventurous spectrum of cultured dairy foods to a wider public. The recent American debut of Icelandic *skyr* or a cousin (page 199) is a promising omen. I have hopes that in the next few years small artisanal American dairies will start to explore the market for exotic kinds of cultured milk or cream—perhaps even real kefir and Scandinavian "ropy milk." Meanwhile, the best way to stop taking cultured buttermilk and sour cream for granted, and gain some perspective on the limitations of the commercial versions, is to try making your own.

SOME CULTURED MILK AND CREAM PRODUCTS: A BRIEF SURVEY

Milk fermented by lactic-acid bacteria is thousands of years older than any system for classifying different kinds. Orderly-minded searchers for correct definitions are always surprised to see how haphazardly the names of different soured or sourish milk-based products are thrown around— and not just in English. (Trying to sort out anything like the meanings of "buttermilk" and "sour milk" in other languages is an exercise in frustration.) You'd think that modern science would have cleared up some of the confusion. In fact, it has muddied things more by bringing standardized strains of particular bacteria from industrial laboratories in, say, Denmark to far-flung parts of the globe, there to figure in packaged commercial versions of local fermented dairy specialties that may coexist with more "primitive," non-uniform handmade originals. For shoppers, there is the additional hurdle that American manufacturers are free to tag all kinds of things with hit-or-miss names unless they happen to be covered by a federal "standard of identity." Even if you read the fine print of labels, you may be completely mystified by the differences between two items bearing the same name.

ACIDOPHILUS MILK Milk soured with a culture of *Lactobacillus acidophilus* to produce something resembling a harsher version of cultured buttermilk. Widely promoted on the unproven though not disproven "probiotic" theory that *L. acidophilus* (which survives in the colon) boosts the immune system and discourages the action of undesirable bacteria. Some manufacturers add a second organism, *Brevibacterium bifidum.*

A "sweet acidophilus milk" has been developed for those who dislike the flavor of lactic acid; the bacteria remain dormant in it until the milk reaches the digestive system.

"BULGARIAN BUTTERMILK" Really more of a yogurt; milk soured with a culture of *Lactobacillus bulgaricus* alone instead of the double action of *L. bulgaricus* and *Streptococcus thermophilus*. Unless it's been tinkered with to soften the effect, it is sourer than ordinary yogurt and much sourer than American cultured buttermilk.

CREMA Literally, just the Spanish word for cream. In much of Central America the word refers to local equivalents of sour cream with a different mix of cultures and a characteristic slightly salty tang. Like all kinds of sour cream, crema must have originated as what hungry neighborhood bacteria did with fresh cream, before it was turned into more standardized factory-made products based on commercial laboratory cultures. Today's crema is a favorite condiment or table sauce for many Mexican *antojitos* and *botanas* ("little dishes" and bar snacks).

Various brands are sold here in Latin American groceries under the general name *crema centroamericana* or more particular names such as *crema mexicana, crema hondureña*, and so forth. There seem to be two main types: a very heavy one based on a cultured cream-milk mixture with cream cheese added, and another kind without the cheese. (I haven't consistently been able to make out special national nuances.) The flavor of all kinds is delightful, though the texture usually relies heavily on carrageenan, modified food starch, and/or rennet for thickening and smoothness. If crema wins enough new fans on this side of the border, some entrepreneur surely will be inspired to make a more truly, if less apparently, rich artisanal version—the taste is too good not to become part of the mainstream American kitchen. Meanwhile, look for commercial brands with the fewest additives listed on the label. Note that it does not contain live organisms, so you can't use it to culture your own.

CRÈME FRAÎCHE In French, just "fresh cream," though it usually refers to cream lightly cultured with particular mixtures of mesophilic lactic-acid bacteria (i.e., ones that thrive at moderate rather than very warm temperatures). The quality of the cream from which it is made is all-important. Even today, Normandy is considered the premier French source of cream and butter, and Norman crème fraîche has long been the gold standard. It is still occasionally made from unpasteurized Normandy cream (said to have the truest flavor), but pasteurized versions are more common. In the United States, a few small dairies make quite good (pasteurized) crème fraîche. The best is made only from cream and cultures, and has a more blossomy flavor and luxuriant texture than commercial American sour cream. Because of its high milkfat and low casein content, it can be heated to somewhat higher temperatures than sour cream without curdling. Unless the label states that it contains live cultures, it probably doesn't and can't be used for culturing your own.

CULTURED BUTTERMILK Milk soured with a mixture of mesophilic lactic-acid bacteria; for most of us, it is the nearest thing to the naturally soured milk that used to be more familiar throughout Europe and North America than unsoured milk. (If you come across "sour milk" as an ingredient in an old recipe, this is your best bet.) Cultured buttermilk began replacing true churned buttermilk (see the butter and buttermilk recipes in "Butter and True Buttermilk") at least eighty years ago. Most brands are now made from low-fat milk (either 1 or 1.5 percent milkfat; in my mid-Atlantic neck of the woods, Friendship manufactures the best commercial version). It can be a delicious cold drink when made without gums and stabilizers, and is also the ideal culturing agent for cooks interested in experimenting with homemade versions of fresh cheese and several kinds of cultured milk or cream. Cultured buttermilk curdles in cooking unless mixed with a little flour or starch.

Note that today cultured buttermilk often is heated after fermentation, which kills the cultures. Always look for the words "active cultures" or "live cultures" on the label.

CULTURED SOUR CREAM Cream—today, more often a mixture of milk and cream with added dry milk solids, standardized at 18 percent milkfat—soured with a mixture of mesophilic lactic-acid bacteria.

Please do not be bamboozled by the misleadingly labeled

"nonfat sour cream," with its dismal complement of gums and extenders. Low-fat versions differ; ones made with only cultured cream and milk are sometimes fairly pleasant. But the only skinny version of sour cream I really like is made by draining plain, additive-free cultured buttermilk and stirring it smooth. (Follow directions for Hangop, page 226, but leave the buttermilk cream unsweetened.)

Unless the label states that sour cream contains live cultures, it probably doesn't and can't be used for culturing your own. Note: There are not very good versions made by direct acidification rather than culturing.

KEFIR Strictly speaking, milk cultured by the combined action of several specific bacteria, molds, and yeasts, resulting in both lactic-acid and alcoholic fermentation. Kefir, or something like it, may be as ancient as yogurt, but never spread as universally throughout the Diverse Sources Belt. By the twentieth century it had come to Russian cities from the Caucasus (where it probably had been made with cows', goats', or sheep's milk, depending on what was most convenient), having acquired a reputation for healthfulness not unlike that of Bulgarian yogurt in 1920s Europe. It has been a popular Russian drink ever since. Part of the fascination is that, unlike yogurt bacteria, the starter itself is visible to the naked eye. It consists of small whitish blobs clustered into an irregular mass often described as cauliflowerlike. The kefir "grains" contain all the operative microorganisms, ready to flourish together symbiotically in the milk and turn it into a pleasantly sour beverage of gentle fizziness and a slight alcoholic kick. It is not difficult to make; devotees save the grains from one batch—they shrink a little but remain intact—and use them to inoculate the next.

Commercial drinks labeled "kefir" have started showing up in places like the Whole Foods supermarket chain. These products are not at all identical to the original kefir. In the first place, they have been retooled to stop any alcoholic fermentation. They are usually sold in gussied-up, highly sweetened strawberry or vanilla versions surrounded by nutritional hype and augmented with faddish "nutraceuticals" such as the complex sugar called inulin. Even the plain unsweetened version tastes more like mediocre yogurt than anything worth consuming on its own. If you want to taste real kefir, you're best advised to seek a source of kefir grains, though you may feel as if you'd embarked on a "Joe sent me" search for a speakeasy. The New England Cheesemaking Supply Company (page 317) can put you in touch with a source.

Note: "Kefir" is one of several words that can land you in misunderstandings in Hispanic groceries. It is sometimes an all-purpose name for any vaguely yogurtlike fermented dairy product.

KUMYS, KUMIS, KOUMISS By whatever Anglicized spelling, this was another Russian link with the ancient dairying past. Like kefir, it was milk fermented by a mixture of different organisms, including bacteria and yeasts, and produced alcohol as well as lactic acid in the fermenting process. But apparently kumys had a stronger connection with nomadic civilizations of the former Silk Road that eventually fell under Russian domination. It was classically made from mares' milk, which has plenty of lactose for producing alcohol. There was also camels' milk kumys (probably less alcoholic). In modern times there has been some Russian production of kumys from cows' milk, though it is weak if not fortified with sugar to boost alcohol content. Memories of real kumys were growing rare by the late 1960s, when Helen and George Papashvily went to Kazakhstan while researching the Russian volume in the Time-Life Foods of the World series and were told by a nonagenarian recalling her youth, "One mouthful of *kumys* and I could name the mare from which it came." Today mares'-milk kumys is reported to barely survive in a few parts of the Central Asian republics and Mongolia. People who have tasted it describe it as distinctly acid, pungent, and fizzy.

As with "kefir," Latin Americans loosely apply the name "kumys" to some yogurt cousins with no connection to the Silk Road original.

SKYR An almost-cheese or not-quite yogurt from Iceland that involves skim milk cultured by a combination of several lactic-acid bacteria including the most important yogurt-making organisms, along with several commonly used for cultured buttermilk, before being lightly renneted and drained of whey. Recently several American manufacturers have introduced agreeable plain versions, as well as others given the sweetened-yogurt treatment. Take a leaf from the Icelanders and eat plain skyr with fresh berries, lightly sprinkled with sugar and doused with cream.

SMETANA The Russian word for sour cream, adopted into French culinary parlance as *smitane*. Emigration from the ex–Soviet Union has brought Russian-style smetana to these shores, and it's a huge improvement over most commercial American sour cream. The flavor is rounder and less sour. The cream doesn't set up as firm, but keeps a buttery softness that I find more pleasing. So far it seems to be sold only in bulk, not prepackaged.

HOMEMADE CULTURED BUTTERMILK

Though by now it should be clear that cultured buttermilk is "buttermilk" only by courtesy, it can be both flavorful and useful in its own right. If only manufacturers and consumers had more respect for it as an excellent food instead of some kind of dieter's ration to be tortured into a travesty of honest sour milk! Make up a batch at home with some good unhomogenized whole milk, and you will get an inkling of what it can taste like. Even homogenized whole milk will give you buttermilk with more body and flavor than the usual supermarket brands.

As long as supermarket buttermilk contains live cultures (and says so on the label), it is your ticket to better things—meaning home culturing of milk and cream for fresh cheeses as well as good versions of cultured sour cream and buttermilk. As with cheeses, I see no reason for sending away to a specialty supply company for cultures when you have this perfectly respectable source of mesophilic bacteria. Try to check expiration dates and delivery schedules in order to buy the buttermilk as fresh as possible.

YIELD: 1 quart

1 quart whole milk, preferably unhomogenized and very fresh
¼ cup commercial cultured buttermilk with active cultures,
    well shaken before measuring

Culturing will take place a little faster if you begin by warming the milk to between 85° and 90°F. But it will happen sooner or later as long as the ambient temperature stays above about 70°F (preferably a little warmer). In any case, mix the milk and buttermilk and let stand undisturbed at room temperature, loosely covered, until the milk thickens slightly and the taste is lightly but distinctly sour (usually between 12 and 18 hours). Store in the refrigerator, tightly covered, for up to about a week. As with yogurt, you can use the last of one batch as starter for another, though—also like yogurt—it loses some bacterial activity with long keeping.

VARIATIONS: You can make cultured buttermilk from either all skim milk, whole milk mixed with skim in any desired proportion, or whole milk mixed with half-and-half (nonultrapasteurized, please) in any desired proportion.

I usually don't add salt, but if you like, mix in anything from a pinch to half a teaspoon per quart after culturing. If you have used unhomogenized milk, stir the top cream into the rest of the buttermilk before drinking or using.

HOMEMADE SOUR CREAM

Call it "Homemade Crème Fraîche" if you like, though the name is a stretch. A major difference between American commercial sour cream and the better versions of crème fraîche sold in this country is that the latter are made from richer cream and don't need the extraneous thickeners that manufacturers add to offset the relative thinness of sour cream.

Make sour cream at home without such disguises, using light cream that contains the usual commercial minimum of 18 percent milkfat, and you will end up with something that tastes okay but has little body. Make it with heavy cream as suggested here, and you'll see what you've been missing.

As for flavor—well, sour cream inoculated with cultured buttermilk has great sour cream flavor. Will it taste just like your favorite brand of crème fraîche? Probably not. Today's American makers often play around with different combinations of mesophilic bacteria in order to bring out certain notes of fragrance and flavor in the finished crème fraîche. This is one case in which real perfectionists may want to try ordering a direct-set culture from a cheese-supply company (page 317). Remember, however, that the mixture of bacteria you end up buying may or may not resemble that used by a particular crème fraîche maker. Meanwhile, you can rejoice in the ease of making really excellent sour cream.

As always, check labels for the presence of live bacteria—which is why you can't just use commercial sour cream or crème fraîche to inoculate cream for your own. Usually they have been pasteurized or subjected to some heat treatment after packaging, thereby inactivating any cultures. If you find a brand that works, you're luckier than I've been.

YIELD: 2 cups

2 cups nonultrapasteurized heavy cream, preferably unhomogenized
¼ cup commercial cultured buttermilk with active cultures,
    well shaken before measuring

Mix the cream and buttermilk and let stand undisturbed at room temperature (70° to 80°F, preferably above 75°F) until thickened and lightly soured, just as for the preceding Homemade Cultured Buttermilk. Refrigerate, tightly covered, for up to a week.

HERRING WITH SOUR CREAM SAUCE

For centuries both soured milk (or cream) and salt fish were eaten by everyone in the Northeastern Cow Belt—peasants and princes, shtetl dwellers and their oppressors. Together they formed one of the region's archetypal flavor marriages. The pairing of cured herring and sour cream crossed the Atlantic along with Ashkenazic Jews, Poles of all religious beliefs, and assorted Scandinavians. It even made it to American soi-disant "gourmet" circles as an appetizer for a generation or so after herring with mild sweet-and-sour cures appeared for sale in jars around 1940. Then cured and pickled herring vanished from favor among the leaders of taste. Today there are all-purpose kitchen bibles, up-to-date Jewish cookbooks, and even some would-be encyclopedic fish cookbooks with no mention of herring, period, let alone the once-popular combination with sour cream.

Please be persuaded to give this immensely satisfying appetizer another lease on life. There is a problem: finding the fish. You need to live within reach of an old-fashioned store selling cured herring in barrels to a Polish, German, Russian, Dutch, Eastern European

Jewish, or other ex-Baltic and North Sea clientele. Some Russian-American groceries sell decent pickled herring in large jars or plastic pouches. (Ignore all recipes that tell you to simply start with a jar of ordinary commercial pickled herring—one look at typical lists of ingredients should send you fleeing from these syrupy products.)

Try to buy fillets of plain salted herring. If you don't see these labeled, are not clear on what different labels like "schmaltz" and "matjes" mean, or run into language barriers in the store, just get whatever looks appealing. If only whole herring are on sale, ask someone to fillet them for you. When you get home, taste what you've bought to see whether it's powerfully salty, mild, or sweet-and-sour. You can get good results with any of these.

Fans of herring with sour cream are wholly non-unanimous on such details as the preferred variety of onion or how sweet or sour the sauce should be. I give the onion (the usual yellow kind) a brief preliminary soaking in slightly sweetened ice water to crisp it and take out a bit of the oniony sting, and I make the sour cream sauce fairly but not overpoweringly sweet. Taste as you go along and adjust the sugar and vinegar to your preference. The grated apple is a Polish touch that splendidly complements the fish and sour cream flavors.

YIELD: 4 to 6 servings as appetizer

8 large cured herring fillets, preferably from plain salted herring (about 12 ounces in all)

Half of a medium onion

About 2 tablespoons sugar, or to taste, with a little more for soaking the onion

2 tablespoons red or white wine vinegar, or to taste

2 cups sour cream, preferably Russian-type smetana, or 1 cup each sour cream and very good crème fraîche (I use the Vermont Butter and Cheese brand.)

Half of a large, crisp, juicy tart apple (Omit if good apples are unavailable.)

½ to 1 teaspoon salt, or to taste

1 or more tablespoons of prepared (not creamed) horseradish or Polish-style mustard (optional)

Fresh dill for garnish

First rinse the fish well under cold water and taste a tiny bit. If it is mild-flavored enough to be eaten as is, simply blot it dry and proceed. Otherwise, place it in a large bowl, cover well with cold water, and let soak, refrigerated, for anything from 2 to 24 hours. Change the water at frequent intervals, tasting the herring, until it is mild enough to suit your preference. Drain, blot thoroughly dry with plenty of paper towels, and cut into 1-inch pieces.

Slice the onion into paper-thin half moons and drop the slices into a bowl of ice water with 1 to 2 teaspoons of sugar dissolved in it. Let soak for about 5 minutes before draining and blotting thoroughly dry. Layer the herring and onion in a small glass or crockery bowl or container.

Put 2 tablespoons each of sugar and vinegar in a small nonreactive saucepan, and heat, stirring, just long enough to dissolve the sugar. Whisk the sour cream smooth in a bowl and whisk in the sugar-vinegar solution.

Peel and core the apple half, grate on the coarse side of a box grater, and stir into the sauce. Taste for salt (the herring after enough soaking will contribute next to no salt, so overkill is unlikely) and gradually mix in enough to balance the other flavors along with a little more vinegar if you like, or more sugar dissolved in a teaspoon or two of warm water. If desired, add horseradish or mustard to taste. (These are an improvement only if the fish needs perking up or no tasty apples are to be had.) Pour the sauce over the herring and onion and refrigerate, tightly covered, overnight or for at least 6 hours. Serve garnished with fresh dill. It is wonderful with coarse-textured black or sour rye bread.

SMOKED WHITEFISH SALAD

More properly, "smoked whitefish dip" or "spread"—but as a staple of New York Jewish brunch tables it's universally known as "salad." If you don't already understand the harmony of smoked fish with something creamy and slightly sour, this simple combination is the perfect example. The only messy part is removing the whitefish bones, which are many and stubborn.

YIELD: About 2½ cups

2 pounds smoked whitefish
½ to 1 cup sour cream
2 to 3 scallions or 1 small onion, minced
1 celery rib, minced
1 tablespoon prepared horseradish (optional)
Fresh dill for garnish

Remove and discard the skin and bones from the fish. Flake the meat with your fingers; you should have about 2 cups. Put it in a bowl and mix in enough sour cream for a spreadable consistency. Stir in the scallions, celery, and optional horseradish. Scoop the mixture into a serving bowl, sprinkle a little chopped dill over the top, and serve with coarse dark rye or pumpernickel bread. It will keep in the refrigerator, tightly covered, for two to three days.

BUTTERMILK-CARAWAY SOUP

It would be impossible to overstate the importance of utterly plain, bare-bones milk dishes in peasant diets throughout much of Europe well into the twentieth century. Bread or potatoes with milk or sour milk once made up a very quick square meal in millions of households from Ireland to Lithuania, Switzerland to Siberia. This caraway-spiked Austrian and Bavarian soup gives you an idea of just how minimalist a country breakfast or supper could be—though with well-flavored buttermilk and sturdy black bread I'd take it over American breakfast cereal and milk any day.

If you should go on a buttermaking kick and have some thick, tasty ripened buttermilk to dedicate to this purpose, you will be astonished at the goodness of the soup.

YIELD: 4 large servings

4 thick slices of sour pumpernickel or rye bread, or any coarse-textured
    sour-flavored bread, broken or cut into chunks
2 cups water
2 teaspoons salt, or to taste
2 to 3 teaspoons caraway seeds, lightly bruised with mortar and pestle
2 tablespoons flour
2 cups cultured buttermilk
Any preferred green herb (dill, chives, marjoram), minced or snipped

The bread must be hard and stale, so slice it and let it sit for a day or two before starting the soup.

Bring the water to a boil with the salt and caraway. Mix the flour to a smooth paste with a little of the buttermilk, then stir in the remaining buttermilk. (This keeps the soup from curdling.) Whisk the buttermilk into the water over medium heat and let come to a boil. Distribute the bread in serving bowls, pour the soup over it, and serve scattered with the herb of your choice.

VARIATION: By thrifty consensus this soup was generally made with equal parts of buttermilk and water. You can, however, use all buttermilk. Stir the flour with a little of the buttermilk, combine with the rest, and add the salt and caraway. Heat just to a boil over low heat and serve as directed.

MICHAEL FIELD'S "CHŁODNIK"
(COLD SAVORY BUTTERMILK SOUP)

Decades ago, this recipe in *Michael Field's Cooking School* (1965) provided my first glimpse of the magic that results when you combine fresh, slightly sour forms of milk or cream with strong, provocative flavors like garlic and pickling brine. It is still my favorite cold soup, though I now know that Field's description "a poem of a Russian iced soup" needs some correcting. Russians call this and a family of similar soups *okroshka. Chłodnik* (pronounced roughly "huh-WOD-nik") is the Polish counterpart (see page 207 for a gorgeous version with beets).

Over the years I have replaced Field's canned shrimp with fresh shrimp and dropped the fennel that was in the original recipe. I also usually leave out the hard-boiled egg garnish (though it's a classic part of such soups), and wilt the cucumbers in salt because they then marry better with the other flavors. Use sauerkraut juice from good delicatessen sauerkraut or a brand put up in glass jars or plastic pouches, *never* cans.

YIELD: 8 to 10 servings

½ pound medium shrimp, briefly poached in the shell
4 small Persian-type or 2 American-type cucumbers
1 tablespoon salt
2 garlic cloves
2 cups sour cream, preferably Russian-type smetana (page 200)
5 cups cultured buttermilk, at least 1.5 percent milkfat
    and made without salt or gums
½ cup sauerkraut juice
4 scallions, whites and part of green stalks
Freshly ground white or black pepper
A large handful of fresh dill
2 hard-boiled eggs (optional)

Shell and if necessary devein the shrimp. Cut into coarse dice.

Peel and seed the cucumbers. Cut into medium dice (about ¾ inch), toss in a bowl with the salt, and drain in a colander for 20 to 30 minutes.

Mince the garlic very fine and place in a large nonreactive bowl with the sour cream, buttermilk, and sauerkraut juice. Whisk to combine thoroughly. Rinse the salted cucumbers under cold running water, squeeze as dry as possible, and stir into the buttermilk. Trim the scallions, chop fine, and add along with the reserved shrimp. Season with pepper to taste and a little salt if desired (it may need none). Refrigerate, covered, for 4 to 8 hours; I find that it gets harsh if kept longer than overnight.

When ready to serve, snip the dill into bits, chop the optional hard-boiled eggs, and scatter a little of each over every portion.

CHŁODNIK LITEWSKI
(POLISH COLD BEET SOUP)

Borscht" is what many American cooks will want to call this soup. But it couldn't be more different from the sweet kinds that often represent the Russian *borshch* in American kitchens. It belongs to a family of cold soups, known in all countries of the Northeastern Cow Belt, that are based on sour milk or cream and some other sour principle, usually sauerkraut or pickle brine or some version of the fermented drink called *kvas* in Russia, *kwas* in Poland. Beets are just one of the things that can go into them.

Poles are particularly dedicated to this kind of cold soup ("chłodnik" in Polish), which they make in an amazing spectrum of different guises. The original secrets of flavor are two: Chłodnik used to be made from sour whole milk with all the butterfat intact—in other words, something at least two or three times as creamy as the usual American cultured buttermilk. To come close, you must throw in a good slug of sour cream. In addition, Poles and most other Eastern Europeans have a summer-fall tradition of pickling nearly anything that can conceivably be pickled, from apples to tomatoes. Cooks thus regularly have (or used to have) several different kinds of brine on hand to add to chłodnik—or they might put in some kwas/kvas made from bread or beets. The resulting soups, often enriched with crunchy raw radishes or cucumbers, are liquid quasi-salads as gloriously varied and wonderfully refreshing as the gazpachos of Spain. Perhaps the most famous and certainly the most dramatic-looking of the Polish chłodnik tribe is this classic version made from beets and beet greens. Poles attribute it to Lithuania, at one time a Polish possession (hence the name "Litewski").

If you live near Polish, Russian, or Serbian communities with stores selling barrels of summer vegetables and fruits in brine, be sure to get some in season and add a little of the brine to the soup in lieu of sauerkraut juice. The color is most beautiful when a grated raw beet is mixed in at the end.

YIELD: About 2 quarts (8 cups)

4 to 5 medium beets, with leafy tops
4 to 6 radishes
3 to 4 small, thin-skinned Persian-type cucumbers, or an
    8-inch piece of an English hothouse cucumber
6 to 8 scallions, whites and part of green tops
2 garlic cloves, or to taste
1 quart cultured buttermilk, at least 1.5 percent milkfat and
    made without salt or gums
1 cup sour cream, preferably Russian-type smetana
½ to ⅔ cup juice from sauerkraut or full-sour kosher-style dill pickles
2 to 3 teaspoons salt, or to taste
A large handful of fresh dill
2 to 3 hard-boiled eggs, chopped (optional)

Cut off the beet tops at least half an inch above the root and rinse thoroughly. Scrub the beets well. Bring a large saucepan of water to a boil and add 3 or 4 of the beets along with the greens. Reduce the heat to medium-low, and cook, covered, until the beets are tender when probed with a knife, usually 25 to 40 minutes. Drain the beets and greens separately, and let cool.

Meanwhile, scrub the radishes and cucumbers and grate both on the coarse side of a box grater. Clean, trim, and mince the scallions. Mince the garlic, or crush it to a paste using a mortar and pestle.

Chop the drained beet greens fairly coarse. Peel the beets, and cut into fine slivers or dice.

Now combine the buttermilk, sour cream, ½ cup of the sauerkraut juice, and 2 teaspoons of the salt in a large bowl, whisking to a smooth consistency. Stir in all the vegetables. Grate the remaining raw beet on the fine side of a box grater and add the pulp and juice to the soup. Taste for seasoning and add more brine or salt as you prefer. Refrigerate, covered, at least 4 to 6 hours or overnight. Serve very cold, garnished with plenty of fresh dill and the optional chopped hard-boiled eggs.

KADHI OR KARHI
(NORTH INDIAN THICK BUTTERMILK SOUP)

This soupy sauce or saucelike soup from the Punjab and northern India is one of the many dishes caught up in the great Indian-American confusion about the difference between buttermilk and yogurt (see page 179). Having first encountered it (in Madhur Jaffrey's *An Invitation to Indian Cooking*) made with cultured buttermilk, I've remained fond of that choice.

Kadhi is usually made with a flotilla of small chickpea-flour dumpling-fritters called *pakodis* or *pakoras*. I think it is also good either by itself or with a medley of vegetables. Don't hesitate to omit any of the suggested choices or add more.

YIELD: About 8 servings

⅔ cup Indian chickpea flour (besan)
6 cups water
2 cups cultured buttermilk or plain whole-milk yogurt
4 tablespoons ghee (page 251) or vegetable oil
A pinch of ground asafetida
¼ teaspoon each fenugreek seeds, Indian brown mustard seeds, cumin seeds, and nigella (you can use more or less of any)
6 to 8 fresh curry leaves
4 small dried hot peppers (or to taste)
½ teaspoon ground turmeric
4 small waxy potatoes, peeled and cut in half
4 ounces cauliflower, broken into bite-sized florets
1 medium onion, cut into 8 wedges
4 ounces green beans, trimmed and cut into 1-inch lengths
2 small zucchini, scrubbed and cut into ½-inch chunks
2 teaspoons salt, or to taste
¼ cup sour whey from drained yogurt (page 158) or 2 to 3 teaspoons freshly squeezed lime juice (optional)
Cilantro for garnish

Put the chickpea flour in a bowl and mix to a paste with a little of the water. Add the rest of the water and the buttermilk and mix as smooth as possible.

Heat 2 tablespoons of the ghee until fragrant in a deep saucepan. Add the pinch of asafetida along with the fenugreek and mustard seeds. When the mustard seeds begin to pop, stir in the cumin seeds and nigella, then (in a few seconds) the curry leaves and dried peppers. Stir in the turmeric and let it sizzle a

KADHI (CONT.)

few seconds. Add the thickened buttermilk, and stir to distribute everything. Let the soup simmer over very low heat, partly covered, for 30 to 35 minutes.

While the soup cooks, heat the remaining ghee in a deep skillet or wide saucepan. Add the potatoes and sauté, stirring, for a few minutes. Stir in the other vegetables and sauté until the onion is translucent. Add 1 cup water and cook, partly covered, over medium-low heat, stirring occasionally, until the vegetables are tender, about 20 to 25 minutes.

Transfer the vegetables to the buttermilk soup and stir to distribute everything evenly. Taste for seasoning; add salt and—if you think it can use a dash of acid—some sour whey or lime juice, a little at a time. Serve hot, garnished with cilantro. It's lovely spooned over plain rice.

MORU KOZHAMBU
(SOUTH INDIAN BUTTERMILK SOUP)

This dish, also anglicized as *mor kozhambu*, is the South Indian counterpart of kadhi (page 209). It, too, is often served with chickpea- or lentil-flour dumplings, but vegetables are just as usual. I use the same mixture as for kadhi, but one or two of the following would be more authentic: okra, plantains, small eggplants, tomatoes, taro, Indian bottle gourd, "ash gourd" (winter melon).

Because of the coconut-laced mixture of ground seasonings and the smaller amount of starch, the "soup" will be thinner and quite different in flavor.

YIELD: 6 servings

Vegetables as for the preceding kadhi (potatoes, cauliflower, onion, green beans, zucchini)
1 tablespoon toor dal ("red gram," hulled split pigeon peas)
1 tablespoon channa dal ("yellow gram," hulled split Indian chickpeas)
4 to 6 small hot green peppers, deseeded if desired
A 1-inch chunk of peeled fresh ginger, coarsely chopped
2 teaspoons cumin seeds
2 teaspoons coriander seeds
⅓ cup grated coconut, fresh or frozen
A pinch of asafetida
¼ teaspoon ground turmeric
4 cups cultured buttermilk or plain whole-milk yogurt
3 tablespoons ghee or vegetable oil
1 teaspoon Indian brown mustard seeds

6 to 8 fresh curry leaves
2 small dried red peppers, deseeded if desired
1 to 1½ teaspoons salt, or to taste

Prepare and cook the vegetables as directed for kadhi. Meanwhile, soak both kinds of dal in a small bowl of water for 30 to 40 minutes. Drain well and put in a blender or food processor with the hot peppers, ginger, cumin seeds, coriander seeds, grated coconut, asafetida, and turmeric. Process to a paste, adding water if necessary to help the grinding. Mix the paste into the buttermilk.

Heat the ghee in a saucepan until fragrant. Add the mustard seeds and cook until they start to pop. Add the curry leaves and dried red peppers. Pour the buttermilk mixture into the pan, and cook over low heat, stirring, just until heated through. (It will curdle if allowed to boil.) Stir in the cooked vegetables, let heat through, and serve at once. This also is perfect with rice.

COLD BLUEBERRY SOUP

Cold fruit soups, among the most refreshing of summer dishes, flourish vigorously in eastern and northeastern Europe. They fall into several families—starch-bound, creamy, or based on sour milk. This version with blueberries is a nontraditional composite of the latter two approaches that I found long ago in *The Berry Cookbook* by Barbara R. Fried. The original called for two cups of sour cream. I now find this too heavy and replace it with part buttermilk. Vary the proportions of sugar, sour cream, buttermilk, and wine according to your preference and the flavor of the berries.

Americans have great difficulty figuring out just where to fit fruit soups into a meal. I think they make excellent first courses for a summer lunch menu featuring a light main-dish salad or vegetarian grain dish. They also win converts as dessert, accompanied by crackers or plain, not-very-sweet cookies.

YIELD: About 6 cups (6 servings)

2 cups blueberries, rinsed and drained
½ cup sugar, or to taste
A 3-inch piece of cinnamon stick
1 lemon, sliced thin
½ cup red wine (any preferred kind)
1 cup sour cream
1 cup cultured buttermilk

COLD BLUEBERRY SOUP (CONT.)

Put the berries in a nonreactive saucepan with 2 cups water and the sugar, cinnamon stick, and lemon. Bring to a boil and simmer, uncovered, for about 10 minutes or until the berries are cooked; add the wine during the last minute or two. Pour through a mesh sieve into a bowl, pushing with a spoon to extract as much liquid as possible. Discard the solids. Let cool to room temperature. Whisk in the sour cream until smooth. Add the buttermilk, a little at a time, until it is thinned to your taste. Taste for sweetness and acidity, adding a little sugar (dissolved in water for easier mixing) or lemon juice if desired. Chill in the refrigerator for 2 to 3 hours before serving.

VARIATION: During the brief summer season of sour cherries, I sometimes turn this into a cold cherry soup very inauthentically based on the celebrated Hungarian *meggykesköce* or *meggyleves*. Use 2 pints (about 1½ pounds) fresh sour (*not* sweet!) cherries, ¾ cup sugar or to taste, 3 inches of cinnamon stick, the juice of 1 large lemon, a dash of red wine, a dash of almond extract (bitter almond, if you can find it), 1 cup sour cream, and a little heavy or light cream. (Hungarians mix the sour cream with flour to prevent curdling and stir it into the hot soup, but I prefer it flourless.) Pit the cherries, saving a handful to add at the end; place the rest and their juice in a saucepan with 3 cups water, the ¾ cup sugar, and the cinnamon stick. Bring to a boil and gently simmer, uncovered, until the cherries are very soft, 15 to 20 minutes. Remove the pan from the heat and stir in the lemon juice, wine, and almond extract. Fish out and discard the cinnamon stick; puree the soup in a blender or food processor. Pour it into a bowl and let cool to room temperature. Whisk in the sour cream until smooth. Taste for the balance of sugar, acidity, and creaminess, and add a little sugar (dissolved in water for easier mixing), lemon juice, or sweet cream until you like the result. Add the reserved pitted cherries and chill in the refrigerator for 2 to 3 hours before serving.

SOUR CREAM/CRÈME FRAÎCHE AS
COLD SAUCE AND DIP

Sour cream, crème fraîche, Russian smetana, Latin American crema, and the rest of the family can effortlessly be turned into cold sauces and dressings perfect for a hundred purposes. The story is different as regards hot sauces, because of the ease with which heated sour cream curdles. The richest versions of crème fraîche (unfortunately, different brands vary) are more heat-resistant, as is crema. But in most cases coldness itself is part of what's delightful in their pairings with other foods, hot or cold.

The parade of marvelous table sauces or dressings begins with plain sour cream itself, simply mixed smooth or given a brief draining as with yogurt. (Draining is helpful if it is to be combined with anything a little watery.) It responds happily to minimal additions like salt, lemon juice or wine vinegar, and/or sugar, with or without some enriching egg yolk. One basic formula for a savory sour cream sauce—you can omit anything except the sour cream—would be an egg yolk whisked smooth in a small bowl and combined with a large pinch of salt, 1 cup sour cream, ¼ to 2 teaspoons sugar, 1 to 2 teaspoons grated onion, and 1 teaspoon to 1 tablespoon lemon juice or vinegar. Whisk in the sugar and acid a tiny bit at a time until you like the balance of flavors.

Many other seasonings can be used with or instead of these. Dill, fresh or dried, is the classic herb, but minced chives or scallions are also popular. Caraway seed has the same affinity for sour cream as cumin for yogurt. Other wonderful additions include grated apple, minced sour pickles of all sorts, and strong-flavored accents like prepared horseradish or mustard, Tabasco or chipotle sauce, cayenne, curry powder, capers, and anchovies. Chopped hard-boiled egg is a natural. If you can find the Balkan sweet red pepper and eggplant sauce called *ajvar,* mix it with sour cream in any proportion to make a pretty and delicious relish (or spread for rye toast).

The foods that such sauces go with are numberless. In the Ashkenazic Jewish kitchen, a bowl of plain or (less often) flavored sour cream regularly accompanies blintzes, potato pancakes, and—a truly lovely marriage—pot cheese or farmer cheese. (Whenever possible, try to look for the best of all sour-cream versions, smetana, in Russian stores.) It is nearly mandatory with Russian blini, and I prefer it to syrup on most kinds of pancakes or fritters. Everyone knows that sour cream goes perfectly with hot baked potatoes, but it's just as good with boiled potatoes (dill is great here), braised red cabbage, or braised sauerkraut. It's among the best of all salad-dressing bases; try sour cream instead of mayonnaise in potato or egg salad as well as cole slaw. Mix it with sliced or chopped cucumbers or radishes (especially black radishes). Combined with cured herring, sardines, or smoked chub or whitefish, it magically cuts their fishiness. And please follow Mimi Sheraton's suggestion (in *From My Mother's Kitchen*) of mixing chunks of pumpernickel or rye bread into a bowl of sour cream.

When it comes to sour cream or crème fraîche as dessert sauce, all I can say is the plainer, the better. Most seasonings except for maybe—*maybe*—a touch of lemon juice, sugar, and/or ground cinnamon or allspice are just so much lily gilding. All by itself it's the ideal dressing for mixed fruit salads (leave out the pineapple unless it's cooked or canned) and a heavenly foil for blueberries, raspberries, strawberries, and sliced peaches or nectarines. Put some on a dried-fruit compote. Or make an instant and excellent pseudo-mousse by mixing it into cooked-down fruit pastes like apple butter and prune or apricot lekvar.

A final use invented by the late Helen Evans Brown and immensely popular for a couple of generations: For the world's simplest chocolate frosting, melt 5 ounces of semisweet chocolate in the top of a double boiler and stir in ½ cup sour cream.

BUTTERMILK SALAD DRESSING

Sorry if hopeful cooks coming on something called "Buttermilk Dressing" expect a cousin of Hidden Valley Ranch Dressing. Mine was designed with potato salad in mind, though I expect it would also be good with coleslaw.

YIELD: About 1 cup

1 scant cup walnut oil, or any combination you wish of peanut and
   walnut oil
3 tablespoons cultured buttermilk
1 tablespoon sour cream
2 to 3 tablespoons sour pickle brine (from half-sour kosher dill pickles,
   sauerkraut, or brined capers)
1 garlic clove, mashed to a paste with a knife blade
3 to 4 tablespoons grated onion
1 teaspoon caraway seeds, lightly bruised with a mortar and pestle

Salt if needed (there may be enough in the brine)
Freshly ground pepper

FOR GARNISH:
3 large scallions (whites and some of the green parts), minced
Fresh dill
A handful of walnut meats, coarsely chopped (optional)

Whisk together the oil and all other dressing ingredients. To use for potato salad, toss with the freshly cooked potatoes while they are still warm. Scatter the salad with minced scallions, snipped dill, and (if desired) some chopped walnuts.

CUCUMBER-RADISH SOUR CREAM SAUCE

If you are fond of cold yogurt sauces or sauce-salad-relishes like Turkish Cacık or Indian Raitas (pages 163 and 164–166), probably you will enjoy this sour-cream counterpart. One of my long-time favorites is this fresh, summery version in *The Book of New New England Cookery* by Judith and Evan Jones. I generally use one of the small thin-skinned Persian-type cucumbers and—because I like the sharp flavor of black radishes—substitute a chunk for one of the red radishes. This is especially luscious if you use Homemade Sour Cream, page 201.

YIELD: Makes about 1½ cups

½ cup grated cucumber, peeled, split in half, and seeded by scooping out center
3 fat radishes, grated
2 teaspoons minced fresh dill
2 minced scallions, including tender greens
1 cup sour cream, or 1 part plain yogurt to 1 part sour cream
Salt
3 to 4 shakes Tabasco sauce

After you have grated the cucumber and radishes, squeeze them dry in a towel. Then mix all of the ingredients together, salting to taste. Refrigerate for an hour or so before serving.

MENNONITE BUTTERMILK "SALAD"

One of my favorite historically oriented international cook-books is *The Melting Pot of Mennonite Cookery 1874–1974* by Edna Ramseyer Kaufman, happily back in print after a hiatus. It traces the wanderings of the Mennonites from the Low Countries and Switzerland to parts of the old Prussian, Russian, and Austro-Hungarian empires and eventually the New World. It's remarkable to see the cooking traditions that survived the many journeys of this sect, some of whom were among my family's oldest neighbors in Pennsylvania.

The book contains no fewer than three versions—from three separate parts of the Mennonite diaspora—of a "salad" that must stem from a very ancient shared tradition. It takes some explaining to people who have never seen this kind of peasant dish: You first soured fresh milk by letting it stand, then added freshly torn or cut lettuce and sliced or chopped hard-boiled eggs to it. (There were versions with homemade noodles or cucumber and scallions.) The resulting soup-salad was seasoned with salt and eaten very cold, sometimes with a little sugar and vinegar. A bit of sour cream might enrich the sour milk. It was a summer dish, considered extremely refreshing and healthful in hot weather.

I tried it for myself one hot July when I had some freshly made cultured buttermilk and sour cream on hand. It was indeed beauti-fully restorative. You won't, however, get the same delicate fresh-ness with commercial buttermilk and sour cream. Made with the homemade articles, it gives you one of those startling glimpses into the past achievable by nothing except firsthand tasting.

Have everything well chilled and mix only at the last minute. The amounts per person are about 1 cup Homemade Cultured Buttermilk (page 200) stirred smooth with ¼ teaspoon salt (or to taste) and a few spoonfuls of Homemade Sour Cream (page 201); a dash of cider vinegar and/or sugar, if desired; 1 sliced hard-boiled egg; and a large handful of tender lettuce (Boston, Bibb, or any young leaf lettuce), torn into bite-sized pieces. Eat it from a soup bowl.

BEEF STROGANOFF

Beef Stroganoff, named for a family of long pedigree in czarist Russia, was a reigning party favorite a generation ago and is one of my leading nominees for a return from limbo. The dish started being extolled in the 1930s by members of the self-styled "gourmet" movement in the United States. Its distinguishing features are thin strips of rapidly seared beef, a sauce enriched with sour cream, and an otherwise complete absence of agreement on the necessary ingredients.

It takes a lot for any beef Stroganoff to be certifiably "inauthentic," though I'd probably draw the line at the addition of habanero salsas or *herbes de Provence*. Most recipes have onions and mushrooms, but there are cooks who reject either or both. One extremely lofty recipe has you fry some onions in the pan "for flavor," then throw them out lest they mar the noble simplicity of the beef. The amount of sour cream (a few atypical recipes have sweet cream) can be half a tanker or a few tablespoons. I have seen Stroganoffs from several continents with or without tomato paste, catsup, condensed mushroom soup, tarragon vinegar (not a bad idea, that), Tabasco, cayenne, paprika, wine marinades, flambéed brandy, sugar, Madeira, and moose meat (this last in a marvelous book titled *Cooking Alaskan*).

All I can say about the following version is that I like it. If that much filet mignon or sirloin is a financial impossibility, try thin-sliced flank steak for a chewier but still excellent result. The classic accompaniment is noodles or a rice pilaf; some people sauté the mushrooms separately and serve them as a garnish or side dish.

YIELD: 6 to 7 servings

2 pounds filet mignon or beef sirloin
3 to 4 tablespoons flour
1 large onion
½ pound (or more as desired) fresh white mushrooms, cleaned and trimmed
6 tablespoons butter
½ cup strong beef broth, preferably homemade
2 to 3 teaspoons Dijon mustard
1 cup sour cream, *at room temperature*
Salt and freshly ground pepper to taste
Parsley or fresh dill for garnish

Cut the meat into strips about 2 to 3 inches long and ⅓ to ½ inch thick. This is easier if you first put it in the freezer for about 30 minutes. Put the strips, well separated, on plates or a work surface and dredge with flour, turning them to coat lightly on all sides. Chop the onion fairly fine and cut the mushrooms, stem and all, into thin lengthwise slices.

Heat half the butter over high heat in a large heavy (preferably cast-iron) skillet. When it is sizzling and fragrant, reduce the heat to medium-high, add a few strips of meat at a time, and brown them very quickly on both sides, stirring with a wooden spoon. As each batch is done, remove it to a plate and add a few more strips. From time to time add a little more of the butter to moisten the pan. The trick is not to crowd the pan (which makes the meat stew in its own juice) and to brown the meat rapidly without letting the flour scorch; keep adjusting the heat as necessary.

When all the meat is browned, sauté the onion in the same pan over medium heat, stirring, until translucent and lightly browned, about 5 minutes. Add the mushrooms and cook, tossing and stirring, until they begin to release their juice, another 5 minutes or so. Raise the heat to high and cook until the liquid is nearly evaporated. Stir in the broth and mustard; cook, stirring, over medium heat until the sauce is a little thickened, about 5 to 7 minutes. Add the browned meat with any juices and cook, stirring and tossing, until it is heated through, 2 to 3 minutes. Now reduce the heat to very low and stir in the sour cream. It will curdle if it is too cold or if the sauce boils, so you must let it warm up for only a minute or two. Season to taste with salt and pepper and serve at once, garnished with a bit of minced parsley or snipped dill.

CHICKEN PAPRIKÁS, OR PAPRIKAHUHN

Paprika didn't exist until chile peppers reached Hungary from the New World and were bred to a uniquely rich-flavored form suitable for drying and grinding. As part of what George Lang's magisterial *The Cuisine of Hungary* calls "the holy trinity of lard, onion, and pure ground paprika," the new spice worked its way into various families of traditional braised dishes. Nothing proved to be a more inspired match for the famous trinity than the sour cream that is added to certain mild and delicate offshoots of the classic stew *pörkölt*. In Hungary this kind of dish is called *paprikás* together with the name of the main ingredient (usually chicken, veal, or fish). All parts of the Austro-Hungarian empire eventually adopted chicken versions marked by such minor wrinkles as the use of browned or unbrowned chicken, thrift or profligacy in the

amount of sour cream, and the presence or absence of green peppers, garlic, and tomatoes.

The following recipe for Viennese *Paprikahuhn* is broadly modeled on a version in Franz Maier-Bruck's *Das grosse Sacher-Kochbuch*.
The original uses butter; I think lard as the foundation of the "holy
trinity" can't be improved on except perhaps by rendered fat from
double-smoked Hungarian bacon.

YIELD: About 4 servings

2 tablespoons lard, preferably from a Middle European or Hispanic
   pork butcher
A 3½-pound chicken, cut into serving pieces
2 medium onions, chopped
1 garlic clove, crushed or minced
1 Italian frying pepper, cored, seeded, and cut into thin strips (optional)
½ cup water or chicken stock
2 to 3 tablespoons sweet Hungarian paprika
A dash of hot Hungarian paprika (optional)
A long strip of lemon rind (optional)
1 teaspoon salt, or to taste
1 large ripe globe tomato or 2 to 3 ripe plum tomatoes, peeled, seeded,
   and finely chopped
1 tablespoon flour
¼ cup sour cream, plus more for serving if desired

Heat the lard in a heavy-bottomed saucepan and brown the chicken pieces on
all sides over medium heat. Remove to a platter. Reduce the heat to medium-
low and sauté the onion, garlic, and pepper strips in the remaining fat until
slightly softened. Deglaze the pan with the water or stock. Add the sweet
paprika, optional hot paprika and lemon rind, salt, and tomato pulp. Give
everything a good stir, bring to a boil, and return the chicken pieces to the pan.
Cook, tightly covered, over low heat for about 30 minutes or until the chicken
is tender.

Transfer the chicken pieces to a heatproof dish along with a spoonful or two
of the cooking liquid, and keep warm over low heat while you boil down the
rest of the liquid by more than half. Meanwhile, stir together the flour and a
little water to make a thin paste. Whisk the sour cream into this and stir it all
into the reduced liquid in the pan and heat until warmed through. Serve the
chicken pieces with the sauce poured over them. If you like, pass around more
sour cream in a bowl.

MUSHROOMS WITH SOUR CREAM SAUCE

People of a certain age remember this as a once-elegant brunch or lunch dish served on toast. The suggestion of caraway as a seasoning comes from Craig Claiborne's *The New York Times Menu Cookbook*, where I first encountered the dish.

It is even better made with a mixture of white and shiitake mushrooms (caps only) and/or reconstituted dried porcini. If you happen to have some homemade veal glaze, a teaspoon or so is a lovely addition.

YIELD: 4 to 5 servings

4 to 5 shallots
3 to 4 tablespoons butter
1 pound fresh white mushrooms, cleaned and trimmed
1 to 2 teaspoons caraway seeds, bruised in a mortar (optional)
A dash of lemon juice
2 tablespoons sherry or Madeira
1 teaspoon salt, or to taste
Freshly ground black or white pepper
2 to 3 teaspoons flour
1 cup sour cream, at room temperataure
Parsley or dill for garnish

Mince the shallots and gently sauté them in the butter while you cut the mushrooms lengthwise into roughly ¼-inch slices or chop them fairly coarse. Add the mushrooms to the shallots and cook over medium-high heat, stirring, until the juice they release is nearly evaporated. Stir in the optional caraway seeds along with sherry, salt, and pepper.

Mix the flour and sour cream as smooth as possible. Stir into the mushrooms and cook over very low heat, stirring, for about 6 to 8 minutes. Scatter snipped fresh dill or minced parsley over the mushrooms, and serve on hot toast or as a side dish by itself.

MUSHROOM PIROZHKI WITH SOUR CREAM PASTRY

Dedicated pastry-makers often have a soft spot for sour cream because the lactic acid slightly tenderizes the dough while the cream adds richness. Russians often make pirozhki (small turnover-like pastries) with a yeast-raised dough, but this sour-cream version is a popular alternative. Mushroom pirozhki are a fine party dish, or nice as part of an otherwise light lunch or supper.

YIELD: About 4 dozen

FILLING:
½ recipe Mushrooms with Sour Cream Sauce (page 220); omit caraway, flour, and sour cream
2 hard-boiled eggs, chopped

SOUR-CREAM PASTRY:
3 cups flour
1 teaspoon salt
¾ cup cold butter, cut into small bits
¾ cup cold sour cream, drained before measuring if watery
1 to 3 tablespoons ice water, or as needed
1 egg yolk lightly beaten with 2 to 3 tablespoons water

For the filling, cook the mushrooms as directed and mix in the hard-boiled eggs. Let cool, and refrigerate until ready to use (several hours or overnight).

Make the dough by sifting the flour and salt into a bowl, then cutting in the butter with a pastry cutter or two knives until the mixture resembles coarse grits. Stir in the sour cream with a fork. The mixture will start coming together in a dough. If necessary, lightly mix in ice water a teaspoon or so at a time until you can gather it up in a ball. Wrap the dough in waxed paper or plastic wrap and refrigerate for at least two hours.

Preheat the oven to 375°F. Lightly flour a pastry cloth or work surface and roll out the dough a little less than ½ inch thick. Cut out 3-inch rounds with a cookie cutter or the rim of a glass. Gather up the trimmings, reroll, and cut into more 3-inch rounds. Put about 2 to 3 teaspoons of mushroom filling on one side of each round and fold over the edge to make a half moon. Firmly press the edges together with a fork.

As the pirozhki are filled, place them on baking sheets and brush the tops with the beaten egg. Bake until golden brown, 20 to 25 minutes. Serve hot.

BUTTERMILK POTATOES

The combination of boiled potatoes and milk used to be part of the culinary landscape throughout most of northern Europe. Irish Champ (page 114) is an example made with sweet milk. As explained earlier, soured milk predominated from the North Sea eastward. Cultured buttermilk is the modern substitute.

The general idea is the same in most places: Boil potatoes with plenty of salt, and mash them, while fresh and hot, with sour milk or a mixture of sour milk and sour cream, lightly bound with flour or starch to keep it from curdling. The dish is usually soupy. For the very poor of earlier generations, it contained no other ingredients except maybe a little onion. Better-off people topped it with fried bacon or salt pork and the hot pan drippings. It's particularly good made with Homemade Cultured Buttermilk (page 200).

YIELD: 4 servings

2 to 3 ounces of slab bacon, coarsely diced
1 medium onion, coarsely diced
4 large boiling potatoes, peeled
1 tablespoon salt
4 to 5 cups cultured buttermilk
1 tablespoon flour
Freshly ground pepper

Cook the bacon over gentle heat in a small heavy skillet until the fat is well rendered. Scoop out the crisp bits to drain on paper towels; fry the onion in the bacon fat over medium heat until soft and translucent. Keep warm over very low heat when it is done.

While the bacon cooks, cut the potatoes into large chunks. Put them in a large saucepan of cold water and scatter in the salt. Bring to a boil and cook over medium-high heat until tender, about 20 minutes. Meanwhile, mix a small amount of the buttermilk with the flour until smooth. Pour 4 cups of the remaining buttermilk into a saucepan, stir in the flour mixture, and warm over low heat without quite letting it boil.

When the potatoes are done, drain them thoroughly. Either return them to the pan and mash with a potato masher or put them through a ricer back into the pan. Turn the heat to low and start mashing in the hot buttermilk a little at a time until the dish is slightly soupy, or add an extra cup of buttermilk to make it very soupy. Season with pepper to taste.

Pour the hot bacon drippings and onion over the potatoes, and top with the crisp fried bacon. Serve at once.

VARIATION: A nice Belgian version of this dish ("stampers," or *taatjespap* in Flemish) in Ruth Van Waerebeek's *Everyone Eats Well in Belgium Cookbook* omits the onion, adds a grating of fresh nutmeg, and finishes everything off with Beurre Noisette (page 261) instead of bacon fat.

FRIED BANANAS WITH CREMA

If you are unacquainted with Latin American–style crema, this simple dish is a lovely introduction. The cool saltiness of the crema is irresistible against the melting sweetness of the banana. (If you like, and can get, blackened superripe plantains, they are as good or better.) You may find the crema delicious enough by itself not to need the suggested additional touch of rum and lime juice. Serve it as a side dish in a meal featuring something like Cuban-style roast pork and black beans, or by itself as a very nice dessert.

YIELD: 4 servings

1½ cups Central American–type crema (see page 196)
A dash of rum (optional)
A dash of freshly squeezed lime juice (optional)
1 or 2 pinches of finely grated lime zest (optional)
3 medium bananas, very ripe but not black
4 tablespoons butter, or 2 tablespoons each butter and any preferred
    vegetable oil

Stir the crema smooth in a small bowl, and stir in the optional rum, lime juice, and lime zest. Peel the bananas and slice them into roughly ¾-inch chunks.

Heat the butter in a heavy medium skillet until it sizzles. Add the sliced bananas at once and cook over medium heat, shaking the pan and turning the pieces frequently to brown them lightly on all sides. They are done as soon as browned. Scoop out the bananas before they can burn, arrange in a serving dish, and serve hot with the crema.

SOUTHERN BUTTERMILK PIE

The American South is home to a family of pies consisting of a pastry crust with a very sweet custard filling—a particular sort of custard made from sugar or syrup, eggs, and butter bound with a small amount of some starchy ingredient (cornmeal, cornstarch, or flour). Pecan pie (visualize the filling minus the pecans) is a classic twentieth-century example. Older members of the group include chess pie, transparent pie, Jefferson Davis pie, and lemon or lime pie. (In some recipes you find them shading into one another.) This cousin based on buttermilk harks back to pre-refrigeration days in the South, when unpasteurized milk at ambient temperatures rapidly curdled (clabbered) and was churned to butter in that condition, leaving plenty of nice sour buttermilk for drinking or cooking. Today people use cultured buttermilk.

YIELD: One 9-inch pie

1 cup sugar
3 tablespoons cornstarch
A pinch of salt
4 egg yolks
4 tablespoons butter, melted
1½ cups cultured buttermilk
1 tablespoon freshly squeezed lemon juice
Freshly grated nutmeg
A 9-inch pie shell, made by any preferred recipe and partly baked by any preferred method

Preheat the oven to 350°F.

Sift the sugar, cornstarch, and salt together into a mixing bowl. Whisk the egg yolks in a separate bowl. Stir the egg yolks, butter, buttermilk, and lemon juice into the dry ingredients and grate in the nutmeg. Pour the mixture into the pie shell and bake for about 40 minutes, or until slightly puffed and very lightly set. Let cool on a wire rack. The pie can be served at room temperature or (more often) chilled.

VARIATION I: Many people either incorporate the egg whites into the filling or use them as a meringue. For the first option, beat the 4 egg whites stiff and fold them into the buttermilk–egg yolk mixture before baking. For the second, bake the filled shell for 25 to 30 minutes; meanwhile, beat the 4 egg whites stiff, adding ⅓ cup superfine sugar and a pinch of cream of tartar partway through the beating. Remove the partly baked pie from the oven, carefully spread the meringue over the whole surface, and bake for another 10 to 15 minutes.

VARIATION II: In the nineteenth century, custardy fillings of the general sugar-butter-eggs type were often baked without a crust; both crusted and crustless versions were commonly called "puddings." For a buttermilk pudding made without a crust, use 1½ cups sugar, 4 tablespoons cornstarch, ¼ teaspoon salt, 6 egg yolks, 6 tablespoons melted butter, 2 cups buttermilk, 4 teaspoons lemon juice, and a generous grating of nutmeg; mix as above, pour into a buttered 1½-quart baking dish, and bake in a preheated 350°F oven for 35 to 40 minutes.

Cow and Calf

HANGOP (DUTCH BUTTERMILK DESSERT)

The name means "hang up," and the dish consists of buttermilk poured into a cloth that gets tied into a bag and hung up to drain until it reaches the consistency of sour cream. It is eaten lightly sugared. Nowadays many people in the Netherlands use yogurt instead. I think the flavor of cultured buttermilk goes better with the usual garnish of crumbled Holland rusks. Recently I realized that rusks seem to have become an obscure item, at least in the United States. So has zwieback, my second choice. The best thing to use if you can't find either is plain Italian biscotti.

This no-work dessert is often enriched with a little whipped cream, and it goes beautifully with all kinds of fresh berries. The recipe can easily be doubled, though it's probably quicker to drain it in two separate cloth bags than one. For suggested uses of the leftover whey, see page 313.

YIELD: About 3 cups *hangop*, 5 cups buttermilk whey

2 quarts cultured buttermilk, preferably at least 1.5 percent milkfat
¼ to ½ cup heavy cream (optional)
¼ cup (or to taste) crumbled Holland rusks, zwieback, or plain biscotti
2 to 4 tablespoons sugar or any preferred kind of unrefined or brown sugar
Ground cinnamon

Line a colander with *tight-woven* cheesecloth or other clean cotton cloth and set it over a bowl or pan as for Fresh White Cheese with Cultures, page 291. Pour the buttermilk into the lined colander and let the whey drain until it is only intermittently dripping, usually about 1 hour. Gather up the corners of the cloth and tie them together to make a bag that will hang as compact and high as possible. (If necessary, tie the neck of the bag with butcher's twine to pull it up more.) Hang the bag of curd over a container deep enough to hold the accumulating whey without letting it touch the bottom of the bag.

Let the buttermilk curd drain overnight, or until it has lost more than half its volume in whey and resembles thick sour cream. Turn it out into a bowl, scraping off the last bits that cling to the cloth. Beat the creamy curd smooth with a wooden spoon. If you want to enrich it a little, whip the optional cream stiff and fold it into the hangop. You can fold in a little of the sugar now, but I prefer to pile the unsweetened hangop in a serving dish and scatter it with crumbled rusks, sugar, and cinnamon. Serve with fresh fruit.

BUTTERMILK AS DRINK

For some reason, people who love buttermilk don't always like yogurt. I have on occasion sung the praises of cold yogurt drinks to doubting Thomases whose mood altered completely when I asked whether they liked drinking buttermilk. As mentioned in the yogurt chapter, there's considerable confusion in Anglo-Indian usage about what constitutes "buttermilk" or "yogurt," the reason being the Indian custom of souring milk to a yogurtlike state before churning it to butter. The resulting buttermilk is closer in flavor and consistency to yogurt than our true buttermilk (whether made from ripened or unripened cream) or cultured buttermilk. Indian cooks in both India and this country often cheerfully call for "buttermilk" in a recipe when they're really thinking of yogurt or something yogurty-tasting. This is my idea of a useful and productive misunderstanding. If Americans fond of buttermilk are thereby sparked to try something that they'd otherwise ignore, why not?

So I advise buttermilk lovers to explore its possibilities as a drink by taking a little inspiration from yogurt country. The American ways of using this deeply satisfying thirst-quencher have not been especially adventurous. Some seventy years ago people might mix it with some sugar and ground cinnamon. Occasionally contemporary cooks turn it into a kind of fruit smoothie, thinned or not with some plain milk or water. I suggest going further: Glance through the recipes for Indian sweet or "salt" lassi as well as Turkish ayran in the yogurt chapter, and experiment with buttermilk versions of any that take your fancy. Please be sure to use the richest cultured buttermilk you can find (at least 1.5 percent milkfat), made without added thickeners. It makes a wonderful drink with nothing but a dash of salt and some crumbled dried mint. I think it's even better with Indian seasonings like cumin seeds, cilantro, hot green pepper, and slivered ginger.

BUTTER AND TRUE BUTTERMILK

Butter is one of life's simple pleasures—except that nothing about it is simple but the eating. What you detect in even the most plebeian mass-produced cows'-milk butter has depths only half-fathomed by modern chemistry.

To get a small glimpse of the complexities beneath the surface, take about one or two tablespoons' worth of cows'-milk butter—real 100 percent butter, not something dubbed "light butter" or "spreadable butter"—and plan to sample it at refrigerator temperature, room temperature, barely melted, briefly cooked, and resolidified. It can be salted or unsalted, but there should be no other added ingredients.

Start by unwrapping some cold butter and sniffing it. Depending on the individual batch, you may smell almost nothing or a tantalizing lactic quality without a name. Cut yourself four small pieces. A fraction of a tablespoon each will suffice. Watch the way the knife goes through the clean, cold, waxy substance. Return three pieces (and the stick they came from) to the refrigerator. Carve off a tiny bit of the fourth and put it in your mouth. Like the Cheshire Cat, it will vanish a little at a time, with a long, elusive finish. Eat another bit, trying to register the stages of smiling disappearance: waxy and solid, less solid but mysteriously cooling, more and more melted, nearly gone, gone but not forgotten. Different flavors will blossom in your mouth as all this unfolds. If your sample came from cultured butter, you may fleetingly think of crème fraîche or a soft red wine. If not, those notes will be missing; nonetheless, what you taste will echo what Henry James tasted in the words "summer afternoon."

Now put the rest of the piece on a plate, and leave it in a warm room—close to 80°F, if possible—for an hour or two. Give it another sniff. Any prior aroma will be amplified. Nick off a bit to eat. This time the fatly glistening stuff will offer about as much resistance to the knife as face cream. You will recognize some of what you tasted before, but not the same progression of effects. The first sensation on the tongue will be close to greasiness, and the act of tasting will be somewhat truncated, as if some part of the original butter had just flown off into thin air. (It has.)

Now take one of the remaining chunks out of the refrigerator and prepare to just barely melt it. The best way is to start warming a little water in a small shallow pan, taking it off the heat when it is slightly hotter than lukewarm. Cut the butter into bits no larger than small peas and put it in a heatproof container like a glass custard cup or small measuring cup. Lower this into the pan of water and watch while the butter gradually melts. Don't be in a rush; what you want to see is the moment at which the last identifiably solid bit is gone. Sniff and taste the butter from time to time while this is happening. The fragrance will become less delicate and perhaps almost cheesy. The marvelous fusion of nameless flavors will begin to come unglued, with a bland, oily taste poised against a faint sourness (how faint depends on the particular batch and how it was made). At the same time, you will see the butter resolving itself into clear fat and shoals of infinitesimal white flecks. When it is fully melted, some of the white parts will almost cloud over the top while some float toward the bottom.

Put the melted butter back into the refrigerator to chill until it is completely solid. Taste it a few times during this brief process. When it is hard and cold, take a good look and a good taste. *It will never go back to what it was.* You may be able to thaw and refreeze ice, or melt and recongeal an aspic. Nobody can do anything of the kind with butter. Once it has melted, its major components go their separate ways and can no more be put together again than Humpty Dumpty. As low as the melting temperature was (the last bits would have dissolved at about 99°F), your resolidified butter has lost the silky closeness and marble opacity of the original and is more like some congealed oil. It has a slightly coarse, grainy feel on the tongue, and a trace of sour whitish liquid may cling to the underside.

Now take another chunk of butter from the refrigerator and put it in a small heavy saucepan or skillet. Melt it on low heat, standing over the pan to observe everything as closely as possible. After the stage at which the last piece melted, the white flecks will start to swim around briskly and gather themselves into a sort of foam. Swirl the pan from time to time; stick in a spoon and carefully taste the hot butter once or twice. It will seem less and less recognizable as butter, but the kitchen will be filled with the deep, soul-warming smell that all right-thinking Americans once knew as "buttery." You will see a little steam rising from the butter before the foam dies away. Another few seconds, and the white stuff—now easier to make out as separate specks—will start turning brown. Swirl the pan and take it off the heat just as the fat itself begins to change color, before everything careens down the slippery slope toward absolutely burned butter.

Spoon out a little and taste it, being careful not to burn yourself. The lightly browned fat will be still oilier than the batch you tasted at melting point. But the tiny brown scintillas will have a nutty sweetness unlike anything you've encountered in the earlier samples. Let it solidify at room temperature and taste it before briefly chilling it in the refrigerator and tasting it again. Both times you will find the texture still less whole—that is, grainier, more congealed, less waxy, and further from melt-in-the-mouth suavity—than the barely melted sample you tried before. And the browned bits will just reinforce the nonbutteriness, or ex-butteriness, of the flavor.

And now for something completely different: Take the fourth piece of butter and put it in a small lidded container. Find a good strong-tasting onion, cut off a slice, and put it in with the butter. Cover the container tightly and return it to the refrigerator for a day (or until you next remember it). Remove the lid and take out the onion before smelling and tasting the butter. It will have acquired a distinct onioniness that will remain until the end of its existence. The onion, on the other hand, won't be in the least buttery.

COMPLEXITY COMPOUNDED

You have now proved something known to everyone who works with dairy products: No other food you can name exists in a state of more fragile chemical equilibrium—translating into flavor equilibrium—than butter and the milkfat from which it is made. The old superstitions about butter spoiling or not "coming" if somebody merely looked at it the wrong way aren't far off the mark. It can hardly sit still for a minute without risking intervention from the universe at large. The agents of drastic, irreversible change are all around milkfat as soon as it is removed from the rest of the milk and chemically turned inside out by some form of churning. And the same is true whether the milk comes from a cow, goat, sheep, buffalo, or other animal.

Some of the potential changes are delightful, some ghastly. They would not occur if the chemist's laboratory of the rumen and the finishing shop of the udder did not direct thousands of different substances into the milkfat, over and above those that go into the much less complex casein and whey. Butter is made up of so many components that some probably still don't have names. The slightest shift in balance can mean an immense flavor difference. This incredible delicacy reflects the life-giving importance of milk itself.

Milkfat is the most concentrated source of energy for nurslings. And it is the crux of their first taste experience. As cooks know, fat is the soul of taste. Vegetable fats like olive or walnut oil impart their unmistakable note to anything cooked in them. But when it comes to milkfat—"butterfat" in its pre-butter state—flavor also plays a biological role. Every species of mammal, from mouse to rhinoceros, produces milk with a "lipid profile," or mixture of fat components, peculiar to itself and not to be confused with any other creature's milkfat. This species-to-species variation in the flavor palette of milkfat is the strongest marker by which newborns instinctively *recognize the milk of their own kind.*

Divert milk into the outside world, and all the intricacies of milkfat have a new theater in which to operate. It's a subject to defeat even textbooks of dairy chemistry, which always acknowledge that much remains to be discovered about such-and-such aspects of milkfat. The only aspects I will touch on, as the ones most related to flavor, are globule membranes, fatty-acid content, and true buttermilk.

Milkfat exists in milk as tiny globules surrounded by delicate but surprisingly strong membranes whose composition is still not fully understood because even trying to study them under a microscope distorts their structure. To an extent, the membranes protect the globule contents—a soup of different fatty acids, together with other fat-related substances too complicated to discuss here—against attack by outside forces.

You can think of the membranes as something like the film around soap bubbles, except that they have a much more complex architecture, with microscopically thin outer and inner layers comprising intricate mixtures of fat-related substances and numerous enzymes. If you have tried the mini-experiment in buttermaking at the start of this book, or whipped some cream by the directions on page 84, you have explored one way to knock apart the many substances making up the globule membrane—releasing flavors that would not register as clearly otherwise—while also letting the enclosed fat flow out of the former "bubble."

There are other conditions under which the membrane can be breached and the contents spilled out, but usually with nastier or at least trickier results. Handle milk, cream, or butter without an eye to sanitation, and eventually you will invite certain bacteria or enzymes that dismantle fat globules, releasing the hideously penetrating flavors of rancidity. "Lipolysis," or breakdown of fat, is the technical name. But curiously enough, small amounts of controlled lipolytic action are exactly what's needed to produce the bracing sting of several excellent Italian cheeses—just one instance of the truth that harnessing the flavor potential of milkfat takes exceeding skill and experience.

The next culinary dimension of milkfat that cooks need to know something about is what kinds of fatty acids it contains. Here I must gloss over many niceties of technical definition to explain that any edible fat in our kitchens, from peanut oil to rendered lard, basically consists of compounds properly called "triglycerides." The last three syllables reflect the fact that they all involve a molecule of an alcohol known as "glycerol," which is reponsible for the basic effect of suave fattiness in fats. The "tri" part means that they all contain three fatty-acid molecules tacked on to the glycerol like three pennants waving from a pole. The truly dizzying aspects of the picture are first, that fatty acids come in phenomenal numbers of different configurations; second, that any triglyceride molecule can contain a mix-and-match assortment of any three fatty acids from the whole spectrum; and third, *that all the resulting permutations and combinations will taste different.*

Most of the vegetable oils used in cooking contain at least dozens of individual fatty acids. But by comparison, the fat in cows' milk is now known to have more than four hundred, shuffled like cards in a deck to furnish the different "tri's" in thousands of triglycerides. Undoubtedly, milkfat from other animals is equally complex. But the unique commercial importance of cows' milk means that it's been better studied than any of the others.

There are several ways to distinguish different kinds of fatty acids. Most are beyond the scope of a book like this. Those important enough for cooks and consumers to warrant brief explanations start with volatility, or the tendency to evaporate at fairly low temperatures. Heat a bit of butter barely above luke-warm and, as you have just seen, the more volatile fatty acids will vanish in a puff of fragrance, never to be recovered.

Individual members of the fatty-acid tribe are also often grouped under the rubrics "short chain," "medium chain," and "long chain," referring to the actual length of the molecule as measured by counting basic architectural units. These units consist of carbon atoms—in most cases from four to twenty-two—linked with one another in arrangements that can be very crudely visual-ized as daisy chains with many odd twists and turns in three-dimensional space. Every carbon atom on the chain has hydrogen atoms attached, but here a whole cluster of variables occurs. Each carbon atom could potentially link up with two hydrogen atoms via straightforward connections called "single bonds." When every one actually is so linked, the fatty acid is said to be "satu-rated," meaning that all potential vacancies for hydrogen are filled. If, how-ever, some are linked with only one hydrogen atom apiece by more tricky and unstable connections ("double bonds"), there are unfilled vacancies and the molecule is said to be "unsaturated."

For about half a century Americans have been absorbing news bulletins about the qualities of saturated and unsaturated fatty acids; at times it seems as if more pieces of nomenclature are being added every other week. Gradually the experts began explaining that there are kinds and degrees of saturation, and the names of different classifications—sometimes of different individual acids—started showing up in media coverage of health issues. What generally seems to have got lost in the fog of nutribabble is the culinary picture.

Different fats, as we encounter them in the kitchen, contain different bal-ances of saturated and unsaturated fatty acids. Broadly speaking, the ones more weighted toward unsaturation are liquid at room temperature and are called "oils," while the more saturated fats are solid at the same temperature. But what's unique about butter is that because of the huge number of different sat-urated and unsaturated fatty acids stuck onto triglyceride molecules in differ-ent combinations, it undergoes a uniquely subtle transition between solid and liquid.

You must also take into account that acids of different chain lengths all have their particular flavors. The shorter ones, which also happen to be somewhat volatile, include the pungent butyric acid and the trio of capric-caproic-caprylic acids that in large amounts produces "goaty-sheepy" effects. The longer ones are usually milder-tasting. Imagine the four hundred–plus chemi-cally distinct fatty acids in cows'-milk butter, all contributing separate jots and

tittles of sharpness, roughness, floweriness, waxiness, mellowness, and melta-
bility to what we taste as a single substance.

The butter story involves many other wrinkles that can't be dealt with here;
I have ignored whole categories of compounds that enter into its taste and
smell. I will mention only one final factor that sets it apart from all other culinary fats: the strategic impurities of "buttermilk." If you remember the concept of "phase inversion" (page 70), you know that churning milk or cream to
butter means agitating an emulsion of fat globules dispersed in a water-based
solution, thus breaking up the individual globules enough to let the milkfat
inside them separate—more or less—from the rest of the milk and form the
continuous mass that we call butter. But butter is never pure butterfat, unless
you resort to very drastic industrial separation techniques that produce something lacking the nuances of proper butter. When the formerly dispersed milkfat comes together in a body through churning, it retains minuscule droplets
of "buttermilk," the incompletely separated liquid residue. Even after freshly
churned butter is worked and rinsed to remove the buttermilk, faint traces of it
remain dispersed through the body of the butter. They contain enough of the
original skim-milk solids to contribute a very faint, elusive milkiness without
which butter never quite achieves its full flavor potential.

These same milk solids illustrate just how close the rewards of cooking with
dairy products are to the pitfalls. They have the wonderful property of browning, caramelizing, and developing a heavenly flavor when butter is heated to
fairly low temperatures, somewhere around 250°F. The white stuff that you
saw separating from the clear butterfat in slowly heated butter, then resolving
itself into nutty browned particles, was milk solids from retained buttermilk.
Unfortunately, their burning point is far below the smoking point of the actual
butterfat. Let the temperature increase even slightly, and in a flash the delicious brown flecks will become acridly reeking black flecks, the hallmark of
irretrievably burned butter.

Most butter as sold in the United States is only about 80 to 81 percent butterfat. The makeup of the remainder varies according to such factors as
whether the butter is salted or unsalted and made from sweet or ripened
cream. Most of it is water (either in the retained buttermilk or incorporated in
the process of rinsing out the buttermilk) and milk solids. For some purposes
such as pastry-making (see the recipe for Pâte Brisée, page 272), butterfat content of 82 percent or higher is desirable. In most other kinds of cooking, the
nuances contributed by trace amounts of buttermilk are actually a virtue—
though too much gives the butter a leaky body and a propensity to go bad.

Why does melting butter so irreversibly change its basic consistency? The
answer lies in the breaking up of fat globules in the churning process. Milk or
cream is ordinarily chilled in preparation for churning. Chilling any liquid fat

to a solid state causes it to form crystals. The enclosure of milkfat within membrane-surrounded globules adds another complication. As some of the globule contents become crystallized, the sharp crystal edges are in effect primed to start rupturing globule membranes even before churning, encouraging the formation of a continuous butter mass. But not entirely continuous; even after churning, some of the original fat globules remain intact, distributed throughout the body of the butter. The cold butter takes on a triple interior structure: part crystalline (which makes it brittle), part continuous (which makes it malleable), part globular. When it melts, this unique architecture is effaced a little at a time along with other changes including the escape of volatile components. Once rechilled, the butter hardens into coarser crystals large enough to be detected as a grainy "mouthfeel."

The ease with which butter absorbs the smells and tastes of other foods is yet another effect of membrane disruption. Components that were comparatively impervious to outside influences while they remained locked up in the inner or outer face of the globule membrane are now distributed through the butter. They include various unstable radicals, or unattached fragments of molecules, that are ready to react with whatever they come in contact with. It so happens that raw onions or other alliums, once cut, release their own arsenal of highly reactive volatile sulfurous radicals in search of attachment points on other substances. Put butter in contact with these "allicins" (in fact, nearly anything vigorously smelly), and you have something like the meeting of two desperately lonely people in a singles bar. All fats and oils tend to be affected by foreign aromas and flavors, but the unique composition of butter makes it the most susceptible of all.

Today various foods seem to be the beneficiaries of a backlash against the more naive preachments of yesteryear, and butter is among them. The nutrition vigilantes who spent much of the 1980s and '90s assuring us that various margarines were a far more healthful alternative have changed their tune following a spate of reports about the effects of trans fatty acids, a class of unsaturated fatty acids in which carbon atoms accept extra hydrogen atoms attached by peculiarly angled double bonds that make the resulting compounds look and behave more like saturated fats. (Small amounts of trans fatty acids occur naturally in milkfat, but they represent only a tiny fraction of the volume now pouring into the food supply from commercially manufactured fats.) To an extent, butter is getting cleared of a disrepute that it never should have incurred in the first place. But I should hate to see its fortunes tied only to the fluctuations of pop diet theory. In the end, the best reason to love it and welcome it (with a good dose of common sense) to our diets is that no other food even remotely mimics the unimaginable intricacies we experience in the ravishing effect of butter on bread, butter melted over a baked potato, butter in a frying pan, butter in a sauce or pastry.

Here I should point out that the global diversity of butter is still pretty much a closed book in this country. As far as I know, strong-flavored versions produced by different kinds of handling with lengthy fermentation have not yet arrived here from places like Tibet, parts of the Arab world, or odd corners of Africa. It's not only possible but probable that in a few years Americans will be readjusting their gastronomic compasses to take in kinds of butter far beyond Eurocentric models. Meanwhile, you can learn a lot about international preferences by searching for goats'-, sheep's-, or even buffaloes'-milk butter and registering how greatly they differ from cows'-milk butter. (A few Greek groceries carry imported sheep's-milk butter, and buffaloes'-milk butter from Italy shows up in a few specialty venues.)

SALTED VERSUS UNSALTED BUTTER: SOME HISTORICAL PERSPECTIVE

Unlike most milk and cream, plain butter as it reaches American consumers today in either salted or unsalted state probably is better made and better tasting than most of the counterparts produced on this continent before the twentieth century. I don't mean butter inflated with gases or mixed with vegetable oils, but the ordinary mass-produced kind put up in quarter-pound sticks. It is a very particular, fairly modern artifact of northwestern European culinary culture, and its uniqueness is difficult to understand without some explanation of how butter reached different cuisines at different times. If you harbor strong prejudices about the superiority of either salted or unsalted butter, much of the reason lies in this same past.

I have mentioned that the ancient Greeks, who didn't raise milch animals for butter, puzzled their heads over the butter, or "cow cheese," that they saw being scarfed down by barbarian cattle herders (page 23). It's highly unlikely that this curiosity resembled modern table butter, because it couldn't possibly have been produced under the conditions that make butter waxy and delicate-tasting. Before modern chilling technology, a more important consideration would have been making the butter keep. Butter does last longer than the milk or cream that furnishes it, but that's not very long. People therefore took to salting it, and sometimes burying it underground in pots or casks. To this day people in parts of the Middle East and North Africa bury butter long enough to reach some desired state of fermentation, and the custom of burying it in Irish peat bogs seems to be centuries if not millennia old.

Given the perishablility of butter, it's impossible to generalize about what it tasted like in ancient and perhaps early medieval Europe. Did people clarify it for longer keeping, or mix it with herbs for more complex flavors, as many of the world's butter-eating peoples still do? Was it strong and almost cheesy-smelling like the North African *smen*? We may never know. But we do know that plenty of it was salted, probably to a degree that we would find harsh. And with repeated use the vessels it was churned in (animal skins in earliest times, later unglazed clay and wood) would have acquired penetrating smells and tastes that they then communicated to the butter.

The butter of the Middle Ages was more a humble rural staple than a delicacy. The situation changed with the eighteenth-century rise of specialized modern dairying, when farmstead butter freshly churned for market became something of a luxury article for town-dwellers' tables in England and northern Europe. The buttermaking scene in George Eliot's novel *Adam Bede*, set in 1799, marvelously evokes what might be called the modern European butter esthetic: "it is so pure, so sweet-scented; it is turned off the mould with such a beautiful firm surface, like marble in a pale yellow light!"

But fine, expensive butter made to exacting tastes was very far from most of the butter sold and eaten throughout the nineteenth century. From contemporary accounts, the usual article was likely to be ill-flavored or frankly rancid through poor handling. In countries that put up a lot of butter for mass commercial distribution (especially the United States and Ireland), it was routinely made with gross amounts of undissolved salt worked in before the butter was packed for keeping into large firkins—sometimes meant to last through a winter—that might be topped up with brine, resulting in a further salt crust on the surface. This did not stop poorly made butter from still being rancid or contaminated with foreign flavors.

"America must have the credit of manufacturing and putting into market more bad butter than all that is made in the rest of the world together," announced the domestic science writer Catharine Beecher and her sister Harriet Beecher Stowe in

The American Woman's Home (1869). By their reckoning, "about one pound of salt to every ten of butter" was a usual ratio—not surprising, with salt costing "five cents a pound and butter fifty."

The disdain for salted butter among many modern American food authorities is a remnant of this era. The Beecher sisters, who had tasted exquisite unsalted butter in France and England, saw the matter in better perspective. One could, they wrote, find at least some American butter "salted with care and delicacy, so that it might be a question whether even a fastidious Englishman might not prefer its golden solidity to the white, creamy freshness of his own."

The new dairying technology of the late nineteenth century resulted in butter of much more uniform and, on the whole, better quality, generally produced at centrifuge-equipped industrial creameries rather than on farms. There are advantages to doing some things on at least a modest industrial scale, and buttermaking is one of them. The fact is that being able to precisely measure fat content, buttermilk content, temperature, and other conditions, while using vessels and churning equipment a great deal cleaner than many earlier counterparts, raised the average quality of creamery butter well above any but the very finest farmstead article. (Eventually, batch churning was supplanted by more highly automated continuous-flow processes.) At the same time, revolutions in packaging, transportation, and home storage meant that nearly everyone could frequently buy butter put up in small amounts and keep it for short periods in an icebox or refrigerator. Before that, you either bought whole firkins meant to last you for months or went to the grocer's for a pound or so dug out of a barrel, in either decent or horrible condition.

By the time creameries proliferated, most American consumers had a taste for salted butter that persists to this day. The minority, at around the turn of the twentieth century, included culinary writers who fancied that unsalted butter was an elegant French preference, as well as a rising tide of Ashkenazic Jewish immigrants from the Pale of Settlement.

Today salting is done less for preservation than because of taste preference, and salted butter is almost invariably made with amounts of smoothly incorporated salt that the Beechers would have thought quite delicate. Both salted and unsalted versions have a fine, waxy consistency and gratifying flavor that would have been far from routine 150 years ago. But the question of which kind is preferable still tends to be debated as if we were awash in butter coarsely oversalted to mask awful defects. I think the facts are much misunderstood.

In the first place, good-tasting butter can be salted or unsalted. Setting aside the differences between butter churned from sweet or slightly soured cream (page 241), the most important factors are first, cream without off flavors contributed by the animals' feed or poor handling; second, meticulous control of temperature at every stage of churning and draining; and third, scrupulous working to remove nearly all the buttermilk while leaving just the tiny residue that will lend soul to the butter. Salt does not ruin well-made butter; it imparts something that some people care for and others don't. Its aficionados can taste just as much complexity in salted butter as can the opposite party in unsalted.

Though I was raised on salted butter, I eventually switched allegiances. Still, I've tasted enough good salted butter to disagree with knee-jerk responses about its invariable inferiority for spreading on bread or melting over vegetables. Other purposes are a different story. Unsalted butter is a must in any situation where the salt would tend to crystallize out of the whole and form a crust on the bottom of the pan—Beurre Noisette or Beurre Noir (page 261), any kind of clarified butter, or most dishes involving butter heated to a fairly high temperature for a long time. Pastry-makers say that salted butter often gives poorer results in baking because it tends to retain slightly more water. It also has disadvantages when you're trying to pregauge the amount of salt needed for seasoning, especially since degrees of saltiness vary from brand to brand. If you cook with salted butter, it's always a good idea to use much less salt than is called for in a recipe, then add more to taste if needed.

Supermarket butter today may not be the ne plus ultra of wonderful butter, but whether salted or unsalted it's usually pretty good. And even pretty good butter is a treasure beyond the power of industrial chemistry to imitate by playing games with either animal or vegetable fats.

A SHOPPING AND HANDLING PRIMER

Buying butter is not absolutely a guessing game, but you have to expect much inconsistency in labeling. The fine print may or may not clear things up. Some common terms are:

- Sweet butter: Often incorrectly used as a synonym for unsalted butter. Properly speaking, it is butter made from sweet cream, as in the recipe on page 245. Sweet butter can be salted or unsalted. The basic butter flavor is pure and simple.
- Cultured or ripened butter: In the strictest sense, butter churned from cream that has been lightly soured by culturing with lactic-acid bacteria (see page 247). Whether salted or unsalted, it has nuances of flavor and aroma not found in sweet butter. The genuine article is time-consuming and expensive to produce, and has largely been replaced by easier methods. Small amounts of lactic-acid cultures are often pumped into the butter after churning; this may not be easy to detect from the label, since "cultures," "bacterial cultures," or "cultured cream" can be listed among the ingredients of butter made by either method. A still more convenient shortcut is to buy distillates of the main flavoring substances that would have been developed by ripening and inject them into the churned butter. The most usual is diacetyl, a volatile compound with a bloomy fragrance. Lactic acid may also be directly added. The labels of butter so treated probably will have no clue except "natural flavoring," which is accurate only in a pretty strained sense of "natural." You know that you are getting true cultured butter if the label says that the cream was cultured *before* churning, but perhaps one maker out of dozens will vouchsafe this information.
- European-style butter: A term with no fixed meaning, sometimes referring to cultured butter and sometimes to butter with a butterfat content higher than the usual 80 to 81 percent in American butter.

- Creamery butter: A phrase left over from the late nineteenth century, when buttermaking largely moved from farms to small centrifuging plants called creameries (page 45). People hearing the word "creamery" today usually don't know that its prior associations were industrial, not pastoral, and it's been appropriated by a spectrum of small-scale artisanal milk processors and even a few cheesemakers. "Creamery butter" in itself may or may not be better than any other butter.

- Whipped butter: The dairy industry's pseudo-solution to the pseudo-problem of chilled butter's resistance to spreading. In the late 1960s someone had the idea of pumping butter full of nitrogen gas (sometimes air), which both softened the texture and handily increased the volume. Because of its reduced density, it cannot be substituted for plain butter in cooking. (Anyone who finds that regular butter won't spread easily on bread should either put out a little butter to warm up to room temperature before using it or buy more substantial bread—you can't expect mass-produced stuff with all the sturdy texture of marshmallow whip to be buttered without tearing into holes.) I skip whipped butter, with one odd but delightful exception: a version of the famous Russian butter made in Vologda, frequently sold in stores that carry imported foods from the ex–Soviet Union. It bears the words "Sweet Whipped Butter" prominently printed on the package below a Cyrillic label, and judging by the taste must be made from cream put through something like the English clotted-cream process. It's just as hard to spread as any regular butter, but the flavor is phenomenal.

- USDA butter grades: Marks (AA, A, B) assigned under a Department of Agriculture evaluation system that today unfortunately has no relevance to most of the butter sold in any retail venue. Most manufacturers decline to be involved in the voluntary grading program, and those that do go along don't necessarily make better butter than the nonparticipants.

WHAT YOU SEE AND WHAT YOU GET

Judging the quality of butter from external factors is dicey. Price and distinguished-sounding Old World (or domestic) origins are no guarantee of anything. Neither is color. Butter can be any shade from nearly white to deep yellow, mostly depending on whether the vitamin A in the milkfat occurs in the finished form (colorless) or as the precursor beta-carotene (yellow). Jersey and Guernsey cows give the deepest-colored butter, Holstein-Friesians the palest. Butter from goats', sheep's, and buffaloes' milk is always ivory-white. The color of cows'-milk butter can vary by season, if the animals have access to spring pasturage (which puts more beta-carotene into the milk). Bear in mind that color has no necessary connection with butteriness; in some parts of the country where people strongly prefer a bright yellow, the color may come from dyes such as annatto.

Real quality, as opposed to cosmetics, depends not only on how the butter was made but on whether it has been exposed to air or allowed to stand at warm temperatures between the time of manufacture and the time of consumption. Every few degrees of temperature above about 45° or 50°F mean some loss of volatile compounds, some irreversible shift in the intricacies of the fragile substance. Then there is the question of packaging. The onion experiment shows how quick butter is to react with its surroundings. Let it sit uncovered even at refrigerator temperatures, and it will soon oxidize enough to develop a discolored and greasy-looking outer layer. It also will either pick up the smell of other foods or simply lose its own pristine flavor. Moral: Tight, secure packaging in materials like foil or stout laminated cardboard—or both together—is a big plus in choosing butter. Some otherwise excellent butters come in flimsy, ill-sealed wrappings. If you take the plunge and buy these, then scrupulously rewrap them the minute you get them home in some impermeable arrangement like plastic wrap inside a layer of foil. (And maybe a freezer bag for good measure.) I don't have a home vacuum-seal device, but it sounds like a useful idea for butter.

Well-wrapped butter keeps quite well in the refrigerator and even better in the freezer. Salt butter has a longer life expectancy than unsalted, but it's hard to give rules of thumb. Today refrigerated butter almost never goes spectacularly *bad* in the sense meant by the Beecher sisters; rather, it just keeps taking on whiffs of something slightly foreign while losing the *luxe, calme, et volupté* that set butter apart from other fats. It may still be quite good after a week's or two weeks' sojourn in the refrigerator, but the safest thing is to cut off a chunk for immmediate use and store the rest in the freezer, carefully wrapped. Here again there's no hard and fast rule about storage times. Good, fresh butter that's never been taken out of sealed packaging can last in excellent condition for many months.

I have pointed out that the general run of butter available to modern consumers is greatly superior to most butter made and sold before about the mid-nineteenth century. Still, I don't want to leave the impression that that's as good as it gets. Our mostly good and useful factory-made butter isn't the same thing as ambrosial, ethereal, extraordinary butter, which does exist here and there—salted or unsalted, "sweet" or ripened. You are less likely to find it by sampling expensive imported or domestic brands in fancy stores than by exploring butter from small-scale producers. This is elusive, but sometimes to be encountered at local farmers' markets. The critical factors are particularly good cream from herds managed for excellence rather than maximum volume; minute adjustment of temperature through all stages of churning and handling; and freshness so extreme that cooking with the butter seems like a desecration when you could simply sit there and eat it in its pure, virginal glory. When made with care, home-churned butter can match the flavor of this exercise in amazing grace—but I've never produced anything to match the beautiful nuances of the consistency.

RECIPES

HOME-CHURNED BUTTER AND
BUTTERMILK: SWEET-CREAM TYPE

Despite what I consider the better texture of good commercial butter, homemade butter fresh from working and rinsing can't be equaled for delivering the taste of cream to the nth power, cream newly translated to some rarefied spiritual afterlife. Some of this same flavor will linger in the new buttermilk, which resembles the commercial cultured product in name only.

I recommend plain sweet-cream butter for a first effort because it is the simpler of the two main types. If you tried the brief "White Magic" experiment on page 69, you'll already have grasped the general process. But for best results you need to understand a few other things.

To start with, it isn't necessary to use only heavy cream. In many parts of the world people have always used unhomogenized milk (though usually soured), and light cream works fine as long as it isn't ultrapasteurized. The advantage of heavy cream is that it churns faster and more completely, with more butter and less buttermilk to show for your pains. Experiment as you like with combinations of light and heavy cream. Unhomogenized cream "comes" faster than homogenized because of its larger milkfat globules.

The most important factor is temperature control. At a butter-making demonstration, I once saw dozens of pounds of wonderful Jersey cream churned into something like a mound of yellow petroleum jelly because the ambient temperature in a sun-broiled farm shed on a hot summer day was about thirty degrees too high. The cream itself should be well chilled, which increases the proportion of crystallized fat in the complex milkfat structure (page 236) and primes the original fat globules for strategic disruption. Commercial makers call the chilling stage "aging."

Maintaining the proper temperature is many times more predictable with factory-scale machinery churning hundreds of pounds than with home equipment churning small amounts. The speediest and most practical home method for most people—the food processor—is also extremely friction-inducing. The mere action of the metal blades will raise the temperature enough during the churning process to affect the texture of the finished butter. For this reason, you must compensate or overcompensate by keeping all materials and implements as cold as possible at every stage. Old-fashioned buttermaking manuals used to suggest bringing the cream to between 55° and 65°F before starting to churn. In my experience this is a mistake for people working in modern home kitchens; the butter is likely to get well over 65°F before you finish.

Before refrigeration, farm families in my part of Pennsylvania used to store new milk and cream in springhouses built over groundwater springs that generally kept springhouse temperatures somewhere between 55° and 60°F except in extreme weather. People also churned—in the springhouse or the coolest room in the house—using wooden butter churns that provided some temperature insulation. We can't replicate these conditions today, but we can at least seek to ensure that the kitchen is as cool as possible during churning. Never try to make butter in a hot kitchen.

Read through everything and have all equipment organized before beginning; once the butter starts to come, you'll have to work fast.

Note: I am not giving directions for salted butter because it is very difficult for home buttermakers to work in the salt closely without grittiness.

YIELD: About ½ pound (1 cup) butter and 2 cups buttermilk (relative amounts will vary greatly with the butterfat content of the cream)

3 cups well-chilled nonultrapasteurized cream (light, heavy, or any desired mixture), preferably unhomogenized

You will need a food processor fitted with the steel blade, a wire-mesh strainer, a couple of mixing bowls, a rubber spatula, a wooden spoon or two, and a lidded storage container. Chill the processor bowl and blade in the refrigerator along with everything else. Have plenty of ice water on hand.

Set up the food processor, and add half the cream (or all of it, if you have a processor model of at least 11-cup capacity). Leave the rest in the refrigerator. Begin processing and watch closely as the cream thickens and whips. Within a few minutes or even seconds, it will start to look less white. As soon as you see signs that it is breaking into something slightly granular, stop the machine and take a look. Cautiously proceed in stops and starts until the cream is quite definitely separated into thin, cloudy whitish buttermilk and clumps of ivory or yellow (depending on the breed of cow) butter.

Set the strainer over a mixing bowl and dump in the contents of the processor, scraping out any clinging butter particles with a rubber spatula. Put the strainer and bowl in the refrigerator while you repeat the processing with the rest of the cream. Add the second batch of butter to what you have in the strainer. Pour off the buttermilk into another container.

Turn out the butter into another bowl and add roughly as much (strained) ice water as you have buttermilk. Work the butter into a mass with a stout wooden spoon or spatula. (The cheesemaker Jonathan White recommends a potato masher, which is quite efficient. In the day of home buttermaking, the usual implement was one or two wooden butter paddles.) Drain off as much liquid as you can and go on working the butter. You will see it becoming smoother and waxier under the spoon, as butterfat freed from its previous encapsulation in distinct globules comes together in a continuous mass. When no more liquid seems to be coming out, pat the butter dry with paper towels, pack it into a container, and promptly refrigerate it, tightly covered. It is more fragile than commercial butter. To taste its incomparable freshness at the full, you must use it within hours. But up to about four or five days you will still get much of that pure, delicate quality.

Taste the buttermilk, which will be a new experience to most Americans. You can drink it as is, throw it out if you dislike it, or use it for the same cooking purposes as sweet whey (page 313). Store it tightly covered in the refrigerator. It will keep for four or five days.

HOME-CHURNED BUTTER AND BUTTERMILK: RIPENED-CREAM TYPE

Most butter in most parts of the world has always come from ripened cream or milk. In hot climates this is because virtually all milk is soured before use. In the colder environments of northern Europe and North America, pre-industrial buttermakers usually saved the skimmed cream from several days' milking and added one batch to the next until they had enough to justify the effort of churning. When the housewife or dairymaid got around to the week's or half-week's churning, a little of this ripened flavor persisted in the butter while much more remained in the buttermilk.

Today most American consumers tend to have a marked preference for either sweet-cream or ripened-cream butter; I'm a fanatic for the latter. I urge you to try making it once you've had success with the sweet-cream butter recipe.

The process is really the same except that the first step is to sour the cream by bacterial "ripening" (culturing) at room temperature before it is aged in the refrigerator. Ripening not only makes the butter come more efficiently but results in the most wonderful thick white buttermilk, silkier than the sweet-cream version and with a clean but complex lactic-acid flavor. (You may get an inkling of why buttermilk vendors, as described in James Fenimore Cooper's novel *Satanstoe,* used to cruise the streets of colonial New York calling out, "White wine!") The butter itself will retain a lovely, aromatic hint of fermentation.

For home cooks, the best ripening agent is commercial cultured buttermilk containing at least 1.5 percent milkfat and made without gum thickeners or salt. The true buttermilk that you end up with will far surpass this in flavor. I like to use heavy and light cream in about a 2 to 1 ratio, because I get more (and better) buttermilk than with all heavy cream.

YIELD: Roughly ½ pound (1 cup) butter and 2 cups buttermilk (relative amounts will vary with the butterfat content of the cream)

3 cups nonultrapasteurized cream (light, heavy, or any desired mixture), preferably unhomogenized
¼ cup cultured buttermilk with live cultures and 1.5 percent (or more) milkfat, as fresh as possible

Stir together the cream and buttermilk in a bowl and let stand at room temperature until it becomes thick and sour-smelling (usually 16 to 24 hours). Cover tightly and refrigerate for several hours or overnight, until thoroughly chilled.

Now proceed exactly as for the preceding butter and buttermilk made by the sweet-cream method, chilling the equipment and taking the same precautions to keep things cold.

CLARIFIED BUTTERS: A REVISIONIST VIEW

Ninety percent of the time, my general take on clarifying butter in the classic European style is "DON'T." This kind of clarifying—melting butter to separate the clear butterfat and discarding all traces of other milk residue—removes the whole poetry of butter and irrevocably alters the intricate original profile of different fatty acids with their many different melting points. In short, it converts butter into the one form of rendered grease that can legitimately claim to taste somewhat—certainly not completely—like real butter.

True, there is the other ten percent. I grant that clarified butter has advantages for pan-frying meat, chicken, or fish at a brisk temperature without leaving smeary black speckles on the food. But it has no special point in baking, and in emulsions like hollandaise sauce contributes less body and flavor than good butter added as is. Its main virtue is the negative one of not burning when it gets above about 250°F.

The only forms of clarified butter that have positive culinary interest are non-European, and involve their own special approaches. Let's start by explaining what happens in clarifying. With the European method, you melt the butter very briefly and gently until its finely dissolved droplets of original true buttermilk release their contents: dissolved minerals, water-soluble proteins, and tiny particles of solid casein. Some rise to the top while others sink to the bottom. Once you have skimmed the top froth and carefully poured off the butterfat from the bottom residue, you have a cooking fat less temperamental than unclarified butter. It also lasts months longer because the most perishable parts have been removed.

The process of making Indian ghee or spice-infused clarified butters is not at all the same. Instead of pouring off the butter as soon as possible, you let it cook long enough to develop a whole different complex of flavors. At the end you have not a cooking fat partly robbed of its original identity but something ready to make its own unique and decisive contribution to anything cooked in it or served with it. Ghee simmers slowly until the water gradually evaporates and the milk solids start to brown, while the composition of the fat alters far more drastically than with orthodox clarified butter. The result, when strained, is a wonderfully rich and nutty-flavored sublimation of butter. The same is true of the Ethiopian *nit'r kibeh*, but it also contains a marvelous bouquet of aromatics melded with the simmered-butter flavor. I suggest that you experiment with either of these in savory dishes where a recipe calls for regular clarified butter.

EUROPEAN-STYLE CLARIFIED BUTTER

My idea of what to cook in simple clarified butter would be Wienerschnitzel or a large mess of pan-fried trout—large enough that nonclarified butter might be starting to burn by the time you'd finished.

Making up a batch is an education in the vagaries of butter. Starting with a pound of butter, you may end up with more than 14 ounces or as little as 12 ounces of clarified butter, depending on the amount of water and milk solids that were in the butter before clarifying. High-fat, low-moisture butter (83 percent or higher butterfat content, by weight) will give a higher yield than the more usual 80 to 81 percent American butter.

Be sure not to discard the buttermilk residue left from the process! It is quite perishable but absolutely delicious (particularly that from cultured butter), and can be saved in small amounts in the freezer until you have enough to use as a seasoning on vegetables, add to sauces as a flavor enhancer, or put into a batch of bread dough. (Madeleine Kamman's *When French Women Cook* has a wonderful walnut-oil bread using the buttermilk residue from clarified butter—*gape* or *gappe*, as churned buttermilk is known in the Auvergne.)

YIELD: Highly variable, but generally about 14 to 15 ounces (slightly less than 2 cups) per original pound

Use only unsalted butter. A pound or half a pound is the most convenient-sized batch to experiment with, but you can use any preferred amount. If you are starting with a pound or less, use a 2- to 3-quart saucepan. Pouring off the clear butterfat will be easier if it is narrow rather than wide. The bottom must be heavy enough to diffuse heat well without scorching.

Have ready a heatproof storage container for the clarified butter, a smaller one for the buttermilk residue, and a small spoon for skimming. Cut the butter into chunks of 1 tablespoon or less and place it in the saucepan over medium-low heat. Watch as it melts. It must not reach a sizzle; reduce the heat if necessary. Do not shake or stir it. As it fully melts, some crinkly-looking foam (mostly water-soluble whey proteins) may swim to the top. Carefully skim this off into your smaller container, trying to disturb the butter as little as possible. Remove the pan from the heat and let it stand a few minutes, to allow the buttermilk residue to separate from the lighter butterfat by gravity.

Slowly pour the clear golden butterfat into the larger container, being sure to stop before any of the cloudy white liquid at the bottom gets into it. Spoon off as much more of the clear fat as you can. Obsessive types can salvage the last smidgin of clarified butter by pouring what's left into a small cup, refrigerating it until it solidifies into a cake, and scraping the buttermilk residue off the bottom with a knife.

The clarified butter should be stored, tightly covered, in a cool place or the refrigerator. It keeps for months. Add all remaining buttermilk leavings to the container with the skimmed foam and freeze, tightly covered.

Some people clarify butter in the oven. To do this, put the butter in a heatproof glass measuring cup and place it in a preheated 225°F oven until melted. Continue as directed above.

GHEE
(INDIAN CLARIFIED BUTTER)

This is the *usli ghee* (Hindi for "pure ghee") long held holy in Hindu thought, as opposed to the partially hydrogenated vegetable-oil substitute called *vanaspati ghee* ("plant ghee") that is now overtaking it in sales as attachment to former dietary observance weakens in much of India. The special status of real ghee reflected the belief that it had undergone two kinds of refining or subliming process. The cow herself performed the first by distilling milk for butter out of the grasses of the earth; people completed the second by subjecting churned butter to the purifying medium of fire.

In contrast to simple clarified butter, ghee is simmered for a long time to bring out complex flavors that never develop in the briefly melted kind. Once you become familiar with its heavenly toasted aroma and flavor, you may fall in love with it much as many American cooks have fallen in love with things like Vietnamese fish sauce, smoked Spanish paprika, and toasted sesame oil.

Before you begin, please remember that different kinds of butter vary greatly in water content. This makes it difficult to predict the total cooking time for ghee. I've seen recipes blithely estimating less than fifteen minutes; all I can say is that it usually takes me between forty minutes and an hour. The exact yield also will vary. To partly duplicate some of the lactic-acid flavor that churned sour milk imparts to Indian ghee, try to use butter from cultured cream. It's best to start with at least a pound of butter—unsalted only.

YIELD: About 12 to 14 ounces (slightly more than 1⅞ cups) per original pound

GHEE (CONT.)

Have ready a heatproof storage container for the clarified ghee, a smaller one for the buttermilk residue, a small spoon for skimming, and a small strainer lined with several layers of *tight-woven* cheesecloth or a clean cotton handkerchief, set over a small heatproof bowl.

Cut the butter into chunks of about a tablespoon each, and melt it in a heavy-bottomed 2- or 3-quart saucepan over low heat. It must melt evenly so that part isn't sizzling while the rest is still solid; shake the pan to even things out if necessary. When it is fully melted, you can increase the heat slightly, but it should never be higher than medium-low. The butter will crackle and sputter as the watery part starts to evaporate. Carefully skim off as much of the rising foam as you can into the smaller container, and push the rest to one side so that you can see the color of the butter.

The pan can now mind its own business for between 30 minutes and an hour (depending on the amount of water to be driven off), but you must keep checking it at frequent intervals. Gradually the butterfat will become clearer as the water evaporates and the temperature rises; the bubbling and hissing will subside, and you will see the milky residue forming into clumps on the bottom. This must not be allowed to burn; if it becomes darker than golden brown, the ghee will taste scorched. If you see it darkening too fast, briefly remove the pan from the burner and lower the heat before resuming. Eventually the butterfat will be deep golden and have a ripe, walnutlike smell. Set it aside to cool slightly before proceeding.

Carefully pour off and spoon the clear ghee into the larger container. When you're down to the last bit that you can get, strain the rest through the cheesecloth and scrape all the leavings into the container with the skimmed foam. (Save this in the freezer as for the residues from European-style clarified butter. It will taste even better because of the lengthy browning process.) Let the ghee cool to room temperature before covering tightly. It will keep at least six months in the refrigerator, indefinitely in the freezer.

NIT'R KIBEH
(ETHIOPIAN SPICED CLARIFIED BUTTER)

The European-style flavored butters discussed on page 256 place the flavoring ingredients (lemon juice, chives, parsley, anchovies, or whatnot) in strong perspective against the pure, creamy butter vehicle. In much of northern Africa and the Mideast, people have adopted different approaches. Ethiopian *nit'r kibeh* (there are various English transliterations from Amharic) exemplifies one of these. You begin by simmering the butter with various spices and flavorings. In the process, you cook out both the perishable and the creamy qualities, while the strong flavors of many different ingredients fuse into a subtle bouquet that registers less immediately on the palate than the warm, nutty fullness of the transformed butter. What remains when the aromatics are strained out is one of the world's finest cooking fats, as rich-flavored as ghee but with other elusive complexities.

In Ethiopia nit'r kibeh is a favorite sautéing or braising medium for a wide variety of meat, chicken, and vegetable dishes, and serves as a sauce or dressing for *k'itfo t're*, the celebrated national counterpart of steak tartare. Among the usual constellation of flavorings, black or "false" cardamom (the pungent *Aframomum korarima*), *ajowan* (*Trachyspermum ammi*; also called bishop's weed or carom), and fenugreek are available in Indian grocery stores. If you are unable to obtain one or two of the ingredients, simply leave them out; the butter will still have plenty of flavor. If you can find fresh turmeric (also sold in Indian groceries), use a nickel-sized slice, minced, in place of dried ground turmeric.

The recipe can be halved, though I find it easier to make at least a 2-cup batch.

YIELD: About 2 cups

1 pound unsalted butter, cut into small pieces
3 to 4 large shallots, minced
3 large garlic cloves, minced
3 to 4 quarter-sized slices of fresh ginger, minced
Seeds from 3 black cardamom pods (do not substitute green cardamom)
Cinnamon stick (a 1- to 2-inch piece)
1 to 2 whole cloves, bruised
½ teaspoon fenugreek seeds
½ teaspoon ajowan seeds
½ teaspoon dried ground turmeric (or fresh, see above)

Melt the butter over medium-low heat in a small heavy saucepan. When it is hot and fragrant and the sizzling begins to subside, add all the remaining ingredients. Reduce the heat to very low and cook, uncovered, for 45 to 60 minutes, until the shallots and ginger have stopped bubbling and there is a layer of clear golden fat on top. If necessary, push any rising foam to the side so that you can see the butter; do not let the aromatics brown.

Let the nit'r kibeh cool slightly. Place a colander lined with *tight-woven* cheesecloth or a clean cotton handkerchief over a heatproof bowl; pour the contents of the pan into it, letting the clarified fat drain through. Strain twice if necessary to eliminate any cloudy sediment, which would shorten the keeping time. Discard the residue. Transfer to storage containers and let cool to room temperature before refrigerating; store, tightly covered, in the refrigerator. It will keep for four to six months.

BEURRE MANIÉ

Despite its usual name, beurre manié, or "kneaded butter," is not an exclusively French invention. It was perfectly at home in nineteenth-century American kitchens, where people often called it "braided butter." It isn't a sauce in itself but a variation of the same principle—fat plus flour—that thickens roux-based sauces. In both cases the fat protectively coats the separate flour granules so that they will not coalesce into a sticky mass as soon as they meet some hot liquid ingredient. This allows them to gradually soften (by absorption of water) on exposure to heat and progressively release their starch into the liquid. Result: binding of a sauce.

The main difference is that in a beurre manié the flour starts out with a coating of more or less cool, solid butter, whereas in a roux the fat is already liquefied and heating up fast. Melt butter for a roux and add flour, and the mixture quickly reaches temperatures higher than the boiling point of water. But the flour and butter for a beurre manié are worked together off the heat and added to a simmering liquid, meaning that the temperature never will go above 212°F. The flour-fat mixture undergoes a nuanced melting and melding before the butter becomes fully liquefied. Thus the flour granules can first absorb liquid and then release starch into a sauce in gentle stages. In a roux-based sauce, by contrast, the amalgamation of flour and (already heated) fat happens more abruptly, and by the time the liquid is added more of the butter's original qualities have been lost. There is the further wrinkle that flour cooked at high temperatures loses more of its thickening power than at low temperatures, so that a certain amount of flour will thicken a certain amount of liquid more in a beurre manié than in a roux.

There is no use trying to reduce a beurre manié to a set of recipe directions, but this is the gist of the process: Put equal amounts of flour and butter (by volume—say, 4 tablespoons each) on a plate or clean work surface. The butter should be very little softened, if at all. The softer and easier to work it is, the likelier the mixture is to be borderline greasy before you add it to any would-be sauce.

With the tines of a fork, patiently mash the flour into the butter until no loose flour is visible and the mixture is perfectly smooth. (I use a fork rather than my fingers in order to keep it as cool as possible.) If it will have to wait a while in a hot kitchen before use, refrigerate it.

To use beurre manié, whittle off bits equal to about ¼ to ½ teaspoonful each and add them to the simmering sauce over low heat. It is hard to give a rule about how much to use, because any liquid to which you add it—say, unthickened gravy from a roast, or a soup that you want to lightly bind—will have a particular viscosity. After a few times you will learn to judge by eye without laborious measuring. Begin by adding the equivalent of about 1 to 2 teaspoons beurre manié per cup of liquid. Stir it in well (or shake and swirl the pan if it's full of meat or vegetables in large chunks). Watch for signs of thickening and add a bit more if after a minute or two the sauce or soup looks too thin, but remember that it will slightly thicken of its own accord after it reaches serving plates. Once the paste is well incorporated and the sauce thickened to your liking, remove the pan from the heat.

To keep the sauce from acquiring a floury or wheaty taste, either serve it instantly or briefly keep it warm without boiling (for instance, on a heat-deflecting device over very low heat). Or if it fits your schedule, let it simmer at least another 20 minutes. The floury quality develops when a beurre manié–thickened sauce cooks for more than a few minutes, but goes away with longer simmering.

Beurre manié will keep in the refrigerator, tightly covered, for a week or two, but I prefer to make up small amounts as needed.

FLAVORED OR COMPOUND BUTTERS:
SOME SUGGESTIONS

As you saw if you put butter in a closed container with onion as suggested on page 231, it's a magnet for penetrating smells and flavors. Merely "cutting the butter with an oniony knife" was the thoroughly English proposal for getting rid of an unwelcome visitor in one of Arthur Ransome's "Swallows and Amazons" children's books. Of course, there are those of us who *like* raw onion or other assertive, aromatic ingredients just begging to pair up with some of the highly sensitive and reactive chemical components of butter. This affinity is part of the reason that even uncooked butter can be one of the most magical sauces, or sauce bases, in the canon.

Cooked butter can play a similar role when heated with desired ingredients long enough to become infused with their essence. Anglophiles may think of shellfish butter made by simmering the crushed shells of shrimp or lobster in butter, or potted savories in which gently melted butter is poured over a rillette-like mixture of shredded long-simmered meat. I'm a fan of the quite different approach represented by the Ethiopian spiced butter, nit'r kibeh (page 252). But uncooked flavored butters are both easier to produce and much more diverse.

In this large tribe of savory toppings, spreads, and quasi-sauces, the butter is worked with some chosen flavor foil until thoroughly combined. Such mixtures, often called "compound butters," belong to the fill-in-the-blank category of recipes that really amount to no more than "Take some butter and mix it with some (insert name) to suit your taste." The partnering ingredients can be in any kind of ground, puréed, mashed, grated, finely minced, or liquid form that permits even distribution.

For practice purposes, try making up a small amount as follows: Put about ¼ cup of butter in a mixing bowl and let it warm to the temperature of a cool room. (It can be salted or unsalted, but the latter is better if you'll be adding a salty ingredient.) When it's just soft enough to work with, before it turns greasy and squishy, cream it with a stout wooden spoon and work in about 1 teaspoon of freshly minced chives. Taste it and add more chives if desired. Refrigerate it, covered, until dinnertime. Let it come to room temperature and serve with baked potatoes.

That's really all there is to it, though you'll usually deal with larger amounts. One caveat: When you mix perishable raw aromatics into butter, the insulating fat provides nice growth conditions for anaerobic bacteria, so you should plan on using (or freezing) the mixture within twenty-four hours. Dried spices and most things that have been cooked or pickled present no problem.

The following list of flavoring suggestions is far from exhaustive. The sky's the limit, but simplicity is better than overkill. Note that a little freshly squeezed lemon juice will pep up many butter-herb combinations. Usually I like to keep to fairly Eurocentric ingredients, though I have to say that minced Chinese salted black beans make a great flavored butter. I prefer to work with ½ to 1 cup of butter, depending on the destined use.

Judgment calls on how much or little of a flavoring ingredient to use are difficult. Always start with a small amount and add more to taste. The amounts given here are minimums, meant to be enlarged at your own discretion.

- Minced or grated raw onion (red, yellow, white); finely minced raw or blanched garlic; finely minced scallion (whites, greens, or both). Start with 1 to 2 teaspoons per half cup of butter; use within a day.
- Good meat glaze (beef or veal). With a dash of lemon juice, this is the most luxurious thing you can put on poached fish or asparagus. Start with 1 teaspoon per half cup of butter.
- Balsamic or other preferred vinegar; start with 1 to 2 teaspoons per half cup of butter.
- Any preferred fresh herb or combination of herbs, such as parsley, oregano, chives, cilantro, rosemary (sparingly), basil, *shiso*, tarragon, minced very fine. Start with 2 teaspoons or less per half cup of butter; use within a day.
- Any preferred dried ground spice or spice mixture, especially "savory" or versatile "sweet-savory" spices such as cumin, paprika or ground red pepper (Hungarian or Turk-

ish), Spanish smoked paprika, black or white pepper, cardamom, allspice, garam masala, curry powder, various homemade dry spice rubs. Start with ½ to 1 teaspoon per half cup of butter.

- Minced or puréed fresh chiles, canned chipotles, roasted sweet red peppers. Start with ½ to 2 teaspoons per half cup of butter, more for sweet peppers.
- Prepared mustard, *harissa*, sun-dried tomato paste, anchovy paste, hot pepper sauces, miscellaneous herb-based seasoning pastes meant as rubs or marinades for grilled foods. Start with ½ to 1 teaspoon per half cup of butter.
- Minced anchovies or anchovy paste, sardines (sparingly), smoked ham or prosciutto, smoked salmon, salmon "caviar." Start with ½ teaspoon per half cup of butter for anchovies, 1 to 2 teaspoons for the rest.
- Pesto or fresh Mexican salsa, minced dill pickles or other pickled vegetables, minced capers. Start with 2 teaspoons per half cup of butter.
- Freshly ground pistachios or other nuts. Start with 2 to 3 teaspoons per half cup of butter.
- Finely grated lemon or other citrus rind. Start with ½ teaspoon per half cup of butter.
- Finely grated aged cheese (e.g., Parmesan, aged Gouda). Start with 2 to 3 teaspoons per half cup of butter.

BEURRE BLANC/BEURRE ROUGE

What happens if you half-melt butter while combining it with a small amount of some water-based liquid such as vinegar, white wine, or lemon juice? You get a fragile emulsion, pale and opaque, that makes the best of all sauces for fish (especially pike or shad), poached shellfish, and some vegetables (especially artichokes, asparagus, or leeks). From the miracle of butter chemistry as described earlier, you know that the unique manner in which warmed butter gradually changes from solid to liquid is a heaven-sent gift to cooks, a subtle transition that can be stopped at different points for certain purposes. At about 125° or 130°F the balance of barely solid and fully liquid components creates the richly satiny but ethereal effect synonymous with a proper beurre blanc. Not surprisingly, it can't be held for more than minutes and does not bear reheating.

The idea is quite old. The sauce for "buttered eggs" (hard-boiled and sliced) in John Murrell's 1621 *A Booke of Cookerie* is "sweet butter drawne thicke with faire water." Something like this was the usual "drawn butter" or "melted butter" of eighteenth- and early nineteenth-century English and American cookbooks, but by then it had become standard practice to hedge the bet by adding a little flour to stabilize the mixture at a higher temperature. (In fact, in some cookbooks "drawn butter" later was degraded into a roux thinned with water.) The flourless French beurre blanc in the style of Anjou became familiar to American cooks only about a generation ago. The splendid food writer Sheila Hibben was already presenting a flourless "white butter" as a New Orleans fish sauce in *The National Cook Book* in 1932, but I don't know of any Angevin-type "white butter" in a major all-purpose American kitchen bible before the 1962 *Joy of Cooking*.

The sauce is not at all tricky. It is both better-flavored and more stable if made with a dash of acid, which usually comes from boiling down a little vinegar, dry white wine, or a combination to a few tablespoons. You then start beating the butter into the hot liquid a little at a time. Adding the fat faster won't ruin the sauce as with mayonnaise; it just makes the deliberately incomplete melting process slightly harder to supervise. What you want is to keep the butter continually starting to *melt* without starting to *cook*. If fully liquefied, it will break the emulsion and turn a velvety sauce into grease, albeit good-tasting grease. (If this happens on your first try, say nothing and serve it anyhow—just remember where things went wrong for next time.) Have the food piping hot when you pour the sauce over it.

The proportions of wine and vinegar can be altered to taste—1 to 1 as given here, or 2 or even 3 parts wine to 1 of vinegar. Some people add a tablespoon of heavy cream to the reduction before starting to add the butter, on the theory that it stabilizes the emulsion, but it isn't really necessary. Nor do you have to strain the sauce before serving. The bits of shallot accentuate the flavor.

YIELD: 1 cup

½ pound (2 sticks) butter, preferably unsalted and made from cultured
    cream
1 medium shallot
¼ cup white wine vinegar
¼ cup dry white wine (Muscadet is traditional)
¼ to ½ teaspoon salt (omit if using salted butter)

Cut the butter into tablespoon-sized pieces, and keep it cold.

Mince the shallot very fine. Bring the vinegar and wine to a boil in a small heavy-bottomed saucepan. Add the shallot and simmer over medium heat, not letting the edges scorch, until only 1 to 2 tablespoons of liquid are left. (If the liquid evaporates completely, add 1 to 2 tablespoons water.)

Remove the pan from the heat, let stand for a minute or two, and beat in 1 to 2 tablespoons of cold butter with a wooden spoon or wire whisk. When it is almost completely melted, return the pan to the stove, either keeping the heat very low or being prepared to snatch it off the burner. Begin vigorously beating or whisking in the rest of the butter, 1 or 2 tablespoons at a time; the sauce will thicken and turn pale as you proceed. Keep watching the consistency; the sauce should never become fully liquefied. If the butter seems to be melting too fast, quickly remove the pan from the heat and set it in a larger saucepan of cold water before proceeding. Add the salt (if using) just before the last few tablespoons of butter. Whisk the sauce for a few seconds off the heat, and serve at once.

VARIATIONS: For Beurre Rouge, replace the white wine with red wine. You can also use lemon juice (for Beurre Citronné).

BEURRE NOIR/BEURRE NOISETTE
("BLACK BUTTER"/"BROWN BUTTER")

Probably everyone who has cooked with butter has burned it on at least one occasion. In fact, you can learn a lot about the chemistry of butter by following the process to the smelly and bitter end. But if you break off shortly before the smoke-alarm stage, the result is one of the simplest and best butter sauces. It's something like the early steps of making either clarified butter or ghee, where you sacrifice the creamy lusciousness of barely melted butter for other effects.

The heavenly butteriness of butter, you will remember, rests on the wheels-within-wheels circumstances of its composition: a complex emulsion of compounds with many different melting points, holding tiny droplets of water-based true buttermilk that in turn contain various suspended milk solids. Above a temperature of 212°F any water starts boiling off. In unclarified butter the solid particles remain in the hot fat, where they would eventually darken and burn if allowed to get much hotter than 250°F. But before this happens, some of the melted milkfat lipids become hot enough to volatilize, or escape as gases that release a hazelnutlike fragrance (hence the French name "noisette"). At the same time, the milk solids begin to caramelize and acquire a wonderfully nutty flavor, while the golden color of the butter deepens to a light brown. (Clarifying the butter after melting it, as some American writers suggest, certainly lessens the risk of scorching, but it also eliminates something intrinsic to the sauce.) You can just get by with beurre noisette as a sautéing medium for something such as very rapidly scrambled eggs—but not with beurre noir, which is what you get if you let the cooking proceed even half a minute longer. This so-called black butter actually is a rich dark brown from almost-burnt milk solids, and has a stronger flavor than brown butter. At this instant (or seconds before), the pan must be snatched from the stove before you have really black butter, which would be inedible.

The main difference between "brown" and "black" butter is not so much the degree of cooking as the way they are then treated. Black butter is invariably (and brown butter almost invariably) used sizzling hot, as a sauce for already cooked foods—cauliflower, artichokes, poached or fried eggs, cooked brains or sweetbreads, and most classically pan-fried fish such as skate, tinker mackerel, and smelts. Brown butter can be served as is, but usually includes a dash of lemon juice and sometimes chopped parsley (in which case, it is often called *beurre meunière*.) Black butter is always given a contrasting accent of vinegar (usually reduced) as well as a final handful of parsley. Capers can go into either, but are more usual with black butter.

The procedure is as follows: Put some unsalted butter in a small, fairly heavy saucepan or skillet. The amount depends on how much food you want to sauce; I'd allow about 1½ to 2 tablespoons per serving. Have the cooked food within easy reach, along with a small handful each of capers and minced parsley if you want to include them. For beurre noir, you should also have a few tablespoons of wine vinegar (any preferred kind) in a separate small saucepan; for beurre noisette, have a halved lemon ready for squeezing.

Melt the butter slowly over low heat, shaking the pan occasionally and watching it like a hawk. After the foam dies away, you will see it gradually change to a pale brown. If you are making beurre noir, bring the vinegar to a boil while the butter heats and let it reduce by about half. Keep it hot.

There are various ways of combining the butter and vinegar or lemon juice. For beurre noisette, the simplest is to promptly empty the pan of hot butter over the food, squeeze on a bit of lemon juice, and serve at once with or without parsley and capers scattered on top. Beurre noir takes a little more logistics to avoid a boil-over of something uniting the worst features of burnt butter and burnt vinegar. I find it easiest to let the butter cool for a few minutes before adding the hot vinegar, then returning the butter to the stove just long enough to make it sizzling hot. You can either toss the optional parsley and capers into the pan or scatter them over the food. In either case, pour the butter mixture over the food and serve at once. It should be eaten as hot as possible, before it loses its élan.

If either brown or black butter threatens to darken too fast, immediately arrest the cooking by setting the pan in a larger pan of cold water. Some people routinely do this the minute the butter is approaching the desired point. But be sure to reheat it before pouring it over the food.

Once you know how to make brown butter, you can experiment with melting it directly in a skillet that you have just used for fried eggs, pan-fried fish, etc. (I wouldn't try it with black butter.) The goal here—a matter of practice—is to pick up nice browned flavors from the sautéing residues in the skillet, without letting them burn.

VARIATIONS: Butter cooked to the brown stage with no added ingredients is a wonderful sauce or hot topping for hot cooked spinach or other greens. It is also great splashed over dishes topped with Yogurt-Garlic Sauce (page 162). Goats'-milk and sheep's-milk butter are particularly delicious for this purpose. A similar and very pretty last touch in Turkish cooking is to stir Aleppo pepper or other red pepper flakes into melting butter, take it off the heat just before the pepper burns, and drizzle it over a dish.

ABOUT BUTTER-AND-EGG CUSTARDS

The custard tribe is familiar to most of us through mixtures of the crème anglaise kind (page 132), in which milk or cream dilutes eggs to a point where they become fairly stable under at least gentle cooking and will thicken to a smooth amalgam. But there is another custard-family branch based on subjecting butter and eggs to heat under conditions that stop them from curdling. The addition of sugar is one means. Highly sweetened butter-egg custards can take quite a lot of heat without breaking down, an aptitude that makes possible "sugar pie" fillings like those for pecan pie, Southern chess pie, and the famous Canadian butter tarts. (The Southern Butter-milk Pie on page 224 is a cousin with more added liquid.)

Acid also helps increase the tolerance of egg proteins for heat; hence the allied clan of butter custards involving a com-bination of sugar and acid added to egg and butter. Like the sugar pie fillings, these can be cooked to higher temperatures than plain egg-and-butter mixtures without the egg proteins congealing into a curdled mess. Lemon Curd (page 269) is the best-known acid- and sugar-stabilized custard.

Take away the sugar and you have something more fragile. Hollandaise sauce, with only a small amount of acid to temper the effect of heat, is the classic example: a delicate emulsion that needs just the right degree of cooking in order not to be ruined. Still trickier and more demanding is the ultimate in butter-custard minimalism: butter and eggs with no added ingredients, turned into a rarefied transformation of scrambled eggs that must cook at a snail's pace over the lowest possible heat until it slowly thickens to a rich-flavored, barely runny custard.

What all these butter-egg custard dishes have in common is a magical way of melding the most delicate, evocative qualities of fresh butter and eggs into something more sensuous than either one alone. Aside from butter itself, eggs have a more intrinsically buttery flavor than almost any other food I can think of. Cooking the two together by gentle methods that let the egg proteins retain a fine, smooth continuity without degenerating into coarse clumps seems to take butter to another dimension.

HOLLANDAISE SAUCE

Why we stopped calling this "Dutch sauce" and started assuming that it was French in origin, I have no idea. It did indeed reach something like perfection when French cooks took to making it with Normandy butter, but it really dates back to the spectacular success of the seventeenth- and eighteenth-century Dutch in grazing cattle on reclaimed sea bottom and selling butter and cheese to the rest of Europe. At the time, butter happened to be a surefire choice as an exportable cash crop; it had recently taken on new elegance and cachet as a sauce foundation in the cuisines of England, France, and the rest of northern Europe.

An influential kitchen preference of the day (especially in the Low Countries) was for sauces of melted butter combined with some acid element. A stewed-eel recipe in the celebrated seventeenth-century Dutch kitchen manual *De Verstandige Kock* mentions a sauce involving butter and vinegar mixed with a binder—in this case, egg. Here we have in at least rudimentary guise the elements of the later hollandaise, drawing on both the butter-based and the egg-based emulsion principles. But this didn't instantly become the standard form.

Early "Dutch sauces" in English cookbooks often call for a strong-flavored vinegar mixture as the acid element and flour rather than egg as the binder. Though Eliza Acton's magisterial *Modern Cookery for Private Families* (1845) presents a "Dutch sauce" that any cook today would call a classic hollandaise, various roux-based mixtures continued to share the title. Toward the end of the nineteenth century the name "Dutch" was universally replaced by "hollandaise" in English and American cookbooks, and by the time of Fannie Farmer's *The Boston Cooking-School Cookbook* (1896), the sauce was generally understood to be an egg, butter, and lemon-juice emulsion.

That much is still generally understood, but otherwise it would be hard to find any classic sauce whose making is the object of as many disagreements. Any search of a few basic cookbooks will give you close to a dozen hollandaise philosophies. Before getting to my own preference, let me state that people who are already happy with another should stick to it. Good hollandaise can be made with the butter solid or previously melted, over direct heat, in a double boiler, altogether off the heat, with a whisk, with a wooden spoon, in a blender, in a food processor, with plain lemon juice or vinegar, with lemon juice or vinegar diluted with water and slightly reduced. . . . To cut to the chase, all these have been known to work just fine in plain hollandaise or its two most popular variations: béarnaise, made with a tarragon- and shallot-flavored vinegar reduction; and maltaise, where Seville orange juice replaces lemon juice. The only approach that I strongly quarrel with is using clarified butter. According to one wing of opinion, this produces a thicker sauce and eliminates any off flavors lurking in the residual buttermilk. I submit that (a) plain butter tastes more buttery; (b) there's nothing wrong with a thinner sauce; and (c) if you don't trust the butter to be delicious you shouldn't be using it. It does, however, seem smart to use the kind of high-fat, low-moisture butter favored by pastry chefs, the fresher the better.

What to put it on? Addicts may wonder what *not* to put it on. It is a peerless partner to grilled, poached, or steamed fish, shellfish, and vegetables (especially asparagus). I have eaten it with plain poached chicken, broiled lamb chops, baked and boiled potatoes and sweet potatoes, and believe it or not, rice. Given the opportunity, I'd probably eat it with boiled newspaper.

I always use lemon juice, not vinegar, in hollandaise. If you'd like to try vinegar, I suggest the plainest possible white wine vinegar rather than something syrupy or herb-infused. I add the lemon juice straight and probably would do the same with vinegar, but there's something to be said for an acid reduction with a slight concentration of flavors, as long as it's not allowed to become too metallic-tasting. If you want to try it, replace the plain lemon juice in the following recipe with 2½ tablespoons white wine vinegar and 2½ tablespoons water. Put these in a small saucepan, carefully boil down to half the starting volume, and stir in a dash of cold water before adding the reduction to the eggs and proceeding as directed.

The following recipe is based on a version that I encountered decades ago in Elizabeth David's *French Provincial Cooking*. I have never had the courage to make the sauce directly on the heat instead of in a double boiler. I have also found that it's a blessing and a reassurance to have a few emergency rescue measures—as suggested below—in place before you start, so that if the dread signs of curdling from excessive heat appear you can quickly stop or temper the cooking.

YIELD: About 1 cup

6 ounces (12 tablespoons, 1½ sticks) very fresh high-fat (about 83 to 85 percent) butter, either salted or unsalted
2 tablespoons freshly squeezed lemon juice (or the reduction described above)
½ to ¾ teaspoon salt (omit if using salted butter)
3 or (for more richness) 4 egg yolks
A pinch to ⅛ teaspoon cayenne pepper (optional)

Cut the butter into about a dozen pieces, and set it on a plate to warm to room temperature.

Heat a little water—it should be less than an inch deep—in the bottom of a double boiler and turn it off when it comes to a boil. Mix the lemon juice and salt in the double boiler top and set it over the bottom. Whisk in the egg yolks. Turn on the heat but keep it low, so that the water remains hot without boiling. Whisking steadily, add a piece of butter and work it into the eggs as it melts. Give it a moment to become warmed and fully incorporated before adding another piece, whisking it in, and adding another. The trick is to add butter a little at a time while gradually achieving a temperature (about 160°F) that will semi-cook the egg protein without either thickening it so rapidly as to make it curdle or letting it languish in a cautious coolness that won't thicken it at all.

If you think the mixture is heating too fast, there are four ways of slowing it down: (1) Whisk in a tablespoon of hot water; (2) take the whole double boiler from the burner and place it on a Flame Tamer over low heat; (3) briefly lift the top off the bottom and set it aside; or (4) put the top in a pan or bowl of cold water. Whisk furiously while performing any of these measures, then put everything back on the stove as before. At intervals, check to see that the water is not boiling in the bottom of the double boiler. By the time you have incorporated all the butter, the sauce should have a beautiful satiny sheen and the consistency of a light mayonnaise.

Quickly remove the double-boiler top and taste the sauce for seasoning. Add a little more salt or lemon juice to taste. If desired, add enough cayenne to give it a mild kick. Use it promptly, while still warm. Hollandaise is by nature a last-minute preparation, one of those things that people wait for instead of having it wait for them. If held for more than a few minutes it may break, but if it isn't too far gone you may be able to salvage it by whisking in a little boiling water, or whisking a fresh egg yolk in a bowl and beating the sauce into it.

VARIATION: The hollandaise is just finished, the kitchen is steaming like a cauldron, and the dinner timetable has been thrown into chaos by some unforeseen glitch. How to avoid ruin? On such an occasion I discovered an out that actually proved to be a useful cold sauce in its own right: Scrape the warm hollandaise into a small pitcher or glass measuring cup. Pour in enough cold heavy cream to cover the top by barely half an inch. Set it in the refrigerator, where the hollandaise will quickly thicken. When it is nearly solid, work the cream into the sauce with a fork or whisk, adding a little more cream if necessary to bring it to a spreadable consistency. Stir in an extra dash or two of lemon juice and salt. Serve cool or at room temperature. Unlike freshly made hot hollandaise, this daughter-of-necessity version is blessedly stable. It goes beautifully with any of the usual hollandaise partners in their cold (or room-temperature) poached form.

"BUTTERED EGGS"
(SKILLET-CUSTARD EGGS)

The plainest of all egg-and-butter custards is also the most demanding to make, because there is nothing to hinder it from curdling except low heat and endless patience. Scrambled eggs cooked in this manner are to ordinary scrambled eggs as quenelles are to fish burgers, and are the one reason I see for anybody to own a nonstick pan. The only elements are eggs and butter very slowly stirred over the lowest possible heat until the whites coagulate in small, delicate bits and—this is the tricky part—the yolks and butter set to a thin custard, about the consistency of a faintly runny lemon curd without the lemon. If you are willing to dedicate three-quarters of an hour to standing over a nonstick skillet and don't mind eating the result with a spoon, it is the holy grail of scrambled eggs. Needless to say, the freshest eggs and butter will taste the best.

    For each serving

    2 tablespoons butter
    3 eggs
    1 to 2 tablespoons heavy cream (optional)

The frugal-minded can cut back slightly on the butter and use two eggs. Since I make this only about twice a year, I usually splurge on three. Gently melt half of the butter in a heavy nonstick skillet, tilting the pan to coat the sides. Turn off the heat and let the pan cool to room temperature. Break the eggs directly into the pan and turn the heat to the lowest possible setting— and I mean lowest; if necessary, use a heat diffuser such as a Flame Tamer. With a wooden spatula or spoon, break up the yolks and begin stirring as slowly and evenly as possible. Keep stirring . . . and stirring and stirring. It's like watching paint dry, but there are no shortcuts. The eggs and butter will at first look like a blotchy and very peculiar soup. The egg whites will appear at least partly cooked after 10 or 15 minutes, but the yolks have a long way to go. Keep breaking up any clumps that threaten to form on the bottom of the pan. After 25 to 30 minutes of cooking, stir in the remaining butter along with the optional cream. By degrees the mixture will get smoother and slightly thicker, first starting to coat the back of a spoon, then throwing off a wisp of evaporation and leaving a clean track as you draw the spatula across the bottom of the pan. Keep going until it has cooked for 45 to 50 minutes in all and is a little thinner than a crème anglaise, then pour it over any preferred kind of toast and eat at once. Let everyone season his or her own with salt and pepper.

VARIATION: The scrambled-egg recipe in M. F. Fisher's *How to Cook a Wolf* is a very similar but less labor-intensive dish of custardy eggs made with cream instead of butter. The ingredients are eight eggs and a cup of cream. The cream makes the mixture a little more tolerant of heat than the butter-custard version.

Fisher's general instructions are to break the eggs into an unwarmed iron skillet before adding the cream, then begin to stir—not beat—from time to time "from the middle bottom" over very gentle heat without letting it boil. Continue to stir occasionally for about half an hour; some optional enrichment like herbs, cheese, mushrooms, or chicken livers ("and so forth") can be added halfway through the cooking. Don't try to hurry it. Stir in any seasonings at the very end and serve, just about set, on toast.

LEMON CURD

A few years ago Regina Schrambling wrote a piece for the *Los Angeles Times* food section announcing that she couldn't understand why people swoon over killer chocolate desserts when such a thing as lemon curd exists on this earth. A woman after my own heart! Like Regina, I was born without the chocolate gene—but put me in front of anything made with lemon curd and I go wild. For me, it's the most magical application of the custard principle that enables egg yolks to thicken a liquid (here, lemon juice) in the presence of heat.

Lemon "curd," which technically isn't a curd, contains neither milk nor cream. The eggs are coaxed to maximum thickening power, without turning into a grainy mass, through an acid-sugar combination that allows the egg protein to coagulate smoothly without breaking, and to emulsify with melted butter at a higher temperature than is possible with most egg-based emulsions. The flavors of the result are simultaneously buttery, sweet, sharp, and silky, all fused into one angelic whole. And it is amazingly easy to make, far easier than any milk- or cream-based egg custard. The one technical necessity is a double boiler or some equivalent arrangement.

Lemon curd is the best of all fillings for a Lemon Tart (see page 274) and marvelous in layer cakes. It also makes a glorious mousse when whisked together with whipped cream (in any proportion you want), an excellent topping for bar cookies, a magnificent breakfast jam for toast or scones, or—all by itself—a piece of shameless indulgence for anyone equipped with a spoon. It would also be a natural for the old Southern "pinch pie" or "angel pie," which consists of a baked meringue shell (voilà—a fine destination for the leftover egg whites) with a rich filling such as ice cream or lemon custard. On occasion I have successfully improvised a sort of trifle using lemon curd and day-old angel food cake (another use for the egg whites).

I always make a large (3-cup) batch using only egg yolks; other people may want to halve the recipe or use whole eggs. Note that the number of lemons needed for a given amount of juice varies phenomenally between different seasons of the year. You will need more in summer, fewer at the height of the winter citrus season. Some people prefer to use much more lemon zest, not peeled in strips but finely grated and added directly to the curd after it has been cooked and strained.

LEMON CURD (CONT.)

YIELD: About 3 cups

12 tablespoons unsalted butter (1½ sticks), cut into small bits
12 large egg yolks or 6 large eggs
A pinch of salt
1⅓ cups sugar
⅔ to ¾ cup freshly squeezed lemon juice, from 3 to 4 (in winter)
   or 7 to 8 (in summer) large lemons
Zest of 2 lemons, peeled off in strips

Melt the butter in a double boiler over simmering water; whisk in the other ingredients and cook, stirring or whisking constantly, for 15 to 20 minutes, until the mixture thickens enough to coat a spoon. Pour the curd through a fine-mesh strainer into a heatproof bowl, and let it cool with a sheet of plastic wrap pressed over the surface (to prevent a skin from forming). It will keep in the refrigerator, tightly covered, for three to four days.

VARIATION(S): For Lime Curd, use limes instead of lemons. Any citrus juice will work, though with orange juice you should slightly reduce the amount of sugar. In fact, you can make this from just about any tart, fresh fruit juice.

ABOUT BUTTER IN PASTRY

I'm reluctant to give advice about things that I never make myself, and this is why bakers will find no recipes here for butter cakes or butter cookies. On the other hand, I do occasionally make pastry—not the tour-de-force kinds like puff pastry or strudel dough, but simple versions for pies and tarts. And no lover of these could live without butter.

From a flavor standpoint, butter is the ideal fat for pastry. But the technical standpoint is another matter. The very complexities that make butter a wonderful partner for flour in sauces have difficult effects on its interactions with flour in pastry doughs.

When you work butter into a dough at ordinary room temperatures, it will perform its usual subtle transitions between the solid and melted states—unfortunately meaning that some of the fat will prematurely melt into the flour particles while the rest is still solid enough to simply coat them from outside. It's the external coating action that's important for tender, flaky pastries such as the kind used for American pies. The thin shielding of fat retards the development of gluten during the initial mixing of the dough. There is the added problem of water content in butter. It comes mostly from the dispersed buttermilk droplets, but sometimes also from rinsing water that wasn't completely expelled in the final working of commercial butter. The leakage of fat and water into the flour is what often makes all-butter pastry brittle, tough, or both.

Lard and partially hydrogenated shortenings don't share these disadvantages. In the first place, they liquefy more uniformly and at higher temperatures than butter, so that melting can be delayed until the pastry actually goes into the oven. They also contain virtually a hundred percent fat, and so have no water to release into the dough and throw off a cook's calculations about how much water to add in mixing. Shortenings like Crisco have long been the mainstay of cooks devoted to the goal of tender, flaky American-style pie crust. (I don't know whether recent reformulations to eliminate trans fatty acids have changed these products' baking qualities.) A few, like me, rely on a combination of butter and lard to offset the problems inherent in using butter alone.

But there's another family of pastry doughs in which butter is not only the best but the only fat you can use: the very fine-textured, almost shortbreadlike ones such as French pâte brisée and German *Mürbeteig*. Higher in fat content than American pie doughs, they start with butter being worked into dry ingredients in rather coarse bits at as cold a temperature as possible. A small amount of water with or without some other liquid (egg yolk is the most usual for pâte brisée) is then added, and the dough loosely gathered together in a mass. It is now ready for the crucial stage of *fraisage*—in this context, something like "rumpling." Fraisage is accomplished by rapidly and firmly smearing the dough across the work surface with the heel of your hand in order to amalgamate the fat and flour very closely. The dough is then chilled for at least an hour (preferably longer) before the final rolling out. Pastry made by this method is simultaneously firm and crumbly, with just enough gluten development to hold together. And it practically sings of the butter that went into it.

Some version of pâte brisée is the backbone of classic

French tart shells. For savory tarts like quiche, the pastry is usually unsweetened or made with only a tiny bit of sugar. For dessert tarts it can be sweetened or not. The reason for adding sugar is not only flavor but ease of working; it tends to inhibit the development of gluten and lets the cook handle the dough more swiftly and decisively without causing the pastry to toughen. Moderately sweetened pâte brisée is usually called *pâte sucrée*. An especially crumbly version, *pâte sablée*, uses more sugar for a more cookie-like effect.

BASIC PÂTE BRISÉE

It is important to start out with very cold butter and take all precautions against letting it get warm and greasy. Have the kitchen as cool as possible while you work. To mix the dough ingredients, handle them as little as you can and use only your fingertips or a pastry blender.

If possible, use unsalted butter (salted butter often retains more water after churning) with a butterfat score of at least 83 to 85 percent.

YIELD: Enough for a 9- or 10-inch tart

1 ¼ cups all-purpose flour
¼ teaspoon salt
2 teaspoons sugar (optional)
1 stick (¼ pound, 8 tablespoons) unsalted butter, cut into bits no larger than ½ inch
1 large egg yolk
1 to 2 tablespoons ice water, or as necessary

Sift the flour, salt, and sugar (if using) onto a work surface or into a large bowl. Make a well in the center and put the butter into it. Work the butter into the flour with your fingertips or a pastry blender, gradually sweeping everything from the edges of the well toward the center as the mixture starts to come together. Add the egg yolk, thinned with 1 to 2 teaspoons of the ice water; quickly work it into the flour and butter until you have a loose dough. Add just as much more ice water, a teaspoon at a time, as you need to make the dough hold together. Put the dough on a lightly floured work surface. Working with a little at a time, use the heel of your hand to push the dough straight away from you with a strong, rapid pressure that nearly mashes it into the work surface. You are trying to eliminate lumps of butter and make the texture somewhat smoother than for an American flaky pastry.

When you have finished this stage, gather the dough up into a ball. Flatten this into a 5- to 6-inch disk, quickly rounding off the edges as evenly as possible. Wrap the dough in plastic wrap and refrigerate for at least 2 hours, preferably longer.

Put the chilled dough on a lightly floured work surface or pastry cloth. Whacking it a few times with a rolling pin may make it cooperate more in the next stage: Roll it out into an 11- or 12-inch circle. Carefully lift the sheet of dough to a 9- or 10-inch tart pan with a removable bottom. Ease it into the pan as gently as you can; press to anchor the base and sides firmly to the bottom and rim of the pan. Trim away the excess of dough from the edges, leaving at least a ½-inch overhang that you can press to the sides.

Use a fork to prick the bottom and sides of the pastry shell all over. It is now ready to use in recipes from any cookbook that call for a shortcrust tart shell. Consult particular cookbooks to decide whether to use the crust as is or to give it a preliminary "blind" baking. It is the ideal crust for Lemon Tart (page 274).

VARIATION: For Pâte Sucrée, use 3 to 4 tablespoons sugar and proceed as directed.

NINETEENTH-CENTURY
GERMAN BUTTER CASK

LEMON TART

Possibly the most elegant use to which lemon curd can be put.

YIELD: A 9- or 10-inch tart

1 recipe Pâte Brisée or Pâte Sucrée (pages 272 and 273)
1 recipe (3 cups) Lemon Curd (page 269)

Prepare the pastry and fit it into a tart pan as directed. Prick the bottom and sides all over with a fork while preheating the oven to 400°F. Line the pastry shell with a round of parchment paper or aluminum foil and add several cups of something that will weigh it down without imparting peculiar flavors—dry beans or lentils, rice, ceramic pastry weights. Bake it for 10 to 12 minutes to set the pastry. (Either a pie-crust shield or a narrow band of aluminum foil carefully crimped around the rim of the pan is a great help in preventing the edges from burning.) Remove from the oven, and reduce the oven temperature to 375°F.

Take out whatever baking weights you used and let the partly baked tart shell cool to room temperature. Brush the bottom and sides with lightly whisked egg white thinned with a tablespoon or so of water. Pour in the lemon curd and bake for 25 to 30 minutes. Remove from the oven and let cool to room temperature.

There are various currently popular ways of finishing and serving a lemon tart; most kitchen bibles today will have some suggestions. My own strong preference is to simply let it cool thoroughly, cover (or dot) the top with plain whipped cream, and set to chill thoroughly in the refrigerator. Let warm up not quite to room temperature before serving.

Milking the Cow

CANADIAN BUTTER TARTS

I didn't know anything about Canadian butter tarts until I happened to be in the vicinity of Toronto about two years ago. One bite, and I wondered why they haven't become a mad passion here, as they certainly are north of the border.

The general idea is very simple: Line small tartlet pans with any preferred pie or tart crust pastry and fill them with a delectable butter-based custard somewhat resembling pecan pie or other "sugar pie" fillings; bake until the filling is well set. In Ontario, butter tarts are often made with additions like plumped raisins or chopped nut meats (generally walnuts or pecans). I like them plain. The usual filling uses sugar (white or brown) and corn syrup (light or dark) combined with eggs and butter. Cane syrup is a nice substitute for corn syrup.

Since I don't have a set of tartlet pans, I use standard muffin tins with cups of about ½ cup capacity. Slight differences in depth and width between different models can affect the exact yield.

YIELD: 18 to 20 individual tarts

Pie or tart crust from any preferred recipe, enough for 1 double-crust or
    2 single-crust pies or tarts (I like Pâte Brisée, page 272)
3 eggs, lightly beaten
1 cup white sugar or any preferred kind of dark sugar
    (light brown, dark brown, or unrefined)
1 cup golden syrup, light corn syrup, or dark corn syrup
⅓ cup butter, barely melted
¼ teaspoon salt
1 to 2 teaspoons pure vanilla extract, rum, or rye whiskey

Make and chill the pastry according to your chosen recipe. When you are ready to bake, preheat the oven to 400°F. Roll out the dough about ⅛ inch thick (a tiny bit thicker for Pâte Brisée). Use a round cookie or vegetable cutter to cut it into circles about 4 inches in diameter. Fit and pat these into muffin tin cups; don't worry if they look a little misshapen.

Beat all the filling ingredients into the eggs to combine smoothly.

Pour about ¼ cup of the filling into each tart shell, topping it up as evenly as possible with what's left over. Bake for 15 to 20 minutes, or until the filling is set and slightly browned on top. Cool on a wire rack. Serve plain or—for an inauthentic touch—with whipped cream.

FRESH CHEESES
(INCLUDING BRINED CHEESES)

Introduction

Sorting Out Names and Cheeses

About Brined Cheeses

Getting Organized for Cheesemaking

Fresh White Cheese: Kindergarten Version

Fresh White Cheese with Cultures

Fresh White Cheese with Cultures and Rennet

About Cream Cheese

Cream Cheese: Creamy

Cream Cheese: Light

Cervelle de Canut

Cream Cheese–Scallion Dip

About Liptauer Cheese

Liptauer Cheese I

Liptauer Cheese II

Tyrokafteri or Htipiti (Whipped Feta-Cheese Spread)

Syrniki or Tvorozhniki (Russian Pot-Cheese Fritters)

Savory Lokshen Kugel (Noodle Pudding)

Non-Nursery Junket

Paskha (Russian Easter Dessert)

Uses of Whey

Bulgur Pilaf with Whey

Fresh cheese is one of those things that nobody had to "invent." It undoubtedly invented itself many times over in the original dairying lands that I call the Diverse Sources Belt—and later just as often in other regions—when someone let soured milk sit around too long for drinking. Sooner or later it would have become two substances, one of which could be progressively drained off to leave the other more and more solid. Before draining, it was curds and whey; afterward, the first version of fresh cheese.

The first cheeses were from sheep's and goat's milk. Other animals—chiefly camels, cattle, and water buffaloes—got in on the act later in different reaches of the Diverse Sources Belt. Eventually, cheesemaking would spread to northerly Old World climates—but not the biggest southerly dairying region, the Indian subcontinent. The closest Indian counterparts of cheese, chhenna and panir, lack the main elements that give true cheeses their curd structure: fermentation by lactic-acid bacteria and/or coagulation by enzymes.

Fresh cheeses produced by one or both of these means gradually proliferated through a wide geographical range, and other refinements appeared over time. They came to exist in a range of forms that defied logical classifications. At one time there were not only regional but neighborhood-to-neighborhood or household-to-household variations. Even today, when most of this diversity has been ironed out, it is difficult to line up fresh cheeses in strict categories. One type has a way of shading subtly into others.

The two main ways of turning milk into curd have both existed since prehistoric times. The older was bacterial fermentation—a prolonged version of the process responsible for the earliest counterparts of yogurt. What happens partly resembles what happens in a nursing infant's stomach where acid is being secreted: Lactic-acid fermentation eventually creates a low enough pH (or high enough acidity) to knock out the negative electric charge that keeps casein particles separated from each other in fresh milk. As they become free to precipitate, or start coming together in a body, the milk first takes on the consistency of thin yogurt and then, with increasing acidity, forms a defined curd with somewhat more distinct separation from the whey.

The second means of curd formation also mimics something that happens in actual digestion—at least, digestion of mothers' milk by nursing infants. Much of the business is carried out by enzymes specifically tailored to reconfigure casein—the most important source of protein in milk—so that it will be more slowly, complexly, and completely absorbed than if the enzymes weren't there. After weaning there is a general rearrangement of digestive enzymes, with the original milk-digesting ones ceasing to be produced. In infant ruminants like lambs, kids, and calves, there is another wrinkle: Unlike adults, they receive food straight into the fourth stomach, or abomasum (see page 41), bypassing the three other ruminant stomach chambers that will take over digestion when they are old enough to eat grass.

The milk-digesting enzyme secreted by the lining of the abomasum is chymosin ("rennin" in older sources, but latterly rechristened). It snips off certain parts of the casein micelle more neatly and predictably than acid alone, though actually it is better activated in the presence of digestive acids. The newly pruned casein particles gather together in a firm curd that can be digested in gradual stages.

How did people first learn about this mysterious milk transformer? Our best guess is that someone either inadvertently discovered the curdled contents of a young lamb's or kid's stomach bag in butchering the animal or tried using the bag as a container for previously drawn milk and found that the milk had turned into something else. In any case, long before classical times the layer of tissue that produced the effect had become a prized cheesemaking resource, and remains so to this day under the name of "rennet."

Until a few centuries ago, cheesemakers used dried pieces of the actual abomasal lining, or sometimes soaked it in brine to make an extract, or ground it to a paste or powder. This comparatively unrefined rennet had strong effects on the character of the finished cheese. Unlike modern purified rennets or rennet equivalents, it contained not just chymosin but a bouquet of other enzymes designed to tackle other parts of the milk besides casein. From a flavor standpoint, the most important ones are lipases, or fat-digesting enzymes. Part of their role is to chop up the long, mild-tasting fatty-acid molecules into shorter ones that are aggressively pungent. Short-chain fatty acids are responsible for the piquant bite of provolone and a few other Italian cheeses (nowadays, manufacturers add lipase to cheesemilk in refined form for just this purpose). We can pretty certainly surmise that fresh cheeses made with older versions of lamb, kid, or calf rennet were not as bland and unindividualized as the ones we're used to. Their flavor must have varied sharply with the lipase content of the rennet and the way different farmers prepared the rennet for use.

Wherever fresh cheeses existed, up to the dawn of modern agriculture they remained simple peasant standbys, only marginally less perishable than the milk from which they were made. The earliest means developed to preserve them more than a few days was brining. Brined cheeses more or less resembling Greek feta are nearly as pervasive and defining a culinary feature of the eastern Mediterranean and lands to the east as yogurt. What sets them apart from the ripened or aged cheeses more familiar to Western cheese lovers is that immersing the curd in brine keeps it from undergoing a progression of further enzymatic changes that would otherwise cause it to knit into a smooth, close, homogeneous texture. Feta and its many Diverse Sources Belt counterparts retain much of the looser casein structure of fresh cheese.

When dairying and cheesemaking moved north to colder environments, the technique of brine preservation didn't. The climate difference meant that unbrined (or only very lightly salted) fresh cheeses had a better chance of lasting more than a few days without spoiling. They assumed great importance throughout both the Northeastern and Northwestern Cow Belts of Europe, where temperatures were generally favorable to fermentation by mesophilic bacteria, or kinds suited to conditions slightly cooler than those needed by the thermophilic kinds endemic to the Middle East. But as pointed out earlier, the role of fresh cheeses was to decline in western regions with the arrival of modern commercial dairying geared toward an urban market. Both drinkable fresh milk and specialized ripened cheeses took on an unprecedented prominence as cash crops. Especially in the English-speaking world, sour milk and fresh cheeses became archaic or marginalized for much of the nonrural population. It was chiefly from eastern Scandinavia through the Baltic lands and Mitteleuropa into Russia and Ukraine that they remained a universally loved everyday sustenance.

Fresh cheeses must have existed in North America as early as colonists and cows, but they certainly were not stars of the commercial dairying scene that emerged within half a century of independence. Nineteenth-century American cookbooks occasionally give recipes for making some kind of fresh cheese—sometimes called "cottage cheese"—at home. Often there is a Philadelphia or Pennsylvania connection, as shown by the fact that nearly all authors mention "smearcase" (from Pennsylvania German *Schmierkäse*) as a familiar if less elegant name. It also came to be called "Dutch," probably meaning "Pennsylvania Dutch." The cheese itself usually is a simple cousin of the Fresh White Cheese with Cultures on page 291—milk soured to a clabber, or soft curd, drained of whey, and worked smooth. A richer cousin, "cream cheese," also has been a Philadelphia specialty since at least the early nineteenth century.

Cream cheese seems to have achieved commercial popularity in the last decades of the century. But Ralph Selitzer's invaluable history *The Dairy Industry in America* reports that cottage cheese was of minor importance until World War I, when the Dairy Division of the Department of Agriculture launched a campaign for "rediscovering" it as a thrifty, nutritious use for skim milk.

The moment could not have been better, because the nation was also being seized by its first infatuation with the cult of extreme slimness. Mass-produced cottage cheese appeared on the scene just in time to be hailed as the dieter's friend, an association that has never vanished. Cream cheese also underwent a timely makeover in the mid-1920s when manufacturers introduced the new "hot pack" technology (page 298) that would extend its shelf life and enable it to emerge as an inexpensive all-purpose "cocktail spread" base.

For the better part of the twentieth century, these two products were virtually the only fresh cheeses known to most Americans. The great exceptions were the Ashkenazic Jews and other immigrants from the Northeastern Cow Belt who began coming to major cities after about 1880 and were entrenched ethnic presences by the time immigration was cut off by congressional fiat in 1924. Fresh cheeses were too important a part of their heritage to be given up, either in their own right or as a cooking ingredient. It was Jewish food lovers who kept alive a taste for more flavorful, meaty alternatives to watery American-style cottage cheese. The usual versions of these well-flavored fresh cheeses were generally called "farmer cheese" and "pot cheese." They went into many kinds of dumplings, pastry or blintz fillings, sweet and savory puddings, and fritters. People often tossed a few spoonfuls with hot cooked noodles, or ate a generous serving as an accompaniment to raw vegetables. For several generations American Ashkenazim also formed a loyal clientele for cream cheese fresher-tasting and less gummy-textured than the hot-pack version.

This heritage was fading fast when reinforcements started to arrive during the final throes of the Soviet Union. With them came not only many of the same cooking traditions but enough of a taste for good fresh cheese to fuel some small-scale manufacturing in major cities. Today domestically produced Russian-style *tvorog* is probably the best choice in nearly any recipe calling for any cheese from the cottage-cheese clan.

Brined white cheeses have continued to occupy the same central role throughout most of the Diverse Sources Belt as nonbrined fresh cheeses in Eastern Europe. They remained little known in this country—people still vaguely call them all "feta" and assume that they are or ought to be Greek—until waves of immigration began after 1965 from many regions where brined cheese was simply an indispensable part of culinary life. You can now buy versions imported from many countries—even France, where cheesemakers have taken to manufacturing brined sheep's-milk cheese for worldwide export, using surplus milk that would otherwise go into Roquefort. Their culinary uses almost exactly parallel those of fresh cheeses in Eastern European traditions, down to pastry fillings (most famously, in such phyllo-wrapped specialties as the Greek *tiropita* and the small cylindrical Turkish *sigara böreği*) and the partnership with fresh raw vegetables.

Generally speaking, American cheesemakers have been slow to recognize what wonderful opportunities await someone with the initiative to make first-class fresh or brined cheese. The inspiring exception is the goat contingent. Goat cheeses are the fastest-growing segment of the artisanal-cheese industry, and the most popular of all are the fresh young versions that most people firmly if illogically assume to be synonymous with "chèvre." In other words, there's a market ready to be instructed in the pleasures of very good fresh cheese. Many of its members would equally adore the brined cousins of fresh cheese if they had ever tasted a really excellent Greek feta or Bulgarian *sirene*. And there is the added advantage that today's small-scale cheesemakers have a sizable pool of knowledge about such subtleties as flavor-affecting enzymes and particular combinations of lactic-acid bacteria. I would not be surprised if something like a minor golden age dawns in the next few years for fresh cheeses. In the meanwhile, making a few simple versions of your own is an eye-opener.

SORTING OUT NAMES AND CHEESES

Forewarned is forearmed: There is no such thing as consis-
tency in popular names for the many different fresh cheeses. None except cottage cheese and cream cheese has been assigned a formal "standard of identity" in the FDA Code of Federal Regulations, and even those specifications are broad enough that things barely resembling the most familiar super-market cottage and cream cheese versions could conceivably qualify. Besides, shopkeepers and restaurateurs trying to explain the unfamiliar to English-speaking patrons inevitably get their own off-the-cuff translations going—e.g., "cottage cheese" for Indian panir (which isn't a cheese at all, much less cottage cheese). I hope that the following list will help you either make sense of some terms or accept the limitations of sense. All entries are for varieties of fresh cheese—meaning unripened cheese made by the action of lactic-acid bacteria, enzymes, or both—with the exception of ricotta and *queso blanco*, which defy easy classification.

BRINED OR PICKLED CHEESES See page 288. You will most often find them labeled "feta." As of 2008 the use of that name on labels will be (illogically) restricted to brined cheeses made in, or at least shipped from, Greece. I doubt that this will affect informal signs on store shelves, but you may want to know some other names by which to search for brined cheeses in ethnic groceries. In most stores catering to émigrés from Russia and parts of the former Soviet Union, look for "brinza" or "bryndza." In many parts of the old Diverse Sources Belt, from the Balkans to the Central Asian republics, brined cheeses are so universally taken for granted that people simply call them "cheese"—e.g., *sirene* in Bulgaria, *gibneh* or *jibna* in much of the Arab world, or "white cheese"—as in Turkey, where they're collectively *beyaz peynir.* This makes for communication problems in some neighborhood shops. Try to find out the source of the milk; the most lusciously creamy brined cheese comes from sheep's milk.

CHÈVRE In American parlance, fresh young goat cheese, though in French any goats'-milk cheese is *fromage de chèvre.*

CLABBER OR CLABBERED MILK A regional (mostly Southern) term for milk curdled by the natural action of ambient bacteria. Before pasteurization became universal, this happened pretty quickly in all parts of the Deep South, especially during the warm months. People either drank clabber while it was no thicker than cultured buttermilk or let it sit until the curd was firm enough to eat as fresh cheese, often sweetened and accompanied with rich cream.

COTTAGE CHEESE This has come to be the standard American term for most fresh cheeses made by lactic-acid fermentation, usually in combination with curdling by rennet or some other enzyme source. But a shortcut version can also be made through direct injection of an acid, which eliminates the small amount of flavor nuance that most mass-produced cottage cheese has to begin with. Read labels and look for the words "cultured milk" and "enzymes" (not some weaselly term like "natural flavoring"). The main thing that distinguishes American cottage cheese from most other fresh cheeses of the world is that the curd remains in small, slightly chewy bits instead of forming a smooth paste.

   There is really no way to tell what any brand will taste like except by buying some and sampling it. The milk is usually nonfat or reduced-fat, often with the addition of nonfat milk solids. Manufacturers loosely distinguish between "large-curd" and "small-curd" cottage cheese, referring to the way the curd is cut during heating. The large-curd kind contains more rennet and has a shorter setting time, meaning that it stays blander. The other develops more acidity—that is, a livelier flavor—through longer fermentation. "Creamed" cottage cheese has a small amount of cream (usually thin half-and-half) worked in to moisten the finished curds. Most cottage cheese is also lightly salted.

In American usage, POT CHEESE AND FARMER CHEESE are slightly different versions of cottage cheese, but there is no general agreement on how they differ from one another. Get them all figured out in one part of the country and you may scratch your head when you encounter them someplace else. But broadly speaking, both have more flavor and character than the usual run of supermarket cottage cheese. In the Northeast, farmer (or farmer's) cheese usually has a fine, grainy, homogeneous texture while pot cheese contains larger and more distinct curds. Both are usually drier and cheesier than other versions of cottage cheese. One kind of farmer cheese is pressed very firm and dry (somewhat like the lean, meaty old-fashioned fresh cheese called "hoop cheese") and sold in a kind of flat lozenge shape. Most farmer cheese, however, is softer and moister. I usually find American pot cheese and farmer cheese much better for both eating and cooking than other forms of cottage cheese, though not as good as Russian-style tvorog (page 287).

In all versions of cottage/pot/farmer cheese, I look for a good lactic-acid flavor and a bit of texture or bite. Without these, it's pretty vacuous.

CREAM CHEESE Any bland, rich-textured fresh cheese made with a cream-milk mixture can technically be labeled "cream cheese." But today the name almost universally refers to the standardized result of "hot pack" processing (page 298)—not just in the United States but in dozens or hundreds of other venues, testifying to the global reach of Kraft's "Philadelphia" brand. Its characteristic feature, aside from the somewhat gluey texture conferred by stabilizers, is a distinctive cooked flavor irresistible to fans. Explore cheese stores for the unfortunately rare "cold pack" versions, or make your own for a real revelation. Ignore anything purporting to be nonfat or reduced-fat cream cheese.

CURD CHEESE General British term for all fresh cheeses of the cottage-cheese type.

FROMAGE BLANC, FROMAGE FRAIS French for "white cheese" and "fresh cheese," referring to various unripened French cheeses of fresh, delicate flavor and smooth, close texture. Several United States producers now make similar cheeses labeled "fromage blanc." Be warned that there is no single agreed-on standard, so one maker's version may differ markedly from another's.

JUNKET Originally, a loose term for fresh curds from cream or milk, lightly drained in a rush basket (French *jonquette*). By the early nineteenth century it usually meant sweetened milk curdled with rennet and eaten while barely set with a topping of fresh or clotted cream (see recipe, page 89). "Curds and whey" as a sales pitch often referred not to plain curds and whey but a heavily sweetened kind of junket sold by London street vendors (Henry Mayhew's 1851 survey of London street sellers gives the usual proportions as half a pound of sugar to eight quarts of milk). In 1915 a canny manufacturer registered "Junket" as a trademarked name for its rennet tablets, thereby taking the term out of circulation as a general description. As explained on page 289, plain Junket brand rennet tablets are what I prefer for renneting fresh cheeses.

NEUFCHÂTEL Another good name traduced by American sales initiative. In France it is an estimable mold-ripened young *appellation contrôlée* cheese from Neufchâtel in the Bray district of Normandy. In this country it now refers to a spreadable fresh cheese made by the same hot-pack method as most commercial cream cheese, but with less milkfat, fewer calories, and if anything a gummier effect.

QUARK OR QUARGEL The general German term for all kinds of fresh unripened cheese. The Austrian equivalent is *Topfen*. On home ground, the character of the cheese varies from region to region—drier, creamier, finer-textured, grainier, curdier. (Usually, however, Topfen more resembles our farmer cheese or Russian tvorog.) Today there are several American-made versions, usually very smooth-textured and mildly tart. As with our "fromage blanc," there are no accepted manufacturing standards, and you should expect great variation among different brands.

QUESO BLANCO, QUESO FRESCO Spanish for "white cheese" and "fresh cheese." In the Latin American countries, these terms can embrace a spectrum of cheeses. In the United States, they don't have an absolutely fixed meaning but nearly always refer to milk completely or partly curdled by acid precipitation. Sometimes queso blanco or fresco also undergoes a little exposure to rennet (or other enzyme sources) and/or lactic-acid bacteria. But it is essentially one of the noncheese cheeses like Indian panir. Very mild-flavored and rather rubbery, it is popular with Mexican and many other Latin American cooks because it keeps its shape instead of melting when cooked.

RICOTTA Also an anomaly on the cheese map. True Italian ricotta differs from real cheese in containing virtually no casein. This is because it is made from what's left after the casein has been removed from milk in cheesemaking: the whey. Reheating whey (hence the name "ricotta," or "recooked") precipitates the water-soluble proteins (lactoglobulins and lactalbumins) to a white substance distantly resembling cheese curd, but moister and more fine-grained in texture. The yield is very low compared to that from true curd precipitation, though it increases slightly with higher acidity (lower pH); vinegar is often added to the whey for ricotta for more efficient separation.

In Italy, industrial ricotta-making is a thrifty form of recycling what would otherwise go to waste. The best comes from sheep's-milk whey. There is also good buffaloes'-milk ricotta. That from cows' milk is the blandest and least interesting. Most commercial American "ricotta" (so called) is a very different, fairly insipid product. This is another of those cases where manufacturers are held to no particular standard, and what most of them seem to have in mind is a sort of imitation cottage cheese made by acidifying whole or skim milk (sometimes part whey) with vinegar or another souring agent. If the result is too watery it gets thickened with gums. The usual recipes for homemade ricotta in American cookbooks are no closer to whey-based ricotta. They call for curdling heated milk with lemon juice, and produce something very like the Indian chhenna on page 107. Real whey-protein ricotta has an altogether different texture, thin-bodied and not particularly cheesy.

I have not tried to give a recipe for true ricotta because none of the fresh-cheese recipes in this book yields enough whey to make more than a few spoonfuls. If you hanker to make your own, chhenna isn't any more inauthentic than the expedients in other cookbooks. But what I really recommend is searching out fresh sheep's-milk ricotta (not to be confused with the hard cheese called ricotta salata) in a cheese store. It will spoil you for other kinds.

TVOROG The Russian word for what we call farmer cheese or pot cheese—a firm-textured small-curd fresh cheese with excellent flavor and little of the extraneous liquid that American cottage cheese often swims in. Salted and saltless versions are now produced, usually in half-pound cartons, by several American manufacturers for a diverse buyership of émigrés from the ex-Soviet bloc. Large Russian-American delis often sell it in bulk. It is the most consistently good commercial fresh cheese that I know; I prefer it in virtually any recipe calling for anything like cottage cheese, especially dishes such as blini, cheese-filled pastries, or noodle kugels. Don't even think of making Russian Paskha (page 311) without good tvorog. It is also perfectly delicious eaten by itself, but even better with a dollop of Russian-style sour cream.

ABOUT BRINED CHEESES

Some rough-and-ready cousin of the "Fresh White Cheese with Cultures" in this chapter was the first of all cheeses, allowing for such circumstances as the absence of cows' milk, or of nice purified cultures to be added in measured amounts. Cheese made by a combination of culturing and renneting came later. But what came next was not cheese ripened or aged by the techniques later developed in northwestern Europe. Once fresh cheeses had become ubiquitous in the Diverse Sources Belt, people discovered the simplest means of *preventing* the onset of ripening: putting the cheese in brine. The modern example that most people know by name is Greek feta.

The curd structure of brined (also often called "pickled") cheeses has more in common with that of fresh cheeses than those that have undergone prolonged, progressive changes through ripening and perhaps protracted aging. The main difference is in the degree to which the original casein gets rearranged. A good deal of the somewhat spongy original casein matrix remains in brined curd. Prompt salting and brining are what keep it from starting down the cascade of reactions known as ripening.

At the stage where a fresh cheese would be deemed ready for eating, brined cheese takes a detour. The curd is cut into slabs or chunks, salted, and left to firm up by releasing more whey for some hours or days before being put into a container with a brine solution of salt, water, and—usually though not always—some of the whey, which lightly acidifies the brine. In this state, it keeps for weeks or months, depending on the strength of the brine. When removed and desalted by soaking in fresh water, it can be nearly as close to the milky quality of the fresh curd as soaked salt codfish is to the character of fresh cod.

GETTING ORGANIZED FOR CHEESEMAKING

I never use any special equipment or ingredients from cheesemaking-supply companies. These expenses may make sense if you're working on a professional scale with dozens of gallons of milk at a time. But for one or two pounds (roughly two to four cups) of cheese, anybody can get equally good results with pretty ordinary kitchen resources and a little planning. (If you decide to explore fresh cheeses more zealously, see the Note on Shopping Sources on page 317.)

The only necessary ingredients are milk or a milk-cream mixture, a source of live lactic-acid bacteria to inoculate and culture the milk, and in three of the following five cheese recipes, an enzyme to help set up the curd.

Very fresh milk from a small dairy is always preferable, but supermarket milk will do. As for the inoculant, I use plain cultured buttermilk. You may need to try a few supermarkets before finding a brand with active cultures and without added salt or gums. My enzyme source is plain unflavored Junket brand rennet tablets, and here some people will have easier hunting than others. Some supermarket chains and specialty food shops still carry this once-common ingredient. If you strike out, I suggest asking the maker of Junket about local sources (Redco Foods, Inc., P.O. Box 879, Windsor, CT. 06095; or e-mail info@junketdesserts.com). Vegetarians and kosher cooks please note: This rennet is an animal product. Luckily you have an excellent alternative in the rennetless cheese on page 290.

The steps you will be going through in most cases are putting the milk in a nonreactive saucepan or other container, warming it to a suitable inoculation temperature (generally between about 85° and 100°F; I recommend an instant-reading thermometer), letting it incubate for a prescribed period of usually between 8 and 24 hours at (preferably warm) room temperature, and draining the whey from the curd. This last part of the procedure is the only one requiring much advance organization. For it you will need a colander or strainer set over a pan or bowl and lined with *tight-woven* cheesecloth—not the loose, flimsy supermarket article—or another good-sized piece of clean cotton cloth such as a large handkerchief or remnant of old bedsheet. The cloth must be large enough to line the colander with some overhang and to tie up into a bag for the final stage: hanging up to finish draining for an unpredictable interval of (usually) several hours. You will need something to hang it on, like the kitchen faucet (if you won't be using it for a while) or a sturdy wooden spoon placed over a pail deep enough for the bag of curd not to touch the bottom. Remember that the curd will be in a messy, sloshy state when you actually start transferring it between the first vessel and the colander or getting the cloth bag hung up. You'll thank yourself later if you can get as prepared as possible beforehand.

The most complex recipe in this chapter, "Fresh White Cheese with Cultures and Rennet," involves an additional stage of cutting the incubated curd into cubes and gradually heating it to a temperature high enough to firm it up by expelling whey more efficiently. The extra equipment you will need is described in the recipe. For the last stage of the two cream-cheese recipes, a weight of several pounds (another whey-expelling measure) is helpful.

FRESH WHITE CHEESE: KINDERGARTEN VERSION

Here is cheese for the scientifically challenged. In somewhat telescoped form, it illustrates the stages of curd formation and draining explained above. I originally came across it in several American-published Russian cookbooks as a resourceful substitute for tvorog, the beloved Russian pot or farmer cheese. Though it's a little tougher than fresh cheese made by more orthodox methods, the flavor is good.

The reason this is easier to make than other fresh cheeses is that you have a head start on the task of precipitating the casein from the whey. It's already been incompletely precipitated by the lactic-acid bacteria added to the milk at the manufacturing plant to make cultured buttermilk. Just heating it speeds up the process enough for better curd formation. Other fresh cheeses require you to add the bacteria yourself, and rest on a much more cautious application of heat that leaves the curd more tender and delicate. Still, the general principle is the same.

YIELD: About 1 cup cheese and 3 cups sour whey per starting quart of buttermilk. (See page 313 for Uses of Whey.)

Go buy a cardboard carton—two, if you're game—of cultured buttermilk. It should be made without salt or gummy stabilizers, and preferably should have a milkfat content of at least 1.5 percent. Place the unopened carton(s) in a deep pan such as a stockpot or asparagus steamer and add enough cold water to come close to the top of the cartons. Bring the water to a full boil over high heat. Remove the pot from the heat and let the whole thing cool to room temperature.

Read the directions on page 289 for preparing a cloth-lined colander set over a saucepan or other vessel, tying the cloth into a bag, and hanging it up to drain. Open the carton(s) and dump the contents into the colander, then proceed with the tying-up and draining stages. When the whey stops dripping, turn out the drained curd into a bowl and briefly work it with a wooden spoon. Work in a pinch or two of salt and a dash of cream, if desired. Store in the refrigerator, tightly covered, for three to four days, and use in any way you would use commercial cottage or pot cheese.

FRESH WHITE CHEESE WITH CULTURES

This version of fresh cheese is somewhat more complicated than the preceding one but has no real hurdles as long as the inoculated milk doesn't get bumped or jounced while incubating. The recipe calls for skim milk not because whole milk won't work but in order to eliminate one variable during a first effort. Later you can try the whole-milk version (page 296). But this cheese actually is one thing that I prefer made with skim milk.

To repeat my inevitable mantra, the flavor will be best if you look for very fresh milk, without added milk solids, from a small dairy that does batch pasteurizing. But freshness really is more crucial with the second essential ingredient: a mixture of several different mesophilic starter bacteria. As explained earlier, my preferred source of these organisms is simply a little cultured buttermilk of at least 1.5 percent milkfat content. If it has been sitting around long enough in the store or your refrigerator to lose a lot of the original bacterial activity, the milk either will take longer to curdle or may scarcely curdle at all. Read labels and don't buy anything that lacks the magic words "live cultures," or that contains gums and salt. If you can find cultured buttermilk at a local farmers' market, snap it up at once and use it that day or the next.

The recipe can be halved if a gallon of milk sounds intimidating, but don't try to cut it beyond that.

FRESH WHITE CHEESE I (CONT.)

YIELD: About 4-plus cups cheese and 11 to 12 cups slightly
soured whey per starting gallon of milk. (Expect wide variation.
See page 313 for Uses of Whey.)

1 gallon skim milk
½ cup cultured buttermilk
½ to ¾ teaspoon salt
A dash or two of cream, if desired

Read the directions on page 289 for preparing a cloth-lined colander set over a
saucepan or other vessel, tying the cloth into a bag, and hanging it up to drain.
Have the kitchen sink clear, to be used as a water bath.

Pour the milk into a 6-quart pot. Run hot water into the sink to a depth of
several inches, set the pot in it, and test the temperature of the milk. Stir it gently, occasionally rechecking the temperature, until it reaches about 85° to 90°F.
If you have to add more hot water or resort to heating some in a kettle, be sure
not to splash it into the milk. And it's better to warm the milk cautiously than
find that you've suddenly gotten it much hotter than you meant to.

Remove the pot of milk from the sink, and set it in a warmish spot (things
will proceed faster if the room is at 75° to 80°F) where it will not be disturbed
for the next day. Shake up the carton of buttermilk in case the thicker part has
settled; stir in ½ cup. Loosely cover the pot with a cloth, and go away and leave
it. The inoculated milk *must not be jostled*, and the room temperature shouldn't
fluctuate wildly.

After about 12 hours, take a look at the milk, without moving or jiggling the
pot, to see whether it has started to set in a curd. Most likely it won't be well set
until 18 to 24 hours after inoculation. You will know it's ready when, as you
cautiously test the edge with a small spoon, you see a bit of soft but definite
curd break from the mass like a very tender custard.

Set the colander, with cloth lining in place, over a bowl to catch the whey.
Very gently ladle the contents of the milk pan into the colander, carefully
pouring in the last bit of whey and scraping out any clinging curd. Let the
whey drain for 1 to 2 hours. When the surface is less flooded, gather up the
corners of the cloth and shift the weight around a little to encourage more
draining. Tie the corners into a bag and hang it up to drain until the whey has
stopped dripping. This will take anywhere from 4 to 8 hours. If you get discouraged, you can hasten things by putting the bag in a strainer over a bowl
and weighting it with something like a heavy can set on a plate. When it gets to
soft-cheese consistency, turn the curd out into a mixing bowl and work it
smooth with a wooden spoon. Work in about ½ to ¾ teaspoon of salt (less for
a half-sized batch). You can also add a very little cream if you like, but I prefer

it without. It will keep in the refrigerator, tightly covered, for four to seven days.

Call it anything you like, from cottage cheese to fromage blanc to Schmierkäse; names for cheeses of this ilk are notoriously unsystematic and imprecise in every language. By all means mix it with any seasonings you like— green herbs, scallions, horseradish, blue cheese, chutney, minced celery or olives, pickled jalapeños, salmon caviar, or anything else that occurs to you— before serving it to guests in the form of a spread (it's great on open-faced sandwiches). Or put the unadorned cheese on the table and eat it with apple butter or prune lekvar. The nineteenth-century cookbook author Mary Lincoln reports that it "is delicious with warm gingerbread."

You are now primed to understand the main factors that make any fresh cheese tick. A little practice with this version will equip you to go on to another "cottage cheese" made with just two added factors: rennet and a little more heat.

FRESH WHITE CHEESE WITH CULTURES AND RENNET

For makers of aged cheeses, renneting is a complex business involving many factors. Those of us interested only in making small batches of fresh cheese have only a few things to keep in mind. First of all, rennet and lactic-acid fermentation reinforce each other's action; second, renneted curd is profoundly affected by temperature. Curd produced by culturing alone is more forgiving of heat. But if you slap a pot of renneted milk on the stove and rapidly heat it above 120°F, the result will be as fresh and tender as boiled rubber. Thus you need to do more advance thinking than for other kinds of fresh cheese, and plan on spending an hour or more at the stove during the heating stage. The advantage is that with a little practice you will be able to better manipulate such factors as degree of firmness or softness, sourness or blandness, than with culturing alone.

Before you begin, read through the directions on page 289 for preparing a cloth-lined colander set over a saucepan or other vessel, tying the cloth into a bag, and hanging it up to drain. But this time you will also have to get together some extra equipment: a pot large enough to hold the one containing the milk, a sturdy rack to set the (heavy) milk pot on inside the larger one, a long thin-bladed knife or metal spatula, a heat deflector such as a Flame Tamer, a stirring implement (wooden spoon or rubber spatula) long enough to reach the bottom of the milk pot, and an instant-reading thermometer, preferably one with a long probe.

You had better try out the rack arrangement beforehand. The top rims of the smaller and larger pots should be at least roughly level. If you don't have a rack high and strong enough for the purpose, use a few empty cans with tops and bottoms removed. Or try my improvised "rack" for setting a 6-quart Dutch oven inside a 12-quart one: two 5-pan sets of 3-x-5-inch disposable aluminum loaf pans from the supermarket, left stacked for extra strength. Use a screwdriver to punch about a dozen holes through the bottoms of each set, and put them in the larger pot, upside down. Luckily they can be endlessly reused for this purpose.

Look when possible for fresh skim milk made without added milk solids, as well as very fresh buttermilk with live cultures. As with the preceding fresh cheese version (page 291), the recipe can be halved.

YIELD: About 4 cups cheese, 12 cups faintly soured whey. (See page 313 for Uses of Whey.)

1 gallon skim milk
½ cup cultured buttermilk
¼ plain Junket brand rennet tablet (see page 289)
½ teaspoon salt, or to taste
A dash or two of cream, if desired

Get together all the equipment listed above. Have the kitchen sink clear for use as a water bath.

Pour the milk into a 6-quart pot, run hot water into the sink to a depth of several inches, and set the pot in it. Stir the milk gently, occasionally rechecking the temperature and carefully adding hot water if necessary, until it reaches about 85° to 90°F. Carefully remove the pot. Shake up the buttermilk before measuring. Crush the piece of rennet tablet in a few spoonfuls of water in a cup, making sure it dissolves thoroughly. Stir the buttermilk and rennet into the milk, then go away and leave the lightly covered pot *completely undisturbed* in a warm spot (preferably at a temperature of 75° to 80°F).

In about 10 to 12 hours the milk will show the first sign of the difference between fresh cheese curdled by lactic fermentation alone and that with a combination of culture and rennet: more rapid curd formation, with clearer separation of whey. This may be hard to judge without jostling the milk. As gently as possible, test it by slipping a thin knife blade just under the surface.

When the curd seems almost to "unzip" in a clean cut revealing fairly clear-looking whey, it's ready. The texture will be slightly firmer than that of simply cultured curd.

Now for the most delicate part of the operation, which will take at least an hour: First, set the larger pot on a Flame Tamer or other heat deflector over a stove burner and put your rack arrangement in it.

Next, use your knife or spatula to very carefully cut straight down through the curd at roughly ⅓- to ½-inch intervals. (Don't worry about mathematical precision.) Make a second set of cuts at right angles to the first. Holding the blade at a forty-five-degree angle to the vertical cuts, make a third set of cuts, this time oblique—an inexact but good enough home equivalent of professional curd-cutting with wire "cheese harps" that do both vertical and horizontal cutting. The aim is to encourage still more curd-whey separation.

Now carefully set the pot of curd on the rack and even more carefully pour enough lukewarm water into the larger pot to come most of the way up the sides of the smaller one (leave a few inches of leeway). This is your equivalent of an industrial-scale water jacket. Turn on the heat, keeping it fairly low, and begin checking the water temperature, which has to rise slowly rather than rapidly. Be aware that once it starts heating you may have trouble slowing it down. When it gets above about 100°F, turn your attention to the milk pot.

You must now bring the curd from about room temperature (say, 75°F) to roughly 108°F at the rate of only two or three degrees every five minutes—thirty-some degrees in about an hour. Begin testing the temperature in different parts of the pot. Every few minutes, carefully stir the curd with a long spoon or spatula. The object is not to agitate or mix the contents of the pot but to let the whey circulate as freely as possible around the pieces of cut curd, evening out their temperature and making the curd firmer by promoting more whey loss. As the casein matrix knits together more firmly, it will literally squeeze out more and more moisture. The longer you continue, the more whey in proportion to curd you will see in the kettle.

It doesn't matter if bits of curd break off in stirring; they will be retrieved in the final straining. Keep checking the temperature and as it reaches about 100°F, turn the heat as low as possible. If the curd seems to be warming up too fast, lift the pot from the larger vessel, turn off the heat, and add some cold water or ice cubes to the warm water before cautiously resuming operations. When the temperature of the curd reaches 108°F (or something between 105° and 110°F—on the whole, better a bit too cool than too warm), try to hold it at that level without further warming for about 15 minutes. (If necessary, add ice to the water bath or briefly lift the milk pot out of it.)

Now set up your cloth-lined-colander arrangement. Carefully ladle in the curd and some of the whey; pour in the remaining whey as gently as possible.

FRESH WHITE CHEESE II (CONT.)

Tie the cloth into a bag for draining as before. It will drain more promptly and completely than the rennetless version, yielding anything from an ounce to a few ounces less cheese and more whey.

When the whey has stopped dripping, decide whether to take or omit a step that I never bother with myself: Fill the sink with ice water and slosh the bag around while kneading the cheese with your hands to rinse out the last remnants of partly sour whey. Many people regard this as standard practice; I can only suppose that they want something as "sweet" and innocuous as supermarket cottage cheese. Personally, I think the small amount of residual whey gives the cheese character.

If you have rinsed the curd, hang it up to drain again (this time it will go faster) before proceeding to the end stage: Turn out the cheese into a mixing bowl, and work it as smooth as possible with a wooden spoon. Work in salt to taste. Some people like to add a little fresh cream at the same time; I usually prefer the cheese without. Store and use as for the rennetless version.

VARIATIONS: I think there is nothing better than either rennetless or renneted fresh cheese made with skim milk. But excellent ones can also be made with whole milk, either homogenized or (as I prefer) unhomogenized. They are nearly creamy enough to pass for cream cheese. If you use unhomogenized milk you will see some melted butterfat appearing on the surface as you heat it. But most of the butterfat will remain with the curd when you drain it in cheesecloth, and any that goes off in the whey can easily be salvaged by chilling the whey and lifting the fat from the surface, to be worked back into the cheese.

The same technique can be used to make a simple culture-and-rennet fresh goats'-milk cheese. But trial and error are even more the rule here than in most home dairying experiments. The huge variations in the chemical makeup of any species's milk that have been partly erased from the modern commercial cows'-milk supply remain glaringly obvious in goats' milk from different herds and dairies. All goats' milk differs from cows' milk in casein structure, the factor that most directly affects curdling behavior. But there is also a range of differences in goats'-milk casein not only among particular breeds but—because of the strongly seasonal tendency of goats' mating patterns—among samples taken at different times of the year. Also, not all processors will label the milk to tell you if it's been frozen. The practical result for a home cheesemaker is that no recipe can reliably tell you the correct amount of rennet for a gallon of goats' milk or the time the milk should be left to curdle after renneting and inoculation. With identical amounts and timings I have ended up with a curd that refused to become curd at all (it tasted great, though, and I successfully presented it to friends as "goat buttermilk"), a curd too unpleasantly tough for anything but throwing out, and a nice soft cheese.

A fresh white goats'-milk cheese is good enough to risk a few failures. I suggest starting to check the degree of curdling after eight hours; do not let the curd become as stubbornly firm as a wrong opinion. Omit the steps of cutting and heating the curd. The cheese will be ready to drain once you have a somewhat (not decidedly) firm curd. When finished it will be very mild, with scarcely a hint of goatiness. (That characteristic emerges only after brief aging.) The main clue that it comes from goats' rather than cows' milk will be the more smoothly, finely knit texture of the curd.

ABOUT CREAM CHEESE

Cream cheese is a great confidence builder for neophyte cheesemakers. Cream is really far easier to work with than milk. Its comparatively small casein content means that even after renneting it never forms a curd requiring to be cut and laboriously brought to a crucial temperature; there's scarcely anything you need to do to the cream once it's set except drain it.

If you have never eaten any kind of cream cheese except Kraft's Philadelphia Cream Cheese and other commercial knockoffs, the homemade version free of gums and stabilizers will require some mental readjustment. Like most other kinds of fresh cheese, cream cheese has meant many things to many people in the last few centuries. We can only guess at what the term referred to before the global triumph of the foil-wrapped product baptized with the name "Philadelphia."

The only wisp of certainty in a vacuum of information is that cream cheese from perhaps the eighteenth century on usually involved cream curdled and drained to a cheesy consistency. As mentioned earlier, something called "cream cheese" had been considered a Philadelphia delicacy for more than a generation before the Empire Cheese Company began selling "Philadelphia Brand Cream Cheese" from a plant in Otsego County, New York, in the early 1880s. ("Dear Longo," the New York bon vivant Sam Ward wrote to his friend Henry Wadsworth Longfellow in 1841, "Just returned from Philadelphia. . . . What took me there? . . . Not creamcheese, nor melons, nor Preciosa [the ballerina Fanny Elssler], but the Chinese Museum, which closes tonight.") One can only guess how much it resembled today's commercial cream cheese. In 1867 the New York market chronicler Thomas F. De Voe described as a Philadelphia specialty one kind of cream cheese "made from rich sour cream tied up in linen cloth to drain, then laid on a deep dish, still covered around, and turned every day, and sprinkled with salt for ten days or a fortnight, until it is ripe. If wanted to ripen quick, cover it with mint or nettle leaves."

De Voe's Philadelphia cream cheese sounds much more interesting (and creamier) than the kind now known from Rome to Rio, which undoubtedly didn't reach anything like its present form until the late 1920s. That was when a series of technological innovations began paving the way for cream cheese made by liquefying a not particularly creamy curd at a temperature well above the boiling point of water, concentrating it in a mechanical separator, standardizing it to a desired fat percentage, and pumping the hot fluid mixture directly into small rectangular foil packages for retail sale. Because the heat-treated cheese tends to leak water, gums such as guar and locust bean are routinely added at the standardizing stage. The end product, "hot pack cream cheese," has a distinctly cooked flavor and gummy consistency that cannot have belonged to cream cheese before the hot-pack revolution. Today even gourmet and health-food shops and some cheese stores are unlikely to carry anything but hot-pack cream cheese, under whatever label.

Given the popularity of cream cheese made by this technique, talk of fresher-tasting alternatives may sound like an affectation. But I honestly recommend looking for gum-free brands, if only to be able to make the comparison. Or for an idea of what really fresh cream cheese can be, try one of the following two recipes.

CREAM CHEESE: CREAMY

Creaminess is a relative concept. Make cream cheese with the richest, heaviest cream you can find, and it may prove a disappointment. The curd sets up more satisfactorily and with better flavor if you aim for a higher protein content and lower fat content than that of heavy cream. (It still won't behave exactly like the curd from cultured and renneted skim milk, but it will make a nice cheese.)

My idea of an agreeably creamy cream cheese starts with a mixture of about two parts whole milk—unhomogenized is best—to one part not-too-rich cream made by combining equal amounts of half-and-half and heavy cream—both also unhomogenized, if possible. Remember that what's labeled half-and-half in one store might pass muster as light cream in another; there is no uniformity in these matters from region to region or even processor to processor.

Your advance planning for cream cheese should include both lining up some small weights and clearing the decks in the refrigerator for the last stage of draining.

YIELD: About 2¼ cups of cheese, 6¾ cups of slightly sour whey
(but every batch may be different; the richer the cream,
the higher the proportion of cheese to whey)

1 ½ quarts (6 cups) milk, preferably unhomogenized and very fresh
1 ½ cups nonultrapasteurized rich half-and-half or light cream,
    preferably unhomogenized
1 ½ cups nonultrapasteurized heavy cream, preferably unhomogenized
½ cup cultured buttermilk of at least 1.5 percent milkfat content,
    as fresh as possible and made without salt or stabilizing gums
½ unflavored Junket brand rennet tablet
½ teaspoon salt, or to taste

Pour the milk, half-and-half, cream, and buttermilk into a saucepan. Set the pan on a heat deflector over very low heat and slowly heat the milk to about 98° to 100°F. Put the piece of rennet tablet in a small bowl or cup, crush it to a powder, and add a few tablespoons of water, stirring to dissolve it thoroughly.

Find a spot in a warm room where the pan of milk and cream can rest absolutely undisturbed for the better part of a day. Remove it from the heat, stir in the dissolved rennet, and loosely cover the pan with a kitchen towel. Let the inoculated mixture sit without jostling or jiggling for 12 to 16 hours, or until you can see by very gently testing the edge with a spoon that it has become about as thick as sour cream. It should smell slightly sour.

Follow the directions on page 289 for preparing a cloth-lined colander set over a saucepan or other vessel, tying the cloth into a bag, and hanging it up to drain. After about 5 or 6 hours of draining you will have something approaching cream cheese, but it will still contain some residual whey. (Cream cheese has less of a casein matrix than milk-based cheese to squeeze out moisture from the interior.) Get the cloth-swaddled curd arranged in the colander so that you can place a weight on it. A few beach stones are good, or something like a few heavy cans set on a small plate. For years I used a couple of my husband's 2-pound lead diving weights (on a plate, natch). Put the whole affair over a bowl in the refrigerator until the curd is about as firm as commercial cream cheese and virtually no whey is coming from it. This may take another 6 to 10 hours—some batches drain more cooperatively than others. Check it at intervals.

Turn out the drained cheese into a mixing bowl and taste it. It should be beautifully creamy but not cloying, with a fresh lactic-acid flavor. Beat it smooth with a wooden spoon and work in a little salt. It will keep in the refrigerator, tightly covered, for about a week.

CREAM CHEESE: LIGHT

Light," that is, by comparison with the previous example. But please don't expect anything "lite." To me this is the ideal cream cheese. I think it strikes just the right balance between creamy and cheesy. It also spreads a little more easily than the preceding version.

The yield is nearly the same as for "creamy" cream cheese (a tiny bit more whey and less cheese). The procedure is identical. The ingredients are 7 cups unhomogenized whole milk, 1 cup rich half-and-half or light cream, ½ cup gumless and saltless cultured buttermilk (at least 1.5 percent milkfat), ½ unflavored Junket brand rennet tablet, and ½ to ¾ teaspoon salt. Follow the directions in the preceding recipe; the cheese will drain a little more quickly and more completely. It will also be slightly more perishable. Allow a day or two less keeping time.

CERVELLE DE CANUT

In the heyday of the Lyon silk industry, *canuts* was local slang for weavers in the region's mills. Apparently some wag decided that this strong and highly seasoned cheese spread—clearly a counter-part of Liptauer cheese and Greek *tyrokafteri*—resembled what silk weavers used for brains.

Any unripened curd cheese will do as the foundation of a pleasant copy, but American-style cottage cheese or ricotta should be well drained of whey and either beaten smooth in a food processor or worked through a fine-mesh strainer. Of course it tastes best when made with a homemade fresh white cheese or good commercial fromage blanc. The seasonings can vary widely as long as shallot and chives predominate. I tend to think that the fewer herbs, the better.

YIELD: About 2 cups

2 cups fresh white cows'-milk cheese, or any preferred mixture of
   fresh chèvre and cows'-milk cheese
1 to 2 shallots
1 small garlic clove (optional)
A bunch of chives
A small handful of chervil, tarragon, and/or flat-leaf parsley (optional)
1 to 2 teaspoons salt, or to taste
Freshly ground white or black pepper to taste
1 tablespoon dry white wine or white wine vinegar
2 to 3 tablespoons olive oil
2 to 3 tablespoons heavy cream or crème fraîche

Work the cheese smooth with a wooden spoon. Mince the shallots very fine; crush the garlic (if using) to a paste with the flat of a knife blade. Mince or snip the chives very fine, together with the chervil and other optional herbs. Work all these seasonings into the cheese along with salt and pepper. Beat in the wine or vinegar, oil, and cream. Let sit in the refrigerator, well covered, for at least an hour before serving it as a spread for coarse country bread or dip for crudités.

CREAM CHEESE-SCALLION DIP

S ay what you will of commercial American cream cheese made by the standard hot-pack method with an array of gums (see page 298), the fact remains that it is *useful*. This truth dawned on a large public during Prohibition and Repeal, when booze-absorbing cocktail nibbles for one-handed eating multiplied like rabbits. In contrast to the elaborately decorated canapés of the previous era, they tended to require almost no time or attention on anyone's part. Cream cheese turned out to be the perfect all-purpose vehicle for many of the new filler-uppers. Having a pleasantly neutral flavor that clashed with nothing, it could be almost instantly mixed to a kind of cement for chopped olives, bacon, sweet pickle relish, raisins, or some stronger cheese like Roquefort.

Ashkenazic Jews viewed cream cheese a little differently, as uniting the handier qualities of Russian-style sour cream and pot cheese. (A few places on New York's Lower East Side continued to make their own cream cheese—sometimes really creamy cold-pack versions—until the last years of the twentieth century. But by then only a handful of diehards cared about the difference.) People took to putting cream cheese on bread or rolls, either plain or mixed with something else—for instance, some member of the onion fraternity. By the 1950s "scallion cream cheese" or "chive cream cheese" was an indispensable Sunday brunch adjunct to bagels and bialys. By the turn of the twenty-first century it was being presented as a dip for crudités, widely sold in prepackaged versions that don't hold a candle to anything you can mix yourself—especially if the cream cheese is homemade or gum-free.

Scallion (or chive) cream cheese scarcely needs a recipe. For every cup (8 ounces) of cream cheese, use a few tablespoons of cream or whole milk and two or three large scallions (the white and a few inches of the green part), cleaned, trimmed, and coarsely chopped. Mash everything together with a wooden spoon, adding cream a tablespoon at a time to make a spread (thicker) or dip (thinner) and using as much or as little scallion as you like. It will keep for several days in the refrigerator, tightly covered, but be sure to let it warm to room temperature before using.

VARIATIONS: There are dozens of other possibilities. I like cream-cheese spread or dip made with a few crunchy raw vegetables, for instance, shredded carrots and minced celery. Clam dip with minced clams (usually canned) and a few seasonings like a little garlic, prepared horseradish, and/or Tabasco sauce is a Superbowl party perennial. People also love smoked fish, especially salmon, in cream-cheese dips and spreads. Roasted red peppers (coarsely chopped) are wonderful. There is a big fan club of blue-cheese dips. In fact, nearly any of the suggestions for sour-cream dips on page 212 can be easily adapted for use with cream cheese, as long as you thin the cheese slightly with cream. Some people add mayonnaise for easier spreading, but I like the flavor better without it.

ABOUT LIPTAUER CHEESE

Like many American cooks, I first met Liptauer cheese as a spread made from ordinary cottage cheese (generally enriched with butter) or cream cheese, with a little paprika, caraway, onion, and/or anchovy paste. And such versions are perfectly good in their own way. But Liptauer cheese really started as something more characterful.

Its historical and culinary career involves many confusing wrinkles. In the first place, the popular Austrian and German name "Liptauer" refers to a Slovakian district that was once a county named Liptó in the medieval Kingdom of Hungary. Long ago it received a large influx of Vlach (Wallachian) sheepherders from parts of present-day Romania and Moldava. Through them, sheep's milk became dominant in local dairying. The cheese called Liptovsky/Liptoi/Liptauer was a version of sheep's-milk "bryndza," or "brinza"—the name for brined cheeses like feta throughout much of Eastern Europe, locally Germanized to "Brimsen"—that came from Romania with the Vlachs. It is still made in the former Liptó county.

The eponymous "Liptauer cheese," meaning the seasoned spread made from the cheese itself, originally was nothing but a western cousin of Greek Tyrokafteri (page 305). Before commercial versions were developed, it was a household or farmstead production whose flavor and texture varied with the quality of the main ingredient—younger/older, milder/saltier, softer/firmer. When the dish caught on along the western Danube, the usual local farmer cheese or pot cheese made from cows' milk generally replaced brined sheep's-milk cheese.

In the course of its Austro-Hungarian adventures, "Liptauer cheese"—the spread, that is—acquired a lacing of sweet paprika and caraway seeds, usually with some chopped onion. There are factory versions with these seasonings or others already mixed in. It usually has a good dose of butter (corresponding to the Greek olive oil) worked into the cheese. Some people consider it incomplete without capers, dry or prepared mustard, or anchovies.

I have come to like Liptauer made with sheep's-milk feta. But Liptauers based on fresh cows'-milk cheese now have a long track record of their own that merits a separate version. The proportions are highly elastic; don't hesitate to use more or less of any seasoning.

LIPTAUER CHEESE I

YIELD: About 2 cups

1 pound feta cheese, preferably a creamy sheep's-milk kind
4 tablespoons (½ stick) butter, at room temperature, cut into 6 to 8 pieces
1 to 2 teaspoons Hungarian sweet paprika
1 to 1 ½ teaspoons caraway seeds, bruised in a mortar to release the flavor
1 small onion, chopped fine or grated
1 small garlic clove, crushed to a paste, or a few chives, minced (optional)

Coarsely crumble the cheese or cut it into largish (1-inch) chunks. Put it in a bowl and let stand, covered with cold water, for between half an hour and 1 hour. Change the water once or twice and taste a bit of cheese for saltiness (but remember that the butter will further dilute the briny flavor). When it is desalted to your liking, drain it in a colander until it stops dripping.

Either process the drained cheese in a food processor or blender with the butter, paprika, and caraway, or use a stout wooden spoon to force the cheese and butter through a coarse-mesh sieve into a bowl. Add the onion and optional garlic or chives and process for a few seconds longer, or work them in with the spoon. Let stand at room temperature 1 to 2 hours, to let the flavors develop. Serve it as a spread for good bread, preferably pumpernickel or Jewish rye; it's also excellent with crisp fresh radishes and scallions.

LIPTAUER CHEESE II

YIELD: About 2 cups

1 pound farmer cheese
2 tablespoons (¼ stick) butter, at room temperature
1 to 2 teaspoons Hungarian sweet paprika
1 to 1 ½ teaspoons caraway seeds, bruised in a mortar to release the
   flavor
1 teaspoon dry mustard or 1 to 2 teaspoons prepared
   German-style hot mustard (optional)
1 to 2 teaspoons capers, drained and chopped (optional)
1 or 2 small anchovy fillets, minced (optional)
1 small onion, chopped fine or grated
1 small garlic clove, crushed to a paste, or a few chives, minced
   (optional)

Omit the soaking of the cheese; otherwise combine the ingredients as directed
in the previous recipe, adding any or all of the stronger-flavored seasonings in
small increments to taste.

VARIATIONS: Many people like cream cheese as a Liptauer base, though I
find it lacking in texture. For this version, omit the butter and use two 8-ounce
packages of cream cheese.

The farmer cheese can also be replaced with an equal amount of a fresh
young goat cheese.

TYROKAFTERI OR HTIPITI
(WHIPPED FETA-CHEESE SPREAD)

I first encountered this silky, pungent stuff as "tyrokafteri" in the
Greek neighborhood of Astoria, Queens. Later I learned that
htipiti is a more common name in Greece. Some people also call it
kopanisti, though that risks confusion with the soft ripened cheese
of the same name. By whatever handle, it belongs to a large family
of whipped feta preparations eaten everywhere throughout the
Diverse Sources Belt. You can't miss the similarity to its Carpathian
descendant, Liptauer cheese (page 303). The irreducible elements
of the many Greek versions are feta cheese, olive oil, and some
kind of hot or sweet peppers, usually but not always charred over a

flame or fried in hot oil. You can use anything from fire-roasted sweet red peppers to small dried hot ones, or even pickled cherry peppers. Once you've tried it, vary the proportions to suit your mood. Some people add lemon juice, yogurt, and/or a favorite green herb. I like garlic, but it's not essential.

The intrinsic creaminess of sheep's-milk feta gives the most irresistible texture. Whatever kind you use, taste it before soaking so that you can gauge the desalting process. The briny sting should be softened, not completely washed out.

YIELD: About 2 cups

1 pound feta cheese, preferably made from sheep's milk
2 long green hot chile peppers (or any preferred kind; see above)
1 to 2 garlic cloves
¼ to ½ cup (or to taste) sharp, peppery olive oil

Coarsely crumble the cheese or cut it into roughly 1-inch chunks; put it in a bowl and cover it well with cool water. Let stand for half an hour to 1 hour; every 15 minutes or so change the water and taste a crumb of cheese for saltiness. (Remember that the oil will temper the salt somewhat.)

While the cheese soaks, roast the chiles over a gas flame until blackened all over. (Alternatively, blacken them, turning a few times, under a broiler, or char them on a dry griddle or in a heavy skillet set over high heat.) Scrape off the charred skin. (Some people recommend first letting them sit briefly in a closed paper bag to soften the skins, but I've never found much difference.) Scrape out and discard the core and seeds. Chop the flesh very fine or mash with a mortar and pestle. Mash the garlic to a pulp with the flat of a knife blade.

When the cheese is desalted to your taste, drain it in a colander until it stops dripping. Turn out the cheese into a mixing bowl and begin vigorously beating it with a stout wooden spoon. (Or process it in a food processor.) Beat in the oil a little at a time, tasting at intervals, and stop when the balance of oil and cheese is to your liking. With a sheep's-milk feta the texture will gradually turn light and creamy, becoming almost like a heavy whipped cream when you have added the full amount of oil. The effect won't be as airy and satiny with goats'-milk or cows'-milk cheese.

Stir in the minced green pepper and crushed garlic. Serve as a spread with good crusty bread or a dip with crudités.

A small dab is a lovely addition to a simple oil-and-vinegar salad dressing.

VARIATION(S): People who don't like feta will be glad to know that similar spreads are frequently made (minus the soaking step) with blander fresh goat and sheep cheeses. Greek *manouri* cheese is one good choice. Or substitute any fresh, soft goat cheese, using just as much oil as you need to make a spreadable paste.

SYRNIKI OR TVOROZHNIKI
(RUSSIAN POT-CHEESE FRITTERS)

Like pancakes or French toast, this useful breakfast/brunch dish can be given any number of sweet or savory spins. Creativity (e.g., rum instead of vanilla or crystallized ginger instead of raisins) will not be misplaced here. Russians usually serve *syrniki* with jam as well as sour cream and/or melted butter; all of these strike me as too much of a good thing. To me they taste better with fresh fruit or an uncooked fruit sauce (say, pureed blueberries or raspberries). Maple-syrup lovers may like to try that pairing. The only indispensable elements are very good pot cheese or farmer cheese—Russian-style tvorog, if you can find it—for the fritters and very good butter for the frying. I prefer cultured butter with a slight lactic tang.

YIELD: 8 small patties (4 servings)

1 pound firm, dry, well-flavored pot cheese or farmer cheese, preferably tvorog (page 287; do *not* use cottage cheese)
½ teaspoon salt
1 to 4 tablespoons sugar (I use 1)
½ to 1 teaspoon finely grated lemon zest (optional)
1 egg or 2 egg yolks
A dash of pure vanilla extract (optional)
¼ cup golden raisins, briefly plumped in hot water and well drained (optional)
⅓ cup (approximately) flour, plus more for shaping the fritters
⅓ to ½ cup (6 to 8 tablespoons) unsalted butter, cut into chunks

If your pot cheese has the least suspicion of excess moisture, wrap it in dampened, wrung-out cheesecloth and place it in a colander under a weight (e.g., a heavy can on a small plate) to press out any whey. If it is not very fine-textured, force it through a coarse-mesh sieve.

Beat the cheese as smooth as possible with a wooden spoon. Beat in the salt, sugar, and optional lemon zest. Whisk the egg lightly and beat it in along with the optional vanilla and raisins. A little at a time, sift the flour over the cheese and beat it in until you have a dough that is almost too stiff to work.

Turn out the dough onto a lightly floured work surface. With floured hands, shape it into a log about 10 to 12 inches long. Wrap it in waxed paper and refrigerate for at least half an hour (it's easier to shape when chilled).

Cut the cheese log into 8 slices. With floured hands, shape these into small hamburgerlike patties.

Melt the butter in a heavy skillet just large enough to hold the syrniki easily in one layer. When it is good and fragrant, adjust the heat to medium and add the cheese patties, which should be half-swimming in hot butter. Fry until nicely browned on both sides, turning several times. Drain briefly on paper towels and serve at once.

Nutmeg is a popular and good seasoning for syrniki; pass a whole nutmeg and a grater around at the table.

VARIATION: For a savory rather than sweet version, cut the sugar to 1½ teaspoons and omit the lemon zest, vanilla, and raisins. Add a handful of minced scallions (or chives), dill, or parsley—or all three—to the mixture before working in the flour.

SAVORY LOKSHEN KUGEL
(NOODLE PUDDING)

The word "kugel" (German for anything spherical, from a cannonball to Planet Earth) covers a lot of ground in the baked-pudding department for Ashkenazic Jews, and for many non-Jewish food lovers who register such things the way they register bagels or "Jewish" rye bread. Probably the earliest versions of kugel were more or less round in shape and tied in a pudding cloth for steaming or simmering. Different kinds made from matzoh, potatoes, various other vegetables, or noodles have their adherents today. But *lokshen kugel,* from the Polish word for noodles, is by far the most popular. It usually contains fresh cheese, sour cream, and eggs, and amounts to a sort of noodle-and-cheese pudding.

Jewish noodle kugels almost surely originated as offshoots of very similar German noodle dishes—which, however, often include such distinctly nonkosher elements as bacon or ham. I much prefer these to the sweet, raisin-studded casseroles that have come to be the favorite American versions of lokshen kugel. The following recipe is a sort of shotgun marriage between a savory kugel and the well-known German *Schinkennudeln* ("ham noodles"). Vegetarians

and people keeping kosher kitchens please note: It may be completely nontraditional, but coarsely chopped walnut meats and/or
chopped green olives make a flavorful substitute for the ham.

YIELD: About 6 servings

4 tablespoons butter
2 medium onions, minced
2 garlic cloves, minced
2 eggs
1 cup sour cream
1 cup coarse bread crumbs, from any preferred sturdy-textured bread
8 ounces broad egg noodles
8 ounces (1 cup) dry farmer cheese, pot cheese, or Russian-style tvorog
    (do *not* use creamed cottage cheese)
½ cup finely chopped smoked ham
Salt to taste
Freshly ground black pepper
Freshly grated nutmeg

Preheat the oven to 350°F.

Melt half the butter in a small skillet and sauté the onions and garlic until
translucent. Scrape the mixture into a bowl; beat in the eggs and sour cream.

In the same skillet, lightly brown the bread crumbs in the remaining butter.

Meanwhile, cook the noodles by package directions in well-salted water,
drain, and return them to the pot. Toss the hot noodles with the cheese, trying
to distribute it evenly. Add the onion–sour cream mixture and ham; toss to
combine. Season liberally with salt, pepper, and nutmeg.

Turn the mixture out into a 1½-quart baking dish, scatter the buttered
crumbs over the top, and bake for 30 minutes or until nicely browned. Serve at
once.

VARIATION: "Kugel Meets Borek," my contribution to the fusion wars, was
inspired by cheese-filled versions of the Turkish "water *borek*" (*su böreği*). Sold
in borek or baklava shops, it's a baked dish of large lasagne-like fresh pasta
sheets layered with a filling. For this hybrid, which undoubtedly would be dis-
owned by Jews and Turks alike, omit the sour cream, ham, and nutmeg, and
replace the farmer cheese with ½ pound feta cheese (preferably Bulgarian
sheep's-milk feta), crumbled and mixed with 2 eggs, ⅓ cup milk, a large handful of chopped flat-leaf parsley, and 6 to 8 large scallions, trimmed and
chopped. Toss the cooked noodles with the cheese-scallion mixture, top with
bread crumbs, and bake as above.

NON-NURSERY JUNKET

The name of this renneted milk dessert—which is essentially an almost-cheese of half-set curd still swimming in its whey—was around hundreds of years before the American branch of a large Danish dairy-supply company trademarked it. As late as my childhood it was a fairly common nursery "pudding" of wan consistency and bland flavor, but that was a fairly recent development. Nineteenth-century English versions commonly included brandy or rum as well as a final dose of cream. Mrs. Beeton's "Devonshire Junket" of 1861 calls for "2 dessertspoonfuls of brandy, 1 dessertspoonful of sugar, and 1½ dessertspoonful of prepared rennet" per "pint of new milk"; when the mixture is set she finishes it with "thick or clotted cream," nutmeg or cinnamon, and a little more sugar.

Like many very simple dishes harking back to an era of better milk, this really has to be made with very fresh unhomogenized milk (or a milk-cream mixture) in order to taste like anything.

YIELD: 4 servings

1 plain Junket brand rennet tablet
2 cups unhomogenized milk, as fresh as possible
1 to 2 tablespoons sugar
A pinch of salt
1 to 2 tablespoons brandy, rum, or Scotch
Heavy cream, preferably unhomogenized
Freshly grated nutmeg or cinnamon
Superfine sugar

Crush the rennet tablet in a tablespoon or so of cold water until thoroughly dissolved. Gently warm the milk, sugar, and salt to 100° to 110°F in a small saucepan, stirring to dissolve the sugar. Add the liquor. Quickly and lightly stir in the dissolved rennet; pour the mixture into four 8-ounce Pyrex custard cups or other small dessert bowls. Let stand with no jiggling or jouncing until lightly set (10 to 15 minutes), then carefully transfer to the refrigerator to chill thoroughly.

To serve, very gently pour or spoon a dollop of heavy cream over each portion without disturbing the surface. Add a sprinkling of nutmeg or cinnamon and let everyone sweeten his or her own with sugar to taste.

PASKHA
(RUSSIAN EASTER DESSERT)

This is as good a place as any to apologize to anyone who has been looking forward to an Ultimate Cheesecake Recipe. I just don't like the ultra-creamy texture of today's cheesecakes. My heart belongs to the lighter, drier filling of cheese *pie* as made in the Pennsylvania of my youth. Alas, I've never managed to duplicate it. But half a lifetime ago I transferred allegiance to the very different charms of *paskha*.

"Paskha"—pronounced "PAHS-khah," with an aspirated "kh"—is the Russian word for Easter, and in Russian Orthodox households the chief glories of the Easter table after colored Easter eggs are a "butter lamb" (butter molded in the shape of a lamb); a tall, round iced yeast loaf called *kulich*, rich with eggs and butter; and this sumptuous cheese creation named for the day.

No, it isn't a cheesecake, though the ingredients resemble those of a cheesecake based on a dry fresh cheese like pot cheese rather than cream cheese. (The difference is that paskha isn't baked and has no crust.) Like the lamb and the *kulich*, it announces the return of foods prohibited in Lent (butter, eggs, cheese, cream, in proportions that vary widely from cook to cook). Traditionally it is made in a pyramidal wooden mold that permits excess liquid to drain from the cheese mixture. Russian émigrés in this country long ago took to substituting a suitably sized flowerpot. In either case it is decorated after unmolding with dried or candied fruit or nuts forming the Cyrillic letters "XB" (for *Kh*ristos *V*oskrese, "Christ Is Risen").

Paskha is not complicated to make, but it takes elbow grease and planning. First, you must round up several pounds of a fresh cheese like Russian tvorog, and reduce it to a smooth texture by putting it through a sieve. You must then beat the heavy cheese as smooth as you can with butter, eggs, sugar, cream, and (usually) vanilla before getting a bulky flowerpot-over-a-rack arrangement into the refrigerator to drain until the paskha is firm enough to unmold, which may take a day. Lastly, you should either make a kulich yourself (there are nice recipes in Darra Goldstein's *A Taste of Russia* and Anya von Bremzen's *Please to the Table*) or go out and buy a super-excellent coffeecake, because for Russians paskha and kulich go together like a horse and carriage.

Note that the recipe calls for uncooked egg yolks, which some people will prefer to avoid. (There are versions of paskha where the mixture is cooked or the yolks are hard-boiled, but I've never experimented with them.) The presence of raw egg yolks is also the reason for draining the mixture in the refrigerator, not at room temperature.

Before beginning the recipe, be sure that you have room for the cheese-filled flowerpot in the refrigerator.

YIELD: 12 or more servings (about 2 pounds)

2 pounds dry, compact farmer cheese or pot cheese, preferably Russian tvorog (do *not* use cottage cheese)
½ pound unsalted butter
1 cup sugar
4 egg yolks, from very fresh and, if possible, free-range eggs
1 cup heavy cream
1 tablespoon pure vanilla extract
Currants, raisins, sliced almonds, or bits of different-colored candied fruit for decoration

Have ready a clean terra-cotta or other ceramic flowerpot of about 2½- to 3-quart capacity, with a hole in the bottom for draining. Also assemble a length of tight-woven cheesecloth, butter muslin, or other clean cotton cloth large enough to line the pot with some overhang; a rack and a deep plate to stand the pot on; and a means of weighting the cheese such as a small plate with a couple of heavy cans or large beach pebbles placed on it.

With a large wooden spoon or a pusher of the type French cooks call a *champignon,* force the cheese a little at a time through a fine-mesh strainer set over a deep bowl. Work it as smooth as possible with a large spoon.

Using a wooden spoon, cream the butter in a large mixing bowl. Beat the sugar into the egg yolks in a separate bowl, then work them thoroughly into the butter. Gradually beat the cheese in until it is smoothly incorporated. Work in the cream and vanilla extract.

Line the flowerpot with the cheesecloth, trying to eliminate wrinkles as much as possible. (The ones that remain will be clearly visible when you unmold the paskha.) Spoon in the cheese mixture, and smooth the top (which later will be the base of the paskha) as level as possible. Fold the edges of the cloth over the top.

Set the flowerpot on the rack over the larger plate, set the smaller plate and weights on top of the paskha, and put the whole arrangement in the refrigerator to drain for 18 to 24 hours, or until it has stopped dripping.

Unwrap the edges of the cloth and unmold the paskha by carefully inverting it onto a serving plate. Gently peel away the cheesecloth and use the dried fruit and nuts to spell out the letters "XB" on the side.

Serve the paskha with kulich (see above). People can either eat it in spoonfuls or spread it on slices of kulich with a knife.

USES OF WHEY

First-time cheesemakers are often dismayed to see how much whey (and how little cheese) they end up with at the end of their labors. Their predicament is also that of the cheese industry as a whole. In a few parts of the world, practical uses have been devised for whey—e.g., the curious boiled-down brown substance that Norwegians adore as *mysost* ("whey cheese"). Or people have learned to recycle the whey in order to make what Italians call ricotta. Farmers used to feed whey to pigs (who love it) in copious amounts. It also has often been a useful aid to home breadmakers, as the liquid in a yeast dough.

In modern times, resourceful American marketers have succeeded in promoting spray-dried whey powder as a nutritional supplement (my advice is "Save your money"). Schemes to put it through alcoholic fermentation to produce "whey wine" have been around for a long time, and today some visionaries claim to glimpse a bright future for whey as a source of ethanol.

For home cooks who find themselves awash in whey after making some simple fresh cheese or Indian panir, I suggest looking back to the time—not much more than a century ago—when it was considered a nutritious, cooling drink.

To me, the most delicious whey for drinking is the soured kind, like that drained from yogurt (page 158). "Sweet" (unsoured) whey from various kinds of cheesemaking with little or no culturing of the milk has much blander flavor. But it makes an agreeable enough drink mixed with a good dash of lemon juice and a little sugar and poured over ice cubes. (People with lactose-digestion problems should know that unsoured whey is a concentrated source of lactose.) Still, I prefer it converted into sour whey by simple culturing: Inoculate the whey by stirring in some plain yogurt or buttermilk with active cultures. (The proportions can be flexible, but about

¼ to ⅓ cup of yogurt or buttermilk to 2 quarts of whey is a good rule of thumb. Yogurt works better if the whey is a little warmer than room temperature when you start.) Let it sit at room temperature until it is well soured; as with other forms of cultured milk, the timing will vary a lot. It is delicious poured over ice with a pinch each of salt and crushed dried mint, or a little sugar and lemon juice as for sweet whey.

BULGUR PILAF WITH WHEY

If you don't want to drink whey, another good use is as a cooking stock in cereal-based dishes such as pilafs. If you are going to make a renneted, not very sour cheese or the chhenna/panir in the chapter on Fresh Milk and Cream, build something like this into the menu plans. The whey makes a pleasantly neutral cooking liquid, adding a little more body than plain water without absolutely taking over as a strong meat stock would. (Caution: Whey that is too acid may make the bulgur remain overchewy even with long cooking.)

Middle Eastern cooks use bulgur in three grades of fineness. Coarse bulgur is the best for pilafs. If you have to settle for the medium grind of most supermarket bulgur, slightly reduce the cooking and resting time.

YIELD: About 6 servings

1 ½ cups coarse bulgur
2 large shallots
1 garlic clove
2 to 3 tablespoons butter
2¼ cups sweet or nearly sweet whey (from making a renneted cheese or panir, page 111; do not substitute whey from drained yogurt or a cheese made only by souring)
1¼ teaspoons salt
½ teaspoon Turkish paprika (optional)
A handful each of parsley and mint leaves
¼ cup pine nuts

Rinse the bulgur under cold running water, and let drain very thoroughly. Meanwhile, mince the shallots with the garlic.

Melt the butter in a saucepan. When it is fragrant and sizzling, add the shallot-garlic mixture and sauté over moderate heat just until translucent. Add the drained bulgur, and stir to coat the grains well. Cook, stirring, just until very lightly browned, about 3 to 4 minutes. Add the whey, salt, and optional paprika, cover the pan, and cook over low heat until the liquid is almost completely absorbed, about 15 to 20 minutes.

While the pilaf cooks, mince the parsley and mint together. In a small heavy skillet, toast the pine nuts over medium-low heat, stirring, until they are lightly browned; remove from the heat.

When the bulgur has absorbed nearly all the whey, put a kitchen towel over the pan, to absorb any condensation, and cover with the lid. Let the pilaf sit, either off the heat or over the lowest possible heat on a heat deflector like a Flame Tamer, for about 7 to 8 minutes. Fluff up the grains and serve at once, garnished with the minced herbs and toasted pine nuts. A little creamy yogurt stirred in at table is a pleasant addition.

VARIATION: For Barley Pilaf with Whey, replace the bulgur with ¾ cup pearl barley. Use 4 cups whey and 3 to 4 tablespoons butter. Increase the cooking time to 45 to 60 minutes (35 to 40 minutes if you like it extremely chewy). Check toward the end and add more whey or water if the barley is absorbing liquid too fast. Omit the resting and fluffing steps.

A NOTE ON SHOPPING SOURCES

I have never found it necessary to invest in specialized equipment for making yogurt, butter, and fresh cheeses. The cultures I use to inoculate milk or cream can easily be obtained from commercial plain yogurt or cultured buttermilk. (The supermarket articles will work just fine as long as they contain live cultures; you may get even better-tasting results using artisanal versions from small local producers at farmers' markets or specialty shops.)

My rennet source for cheeses (plain unflavored Junket brand tablets) is also available in some supermarkets and can sometimes be ordered through pharmacies. If you strike out, it is not difficult to contact the manufacturer online: www.junketdesserts.com/.

The really crucial pieces of equipment—as described in the yogurt, butter, and fresh cheeses chapters—usually have to do with temperature measurement and control, jiggle-proof incubators, and draining arrangements. I've always been content to improvise with inexpensive insulated containers, kitchen colanders, and sturdy tight-woven cheesecloth or cotton handkerchiefs. Still, I'd be delighted if some users of this book were sufficiently bitten by the home dairying bug to try experimenting with specialized bacterial strains and slightly more elaborate equipment. In that case, I recommend the New England Cheesemaking Supply Company (P.O. Box 85, Ashfield, MA 01330), a mail-order source and information center founded and maintained by Ricki Carroll. Send inquiries to info@cheesemaking.com, or telephone 413–628–3808 to request a catalogue.

ACKNOWLEDGMENTS

Among the many people who made this book possible, Judith Jones deserves my greatest thanks for the skill, patience, and insight with which she faced a most eccentric project. Judith's indefatigable assistant, Ken Schneider, salvaged the entire manuscript from an eleventh-hour computer meltdown. (Up to then my nephew, Jorg F. Bauer, Jr., had managed to nurse an aging iMac through innumerable tragicomedies.) Many additional thanks to Iris Weinstein (who designed the interior of the book), Barbara De Wilde (who created such a delightful jacket), and to everyone else at Knopf.

Elisabeth Sifton encouraged me in an earlier version of this project and introduced me to the late Walter D. Howard, who put me on the path to understanding something about cows and dairying. Years later, Colman Andrews and Margo True at *Saveur* brought me back to the subject with a magazine assignment on milk.

Special thanks to my agent, the one and only Jane Dystel.

Thanks to many dairy and cheese professionals, including Art Hill, Allison Hooper, Paul Kindstedt, Paula Lambert, Patrick Longo, John Loomis, Max McCalman, the Murray's Cheese crew (especially Taylor Cocalis), Debra and Eran Wajswol, and Karen Weinberg.

Equal thanks to some probers of nutrition-and-health questions, including Susan Allport (who read a portion of the manuscript in draft), Nina Planck, David Schleifer, and Nina Teicholz.

For assistance in historical research I am greatly indebted to the staffs of the American Museum of Natural History Library, the Bergen County (New Jersey) Cooperative Library System, the New-York Historical Society Library, and the New York Public Library (especially Tom Lisanti, Stefan Saks, and the peerless Dave Smith). Jack Hawley, Andrew F. Smith, Joanna Waley-Cohen, and Nach Waxman helped steer me to needed materials.

More steering came from fellow culinary historians and other dairy-history buffs including Gary Allen, Darra Goldstein, Annie Hauck-Lawson, Lisa Heldke, Ben Katchor, Rachel Laudan, Jan Longone, Sandra L. Oliver, Krishnendu Ray, Laura Shapiro, William Rubel, Robin Weir, and many, many members of the Association for the Study of Food and Society (ASFS) listserv.

My very great thanks to many cooks, culinary experts, and assorted colleagues and friends, including Joan Bolker, Cara De Silva, Naomi Duguid, Nicki Kalish, Leslie Land, Zarela Martínez, Lynda Owen, Maricel E. Presilla, Nachammai Raman, and Susan J. Talbutt.

SELECT BIBLIOGRAPHY

Culinary works for a general audience can't accommodate the sort of reference apparatus that one expects in works of scholarship—a drawback, perhaps, in a cookbook that strays as far into polemical territory as this one. Readers interested in finding out more about milk and its history will find paths to further learning in the works listed below. I will be happy to direct people frustrated by the absence of documentation for particular factual claims to specific sources; please write to me at knopfwebmaster@randomhouse.com.

HISTORICAL, SCIENTIFIC, AND OTHER SPECIALIZED WORKS

Allport, Susan. *The Queen of Fats: Why Omega-3s Were Removed from the Western Diet and What We Can Do to Replace Them*. Berkeley: University of California Press, 2006.

Atherton, Henry V., and J. A. Newlander. *Chemistry and Testing of Dairy Products*, 4th edition. Westport, Conn.: AVI Publishing, 1977.

Aubaile-Sallenave, Françoise. "*Al-Kishk*: The Past and Present of a Complex Culinary Practice," in *A Taste of Thyme: Culinary Cultures of the Middle East*, ed. by Sami Zubaida and Richard Tapper, 2nd edition. London: I. B. Tauris, 2000.

Banerji, Chitrita. *Eating India: An Odyssey into the Food and Culture of the Land of Spices*. New York: Bloomsbury USA, 2007.

———. *Land of Milk and Honey: Travels in the History of Indian Food*. London: Seagull Books, 2007.

Behr, Edward. "Elegy for the Taste of Cream: Low Technology and Old Pastures," in *The Art of Eating*, 1990, no. 15, pp. 1–8.

Du Puis, E. Melanie. *Nature's Perfect Food: How Milk Became America's Drink*. New York: New York University Press, 2002.

Hoffpauir, Robert. "Water Buffalo," in *The Cambridge World History of Food*, eds. Kenneth F. Kiple and Kriemhild Coneè Ornelas. Cambridge, U.K.: Cambridge University Press, 2000; see vol. I, pp. 583–607.

International Dairy Foods Association. *Dairy Facts, 2005 Edition*. Washington, D.C.: International Dairy Foods Association, 2005.

Jensen, Robert G., ed. *Handbook of Milk Composition*. San Diego: Academic Press, 1995.

Kindstedt, Paul, with the Vermont Cheese Council. *American Farmstead Cheese: The*

Complete Guide to Making and Selling Artisan Cheeses. White River Junction, Vt.: Chelsea Green, 2005.

Kosikowski, Frank V., and Vikram V. Mistry. *Cheese and Fermented Milk Foods,* 3rd edition. 2 vols. Westport, Conn.: F. V. Kosikowski, 1997.

Kramer, Mark. *Three Farms: Making Milk, Meat, and Money from the American Soil.* Boston: Little, Brown, 1980.

Lampard, Eric E. *The Rise of the Dairy Industry in Wisconsin: A Study in Agricultural Change.* Madison: State Historical Society of Wisconsin, 1963.

Lampert, Lincoln M. *Modern Dairy Products: Composition, Food Value, Processing, Chemistry, Bacteriology, Testing, Imitation Dairy Products,* 3rd edition. New York: Chemical Publishing, 1975.

Lysaght, Patricia, ed. *Milk and Milk Products from Medieval to Modern Times.* Proceedings of the Ninth International Conference on Ethnological Food Research. Edinburgh: Canongate Academic, 1994.

McGee, Harold. *On Food and Cooking: The Science and Lore of the Kitchen,* 2nd edition. New York: Scribner, 2004.

Mahias, Marie-Claude. "Milk and Its Transformations in Indian Society." *Food and Foodways,* 1988, vol. 2, pp. 265–88.

Nantet, Bernard, et al. *Cheeses of the World.* New York: Rizzoli, 1993.

Park, Young W., and George F. W. Haenlein, eds. *Handbook of Milk of Non-Bovine Mammals.* Ames, Iowa: Blackwell, 2006.

Porter, Valerie. *Cattle: A Handbook to the Breeds of the World.* London: A&C Black/Christopher Helm, 1991.

———. *Goats of the World.* Ipswich, U.K.: Farming Press, 1996.

Sabban, Françoise. "Un savoir-faire oublié: le travail du lait en Chine ancienne." *Zinbun: Memoirs of the Research Institute for Humanistic Studies, Kyoto University,* 1986, vol. 21, pp. 31–65.

Selitzer, Ralph. *The Dairy Industry in America.* New York: Dairy & Ice Cream Field and Books for Industry, 1976.

Simoons, Frederick J. *Food in China: A Cultural and Historical Inquiry.* Boca Raton, Fla.: CRC Press, 1991.

Smith, Bruce D. *The Emergence of Agriculture.* New York: Scientific American Library, 1995.

Trout, G. Malcolm. *Homogenized Milk: A Review and Guide.* East Lansing: Michigan State College Press, 1950.

Tyler, Howard D., and M. E. Ensminger. *Dairy Cattle Science,* 4th edition. Upper Saddle River, N.J.: Pearson/Prentice Hall, 2006.

Walker, Harlan, ed. *Milk: Beyond the Dairy.* Proceedings of the Oxford Symposium on Food and Cookery 1999. Totnes, U.K.: Prospect Books, 2000.

Wilson, C. Anne. *Food and Drink in Britain: From the Stone Age to Recent Times.* New York: Harper & Row/Barnes & Noble, 1974.

Wong, Noble P., ed. *Fundamentals of Dairy Chemistry,* 3rd edition. New York: Van Nostrand Reinhold, 1988.

Wright, Russell O. *Life and Death in the United States: Statistics on Life Expectancies, Diseases and Death Rates for the Twentieth Century.* Jefferson, N.C.: McFarland, 1997.

COOKBOOKS

Acton, Eliza. *Modern Cookery for Private Families*. Non-facsimile reissue of 1855 edition. Lewes, U.K.: Southover Press, 1993.

Batra, Neelam. *1,000 Indian Recipes*. New York: Wiley, 2002.

Carroll, Ricki. *Home Cheesemaking: Recipes for 75 Homemade Cheeses*, 3rd edition. North Adams, Mass.: Storey Books, 2002.

David, Elizabeth. *French Provincial Cooking*. Harmondsworth, U.K.: Penguin Books, 1969.

Diat, Louis. *Cooking à la Ritz*. Philadelphia: Lippincott, 1941.

Field, Michael. *Michael Field's Cooking School: A Selection of Great Recipes Demonstrating the Pleasures and Principles of Fine Cooking*. New York: William Morrow, 1965.

Fried, Barbara R. *The Berry Cookbook*. New York: Collier Books, 1962.

Goldstein, Darra. *A Taste of Russia: A Cookbook of Russian Hospitality*. New York: Harper Perennial, 1991.

Hazelton, Nika Standen. *The Continental Flavor: A Cookbook*. Garden City, N.Y.: Doubleday, 1961.

Hom, Ken. *Fragrant Harbor Taste: The New Chinese Cooking of Hong Kong*. New York: Simon & Schuster, 1989.

Jaffrey, Madhur. *An Invitation to Indian Cooking*. New York: Random House/Vintage Books, 1975.

———. *Madhur Jaffrey's World-of-the-East Vegetarian Cooking*. New York: Alfred A. Knopf, 1981.

———. *Madhur Jaffrey's World Vegetarian*. New York: Clarkson Potter, 1999.

Jones, Evan. *The World of Cheese*. New York: Alfred A. Knopf, 1976.

Jones, Judith, and Evan Jones. *The Book of New New England Cookery*. Hanover, N. H.: University Press of New England, 2001.

Kachru, Purnima. *Kashmiri Kitchen*. New Delhi: Roli Books/Lustre Press, 2000.

Kaneva-Johnson, Maria. *The Melting Pot: Balkan Food and Cookery*. Totnes, U.K.: Prospect Books, 1995.

Kaufman, Edna. *Melting Pot of Mennonite Cookery, 1874–1974*, 3rd edition. North Newton, Kans.: Bethel College Women's Association, 1975.

Kochilas, Diane. *The Glorious Foods of Greece: Traditional Recipes from the Islands, Cities, and Villages*. New York: William Morrow, 2001.

Kremezi, Aglaia. *The Foods of Greece*. New York: Stewart, Tabori & Chang, 1993.

Lambert, Paula. *The Cheese Lover's Companion & Guide*. New York: Simon & Schuster, 2000.

Lang, George. *The Cuisine of Hungary*. New York: Atheneum, 1971.

Maier-Bruck, Franz. *Das Grosse Sacher Kochbuch: Die österreichische Küche*. Munich: Schuler Verlagsgesellschaft, 1975.

———. *Vom Essen auf dem Lande: Das grosse Buch der österreichischen Bauernküche und Hausmannskost*. Vienna: Kremayr und Scheriau, 1981.

Ozan, Özcan. *The Sultan's Kitchen: A Turkish Cookbook*. Boston: Periplus Editions, 1998.

Roden, Claudia. *A Book of Middle Eastern Food*. New York: Random House/Vintage Books, 1974.

Rose, Peter G., trans. and ed. *The Sensible Cook (De Verstandige Kock): Dutch Foodways in the Old and the New World*. Syracuse, N.Y.: Syracuse University Press, 1989.

Saberi, Helen. *Afghan Food and Cookery (Noshe Djan)*. New York: Hippocrene Books, 2000.

Saint-Ange, E. *La Cuisine de Madame Saint-Ange: recettes et méthodes de la bonne cuisine française*. Paris: Librairie Larousse, 1982.

Scharfenberg, Horst. *Die deutsche Küche*. Bern, Switzerland: Hallwag AG Bern, 1980.

Shaida, Margaret. *The Legendary Cuisine of Persia*. New York: Interlink Books, 2002.

Sheraton, Mimi. *From My Mother's Kitchen: Recipes and Reminiscences*, rev. edition. New York: HarperCollins, 1991.

Shroff, Veema, and Vanmala Desai. *100 Easy-to-Make Gujarati Dishes*, 7th edition. New Delhi: Vikas Publishing/Tarang Paperbacks, 1990.

Strybel, Robert, and Maria Strybel. *Polish Heritage Cookery*. New York: Hippocrene Books, 1993.

Uvezian, Sonia. *The Book of Yogurt: An International Collection of Recipes*. Hopewell, N.J.: Ecco Press, 1999.

———. *Recipes and Remembrances: From an Eastern Mediterranean Kitchen*, 2nd edition. Northbrook, Ill.: Siamanto Press, 2001.

von Bremzen, Anya, and John Welchman. *Please to the Table: The Russian Cookbook*. New York: Workman Publishing, 1990.

Wolfert, Paula. *The Cooking of the Eastern Mediterranean*. New York: HarperCollins, 1994.

———. *Mediterranean Grains and Greens*. New York: HarperCollins, 1998.

INTERNET SOURCES

A great deal of information is now available online along with even greater amounts of misinformation, politicking, and rumormongering. Some sites that may be of interest to readers of this book:

http://www.aphis.usda.gov/vs/ceah/ncahs/nahms/dairy/ Web site of the USDA animal health monitoring and surveillance division.

http://classes.ansci.uiuc.edu/ansc438/ Online review and syllabus of Professor Walter L. Hurley's class in lactation biology, Department of Animal Sciences, University of Illinois at Urbana.

http://www.foodsci.uoguelph.ca/dairyedu/home.html Wide-ranging source on dairy science and technology, maintained by the dairy science department of the University of Guelph, Ontario.

http://webexhibits.org/butter/ Extremely diverse and entertaining (if not always factually reliable) site dedicated to butter and its historical/culinary/cultural fortunes.

INDEX

(Page references in *italic* refer to illustrations. Page references in **boldface** refer to recipes.)

Anne Mendelson grew up in southeastern Pennsylvania, in an area where small dairy farms were once common. She is a free-lance writer who has specialized in food and culinary history for the last thirty years. Ms. Mendelson is the author of *Stand Facing the Stove*, a history of *The Joy of Cooking* and its authors. She has collaborated on three Mexican cookbooks with chef-writer Zarela Martínez, and writes for *Gourmet* and *Saveur* magazines as well as the *New York Times* Dining Section. She now lives in a multi-ethnic neighborhood of northern New Jersey.

A NOTE ON THE TYPE

This book was set in Janson, a typeface long thought to have been made by the Dutchman Anton Janson, who was a practicing typefounder in Leipzig during the years 1668–1687. However, it has been conclusively demonstrated that these types are actually the work of Nicholas Kis (1650–1702), a Hungarian, who most probably learned his trade from the master Dutch typefounder Dirk Voskens. The type is an excellent example of the influential and sturdy Dutch types that prevailed in England up to the time William Caslon (1692–1766) developed his own incomparable designs from them.

COMPOSED BY
North Market Street Graphics, Lancaster, Pennsylvania

PRINTED AND BOUND BY
R. R. Donnelley, Harrisonburg, Virginia

DESIGNED BY
Iris Weinstein

p30